D0769182

Realignment of World Power

REALIGNMENT OF WORLD POWER

The Russo-Chinese Schism Under the Impact of
Mao Tse-Tung's Last Revolution

VOLUME I

By

Oton Ambroz

Robert Speller & Sons, Publishers, Inc.
10 East 23rd Street
New York, N. Y., 10010
USA

Library of Congress Catalog Card Number: 73-149631

International Standard Book Number: 0-8315-0114-6

Printed by China Printing Ltd.
Taipei, Taiwan
Republic of China

Dedicated

to

Emma and Alexander

ACKNOWLEDGMENTS

A particular debt of gratitude for the appearance of this book must be paid to Mr. Alfreds Berzins, the only leading statesman and cabinet minister of Free Latvia's last government to have reached the West, Chairman of the Assembly of Captive European Nations for 1969/70, and author of two significant books, *The Unpunished Crime* and the *Two Faces of Co-existence*. A fighter for freedom all his life, he deemed it to be appropriate to recommend the publication of the present work. The cooperation between Mr. Berzins and the author of this book gave reality to the rather romantic Slavic slogan, "From the Baltic to the Adriatic Sea."

It was a pleasure to deal with my editor-in-chief, Dr. John P. Speller, a man of rare knowledge and of instant and clear judgement.

My appreciation also goes to another Balt, Mr. Algirdas Landsbergis, dramatist and professor at Fairleigh-Dickinson University, New Jersey.

I have been fortunate in having access to the following research libraries: Columbia University (Russian, Communist Affairs, East Asian Institutes, Butler), Embassy of France, Consulate General of Italy, Goethe Haus, Radio Free Europe, Radio Liberty, and the New York Public Library.

Among my Chinese friends I am indepted to Mr. Liu Chung-kai, chief of the editorial center of the government information office of the Republic of China, and to Professor Tong Te-kong of the East Asian Institute of Columbia. Mr. Richard Sorich, China bibliographer at the same Institute was of immense assistance in my work as was Mr. Donald W. Klein, research associate there.

Mr. Chris You, general manager of the China Printing Ltd. in Taipei, Taiwan, has my thanks for his fine workmanship in the production of this book. I am much obliged to Dr. Ku Ch'eng-kang, Honorary Chairman of the World Anti-Communist League, and a leading figure of the Asian People's Anti-Communist League, who has been very helpful.

Others whose encouragement and help contributed to this book include Mrs. Milena Hoenig and Mrs. Lydia N. Sienitsky, as well as Messrs. Peter Beales, Gordon H. Evans, Imre Kardashinetz, Anthony Palecek, and Herman Singer.

TABLE OF CONTENTS

Volume I

Chapter I

CONFLICTING NATIONAL-REVOLUTIONARY INTERESTS

Chapter II

DIFFERENT AVENUES OF APPROACH
(A PACIFIC PACT)

Chapter III

THE CHINESE COMMUNIST IDEOLOGICAL CHALLENGE

Chapter IV

MAO'S DOCTRINE EXPOSED
BY YUGOSLAV COMMUNISTS

Chapter X
PRESAGES OF THE TEMPEST

Chapter XI
THE GREAT PURGE: MAOISTS FIGHT THE "RUSSIAN DISEASE"

Volume II

Chapter XII
THE BATTERED IMAGE AND IRREPARABLE HARM

Chapter XIII
TO RECOUP ABSOLUTE POWER

Chapter XIV

THE GUN COMMANDS A SHATTERED PARTY

Chapter XV

THROUGH CULTURE AND IDEOLOGY TO POWER

Chapter XVI

THE NATIONWIDE POWER STRUGGLE

Chapter XVII

TWO MILESTONES OF INTERNATIONAL COMMUNISM

Chapter   XVIII

THE RIFT AND THE WEST

PREFACE

The Russo-Chinese rift is the most important event in the second half of this century. More than that, it represents a new opening for United States' foreign policy. "The greatest asset we have," stated U.S. Senator Henry Jackson, "is the split between the Soviet Union and Red China." This view is shared by Ambassador George Kennan, for whom "the most hopeful fact for the United States in the past twenty years in the international arena has emerged from the position of Mao Tse-tung and his close associates with respect to the world communist movement. It would be silly on our part to sit by idly ... to completely ignore the conflict between China and the Soviet Union and failing to take advantage of the favorable consequences it may have."

The importance of the Sino-Soviet confrontation can be more fully understood only in the context of the past quarter century. World War II did not bury totalitarianism as such, but only its Nazi-fascist variety, while communist totalitarianism emerged even stronger. Ever since it has remained faithful to its goal of conquering the world by infiltration and subversion, direct or indirect aggression, a policy that might provoke a bigger war with all its apocalyptic consequences.

If the 1930's have taught the world anything, it is the vital truth that totalitarians cannot be appeased or bought off by concessions. Therefore, any further communist conquest should not be tolerated as it would merely increase the danger of a global conflagration. Communism and Nazi-fascism may differ in some details, but they are identical in their essence, namely "fascist and communist totalitarian dictatorships are basically alike," said Professors Carl Friedrich and

Zbigniew Brzezinski in their book *Totalitarian Dictatorship and Autocracy.* Both are anti-humanistic, both use genocide as their ultimate weapon, both cannot tolerate anything that deviates from their simplistic monolithic philosophy and total ideocratic control. "The Czechoslovak model of socialism with a human face," actually meant according to Moscow *Kommunist* "the liquidation of the socialist order in that country." ("If there is only one election slate and there is no contest, it is the same as Nazism," as Bukharin, one of the leading Bolshevik theoreticians, had admitted once.) In the Belgrade demonstration against the invasion of Czechoslovakia slogans were seen reading "Brezhnev-Hitler." And the Czech and Slovak people expressed it most tellingly when, following the Soviet invasion of August 1968, they covered Prague and other cities with chalk signs equating the hammer and sickle with the swastika, and thus confirmed Professor Brzezinski's dictum that: "The highest stage of communism is fascism," namely its degeneration into social fascism, rather than evolution toward social democracy.

In a world saddled with a myriad of burning yet unsolved problems, where old doctrines are eroding and traditional values are becoming relative, where believers are turning into agnostics or cynics at an accelerating rate, new approaches are being desperately sought. "Scientific communism" was one of them. But now—on the 120th anniversary of *The Communist Manifesto,* on the centennial of Marx's *Das Kapital* and Lenin's birthday, with the 50th anniversary of the October Revolution still echoing—that new secular faith, as applied in the countries ruled by he communists, stands revealed as having solved nothing and has sadly disappointed mankind's expectations. And yet the communist leaders are claiming in their boundless arrogance that they alone have the answers to all the troubles of the world and that the abolition of private ownership (which actually relegated all wealth to their complete control) has brought about the emancipation of labor and the genuine equality of man.

Their total failure was again manifested during the December 1970 workers' rebellion in the Polish Baltic ports, which was put down by massacre. The local Party headquarters in Gdansk, besieged by thousands of angry shipyard workers, hung a white flag from the top floor, and then the petty autocrats left the building with their hands up, according to Stockholm *Expressen.* The headquarters was set on fire by the workers.

The Western democratic system with its great heritage of liberties has its own considerable shortcomings, but no better alternatives to it are visible anywhere. Communism does offer an alternative—to the worse. That alternative is best grasped by personal experience, one reason why articulate apologists of communism vocalize in the safety of the free world and why the most telling denunciations of the system have come from those who have experienced its blessings on their own skin. It is the latter who know too well that freedom and political slavery cannot be reconciled.

As the contest between the free world and communism was reaching a crisis stage, Mao Tse-tung's unexpected victory in mainland China seemed to make communism invincible on the world scene. Communists hailed Mao's success as the trust of a "monolith" which captured one billion people. This, they claimed, was another proof of the predetermined course of history, moving toward the final victory of communism, and challenged the West to prove the opposite. Surprisingly, and tragically, some in the West seemed to accept the dubious communist thesis.

That psychological disadvantage was one of the reasons why many opportunities to prove the contrary were not utilized: in Albania, Korea and, particularly, in Hungary. After Yugoslavia's expulsion from the Cominform, for instance, the Albanian communist leadership was badly divided between the Soviet and Yugoslav factions and the chances for the restoration of Albania's freedom seemed to be propitious. As we now know one of the men who participated in the drafting of the plan to liberate Albania was a British double-agent who delivered all details to the Soviets, and the Albanian patriots fell into hands of the *Sigurimi,* Tirana's secret police.

In Korea it was the Yalu-complex that prevented the allied forces from giving the Red Chinese a timely lesson. The Hungarian national revolt was defeated not only by Russian tanks but also by Western inaction, although Khrushchev had been wavering for more than a week and was seriously considering letting Hungary go from the "socialist camp". Similarly, the protests against Tibet's subjugation and the genocide perpetrated there were much too few and too faint. How much louder and more persistant are the outcries of communists and fellow-travelers when they castigate the few remaining vestiges of Western colonialism!

Equally deplorable was the failure at the Bay of Pigs. A United States intervention there would have prevented the subsequent dangerous confrontation of the "missile crisis" when a major war was avoided, according to former Secretary of State Dean Acheson, only because of the late President Kennedy's "phenomenal luck" and Khrushchev's "befuddlement and loss of nerve".

Thus, any Western hesitation or concession merely encouraged the communists to undertake new risks and seek new successes. Had the communists gained an all-out victory in Indochina, they would have proceeded further until their advances would have become intolerable to the Western Powers. The formula is clear: communist expansion is "history's law", while any Western attempt to stop or reverse it is an action against history and would be countered by the military might of the Soviet Union, as Foreign Minister Gromyko made clear in the General Assembly of the United Nations in connection with the Czechoslovak events.

Communist China had its own crises. In 1962, a most critical year, Peking was expecting an invasion and many divisions moved to the coastal provinces of Fukien and Chekiang as well as to Sinkiang on the opposite side. The internal situation was disastrous: peasant upheavals looming after the collapse of the "great leap", restiveness in Tibet, mass escape of tens of thousands of Kazakhs from Sinkiang to Kazakhstan, and simultaneously hundreds of thousands of mainland Chinese pouring into Hong Kong. But nobody moved a finger to take advantages of Peking's troubles. And in the fall of the same year India had to pay dearly for her naiveté concerning China's "coexistence" policy.

All of those lost Western opportunities have reinforced the communist belief in their being the incarnation of the "will of history". However, the nations of the free world, according to Milovan Djilas, "are proving to be increasingly resistant to communist 'scientific' prognostications". In his latest work, *The Unperfect Society,* Djilas dealt a lethal blow to Marxism-Leninism as a pseudo-science by refuting any "basic law of the universe" with the help of modern physics, starting with Einstein's relativity theory and the quantum mechanics.

* *

A large portion of this book is devoted to the impact of the Chinese cultural revolution on the Sino-Soviet rift, since the recent convulsion in China appears to be inextricably linked with the conflict between Moscow and Peking. Mao's struggle against the Soviet leadership, now enemy number one, and against his own opposition are interrelated. One of the purposes of the cultural revolution is the fostering and training of the new generation in hostility against the Soviet Union, perpetuation of the present state of affairs, and exclusion of any accommodation in the future, in order to save China from the "quagmire of revisionism".

Thus the cultural revolution represents an ideological upheaval, an attempt to screen China from Russia with the psychological barrier of Mao's thought. Mao is precariously balancing himself on the top of a swaying pyramid in a stalemated power struggle, while China flounders in a continuing instability. As Mao admitted during his secret inspection tour of several provinces in the summer of 1967, according to a Canton red guard tabloid smuggled to Hong Kong: "Some people say there is no civil war in China, but I think this is a civil war, not a war from the outside. This is a brutal struggle, not an ideological struggle".

As a result, China's potential role as a great power was in jeopardy. She was riddled by such bitter dissent, strife and stridency of such dimension that she was incapable of self-assertion for years to come, her limited nuclear capabilities notwithstanding.

Mao's blunders at home and abroad have strengthened the more moderate wing of the Communist Party of China and given encouragement to his opponents. He was obviously not in full control of the entire country. Meanwhile, the opposition in its struggle against the cultural revolution has strengthened its following not only among the Party members but also among peasants, workers and the intelligentsia throughout the country. Chinese nationalists assert that all of these forces represent a popular resistance movement with a basically anti-communist motivation, since Chinese communism is now being equated with Maoist extremism.

What are the prospects for the future? Maoism was temporarily victorious leaning heavily on the military, compelled to abandon the model of the Paris Commune because the new "rebels" were much too weak. Following Mao's demise, his successors, checked by the powerful provincial warlords, will end his messianic mission, an important source of the world's torments, and make China's self-interest Peking's prime concern.

The confusion created by the cultural revolution calls for a new terminology and a new effort at clarification. The old terms and categories are inadequate to describe the rebellion of a minority of leftist communists and non-communists against the communist majority in a communist-ruled country. Anti-Maoist is the most accurate term for the opposition.

Accounts by Western travelers on Red China in turmoil frequently obfuscated more than they elucidated. Travel in China is even much more restricted than in other communist countries and most of the guided tours end up as travelogues on Peking's "Potemkin villages". The same is true about many books about China; the fact that their authors had an opportunity to visit Red China is no guarantee of improved quality. "Why should going to China help one to write about China?" Yale sinologist Professor Jonathan Spence asked in reviewing a volume by K. S. Karol, a French journalist. "He (Mr. Karol) need not have gone to China to write this book." Outside information on communist China was more reliable, confirmed Jules Ray, also a French journalist. In his book he acknowledged: "I had no need to wonder that people in Europe and America knew more about what was happening in China than I did in Peking." Another traveler in China, who reviewed five travelogues in *The China Quarterly,* remarked: "We all visited roughly the same films and operas, and often visited the same schools, communes and factories."

Neither is literary fame a guarantee of insights into China. Alberto Moravia's dispatches on his Peking summer of 1967 in *Corriere della Sera,* Italy's leading daily, were often astute, but his subsequent book in praise of "heroic" impoverishment and austerity was utterly unconvincing.

Conversely, certain travelogues were of some value because their authors had the good sense to study authoritative works after their journey, as in the case of the Swedish journalist Hans Granquist who read the manuscript of a biography of Mao (recently revised) by Professor Stuart Schram, both sinologist and Pekingologist.

Valuable is the source material published by the research institutes in Hong Kong and Taipei, and the endeavors of the University of Chicago's Center for Policy Study, to cite some of them. Penetrating was the account of Mao's "second revolution" by Kuo Hengyü, a young scientist at the Free University of Berlin. Of the periodicals, *China News Analysis* (Hong Kong) and *China Analysen* (Frankfurt am Main) are prominent as research information services.

Among the outstanding surveys of the cultural revolution and its impact on the Russo-Chinese dispute we should mention one compiled by John Gittings of the London School of Economics and Political Science, under the auspices of the Royal Institute of International Affairs. This collection of documents depicting the standpoint of both sides, with a special attention to the polemical exchanges of 1963-1967, is a must for everyone dealing with the subject. This writer fully agrees with Mr. Gittings' conclusion: "It seems unlikely therefore that a change of leadership in Peking will by itself significantly affect the substance of the dispute." Consequently, the same conclusion was made by a task force of Japanese scholars and newsmen after a three-month tour of mainland China in the winter of 1966-1967, sponsored by Japan's giant daily *Yomiuri Shimbun,* best summed up by the title of one of their articles: "Spilt Water Will Never Be Gathered Again."

The unpredictability of Chinese developments may be illustrated by the example of a leading American authority on Chinese communist army affairs who wrote in January 1967, in an epilogue to an excellent book, that the so-called People's Liberation Army would not play a role in the cultural revolution. As it happened, a week or so later Mao called upon the PLA to participate in the three-way alliance of the new powerholders. It is obvious by now that the Maoist headquarters could have hardly remained in existence without the strong support of many military commanders.

*   *   *

The Russo-Chinese conflict has deep historic roots and the communist regimes were simply not able to change the hard geopolitical facts. National rivalries were superimposed on ideological pretensions, exacerbating the former, and standing in a cause-effect relation-

ship. The opposing national and revolutionary interests of Russia
and China are in collision throughout the world and, as a result, a
realignment of world power is taking place. A bi-polarized world is
being replaced by a multi-polarized one. The slow emergence and
crystallization of the pluralistic pattern will very likely dominate the
last decades of the century.

Both Red China and Russia today are competitive yet cautious
fomentors of subversion. Their competition in the developing countries has resulted in expressions of unswerving support by both of
them for "wars of liberation", present or potential. The Chinese
communists especially are advocating a change of the status quo
everywhere. In the tradition of the Middle Kingdom, they are
preaching this "universal truth", however discredited it might be,
and its applicability to three continents, Asia, Africa, and Latin
America.

Russia meanwhile is staunchly upholding the partition of Europe,
a partition that would perennially freeze the division of Germany
and the captivity of the East-Central European nations, thus making
the attainment of a durable peace an impossible dream. With Germany striving for reunification and the captive nations trying to
regain freedom, the European status quo remains enduringly unstable
and the balance of power precarious.

Should Europe or Asia claim the first attention of America's
policymakers? We have seen the center of danger shift from Europe
to Asia. Later events have again put Europe into the center of the
picture. The main strength of Russia, the only power which can
seriously challenge the United States, is concentrated in Europe. In
the shrinking world the communist threat is global, although divided,
as they keep probing the weakest spots to change the balance of
power and the status quo (e.g. South-East Asia). Therefore wisdom
lies not in a Europe-first or Asia-first policy, but in giving priority to
the areas where the danger is gravest. A single borderline goes
around the globe, dividing communist and free world dominions, and
the United States as an Atlantic and Pacific superpower shoulders
the largest responsibilities in Europe and Asia simultaneously. This
is President Nixon's "one world."

The Vietnam war has contributed to widening the breach between China and Russia and has been, on balance, a divisive factor.

Red China is quite naturally much more interested in her perimeter and former tribute territory than Russia could ever be. Desirous of replacing the former colonial domination in South-East Asia with its own, Peking has been trying in vain to eliminate Russia as an Asian country in the Afro-Asian bloc by branding her as just another white colonial power. A "united action" of Russia and China has become utterly impossible not only because of ideological differences, but above all because of their divergent national interests as two competing Asian great powers.

Russia's and China's border, the longest in the world, has to be manned on both sides. And, paradoxically, the United States has partially relieved Moscow's commitments to the defense of her eastern borders. Russia's situation would be much worse without the strong American presence in the Western Pacific and South-East Asia as well as without the formidable military power of the Chinese nationalists on Taiwan. Peking complains about Soviet war games, troop concentrations, and Moscow about China's war hysteria. On the other hand, many Chinese communist divisions were tied down by the Americans and President Chiang Kai-shek.

The two superpowers, the United States and the Soviet Union, shoulder special responsibilities for peace on earth. However, there are still many obstacles to their genuine cooperation. After Khrushchev, the propagandist of "peaceful coexistence", was rebuffed in his attempts to change the status quo in Berlin and in Cuba, Russia seemed to quiet down in Europe until the invasion of Czechoslovakia where she saw her strategical position endangered. Hard pressed by Red China, Russia should pursue a milder line toward the West. Yet Russia's formidable fire power was a greater challenge to the United States in the limited war in Vietnam than revolutionary guerrilla warfare or Mao Tse-tung's thought. Meanwhile, Russia's uneasiness about the potential menace of a two-front confrontation is a tangible weakness that invites a new United States policy of increased pressure on Moscow, instead of attempts to soften her up by new concessions, despite the nuclear stalemate.

Whatever the issues dividing Moscow and Washington, the Red Chinese already saw "Soviet-American cooperation for the domination of the world." Peking's sources have revealed that significant Soviet publications expressing the same idea are being kept in cold storage for an appropriate time. The war in Indochina should not be a hindrance to such a U.S.-Soviet cooperation.

The Chinese certitude is now supported by a change. The Soviet Union still offers very little, too little. Its alleged renunciation of thermo-nuclear warfare is, of course, an important factor, but it simply represents their realization that an atomic war would leave no victors behind—a proof of pragmatic self-interest, yet by no means a concession to the West. Contrasted to the Maoist actual acceptance of nuclear war, based on their trust in China's physical and psychological ability to absorb nuclear punishment and survive, the Soviet stance was a solid gain in public relations versus the West.

For a long time the situation in Europe was frozen, with no solution in sight for all of the problems left over from World War II. (Even General De Gaulle was compelled to admit that reluctantly when during his visit in Moscow he realized that the Soviet leaders were not willing to yield an inch and would maintain the partition of Europe at all costs.) The Sino-Russian rift seemed to have opened new vistas, and it is quite natural that some began considering the Chinese alternative. If there is no way to budge Russia, they reason, why not seek some arrangement with our weaker foe, Red China (especially in its more reasonable stage), in order to disturb and dislodge the main adversary, the Soviet Union? This theory, derived from an old Machiavellian rule of power politics, also holds that a faster industrialization of Red China would make her a bigger threat to Russia. The more intensely Russia would feel the Chinese threat, some argue, the more propitious would be the time for pressuring Moscow for concession. The people who reason thus are those who feel the Soviet shadow over them as a constant chilling reality and for whom there is nothing improper in a policy that would play off one foe against another.

Some observers also believe that the Russo-Chinese developments might help to unfreeze the situation in Soviet dominated East-Central Europe, a group of nations with a population of almost 100 million people and an industrial capacity roughly 40 percent of that of the Soviet Union.

Moscow, pressured by China in the east and, potentially, in its western domain, may eventually be compelled to come to terms with the West. But such prognostications should be tested against long-range prospects and not be undertaken under the spell of recent headlines. In case the Soviets do offer a new deal on the crucial problems, *quid pro quo* should be the governing principle in all dealings with the communist rulers.

*   *   *   *

One of the few positive contributions of Maoist China was her reminder to the world of Soviet colonialism, not only in Asia, but also in Europe, from Riga and Koenigsberg to Chisinau (Bessarabia). The Soviet Union survives today as the only remaining major colonial power in the world. Its Russian population, constituting only one half of the total, occupies the privileged position of colonial masters, and the non-Russian nationalities are subjected to rigorous leveling and Russification. The "soviets" (local administration units) mean little for the Balts, Ukrainians, or Kazakhs who are allowed no real local autonomy or self-government. Thus the Chinese charges were most timely, especially since the Western powers have failed to press the issue adequately. A double-standard concerning colonialism and self-determination has prevailed in the United Nations and most former colonial peoples have shut their eyes to the Soviet brand of colonial oppression and exploitation.

The Russians answered the Chinese in kind, and as a result nationalities in both countries have been singled out for "liberation" from the other side. Territories of Russia and China, claimed as "sacred parts", are being mutually contended. In this competition the Chinese seem to have an advantage, since the Han people, unlike the Russians in the Soviet Union, represent an overwhelming majority. The minorities inhabiting huge and strategically important territories are to be Sinified sooner or later, according to Peking's policy declarations.

Yugoslavia plays a special role in this new configuration of world communism. Peking and Belgrade are antipodal in the red spectrum. Some of the sharpest criticism of the catastrophic collapse of the "three red banners" and of the "great proletarian cultural revolution" came from Yugoslav commentators who evaluated Chinese socialism as weak and constantly getting weaker. Peking's counter-charge was equally devastating, and in their "third comment" to the Soviet Communist Party Central Committee's "open letter", the Chinese leaders asked pointedly: "Is Yugoslavia a socialist country?" Their answer to this rhetorical question was a resounding "No!" Moreover, a booklet recently appeared in Peking entitled: Is the Soviet Union a Socialist State or Not?, with the same perplexing answer.

One may easily argue with the Chinese diagnosis. Yugoslavia *is* a socialist (communist) country, if by it we mean application of Marxist-Leninist principles to national conditions. The Yugoslav communists have been always emphasizing the former, and at the 24th Soviet Party congress and at Lenin's centenary celebrations the Yugoslav League's delegation was listed with all the other ruling pro-Soviet communist Parties. They are part of what is now called the world socialist system consisting of 14 ruling Parties, as defined by the 1969 international communist conference in Moscow. The Soviet armed forces and the thermo-nuclear umbrella are shielding communist regimes, regardless of membership in the Warsaw Pact. Soviet-Yugoslav relations temporarily went on a down-grade following the Czechoslovak events, but this was in no way comparable to the Cominform pressure of the early fifties. Yugoslavia's proclaimed non-alignment is far from being a genuine neutrality between the power blocs because she is ideologically aligned.

Some portion of this book is dedicated to the problem of disputed territories, a powder keg which may touch off a conflagration. One need not go as far as General De Gaulle who in his vision of "Europe to the Urals" conjures an impossible retreat of Russia 350 years back to its past, deprived of her Asian possession. He was impressed by the empty vastness of Eastern Siberia and the Soviet Far East, endangered by Chinese biological pressure, just as the German scientist Starlinger, who had forecast the Sino-Soviet clash, had been once. The blunt fact is that Peking is going so far as to discuss the entire Amur River basin border, the huge areas "east of the Baikal" now suffering from demographic stagnation. The "Chinese Great North-West" in Soviet central Asia is also emphasized. Kazakhstan, for instance, with more than one million square miles has less than two percent of China's population.

Militant and ambitious as Red China is today, its strength should not be overestimated. The Mongol and Moslem minorities also represent a continuous headache for Peking. Russia's military power is overwhelming, and Moscow has had enough time to consolidate the precarious situation before the potential aggressor from the south could undertake any action. On the former "friendship border", riddled with skirmishes and confrontations, the Soviet military preponderance is very strongly felt.

Therefore, the militancy of the tottering Maoists, the nuclear bomb rattling, and China's huge population should be all put in their proper perspective. It is, after all, generally accepted that India's large population has been considerably retarding her advancement. Why should not the same criteria be applied to mainland China? Scarce hard currency must be expended to barely feed an additional 15 to 20 million mouths each year, instead of being invested for faster industrialization. This obstacle, a constant drain on China's economy, is so formidable that it might delay any major Chinese action for many years, and by that time Maoist extremism might have spent itself completely.

More than that, Japan is rapidly advancing as a new democratic world power, and occupies the third place among the leading industrial powers. She may well decide to become an equally strong military power as well and to defend Asia from communist usurpers.

The great communist schism has generated deadly antagonisms and rent the international communist movement in two. An immense gulf now yawns between ascetic Maoism and the "goulash" communism of the Soviet Union and Eastern Europe. Revisionism in the economic sphere (a favorite Chinese accusation) is modest. As not a trace of free enterprise or free economy exists in Russia, the Chinese charges of Moscow's return to capitalism are simply absurd. Stalin's rigid economic system, built upon a foundation of terror, collapsed as soon as the pressure was relaxed. The problem facing Moscow now is how to transform its static socialist economy into something more viable.

*　*　*　*　*

Some sinologists, out of their love for the great Chinese nation, became apologists for Mao's inhuman regime. They close their eyes to the fact that Mao Tse-tung has learned nothing since he has taken over the mainland and that his "thought" has transformed the whole country into a single military settlement. His vision of the Chinese people's future is in terms of silent paramilitary columns of absolutely obedient production crew soldiers satisfied with three meals a day and two blankets for the night. Yet his apologists justify this anachronistic totalitarian insanity by pointing out that throughout China's history its people have never enjoyed personal freedom—as if the Chinese nation should be doomed forever to live under oriental despotism, or as if the world was not progressing towards greater freedom and democracy.

Equally deplorable is the adulation of Mao as a "great man", a survival of the romantic syndrome. Such is the attitude of André Malraux in his *Anti-Mémoires,* where Mao towers as a Herculean hero striving to change the world and human nature.

As a welcome contrast to this dubious hero worship stands the genuine heroism of those enlightened Chinese communist and non-communist writers who were prosecuted for refusing to condone in their writings the enslavement of the Chinese people or their treatment as if they were so much grass (T'ien Han). But while the Western cultural community has, commendably, protested against the violation of human rights in the sentencing of Sinyavsky, Daniel and other Russian and Ukrainian writers and journalists, and the commitment of dissenters to insane asylums, it has remained silent about the imprisonment and extermination of so many eminent Chinese artists and intellectuals. Take the case of Lao She, one of the outstanding writers of our times, a novelist and playwright translated into English, former vice chairman of the All-China, and chairman of the Peking, association of the workers in literature and art, who either committed suicide or was beaten to death by the red guards. Or consider the fate of the world-wide known pianist Liu Shih-k'un, laureate of the international Tchaikovsky competition in Moscow, whose wrists were twisted so viciously by the same savage youths that he will never be able to play again. If the expulsion of Aleksandr Solzhenitsyn from the Soviet writers association was labeled an international scandal and a crime against civilization, what is then the slow physical annihilation of so many Chinese writers, artists and intellectuals? Why are not such resplendent works as The Night Talks Around Yenshan or Notes of the Three-Home Hamlet by Wu Han, Teng T'o and Liao Mo-sha, who dared to offend the tyrant, available in English and other Western languages in book form?

We owe much of the first-hand information on the persecution of writers and intellectuals in China to the testimony of Ma Ts'e-ts'ung (now Ma Sitson), China's greatest living violinist-composer who alone among the persecuted outstanding artists was lucky enough to reach the United States. His haunting composition "Longing for Home", which used to introduce Radio Peking's broadcasts to Taiwan, has thereby lost all its meaning for the mainlanders on the island and was instead broadcast back to the mainland! Ma described the cultural revolution as a movement of violence, terror, cruelty, blindness and insanity. If the Chinese dissenters are so little known in the West, is it not a paramount duty of our sinologists to bring them into the limelight and to make them as well known as the Russian victims of tyranny?

Oriental despotism, however, does not create miracles. Even the regimentation of hundreds of millions of peasant-proletarians failed to make it possible for China to skip the intermediate stages of economic development. Mao's thought was not able to move mountains, make deserts bloom, or change the course of the rivers. Hard facts did not budge in front of the millions of the blue or gray "ants". This industrious and intelligent people could achieve great things— but not under Maoist tyranny. That is why the example of China, so highly touted as a model for the third world, is largely irrelevant. The Chinese revolution, a unique event under very particular conditions, simply cannot be transplanted to other developing countries which have gone through their own national revolutions. Moreover, the "peasant areas" of the world are less willing than ever before to follow such a convulsion course as Mao's, an attitude shared by the free and communist nations alike.

Maoists kept reiterating that the struggle against the United States presupposes the struggle against the "negative example", the Soviet Union. They challenged both superpowers simultaneously until the latest opening to the "American people." Yet Peking's two-front confrontation was not as irrational as it might seem. The American-Red Chinese meetings in Warsaw proved to be useful inasmuch as they widened the Russo-Chinese schism owing to the non-invasion promises by the American am-

bassadors as well as to their assurances that the landings planned by
the Chinese nationalists would not receive U.S. support.   Russia
remains Peking's main hereditary enemy as the heretic of the orthodox
secular faith, whereas Moscow hurls the same invective against the
Maoists. The Sino-Soviet military alliance of 1950 is dead, as will be
demonstrated later in this book. Should Red China become involved
in a war of any kind, Moscow would not intervene. Just as its
predecessor, Imperial Russia, the Soviet Union considers its national
interests of primary importance and pays attention to revolutionary
causes only if they are consistent with Moscow's *raison d'état*. And
a weak China is in the interest of Russia as it has been over the
centuries.

In the middle of the Vietnam War, Mao sowed the whirlwind
which was not less important for him and his closest entourage than
the paramount example of a "people's war". The cultural revolution
provoked such a tension and confusion in the entire life of the country
that economic, educational, and cultural activities were largely dis-
rupted and the whole administrative machinery was seriously
weakened. The intramural struggle in China never managed to save
the Maoist image.

In addition, the cultural revolution has accelerated the deterioration of Moscow's and Peking's relations. The Soviet press has used
a heavy dose of sarcasm and irony in covering the outrages of the
cultural revolution and the veneration of the "demi-God". In retaliation, Maoists accused the Soviet leadership of being "traitors" and
thus formalized the breach.

Will a more moderate Chinese communism emerge after the
passing of the "great helmsman", or will the system collapse completely? The cultural revolution may yet turn out to be the event that
hastened Mao's *Goetzendaemmerung* (Nietzsche) and thus eliminated
the chances for a conflagration. Mao's policies have discredited communism to the extreme and have pushed China into her lowest
standing. After the failure of all these schemes, the great Chinese
nation and the whole world will profit.

*   *   *   *   *   *

Writing current history in flux is more a task of journalists than scholars who some day will have all the complete data at their finger tips. If this book has come close to what Professor Benjamin B. Schwartz of Harvard has called high-order journalism, then the author will have accomplished his task.

A wide variety of sources—Chinese (both communist and nationalist), Russian, Japanese, French, German. Italian, Indian, etc.—were consulted and evaluated, besides American and British sources. Attention was also given to valuable information on China from Yugoslav sources, not available elsewhere. The forgotten prophets of the Sino-Russian clash were given extensive hearing although this writer does not necessarily agree with all they say. The differing schools of Marxism-Leninism and their distinctive viewpoints are exhaustively represented and inferences are drawn as to the sources and nature of the conflict.

Slavic Cyrillic letters have been transliterated, while the Chinese names and notions were romanized in a simplified practical way, differing from the U.S. Congressional Library and Wade-Giles standards, but in accordance with the American Geographical Society ones.

Small portions of the book, now published in a much revised version, were previously used in *ACEN News, Central-East European Papers,* The *China Quarterly* (London), *East Europe, Estudios sobre el comunismo* (Santiago, Chile), *O Estado de S. Paulo* (Brazil), and *Témoignages* (Monaco); in lectures at the Assembly of Captive European Nations in New York City, ACEN seminar in Medellin (Colombia), the seminar of Professor Bogdan Raditsa at Fairleigh-Dickinson University (New Jersey), School of Freedom of the Liberal International at the University of Kingston (Canada); and distributed by the North-American Newspaper Agency.

Oton Ambroz

New York City, 1971, after Lenin's centenary
and in the Chinese year of the pig.

CHAPTER I

Conflicting National-Revolutionary Interests

Nationalism and the Communist Doctrine

Despite the ideological affinities, Russia and China represent—given their completely divergent stages of national development—two very different societies with rather distinct brands of leaderships: Russia is ruled by a Party apparatus which developed in a communist country and was subject to changes of a new class type. She has a government of "clerks." The experience of the stoic first-generation Chinese revolutionaries has been entirely different. They followed Mao Tse-tung and "served under harsh material circumstances and military conditions. For them the austerity of extreme proletarization, the regimentation, improvisation, and reliance on organization and propaganda rather than on objective conditions must appear as natural features of the struggle for communism."[1] However, many of the old veterans do not share this opinion.

In the classics of Marxism lifelike prognoses relating to the possibilities of conflict between socialist countries were expressed. However, under the influence of the Soviet interpretation of the classics, it was taken for granted that when "the class struggle" disappeared there would be no further reason for antagonistic contradictions among socialist nations such as have driven capitalist nations into conflict and war. Conflicts among socialist nations would automatically vanish. Soviet-Yugoslav tensions in the Cominform period, the Hungarian and Czechoslovak invasions, the Russo-Chinese conflict and to a lesser degree Soviet-Albanian and Sino-Cuban differences are the best evidence that this article of their secular faith violates reality. Yet as recently as 1960 the Moscow Statement declared that

1

no conflicts can exist among communist nations. The 1969 international communist conference was more realistic. In the aftermath
of the Czechoslovak crisis in Belgrade it was concluded that communists must "definitely cut the roots of various illusions claiming
that armed conflict is impossible between socialist countries." Here
the Yugoslavs are in accordance with Mao who proclaimed that
"Contradiction is universal and absolute, it is present in the process
of development of all things and permeates every process from
beginning to end ... Every form of society, every form of ideology,
has its own particular contradiction and particular essence."[2]

In the Comintern period it was assumed that whenever communists took power in a country the latter would become part of the
Soviet Union.[3] Such incorporation into the "socialist fatherland" was
viewed seriously as late as after the end of World War II. Yugoslavia
was no exception. According to an official Soviet document, Edvard
Kardelj, now a member of the Yugoslav Federation Council, told the
Soviet Ambassador, I. V. Sadchikov, on June 5, 1945, that "he
would like the Soviet Union to regard them (the Yugoslav communists) ... as representatives of one of the future Soviet Republics,
and the Yugoslav Communist Party as a part of the All-Union Communist Party, that is, that our relationship should be based on the
prospect of Yugoslavia becoming in the future a constituent part of
the USSR."[4] However, in the next few years Kardelj changed his
mind completely.

Later on, Stalin strongly opposed Tito's plans for a communist
Balkan federation under Yugoslavia's leadership, conceding only that
Belgrade might "swallow" Albania.[5] At his last meeting with
Yugoslav leaders in February 1948, Stalin proposed a union between
Yugoslavia and Bulgaria, hoping to subordinate the rebellious Tito
to the loyal Dimitrov, but President Tito rejected the suggestion.
With the victorious Chinese revolution it became completely clear
that it was out of the question for the Soviet Union to ever become
a single all-embracing communist federation.

For too long the Western world, surprisingly enough, believed in
the "unity" of the two big communist powers, as if all the historical
and geopolitical reasons for conflict, lasting for centuries, had disappeared promptly because the communists had come to power. On
the contrary, due to common ideological considerations but dif-

ferences as to their implementation, old rifts of national expansion have become more emphatic and complicated. Both regimes are no longer interested merely in their own *Lebensraum* but are attempting to dominate each other and the world. They not only have conflicting national interests as in the past, but also conflicting revolutionary interests everywhere. Marx and Lenin did not foresee that communist countries would succumb to the baccillus of nationalism, and that this germ would one day shatter the unity of the world communist movement. Nationalism is triumphing over communism!

An identical view was expressed in President Nixon's "New Strategy for Peace" foreign policy message: "International communist unity has been shattered. Once a unified bloc, its solidarity has been broken by the powerful forces of nationalism ... The Marxist dream of international communist unity has disintegrated."

The Lenin centenary theses of the CPSU's CC put the same idea in another way proclaiming "that neither nationalism in any of its forms nor national nihilism are compatible with socialism."

"Marxist doctrine became a camouflage which more or less concealed nationalist and imperialist aims," said the Russian opposition writer and historian Andrey Amalrik reflected in his famous essay on the possibility of war between Russia and China coming in respect to the conflict to the following conclusion:

The absolute antagonism of their national-imperial interests and the conflicting character of the internal processes in each country—"proletarization" and the rise of a fearsome "revolutionary curve" in China and "deproletarization" and a cautious descent along the same curve in the Soviet Union—quickly put an end to any pretense of unity."[5a]

This is what we are witnessing now, an erosion of communist solidarity because of national self-interest. The Russo-Chinese conflict is playing a paramount role in the process. The same socioeconomic system cannot save communist countries from disagreement and contradiction as was once held. The Russians finally had to admit this. The ruling Parties are no longer simply national branches of the communist international. "How is the turbulent flow of national consciousness and national pride ... to be directed along the course of socialist internationalism?" *Izvestia* asked in a theoretical article. The international communist conferences of 1957

and 1960 tried vainly to surmount "the vestiges of bourgeois nationalism and chauvinism."

Further developments have shown that "life has proved to be
more complicated and contradictory" than the formula of "necessary
solidarity."

The actual practice of contact among the countries of socialism
has shown that this homogeneity of socio-economic, political
and ideological structures is a necessary but insufficient prerequisite for the real establishment of the principles of ...
mutual understanding in the relations among socialist states.
Historical experience bears witness to the fact that a complex
intertwining of objective and subjective factors connected with
the considerable disparity in the levels of socio-economic development of the individual countries of socialism, with differences of a historical-cultural and geographical nature and
with varying degrees of cognizance by the various Parties of
the laws of development of socialism, can lead in practice to
deviations from the international principles.
Such a policy is based on the fact that *each socialist state may
have its own national interests* (italics provided) connected
with peculiarities of its history, geographical location, economic development, etc. ... An underestimation of national
interests and requirements and a striving to accomplish inter-
nationalist tasks without regard for the specific nature of their
refraction through the prism of the national consciousness of
socialist peoples can harm the cause of unity of the fraternal
countries.[6]

Again proclaiming strict non-interference in each other's internal
affairs since "each Party is sovereign," the solution was seen in a
harmonious combination of the national and international interests of
"independent and equal countries of socialism in a socialist camp or—
what amounts to the same thing—the world commonwealth of socialist
countries, [where] no one has or can have any special rights or
privileges," to quote the Soviet Party program. All this and many
other similar tracts prove how hard it was for the Russians to theoretically justify the occupation of Czechoslovakia.

The alleged concessions by the Russians are not enough to
establish harmony since the Chinese answer "with abuse and arrogant

dismissal of the opponent's arguments." The trouble is that the Chinese "absolutize their own experience, hold a dogmatic, schematic conception of the Marxist-Leninist theory and show a sectarian yearning to restrict socialism to a narrow range of 'legitimate' forms and methods."

Many examples of mutual accusation are quoted through this book. The Chinese described the Soviet leadership as "sunk in the mire of bourgeois national egoism."[7] The Soviets answered in a Central Committee letter in the winter of 1966 that the ideological-political platform of the Mao Tse-tung group serves "the nationalistic big-power policy of the Chinese leadership" to instigate a world war.[8] To substantiate this thesis a selected number of authorities are quoted: a former U.S. Secretary of State, four American scholars with former high diplomatic responsibilities, a former Asian head of state, the Nestor of American commentators, a writer with long-standing intimate ties to Red China's leadership, two communist leaders and a communist apostate. Similar quotations could be cited indefinitely.

Dean Rusk said, in his statement outlining ten elements in American policy toward communist China, before a closed session of the Sub-Committee on the Far East and the Pacific of the House of Representatives' Foreign Affairs Committee: "The essential nature of this conflict . . . has, if anything, intensified and widened. Its Russo-Chinese national aspects have become more conspicuous."[9]

Roger Hilsman, Department of Law and Government, Columbia University, former Assistant Secretary of State for Far Eastern Affairs, declared at the hearings held by the same Sub-Committee the previous year: "My feeling is that the Chinese communist price for healing the breach will be too high for the Soviets to pay. In the first place, the Chinese will undoubtedly insist on a very large share of the leadership of the bloc and a very large place for Chinese national interests, as opposed to Russian national interests, in deciding on bloc policy—in both cases probably too large a share."[10]

Walt W. Rostow, former special adviser on national security affairs to the President of the United States, stated about the conflict: "It is the power issue that underlies their ideological differences that makes it such a serious fight . . . It is a major historical fact, which is that the communist movement as an international movement has proved itself incapable of organizing on a unified basis."[11]

Edwin O. Reischauer, a reknowned Orientalist and former U.S. Ambassador in Tokyo, said in his recent book:

The Chinese had a deep national pride and long and bitter resentments of the Occident that made the acceptance of Russian domination extremely distasteful to them. Two such huge and different nations, even though joined by the same communist faith, did not necessarily have mutually compatible national interests.[12]

Foy D. Kohler, former Ambassador to Moscow and Deputy Under Secretary of State for Political Affairs, affirmed in an interview:

Even a decade or so ago, anyone who knew the history of the two countries could feel certain that their national antagonisms would eventually prove to be stronger than their ideological ties. I'm glad to say that I made a speech at Columbia University, back in 1951 during the China debate, in which I said it was inconceivable to me that the two would stick together over the long run.

Prince Norodom Sihanouk, the former Cambodian head of state, said in an address to a young socialist rally: "There is a white communism and a yellow communism, and they collide when their nationalist interests diverge."[13]

Walter Lippmann wrote:

I am convinced it is the same conflict which existed when the Emperor of all the Russians and the Emperor of China were still on their thrones. It is a conflict of national interests between the Russians and the Chinese which has gone on for generations, and it is due to a collision between the Russians, expanding across Siberia to the Pacific Ocean, and the Chinese, expanding northward into Manchuria and Mongolia, across the path of the Russians.[14]

Edgar Snow says in his latest book, after interviewing Chinese communist leaders and touring two-thirds of the provinces of China proper: "What recent years have revealed is that nationalism inside the communist system of states threatens to be at least as powerful a factor as the bonds of class solidarity which socialist power would theoretically make unbreakable."[15]

The true nature of the conflict was confirmed by President Tito, who declared in an interview criticized in China and ignored in Russia, that "the differences are less ideological and more political in character."[16]

The Mongolian First Party Secretary, Yumzhagiin Tsedenbal, declared at an extraordinary ideological conference organized by the Central Committee in Ulan Bator that the "Chinese comrades are using a nationalistic ideology as a weapon in the disguise of the pseudo-revolutionary phrase."[17]

Milovan Djilas, after serving nine years in prison under the Tito regime for unmasking the new parasitic communist ruling class and for his revelations about Stalin, declared in New York:

> I know very well that this split in communism between China and them [the Russians] is definite. This is not like a split between small Yugoslavia and Russia. This is a split between great powers. And they cannot find, I am convinced, compromise on an ideological basis. That means they never will be people with the same ideas ... The fact is, we now see that a revolution cannot change a nation, its tendencies and qualities and traits. Revolution only change the form of power and property but not the nation itself.[18]

It is imperative for Western policy not to do anything that might disturb this natural process of disintegration within the communist world. Some propose either a stand-pat position or recognition of Red China. Statesmanship coupled with the courage to make decisions will be required to find the proper solution. It is necessary for the West to wrest the initiative in world affairs and in the struggle with communism. The Russo-Chinese conflict has become an important factor in Western strategy.

Russia Opposed to a Strong China

Stalin was one of the world's great realists. He may have foreseen that a united communist China ultimately would be a menace to Russia. He may not have wanted communism to win all of China, and may have preferred a Red-governed area in the north, a Chinese communist enclave under Soviet control. The victorious Chinese revolution, unexpected even in Moscow, created the second great communist power. It was no longer possible for the Soviet Union to remain the world center of communism. Thus, the Soviet

Party program contains extensive boasts in Khrushchev style about the "invincible world socialist system," while the Chinese revolution, by far the most important event in the communist world since the October revolution, is dismissed with eleven words.

For a long time it was believed that a Chinese nationalist invasion would necessarily provoke Russian intervention and a world war. Later more credence was paid to President Chiang Kai-shek's opinion of its being a purely Chinese affair, as expressed to Ferenc Nagy, the former Hungarian Prime Minister. In his 1967 New Year's proclamation (repeated in his 1970 message), Chiang said very succinctly: "Only by letting Chinese solve the China problem, can we expect to achieve Asian freedom and world peace." And Dr. Ku Ch'eng-kang, Honorary President of the World Anti-Communist League, stated in his address at the 1967 Freedom Day rally in Taipei, commemorating the decision of over 22,000 Chinese and Korean war prisoners in Korea to choose freedom: "Our reinvasion will receive the support of the people on the mainland, and as domestic action to suppress insurgence it will not lead to an international war. Our military action alone can remove the scourge of Asia, safeguard the freedom of mankind and lay the foundation of peace in the world."[19] Some other Chinese nationalist leaders proposed to alter the defensive meaning of the Sino-American Mutual Defense Treaty and give it a more active posture.

A Hong Kong-based American author Robert S. Elegant, could express the following opinion in this country's most influential magazine on foreign affairs: "The Nationalists, for example, might seek to reassert their authority, and might even succeed in a number of coastal provinces. The Russians may tinker with the northern tier of provinces, since Moscow abhors a political vacuum."[20] Russia fears a strong China, and it is highly probable that she would not intervene in such a case.

A Jesuit priest who lived in China for many years, Dr. Louis La Dany, now the top expert on Chinese communist affairs in Hong Kong and Director of the *China News Analysis,* pointed out: "If anybody could establish a bridgehead, solidly, on the coast of the China mainland, there is an 80 percent probability that the whole country would be shaken."[21] There was not yet a cultural revolution in progress at the time.

Peking is nervous about the Chinese national government on Taiwan and has made offers on several occasions to some of its representatives. This anxiety was manifested, for example, when General Li Tsung-jen, former Acting President of China in the critical year of 1949 and a few months after the communist take-over, returned home from a long exile in America. His return was exploited for propaganda purposes to appeal to other nationalists. After the turmoil broke out he was not heard of again and recently died.

It is known that the Chinese communists have even boasted of American guarantees that there will be no invasion either from Taiwan or anywhere else.[22] What they have offered in exchange can be explained by their behavior during the Vietnam war.

The chaos after the total breakdown of the "great leap forward" was not utilized for an invasion which then could have been accompanied by large-scale uprisings in the difficult years of 1959-61. Nevertheless, the Red rulers felt uneasy in those years. Red China was saved from doom twice: first, as a consequence of the American reluctance to violate the Yalu River boundary, and then after the collapse of the commune system. The alleged American guarantees enabled Peking to go so far in the conflict with Moscow as to risk a definite split, and to enter a two-front verbal war against both superpowers. Meanwhile Marshal Ch'en Yi's hair turned grey, as he stated, but the Americans did not come.

To the Red Chinese, imperialists are enemies while the Soviets are "traitors," worse than enemies. Yugoslav sources emphasized that the United States builds its policy in Asia to a considerable extent on the Russo-Chinese conflict. Peking "did not turn a deaf ear" to American assurances despite its public statements. In fact, Red China does not forsee any major clash with the United States in the near future, and "growingly shifts the burden of its main and increasingly only action to the Asian borders of the Soviet Union, and, in a wider context, against world revisionism."[23]

Ideology as an instrument of power is of great importance, above all in the ruling Parties, because it serves to justify totalitarian power; any erosion of it endangers this power. Factions in the communist world cause grave embarrassment and are prohibited at home. It is very unpleasant, therefore, for ruling Parties to have to recognize factions on the international level even if their existence is attested to by hard fact. The struggle for doctrinal authority is as important as the struggle for power, indeed is an essential part of it. With the Chinese preaching *ex cathedra* canons, there are two co-equal centers of authority. Experience shows that ideological and organizational subordination go together in the relations among communist Parties.

"What will the word 'communism' then signify?" asked Professor Brzezinski, Director of the Research Institute on Communist Affairs at Columbia University and a consultant to the State Department. "In the history of ideas, 'relativization' of a hitherto absolute ideology is often the first stage in the erosion of the vitality of the ideology. That is why prolonged Sino-Soviet tension is so ominous for the communist world." Then he continues, "Cynicism combined with institutional interests can for a while support the corrupted ideological edifice, but inside there develops an emptiness and the corrosive feeling that the structure of power no longer has any justification and legitimacy."[24]

The Chinese communists argue that there is a "temporary majority" in the international movement which "persists in revisionism," and a "temporary minority" which resolutely upholds the "truth of Marxism-Leninism." Thus, an impression has been created as though the international communist movement were in a situation analogous to that of the Second International on the eve of its split. There is every evidence the Red Chinese will contribute to the disintegration of the communist world in a way the Titoists never had been willing to do, and that "in the long run . . . the corrosive acids of nationalism may ultimately split the bloc asunder."[25]

When the 24th Soviet Party Congress opened in March 1971, the roll-call was answered by fraternal delegates from 102 communist and sympathizing Parties, who were pro-Soviet without being blindly submissive to Moscow or ready to excommunicate the Chinese. Only a few Parties joined the Chinese in boycotting the Congress although there are about 23 pro-Chinese Party factions, with still others wavering. Pro-Soviet and pro-Chinese Parties are fighting each other in so many countries, forgetting the "class enemy." As Mao said to Chinese students in Moscow in 1957, the occasion of his last visit: "If we do not have a leader our forces may disintegrate."

The two communist great powers may converge in their ends, but diverge in their means and methods. It is impossible to reconcile

Russia's "welfare communism" with China's "warfare communism." They are fighting first and foremost for authority and power in the communist orbit itself, and then in the world as a whole. The Red Chinese are communists as well as nationalists, yet they are more chauvinistic than the Russian communists. To some of them, Mao Tse-tung's regime is the most efficient instrument for restoring the millenia of China's ancient glory. Said the noted historian, Professor Hans Morgenthau: "The basic direction of her [China's] policies is determined primarily by her traditional national interests, and ... communism only adds a new dynamic dimension to the means by which the policies are to be achieved."[26]

Communist propaganda seems to have been unbelievably successful in sowing its myths and legends in the free world. Among them is that of the "monolithic" world communist movement based on ideology. Yet, in the Khrushchev era, particularly in its last years, much was officially revealed on both sides to demonstrate how deep, far-reaching and insoluble the conflict was. And again, right after Khrushchev's downfall, a large sector of the mass communication media in the free world appeared to believe the new Soviet leaders might be able to resolve the conflict. It took only five weeks to prove that nothing had changed. Khrushchev's ouster alone could not pacify the Chinese. They soon discovered that Khrushchevism was still in the driver's seat, *sans* Khrushchev. The Soviets would have had to renounce no less than the de-Stalinization process initiated at the 20th Soviet Party Congress, systematized at its 22nd Congress, and embodied in the new Party program. They would have been forced to engage in public self-criticism and recantation and accept the predominance of the Chinese general line in world communism—a price *no* Soviet leadership could ever pay.

The "Secret Speech", Economics and Sinification

The first Soviet version asserted that serious differences arose between Peking and Moscow after the 20th Congress of the CSPU, Khrushchev's "secret speech" condemning the "personality cult" being the original cause of the conflict. Mao's Stalin-like position in the Communist Party of China was at stake. But according to the Chinese, the conflict unfolded before the whole world on September 9, 1959, when a Tass report regretted a Sino-Indian border incident and condemned China indirectly by depicting the clash as tragic and deplorable. In turn, Mikhail Suslov, the Soviet master ideologue, traced the origins of the rift back to 1958, to left deviationism in China and brinkmanship in the Taiwan Straits, which counted on the alleged shield of Soviet superiority. Here the reasons advanced by both sides stem much more from pure power politics than ideology. However, one fact is indisputable: Khrushchev first raised the issues during a speech behind closed doors and in the presence of international communist leaders at the Rumanian Party congress in the middle of 1960. It was the beginning of the dispute that was to develop into a fight at high noon in mid-1963.

The Chairman himself set the roots of the conflict at 1945, when Stalin opposed the renovation of the civil war and asked for continued cooperation with Chiang Kai-shek. Mao confirmed it in his speech to the 10th CC plenary session in 1962. This and other things were revealed in the Mao papers, compiled by the red guards and other Maoist rebels, consisting of unpublished speeches, directives and letters, and released by the U.S. State Department.[27]

Some Western scholars insist on the ideological character of the dispute and maintain it started, for example, with the publication of four polemical articles in the theoretical journal *Hung-Ch'i* (Red Flag) and *Jen-min Jih-pao* (People's Daily), and the polemical speech delivered by then Politburo member Lu Ting-yi (purged during the cultural revolution) on the 90th anniversary of Lenin's birthday in spring 1960. He stressed the connection between uninterrupted revolution and warfare. The Chinese denied these ideas had anything in common with Trotsky's theory of the "permanent revolution," something the Russians refused to concede. In general, Chinese authors lean more on Lenin's writings before the Bolshevik *coup d'état,* whereas Soviet ideologists rely more on Lenin, the victor, and his concessions during the New Economic Policy period. Chinese communists themselves told West Bengal's Red leader, Konar, that difficulties with the Soviet Party started after Stalin's death.[28]

Other observers believe the earlier "Soviet period" of the Communist Party of China (*Chung-kuo Kung-chan-tang,* hereafter CPC) in southeastern China ended in 1942 with the Party reform *cheng-feng* movement (correction of unorthodox tendencies or rectification campaign) writings,[29] when a specifically Chinese form of communism began taking shape. The CPC, as Liu Shao-ch'i, the now toppled President of the People's Republic stressed, is "a proletarian Party of an entirely new kind . . . built upon the most solid theoretical foundations of Mao Tse-tung in its application to China." Mao's theory was described by the same author as based on the actual practice of the Chinese revolution. In his lengthy report to the 7th CPC Congress in 1945, Liu spoke about Chinese Marxism and Chinese communism. It appeared in book form entitled *On the Party.*

Recently the Russians have finally admitted that it was during the 1942-1944 period that the shift of the CPC to the ideological platform of Mao Tse-tungism was basically completed and the Chinese communists broke with the Soviet Party pattern which they labeled "foreign stereotypes."[30]

Like the recent cultural revolution the *cheng-feng* movement was a large-scale campaign to purge Party cadres. The Soviets accuse K'ang Sheng, now a member of the Politburo's Standing Committee, of having been the executioner who "wantonly labeled 90 percent of the Party, government and military cadres in the liberated areas as spies and traitors or their collaborators . . . K'ang's hatchetmen bloodily oppressed and ruthlessly tortured the righteous communists who criticized Mao's policy and tactics and strived for friendship and close cooperation with the CPSU and the USSR." Mao once boasted to Aidit, the late Indonesian communist leader, about this purge and said: "In northern Shansi, I killed 20,000 cadres at one stroke."

In Mao's entourage an important role is played by K'ang Sheng. He has the delicate position of head of intelligence and liaison with foreign communist splinter groups, a position in which he presumably attempts to lay the groundwork for a pro-Maoist, anti-Soviet communist international, the fifth one. Yet as Djilas predicted, "China will lose every prospect of becoming the hotbed of world communism."

K'ang Sheng, a former graduate from the Comintern school, was also portrayed by the Soviets to Chinese listeners in his present position: "He is an outstanding figure among the handful of adventurists who cluster around Mao and who faithfully carry out his antipeople and anti-socialist policy . . . His hands are dripping with blood of thousands of communists, tortured and killed by him." As the leader also responsible for Maoist cadre policy, and as head of the reinstatement commission to decide the fate of the old Party cadres, he applied sly and cruel measures against communist leaders who displease the Chairman. He advanced from the 25th place in the hierarchy to the fifth place. The Russians call Mao's entourage *oprichnina,* Tsar Ivan the Terrible's palace guard of woeful memory.

Altogether 26 splinter groups, mostly insignificant, were brought together in a roll-call of the pro-Maoists at the 5th Albanian Party congress in 1967. On a visit to China Mehmet Shehu, the Albanian premier, speaking in Wuhan in the presence of Chou En-lai and K'ang Sheng, described the way how to overthrow the pro-Soviet regimes and Party leaderships:

> The great proletarian cultural revolution has become a great example for the communists and people of countries under the rule of revisionist cliques; it shows them how to rise in revolution to overthrow the revisionist cliques, rebuild a dictatorship of the proletariat, and return to the socialist road. It inspires the genuine communists in the communist and workers' Parties where revisionists and renegades have usurped the leadership: it shows them how to rise up and topple the revisionist renegades' leadership and bring their Parties back to a truly Marxist-Leninist road.[31]

A key point of friction in the Sino-Soviet conflict is that the Soviet Union is in large degree a status quo power while Red China is not one at all. Moscow seemingly accepts the nuclear stalemate and keeps promising the peoples of the Soviet Union a better life after five decades of sacrifice. China, on the other hand, demands that Russia renounce this stand and fight for communist conquest of the world. That such a course would lead to mutual destruction of East and West is well realized in Moscow if not in Peking.

The Red Chinese, building empty-stomach socialism, are trying to organize dissatisfied communist factions into an opposition against the developed Soviet Union with its (not yet) full-stomach socialism. The ultimate causes of the present pulling and hauling in the communist world are rooted in economics. This fact was confirmed by the Italian Party chief, Luigi Longo, who stated: "The essence of the conflict lies in the problem of the transition from socialism to communism, or simply: in the pace of development of the Chinese economy." The Red Chinese have never forgiven the Soviets for refusing to provide the large-scale economic aid required to speed their own development. The Russians gave them grants and credits niggardly, less than to small communist countries and India. It amounted to 13 percent of Soviet aid to communist countries generally, and 8 percent to their total aid before being terminated.[32] Was Moscow unable or unwilling? The American geopolitical writer, Homer Lea, predicted in 1904 that "if Russia ever helped China to develop into a major industrial power, this would mean the end of Russia's Asian regions."[33] The Chinese communists claim that the construction of communism in one country is impossible, and that this construction must be proportional and parallel in all socialist countries; the idea is a new version of Trotskyism.

Not until January 1954 did Moscow *Kommunist* acknowledge that China was marching "along the road to socialism." In Stalin's time a transition from feudalism to socialism (communism) was not admitted.[34] Tito's biographer, Vladimir Dedijer, recalls that after the 1927 defeat Mao Tse-tung became an arch-revisionist. He put the main emphasis on the peasantry and his policy was then called agrarianism. But after his victory in 1949 Mao turned out to be an arch-dogmatist. The explanation lay in the harsh Chinese situation. The Polish saying, "Thank God, Russia is between us and the Chinese" is becoming more evident daily, Dedijer says.[35]

Mao Tse-tung has created an amalgam, a Chinese or Asiatic form of communism. He has "Sinified" Marxism. His ideology is a peculiar blend of Marxism, Stalinism, Trotskyism and pragmatism, the definition of Professor Zagoria—without producing a genuine intellectual synthesis. Professor Possony expressed a more peculiar definition holding that "the Chinese Bakunin *modus operandi* is a mixture of Blanqui (the revolutionary socialist), Lenin and Stalin, the late Ch'ing Dynasty, the howling dervishes, terrorism mixed with hypnotism, and Pavlovism (conditioning of people) applied through word magic." The Russians say approximately the same: Maoism consists of elements of Marxism, and it has borrowed from Utopian socialism, anarchism, Trotskyism and populism (Russian pre-Marxist revolutionary movement focused on the "people"—*narodnichestvo*.).[36] And from Confucianism it took the preaching of the spirit of obedience, the praising of authoritarian power and the cult of the supreme ruler.

However, according to Professor Benjamin Schwartz, Maoism

represents a new stage in the degeneration of Marxism. Mao said, in
his report to the 6th plenum of the sixth Central Committee in October
1938, repeating Lenin's dictum: "Their theories (of Marx, Engels,
Lenin and Stalin) are not to be looked upon as dogma but as a guide
to action." He continued: "Marxism must take on a national form
before it can be applied ... What we call concrete Marxism is
Marxism that has taken on a national form ... The Sinification of
Marxism—that is to say, making certain that in all its manifestation it
is imbued with Chinese peculiarities ... We must put an end to
writing eight-legged essays on foreign models."[37] The Russian communists denied this thesis, claiming that Marxism is one and indivisible. They said there is no European or Asiatic, African or American
Marxism-Leninism. The program of the CPSU was allegedly recognized by the fraternal Parties as the "Communist Manifesto of the
20th Century."[38]

There was an enlightening polemic on the originality of earlier
Maoism between Professors Benjamin Schwartz and Karl A. Wittfogel
in 1960. The latter called it a derivation from Stalinism and rejected
Schwartz' viewpoint.[39] But after what has happened in China in the
course of the 1960's there can be no further doubt on the unique
character of latter-day Maoism.

It may be useful, in this connection, to recall the forgotten
prophets of the great schism that has changed the balance of world
power. Their ideas could shed some light on the origins of the Sino-
Russian confrontation. Two well-known German writers on political
affairs predicted the conflict between the two communist great powers
at the beginning of the 1950's, immediately after the Red take-over in
Peking. There was a different appraisal in the Anglo-Saxon world
following the Red Chinese victory. In the prevailing American view
it was futile to suppose Peking could be divided from Moscow. Yet,
inside the State Department one school of thought correctly cham-
pioned the idea of an inevitable dispute between Communist China
and its ideological sponsor, Russia, because Mao's inherently heretical
nationalist drive would lead to a truly independent China.

British Foreign Office experts also foresaw a crisis in Russo-
Chinese relations, but did not expect it to develop for some decades.
The British, furthermore, expected the emergence of two different
kinds of communism, which the West should exploit by making con-

cessions to the new, united mainland China.

The first of our two prophets (both died in the mid-fifties) was Dr. Franz Borkenau, a sociologist, and a former associate of leading communists of the 1920's as well. He wrote most interesting inside stories on the top leadership of the Kremlin. His own experience was very useful in this respect, as are for instance the revelations of Professors Karl A. Wittfogel and Wolfgang Leonhard who sometimes tell us what a writer who has not himself been a communist would hardly perceive. *Newsweek* called Borkenau's writings "brilliantly accurate prophecies." He not only predicted that a Sino-Soviet conflict would develop after Stalin's death, but he raised a highly pertinent question: "How really hopeful for us are their disagreements?"[40] He warned the West against unwise concessions and flaccidity of purpose.

Sino-Soviet Relations Rewritten

Why were the Russians so afraid after unexpectedly acquiring so formidable an ally in the cold war against the West? Borkenau grasped the true nature of Russian fears long before they were exposed to public gaze by the endless exchange of mutual recriminations: The Russians apprehensively and resentfully viewed the threat the Red Chinese victory represented to their exclusive control of world communism, a challenge which contained the seeds of a life-and-death struggle. This was the crux of the conflict. Mao Tse-tung, the "Emperor of the Blue Ants,"[41] would play for the leadership of the entire communist movement.

Among other things, the uneasy Russo-Chinese alliance suffered from Mao's tendency to seek "any and every kind of further conquest short of one precipitating a third world war." In Borkenau's interpretation the outcome of the Korean War deprived the Soviet Union of North Korea. Stalin had prompted the war in the conviction of showing Russian superiority over Mao's China. With the expected conquest of South Korea he would head off Chinese expansion in southern as well as northern Asia. It would be a giant step in gaining exclusive control over Asian communists outside China.

On the other hand, Professor Bela Kiraly of NYC University revealed that "had Korea been overrun, Yugoslavia and Greece would have been attacked" in a speech at ACEN's observance of the Asian

People's Freedom Day. He was a major-general who commanded the Budapest garrison during the heroic Hungarian anti-Soviet revolution.

Furthermore, Moscow had an ally against Mao in the late Ho Chi Minh, an old Soviet hand behind the scenes in the Shanghai bureau of the Comintern. However, the 1954 Geneva Conference delivered Ho into Chinese hands. The obstacle Moscow had interposed to Chinese expansionism disappeared. When the West accepted North Vietnam, the communists could not believe their eyes. The West had temporarily freed the communist alliance from its impasse. This was Borkenau's conclusion in the articles he wrote at the time on Soviet affairs for the *Neue Zürcher Zeitung.*

A top Yugoslav official told John Scott, special assistant to the publisher of *Time* magazine five years ago: "The only way you are going to stop Chinese expansion is through local nationalists, and you have a good one in Ho Chi Minh. I know him well. He hates the Chinese and is afraid they will in any case take over his country. But you keep shooting at him. This is what de Gaulle has been trying to tell you in his remarks about neutralization in Southeast Asia. But you won't listen. You bought Tito as a communist-nationalist willing to oppose the Russians in order to defend his independence; why can't you take the same attitude toward Ho?"[42] Will the situation remain unchanged after the passing of Ho?

This is the so-called Tito-of-the-East thesis. True, the North Vietnamese continue to maneuver against a take-over by China, and the Russians are gaining influence in Hanoi. Traditionally the Politburo members are expansionists. It is a known fact that their final goal is to restore the whole of Indo-China to communist rule. Should South Vietnam ever be united with the North, Laos and Cambodia would soon follow as impossible to defend; their neighbors also would be endangered. The head of the Laos neutralist government Prince Souvanna Phouma declared: "Hanoi is out to establish hegemony over all Indochina, taking the place in Vietnam, Laos and Cambodia formerly held by the French."

At a very early date Borkenau summarized what had happened in the relations between Russian and Chinese communists: The Comintern actually lost control over the Chinese peasant armed uprisings, and the communist-controlled areas, starting with 1928. Mao and his mistakenly-labeled "agrarian movement" were never in

Moscow's special confidence. An independent Chinese communist regime was created in the mountains of South Kiangsi, East China. Moscow never punished any of Mao's deviations, granting them *post factum* sanction at a later date. Collaboration with the *Kuomintang,* insisted on by Stalin for the purpose of diverting Japanese aggression from the Soviet Union, proved to be disastrous for the Chinese communists. Mao was too remote for Stalin to purge, although he was potentially Moscow's most important foe. When the German-Russian war broke out, Mao eliminated all Soviet-Comintern agents within the CPC, including the 28 Chinese Bolsheviks (Wang Ming group), pupils of the Comintern, and others whom Stalin had imposed. At the same time, the rectification campaign meant proclaiming *de facto* independence from Moscow and stressing Chairman Mao's doctrine.[43] Stalinism was banned from Party propaganda. "Mao's attitude of independence deepened to one of hostility." After the war Stalin sought to exert pressure on Mao by installing Li Li-san, a personal enemy of Mao, as political adviser to the Red Army in Manchuria. Li was a former leading Politburo member of the CPC who had been criticized for his unhappy doctrine (and practice) of mounting assaults against cities before communist power had been consolidated in the countryside. The boss in Manchuria was Kao Kang, who unsuccessfully rebelled against Mao. Again defying Moscow, Mao resumed warfare with Chiang and conquered China against Stalin's will. In 1936 Mao had told Edgar Snow: "We are certainly not fighting for an emancipated China in order to turn the country over to Moscow." The dissolution of the Comintern in 1943 was greeted by Mao as bringing to an end its "meddling" in Chinese communist affairs.[44]

Borkenau's intimate knowledge of the communist world and his prophecies were scientifically substantiated by Professor Benjamin Schwartz, a Harvard authority on East Asia, in some early studies. Analysing all primary Chinese and Japanese sources available for the period, Schwartz proved Mao's independence of Moscow throughout the entire period of his rise to eminence. He achieved success by a forceful new strategy unanticipated by Stalin.

Professor Franz Michael of the Institute for Sino-Soviet Studies at George Washington University, however, disagrees. He claims that peasant guerrilla warfare and rural soviets were ordered by Moscow itself after 1927.[45] And the truth is that Comintern instructions changed in contradictory fashion. The 6th Congress of the Comintern and the 6th Congress of the CPC were held in Moscow simultaneously in 1928. The Comintern recommended following the Russian example: quick attacks on Chinese towns and reliance on the proletariat. On the other hand, it could be argued that the CPC Congress envisioned Mao's later strategy.

At the time the CPC was led by Li Li-san, nicknamed the "Stalin of China," Mao was then the first political commissar of the Chinese Red Army. In 1929 the Central Committee of the CPC worked out tactics for simultaneous rebellion in the cities and countryside. For a few days in the summer of 1930 communist troops occupied Changsha, the capital city of Mao's native province of Hunan in south-central China and proclaimed the first Chinese Soviet government under Li's leadership. He displayed independence toward the Comintern which in an open letter condemned him as a *Putschist*. He had to resign his Party posts and make a pilgrimmage to Moscow. A decade later Mao criticized him for having overestimated the strength of the Chinese Red Army and the communist movement in the earlier period. Li returned after World War II, was nominated to the CC, became a cabinet minister and then was relegated to the North China Bureau of the CC. The Public Security Minister in Peking called him a "negative example" of the 9th Party congress.

The Comintern was badly informed on Mao's singular course within the CPC. An obituary on Mao Tsze-dun (Russian spelling) actually appeared in the March 1930 issue of its *International Press Correspondence*. A year later Mao became Chairman of the Provisional Central Government of the Chinese Soviet Republic. Yet, everything did not proceed as smoothly as might seem from the version Mao narrated to Snow. The native's description should be accepted with reservations.

Maoism came to birth as a heresy because the CPC based itself on peasant discontent, quite apart from links to the urban proletariat which is a central feature of Marxist-Leninist doctrine. The Party lost its Marxist identity and resembled—the Utopian socialists. Moving eastward Marxism-Leninism was theoretically in process of decomposition. Nevertheless, Moscow later recognized the *fait accompli*. Tito described the present stage of this process as follows: "Explaining in their own manner, literally, geographically, and mechanically, Lenin's thesis on the shift of the center of revolution from West to East, the Chinese leaders in fact wish to conceal their aspirations to hegemony and ideological monopoly in the workers' movement by saying the center of revolution has moved farther to the East—to China."[46]   Actually, Lenin predicted the road to world revolution would pass through Shanghai and Calcutta.

Mao's first republic was a "soviet" in name only.   Professor Schwartz points out that Lenin favored the soviets only when they fell under Bolshevik control, not as authentic representation of all revolutionary parties. Lenin thought the soviets a form of government best adapted to the psychology of a backward peasant society, like China, without any proletariat. At a later stage the earlier lip service to the soviets became a source of embarrassment to the Chinese communists.   Yet, in the so-called new democracy period of Mao's regime, the pseudo-parties for fellow-travelers provided the communists with useful dupes as elsewhere.

Lenin's theory of imperialism (derived largely from others) was very important, serving as the binding link between Marxism-Leninism and Asiatic resentment to which it gave articulation. The enemy was identified as politico-economic domination by white powers over colonies or semi-colonies (today blandly described as developing countries). But what is today sometimes called the "enrichment" of theory by leftist dogmatists and rightist opportunists in the communist movement actually means disintegration of what the classics taught.[47]

CHAPTER II

Different Avenues of Approach (A Pacific Pact)

An Ominous Shadow

The second German writer to predict the Sino-Soviet conflict was Dr. Wilhelm Starlinger, former professor of the Faculty of Medicine of the University of Koenigsberg, East Prussia (now Soviet-annexed and called Kaliningrad *Oblast*). His reminiscences of the seven years he had spent working as a physician in Russian concentration camps—an excellent listening post—were published posthumously in 1957 as *Hinter Russland, China* (Behind Russia, China) and created much stir both in the original and in the French version. Never translated into English, the book might have initiated a new outlook on the Sino-Soviet problem in the United States and Great Britain, and in the English speaking world in general.

In the camps Starlinger's co-inmates were not only *"kulaks"* but also former members of Soviet cabinets, *apparatchiki* of the Central Committee, generals and other officers of the Red Army, as well as ex-officers of the White Army. The latter, exiles in China between the world wars, had been extradited to the Soviets by the Red Chinese following their victory. All had been sentenced to at least ten years of forced labor and faced permanent exile in remotest Siberia even after an eventual release. Since they were "living dead" in the truest sense of Solzhenitsyn's term, they spoke quite freely and the camp authorities did not give a hoot about their political palaver. But the German physician, who became their confidant, absorbed every word.

Starlinger's concentration camp years coincided with the final stages of the Chinese civil war, the take-over by Mao's forces, and the first years of the People's Republic of China. At that time Russians were generally pleased with the success of the Chinese revolution and, simultaneously, apprehensive about the portents of these changes for Russia. Thus Starlinger had a rare opportunity to study the outlook of the Russo-Chinese relations through Russian eyes. At the early juncture, Russians were already aware of an ominous shadow.

Instead of concentrating on "reason of state" and ideology, Starlinger tried to analyze Russo-Chinese relations and the bio-geopolitical background of China in the light of the teachings of Karl Albrecht Haushofer, the famous geopolitician. Starlinger reminded his readers about the lasting impact of the Mongolian rule over Russia in the 13th-15th centuries, an era that left the Russian soul in constant fear of new storms and conquests coming from the East. (This fear was counterbalanced in the past one-and-a-half centuries by three invasions from the West). One of the confirmations of Starlinger's diagnosis came in the late 1960's with the outpouring of Russian nationalistic poems evoking the trauma of the invasions of Mongol khans and denouncing the "yellow peril," past and present.

According to Starlinger, Marxism-Leninism acquired its second center already in 1950, with the victorious Chinese revolution. Moscow, the original center, was no more in power to suppress the new center, because the latter "was not only ideological, but had its own firm political and military foundations."[1]

Since Mao Tse-tung did not take orders from Moscow in Stalin's times, who could then believe, Starlinger asks, that he would accept orders from Stalin's successors. In Starlinger's opinion, the top Party leadership in Peking was more firmly united at that time than in Moscow. Mao, as any dictator who needs a camouflage of "collective leadership," had surrounded himself with outstanding leader-figures. He was also able to keep Russian agents out from his inner circle. Xenophobia ("the foreign devils") proved itself stronger in China than class hate, and the Russian experts, while they were still in China, lived in a ghetto-like isolation.

In contrast, the United States has traditionally helped China and has been her friend. This fact was recognized by the Chinese communists and by Mao himself, as reported in the 1940's by the U.S. State Department liaison group in Yenan. The Chinese communist leaders had maintained then that "American friendship and support is more important to China than Russia," because "the Soviet Union would be unable to provide the needed large-scale economic assistance to China, and that the United States was the only country in a position to do so."[2]

As recently as in 1965, before Mao had started the cultural revolution, he told to Edgar Snow that time was needed, but that it was inevitable that history would bring the two nations closer together. The "traitor" Liu Shao-ch'i was later accused of the same tendency.[3]

One should never forget that in World War II the Americans helped China in its struggle against Japan. Russia instead was historically China's foe. Over one hundred years ago the Amur was still a Chinese river, until the Emperor in Peking was forced to transfer its north shore and the Maritime Province east of the Ussuri River to Russia, thus sealing the division of Manchuria from the Sea of Japan. (This is a Chinese thesis in contradiction with the Russian one.) The Russians then arrogantly went on to found Vladivostok, "The Master of the Orient," in that area. Next came the Russian extortion for the building of the Eastern Chinese Railway. After World War II, Chiang Kai-shek had to restore all former Russian privileges in Manchuria, lost by St. Peterburg after the Russo-Japanese war; shortly before the Chinese communist take-over the Soviets stripped Manchuria almost completely of its plants and machinery. Outer Mongolia under Russian influence has been described as a "fist in China's back", and Mao declared in 1936 that it would be "automatically" incorporated into China in case of a communist victory.[4] No wonder therefore that for Stalin the unification of China, under whatever flag, spelt danger.

The Korean war provided China with an excellent opportunity to establish her dominance, although temporary, in North Korea. Starlinger interprets the collapse of French rule in Indochina as another triumph for Peking. The lack of determination of both superpowers to reach a final settlement enabled Red China to turn the situation in her own favor and to the disadvantage of the superpowers.

As for Russia's investment of less than two billion rubles for the first five-year plan of China's industrialization, Starlinger regards it as Moscow's "tribute" to Peking for the temporary security of the USSR's eastern borders. In a short time Russia helped China to erect

198 major industrial enterprises—a whole industrial system, in
Khrushchev's words, equipped with up-to-date machinery. Soviet
China expert Sergey Tikhvinsky claimed more, 256 such big enter-
prises. The Russian move was in line with the traditional Tsarist and
Soviet policy of avoiding a double confrontation, East and West.
"To act in both directions at the same time would overtax even
Russia's power . . ."[5]

Professors Richard Loewenthal (Free University of Berlin) and
Robert Scalapino (University of California) correctly anticipated at
the hearings held by the Subcommittee on the Far East and the
Pacific of the Committee on Foreign Affairs, U.S. House of Representatives, in March 1965, that "if China becomes truly powerful in
military and economic terms, the Russians will be less able to play
the game of a two-front war."[6] In fact, the Soviet leadership has
tried everything to avoid the new situation. With China's backing in
the East, Starlinger says that Russia was in the position to maneuver
in the West, i.e. in Berlin and in the rest of Europe. Recognizing the
wisdom of the old dictum that even great powers should not fight on
two fronts simultaneously, the Soviet Union was compelled to cede
to China much of what had been set up in the Far East, from Port
Arthur to Sinkiang, by the Tsarist and Soviet regimes during the
past century.

No preacher of geopolitics could have been more outspoken than
Khrushchev, says Starlinger, when in October of 1954, shortly after
returning from the fifth anniversary of the Chinese communist take-
over in Peking, he told the settlers departing for the Virgin lands:
"You must go far to the East, to plow it, but also to remain there,
to establish families, to have children, because even if our 200
million will grow to 300 million, it will still not be enough." And in
April 1956 he emphasized to the All-Soviet Congress of young
construction workers: "We will build our new plants first of all in
Siberia, in Kazakhstan and in the Far East, which are so far from
Moscow and so near to its heart."

Too Many People, Too Little Farm Land

The Chinese-Russian tensions can be clearly read in the basic
statistics. With its burgeoning population, mainland China has only
one half of Russia's arable land. Russia's reserves of iron and coal

are four times larger. The average Chinese industrial wage income amounts to one-fifth of the Russian one, and of the peasants a fraction of it only. Incomes have reached a new low point during the period of the "great leap forward" and the ensuing cultural revolution. The peasants and laborers of China had to forge ahead the industrialization of their country with sweat, tears and blood.[7] The key problem of China remains: too many people and too little farmland. There is no voluntary acceptance of socialization among the peasants, Starlinger says, and they will never lavish their care on public land.

The census of 1953 (583 million), followed by another secret census in 1964, set the average population at 650-700 million. The latter figure was claimed by the mainland press during the "great leap." On later occasions, however, the total was reduced to 650 million and repeatedly announced during the mid-1960's.[8] The magazine *China Today,* published in Peking, even mentioned 600 million. During the cultural revolution 700 million again became a routine figure.

Back in 1938, Mao spoke of "a great nation of 450 million." The carnage of twenty-five years of civil and foreign wars claimed almost fifty million Chinese. The reign of terror was of extreme severity during the first years of the communist regime, especially in 1951. Estimates of the total number of victims were published in the 1950's by Western sources, followed much later by Soviet sources in the late 1960's. Early sources range from 20 million (Chinese nationalist claims), to 15-18 million (U.S. Assistant Secretary of State Walter S. Robertson, U.N. data and Swiss labor experts estimates), 13,394,000 (American labor sources), and to 1-3 million (French General Guillermaz). Mao himself admitted that no more than 800,000 were killed.

It was never officially disclosed how many died of famine in the bitter years following the "great leap", but Chinese nationalist sources claim as many as during the civil and foreign wars years. Even twenty million would be enough to call it the worst famine in a hundred years. Soviet calculations put both physical liquidations and famine victims at 25 million, and on another occasion "bestial killings" alone before the cultural revolution at 26.4 million.[9]

Soon after the new revolutionary committees had taken over the mainland in the fall of 1968, a Japanese radio monitoring agency tabulated all provincial reports from Peking and arrived at a figure of 712 million. Mao spoke to Edgar Snow of 680-690 million Chinese a few years before, a figure that appeared "incredibly high" for the Chairman. Chou En-lai informed Snow that the government hoped to reduce the annual rate of growth from the usual two percent to one percent. This neo-Malthusian program was put into effect and the annual population growth allegedly did decline. The American demographer Leo Orleans predicted a rate of natural increase of 1.5 or 1.6 percent in the next years, and estimated the Chinese population at 746 million by the end of 1969.[10]

Demographic investigations are made especially difficult by the official Chinese attitudes towards statistics. The head of the Chinese State Statistical Bureau, Chia Ch'i-yün, for instance, said at a conference of statistical officials in Peking, in the fall of 1959: "Statistical work is a weapon of class struggle ... Our statistical reports ... certainly should not be a mere display of objective facts." It is no wonder therefore that Western demographers take a rather critical view of Chinese official statistics. Some conclude that the present population figure should be higher,[11] while others put it much lower, claiming that the census served propaganda purposes and was consequently of dubious value. The 740 million figure in the U.N. Bull. of Statistics (Apr. 1971) is an expression of the former view.

The population explosion, a much more grave problem for China than for smaller countries, represents a dangerous source of weakness, and not of strength. Both persuasion and economic pressure have been applied in the effort to curb births. State food and clothing allowances have been withheld for the third child in a family. Many government institutions refuse to grant maternity leave after the third child. Production teams in the communes are using all kinds of pressures to restrict peasant families. The main reason for this governmental effort to enforce birth control (an effort that, as former Foreign Minister Ch'en Yi had complained to newsmen, is ignored in the West) is that the present birth is slowing down the progress of the country and wheat has to be bought abroad in large quantities instead of machines.[12] The present population-production ratio is still such that capital to launch a modern industry could hardly be accumulated.

The historical Chinese drive southward has been frustrated by the opposite biological pressure. If the existing conditions are not altered, Starlinger concludes, China can advance to the North and North-West only.

Starlinger's theory was substantiated by many experts a decade later. Here are some of their statements:

· The noted British historian Arnold Toynbee: "Much of Siberia will become Chinese. If one were a Russian these days, he would have to be alarmed by what the Chinese are going to do."[13]

Cyrus L. Sulzberger of *The New York Times*: "De Gaulle conjectures that the mighty China whose rise he foresees will some day preempt Russia's Siberian and Central Asian territories, which he considers artificially administered by Moscow since they result from 'colonial' conquests".

Harrison E. Salisbury, after completing an extensive tour on mainland China's perimeter, came to the same conclusion: "For the countries on China's Asian frontiers, particularly those with food surpluses, like Burma and Indochina, or uncultivated lands like Mongolia and eastern Siberia, the index of China's food-population ratio is the key barometer. So long as China is unable to resolve the problems of food and population, China's neighbors believe that the temptation of Chairman Mao, his associates or successors to seek land beyond their frontiers must inexorably grow."[14]

Victor S. Frank, a writer of Russian extraction in his article "The Soviet Citizen and the Threat from the East" spoke about the Russian ". . . fear that the Chinese human sea may flood its shores and spill over into under-populated Russian territories."

C. P. Fitzgerald, Professor of Eastern History, Australian National University: "The Amur is a thin barrier against such a flood . . . The Russians may well fear that the eastern Siberia might be next."

Milovan Djilas: "China cannot find room for expansion except in Russia, and at the same time she shares some historical, even some national rights, for example to Mongolia and some parts of Siberia."[15]

Moscow's *Pravda,* the organ of the Soviet Party Central Committee, observed in an important editorial on the Chinese version of *Lebensraum*: "His (Mao's) thesis actually boils down to the fact that the population of the world is distributed unevenly and therefore, allegedly, justice demands a reallotment of territory."[16]

Thus Manchuria had been for half a century a bone of contention between Russia and Japan. Meanwhile the immigration of more than 50 million Chinese have transformed it into three Chinese provinces. The same has happened with the formally autonomous region of Inner Mongolia. Therefore Starlinger holds that such trends could continue elsewhere. The Soviet Union's 4,150 miles of boundaries with China are weak and disputed by Peking. To the west is the Sinkiang-Kazakhstan-Kirghizia-Tadzhikistan boundary from the People's Republic of Mongolia to Afghanistan (1,850 miles). To the east, the Siberian-Amur-Manchurian boundary extends to the Sea of Japan (2,300 miles). Outer Mongolia's southern frontier of 2,700 miles bulging into China proper was recognized by the Chinese communists—perhaps with the second thought of it being just a province border.[17]

Mutual Reinsurance Among World Powers?

In the first chapter of *Hinter Russland, China,* Starlinger presents a résumé of the last, political part of his first book, *Grenzen der Sowjetmacht* (The Limits of Soviet Power), which had made quite an impact in West Germany and in Western Europe in general. He, already in 1954, emphasized that the Soviet leadership was following with concern the Chinese political development as well as its growing biological predominance. Red China's rise was a surprise for the Soviet Union and was frustrating its own plans.

Old Russian-Chinese disagreements came to surface again and were intensified by biological and geopolitical circumstances. The relaxation of tensions between Moscow and Peking was only temporary, the "settlement" merely illusory, since they lasted only as China's military, political and, above all, economic position was too weak to initiate an active anti-Western and anti-Russian policy simultaneously.

Starlinger could not expect that Mao Tse-tung would dare to commit the folly of challenging both superpowers instead of playing them off against each other. Such an attitude, according to Professor Fitzgerald is contrary to the axiom of traditional Chinese policy "that it is unwise and very dangerous to quarrel at the same time with the power which dominates the northern borderlands and the power which rules the Pacific Ocean."

Or could it be that Peking was so sure that the Americans and our Chinese nationalist friends would never attack so that mainland China could concentrate in her struggle against the Russian "heretics"? After all, Russians were China's enemies long before Japan's appearance on the world scene and are hated more than anybody else.

President De Gaulle was the only Western statement to attempt playing off not only Russia against the West, but also China against Russia—to the displeasure of the Kremlin. Would not such a game be profitable for the United States as well? For Senator McGovern, Peking's "struggle against the Soviet Union will increase China's gravitation toward contacts with Western countries."

If China could come to an accommodation with the United States, Starlinger maintained, the situation of the Soviet Union would dramatically change. The potential two-front threat would become a reality, especially along the already politically endangered Asiatic boundaries. What is the Soviet Union to do? In Starlinger's opinion, she must accomplish in some form a concert of the Big Three world-powers regarding mutual reinsurance (*"das grosse Dreiweltmaechte-konzert der wechselseitigen Rückversicherung"*) between Russia-U.S.A., U.S.A.-China, and China-Russia.

In a similar vein, the British economist Barbara Ward, in a conference of the Foreign Policy Association in New York City, envisioned a balance of power in which the three powers would act as countervailing forces—the so-called "doctrine of the three elephants."[18] As regards in particular the nuclear deterrence, the relationship among the "elephants" has become a rather perilous triangular affair.

Speaking at the same conference, Professor Donald Zagoria, director of the Research Institute on Modern Asia at the New York City University made the following statement:

The first point to make is that the United States has inescapably been a silent, if largely unwitting, participant in the Sino-Soviet dispute. The Russian-American-Chinese relationship is a triangle in which a change in the relationship of any two of the powers unavoidably affects the third. Moscow's improved relationship with Washington has in fact been one of the key factors leading to the serious deterioration in Moscow's relations with Peiping.

The main reason for Red China's intense hostility toward the
United States is that the United States protects and supports
an alternative Chinese regime a scant 100 miles off the coast
of China which proclaims its intention to reconquer the
mainland.

He went on to describe the American impact on the split and
the strange triangle in terms of domestic melodrama. Peking played
the part of the aggrieved spouse betrayed by Moscow's 'liaison' with
Washington, complaining about the fumbling response of the West.

Professor Loewenthal expressed the same idea by stating: "Seen
from Washington, the constellation of world affairs no longer appears
bipolar but triangular, offering the West a chance to side with one
communist giant against the other in order to gain its most important
objectives and avert the most urgent dangers."[19]

The Soviet Union remains the most exposed partner, because
directly imperiled boundaries exist only between her and China.
Moscow must first secure the Western side. That could become a
topical political consideration, overnight, should a Pacific accord
succeed. In the opposite case, wrote the German scientist in the
early fifties, China will be compelled to take the most serious internal
decisions in order to starve herself to greatness in solitude. One
should keep in mind here that the gross national product of the three
countries compares approximately as follows: USA (100), USSR
(47), and China (10).

In the last chapter of his book Starlinger sums up his train of
thought by reminding us that a supranational ideology has never yet
been capable in history to preserve its unity for a long time, and that
ideology was shunted aside when it became an obstacle for the conflicting reason of state of an emerging nation. The "most Christian
King" of France had never hesitated to fight "His Catholic Majesty"
of Spain or "His Apostolic Majesty" of Austria when he deemed it
necessary for the sake of France. The same has happened in the
Protestant and Islamic worlds.

This idea was restated by Professor R. V. Burks, Wayne State
University, who wrote: "What the present historical period suggests
is that the true framework of power is not the international communist movement but the nation-state. Only within this context is it
possible to create a viable regime."[20]

When an ideology first unites nations of a different kind, then it must not only preach the "pure doctrine" from one center, but decide it and proclaim it, too. But if, beside that original center, a second center establishes itself, and the first one does not succeed in destroying it, then a schism comes into being. A real schism can be concealed only temporarily; sooner or later it bursts open and generates struggles that surpass any others in ferocity and intensity. The result is, in Dean Rusk's words: "The intense and deadly antagonism that has always characterized schisms in the Marxist world."

Why should national differences and emotions be valid in the Occident only? China's xenophobia is worse than occidental chauvinism. Do not contradictions between allies sometimes degenerate to warfare? Any alliance was valid and proved effectual only *rebus sic stantibus* (things being as they are) and has been frequently changed, Starlinger tells us.

Anyway, Russia's aid to China was small in comparison to the political advantage of Peking's backing which Moscow received for it but, above all, in view of the importance for Moscow of a harmonious Red camp. Should China find an accord with the United States, Russia would be isolated—an isolation she fears more than anything. Russia would not only lose its maneuverability vis-à-vis the West, which she had enjoyed previously, but she would have to secure her western flank and simultaneously meet the full menace from the East.

In Starlinger's opinion (after his nine years of "first hand" experience with the Russians) communism is an anachronism of the last century and has no future. The communist state is based on power only, and without that power "world Bolshevism of the professional revolutionaries" would collapse like a house of cards.

Starlinger's diagnosis was confirmed by Professor Brzezinski: "Communism is dead as an ideology in the sense that it is no longer capable of mobilizing unified global support." Harrison Salisbury made the same conclusion when he was touring the Soviet Union to gather material for a book on the 50th anniversary of the October Revolution: "The cause of the world revolution is dead." And Milovan Djilas also seconded: "When we talk about communists, we are talking about phantoms. The communism of old is dead.

Only the structures it created remain behind."[21]

The Russians as well as the Chinese communists, Starlinger says, would like to conquer "the world empire of tomorrow," but it would be an empire "of the Russian" or "of the Chinese nation" (just as the Holy Roman Empire of the German nation of long ago). In their striving and rivalry, they would inevitably split apart, unless outside pressure compels them to remain in the same fold.

Starlinger's views had an impact on the thinking of some West European governments. The late Chancellor Konrad Adenauer repeatedly consulted him and shared his ideas. (As revealed in the second volume of Adenauer's *Memoiren,* a few years later, in September 1955, Khrushchev confidentially appealed to the Chancellor for help in his attempts to solve the Chinese problem.) Former President De Gaulle has expressed similar views on China and Russia. Thus almost everybody has agreed that Moscow and Peking are involved in a naked power conflict. The exception are some scholars seemingly bent on defending the integrity of the Soviet Union in disregard of facts.

Since the Sino-Soviet rift, according to Starlinger, is in essence rooted in the conflicting national interests of Russia and China, it is therefore permanent. The apparent ideological differences are also an emanation of that clash of national interests. Conflicts are induced, Professor Brzezinski maintains, "by a mixture of ideology and nationalism."

The Maoists might lavish endless phrases about world revolution, but what they have in mind is, above all, China as the revolutionary center of the world.

"The ideological commitment of the Chinese communist leaders is centered on China," according to Oliver M. Lee, an expert in the field. "In a world of sovereign nations, national interests shape the foreign policy."[22]

A subtle form of Soviet propaganda on China was developed in the Khrushchev era. Particularly after the conclusion of the partial nuclear test ban treaty, Soviet diplomats in the West suggested informally to their Western contacts that Russia was indeed deeply worried over China. They went on to say that it was in the interest of both Russia and the West to join ranks more closely in order to face a common danger from China. Thus the Soviets were trying to implant a notion which would allow them to make the best of a bad situation. Since Russia may expect more trouble with China, it will be in Moscow's interest to be on better terms with the West.

The collective leadership after Khrushchev was less eager in this respect, although also ready for an agreement on their own terms. Unlike Khrushchev, they did not lose all hope with China. Moreover, they worried about a possible accommodation between the United States and China.

Starlinger saw in the Sino-Soviet rift an opening for great opportunities for the West. If he is correct, would not the West, and especially the United States, commit an error in coming to terms with Moscow too early in the game? This explains why the Germans have shown such exceptional interest in Starlinger's theory, which among others, offers a way for a potential recovery of East Germany, now a Soviet protectorate. The issue of self-determination in East-Central Europe is also tightly linked with the further development of Sino-Soviet relations. Soviet propaganda has done its best to obscure any such possibilities by clamoring for an agreement with the West *before* Moscow's relations with Peking become critical. Their hope is to freeze the status quo in Russia's favor.

In contrast to the Soviet siren song, Dr. Abraham Halpern bade the West to bear in mind "the ancient principle of power politics that when your enemies are divided you should support the weaker against the stronger."[23]

Chairman Mao commented about such dual tactics more than thirty years ago in his article "On Policy", now resurrected. What he called the enemy's counterrevolutionary dual policy should be countered by a revolutionary dual policy, taking confrontation and negotiation as two aspects of the same policy. This is his "tit for tat" dialectical rational for the recent shift in course. The Chinese horse is running, although the Russians desperately tried to lasso it, in Chou En-lai's metaphor.

CHAPTER III

The Chinese Communist Ideological Challenge

The Rearguard Becomes the Vanguard

Several years ago Moscow seized on Mao Tse-tung's conversation with a group of Japanese socialists to condemn the struggle of the Chinese leaders against the CPSU and the USSR: ". . . in its fierceness, scale and methods it does not differ from imperalism's cold war against the countries of socialism."[1]

As far back as 1951, the year the CPC celebrated its 30th anniversary, Franz Borkenau interpreted the theses promulgated then by its Central Committee as an ideological declaration of war because they stressed the differences between Maoism and Leninism-Stalinism. They asserted the Chinese revolution offered the right path to all non-white, colonial, semi-colonial and industrially backward and dependent peoples living in Africa, Asia and Latin-America. Naturally, such a development would open the door to Chinese world domination. In fact, Liu Shao-ch'i had already proclaimed the Chinese pattern for the seizure of power in such areas in his opening speech on November 16, 1949, to the Trade Union Congress of Asian and Australasian countries meeting in Peking under the sponsorship of the Executive Bureau of the World Federation of Trade Unions.[2] Liu was faithfully repeating ideas expressed by Mao for the first time in 1936.[3] *Pravda*[4] reprinted Liu's speech without comment while the Cominform organ, *For a Lasting Peace, For a People's Democracy,*[5] supported it.

Unlike Marx, Lenin and Stalin who always stressed the leading role of the proletariat in the world revolution, the Chinese assign primary importance to the developing nations on the three continents, declaring that "the rearguard has become the vanguard."[6] This is indeed a "great leap forward" from the modest change made by the Communist International in 1920 when it expanded the Communist Manifesto's slogan to read "Proletarians and oppresssed peoples of all countries unite".[7]

Marx once said, "being determines consciousness." This may help explain why the Chinese extol the revolutionary virtues of developing countries and peoples. They, too, fall into the same category. Even now, after some industrialization with initial Soviet aid, workers account for less than three percent of the Chinese population; the figure was below one percent before the communist take-over. With their "class" bias the Soviets insist the urban proletariat participated in the "liberation" of South China.[8] Professor Schram however contends the Chinese workers contributed nothing to the 1949 victory.

Peking's claim to ascendancy in fostering communism in two-thirds of the world is part of the struggle for power in the international communist movement. The Soviets rejected it during Stalin's lifetime. After the Red Chinese take-over, at a conference held in Moscow under the auspices of the Soviet Academy of Sciences (November 1951), the historian E. M. Zhukov declared: "It would be risky to regard the Chinese revolution as some kind of model for popular democratic revolutions in other Asian countries".[9] Of course, the Chinese delegates present were bitterly disappointed.

However, Khrushchev made a concession to the Chinese. It was a last and unsuccessful attempt at accommodation in what Tito called the "rotten compromise"[10] of the 1960 Moscow Statement issued at the close of the conference of 81 Communist Parties. The document contained a "Chinese codicil," reading as follows: "By giving the national liberation movement a strong impetus, the victory of the Chinese revolution exerted a tremendous influence on the various peoples, especially in Asia, Africa and Latin-America."

Since the Chinese propagate their revolution as *the* valid model for all developing countries, armed struggle is the chosen instrument. This theory has been provided with a pompous ideological rationalization. There are two intermediate zones in the world, Mao told a group of Japanese socialists. Asia, Africa and Latin-America constitute the first, and the whole of Western Europe, Japan, Canada, Oceania and other capitalist countries "trying their best to free themselves from American control," the second. These are areas of a struggle for influence by representatives of two poles. At one end is the United States with, say the Maoists, its covert ally, the Soviet Union. At the other is China and those whose views resemble hers.

The Soviets reject the theory as anti-Marxist-Leninist since it lacks a class approach. They, in turn, arbitrarily shrunk it into just two zones. The major arena in which Soviet-American antagonism is being played out "peacefully," and an intermediate one which includes China.[11] In fact, this Chinese theory contradicts the idea of "people's war."

In his long anti-Chinese diatribe at the February 1964 CC plenum, Party Presidium member and chief Soviet ideologist, M. A. Suslov, said that this global redistribution of friend and foe "objectively whitewashes the imperialists of Britain, France, West Germany and Japan, who find this advantageous" since it negates the division of the world into two conflicting social orders. This faulty vision, he charges, is the consequence of a Peking leadership "blinded by nationalist arrogance."[12]

Nationalism and race hatred inspired the anti-white Chinese formula on how to seize power in developing countries. The Chinese leaders did not primarily direct their messianic propaganda against Western Europe and the United States, but against Russia in order to challenge Moscow's leadership. The importance of the racist ingredient has emerged clearly in the last years as a result of the open rift. The struggle between them for the leading role in Asia, Africa and Latin-America is going on with no holds barred.

The Chinese have had some eager if not very apt pupils. It has been pointed out that the Chinese communist first established their power in the countryside, and then advanced from there to conquer the cities. The Indonesian Communists gave this strategy grandiose world-wide dimensions by way of a metaphor: Now, they said, the developing countries of Asia, Africa and Latin-America represent the countryside of the world and surround the cities, that is, the industrial nations of North America and Western Europe.[13] However, when the Indonesian communists tried to apply the strategy at home they were annihilated.

The Soviets and Mao's "Close Comrade-In-Arms" Thesis

Exaggerated significance has been attached in the free world to a marathon treatise of some 30,000 Chinese characters by Defense Minister Marshal Lin Piao,[14] proclaimed Mao's close comrade-in-arms and heir-apparent during the cultural revolution. In his speech, Lin universalized Mao's guerrilla strategy, calling for "people's war" by the world's countryside against the cities with destruction of the United States as the main target. The document is sometimes termed Mao's "last will." Actually, its key idea is not Chinese in origin at all and can be found in an old thesis written by Bukharin for the 1928 Comintern program on the role of the colonies and semi-colonies of the period. A Soviet delegate, Solomon Lozovsky, secretary-general of the Profintern (left-wing trade union international federation), objected on the ground that it renounced the primacy of the proletariat. In fact, these were notions used by young Lenin, and two years before in the Chinese general line.[15]

Almost four decades later the CPSU's Central Committee voiced the same objection, this time against the Chinese. It did so in a confidential letter dated February 12, 1966 and entitled "Information on the Splitting Activity of the CPC leaders," which it circulated to the ruling Parties of East Europe and Party committees in the Soviet Union on the eve of the 23rd Soviet Party Congress. The authenticity of the text has been verified by comparing three separate versions which reached the West. The Chinese confirmed it in their own way.

Lin Piao's panegyric to "people's war" is described as a complete revision of the Marxist-Leninist doctrine "of the world-historical mission of the working class." It rejects the Chinese estimate that the world is ripe for violent revolution, charging that the latter not only ignores the very diverse developments in Asia, Africa and Latin-America, but the fact as well that patriotic and revolutionary-democratic forces hold power in a number of former colonial and semi- colonial countries. The Maoists are imposing "*putschist,* conspiratorial tactics" on the communist movement.

The Soviets assert the Maoists are not really concerned about world revolution but are "attempting to acquire a cheap popularity through flattery among the Asian, African and Latin-American peoples, to establish hegemony over them and exploit them for egoistic, great-power purposes."[16] But to the Maoists such arguments prove Moscow's revisionist blindness. According to Mao, "a new democratic revolution" spearheaded by communists is under way on these three continents which threatens the power of all the nationalist leaders and political parties of the old and newly-established independent countries. This again closely resembles Trotsky's theory of permanent revolution.

Lin, quoting Mao, connects the spread of communism with war: "War can temper the people and push history forward. In this sense, war is a great school." But Lin's thesis of wars by poor peasants on an international scale is heatedly challenged by Soviet Academician T. T. Timofeyev, Director of the Institute of the International Workers' Movement in Moscow:

> The incorrect assessment of motivating social forces and paths of development of revolution on an international scale is typical of the ideologists of petty-bourgeois socialism, as is the overestimation of the independent significance of the non-proletarian masses' struggle against imperialism. What, for example is the worth of the anti-Marxist thesis that a 'people's war' is the chief path of development of world revolution in our epoch? This thesis is the basis for the concept of 'encircling' the industrial capitalist powers with a 'world countryside' to destroy imperialism. The essence of this idea lies in its oblivion of the laws of class struggle; in its skepticism about the revolutionary potentialities of the proletariat in capitalist countries; in its attempt to replace the fundamental conflict between labor and capital with the contradiction between 'poor' and 'rich' nations; in its absolutization and transference to the world arena of definite specific features of the guerrilla war tactics used in agrarian countries. Such attempts to counterpose the actions of the peasant masses to the revolutionary workers' movement are alien to Marxism-Leninism.

Marxism defined civil war as the continuation of the class struggle by military means. Mao has extended this formula to the breaking point. Not only do wars for national liberation have a class character, but war *per se* is the highest form of class struggle.[17] The Soviets deny this proposition holds true in the international arena: there peaceful competition between the socialist and capitalist camps is the new form taken by the class struggle.

Two years before Lin Piao echoed Mao's doctrine of military conquest of the world, the Soviets demolished China's overall strategy in the theoretical journal of the Soviet general staff, *Voennaya mysl* (Military Thought).[18] They stated that the Chinese are captives of their past experience, the "Peking supermen" do not recognize the "balance of real material forces" in the world. Therefore, say the Soviets, Chinese military science is obsolete. Lin cherishes the illusion, contrary to historical fact, that the Chinese people's war of resistance against Japan decided the outcome of the Pacific war. The touchstone of Mao's military thinking is described as "an eclectic mixture" by the Russians.

With somewhat guilty conscience the Soviets criticize the Chinese for exaggerating political and ideological factors, popular morale, in time of war. When Hitler attacked the Soviet Union Stalin rallied the masses by appealing to their patriotism, by invoking the "great war for the fatherland." Russian nationalist slogans supplanted socialism and the communist system was practically not mentioned during the war years. Certainly China would appeal to such sentiments in a future war even though, or, more precisely, because the Chinese people as a whole oppose Mao's tyranny or communism of any kind. The fact is we already have the proof in the violent nationalist propaganda campaigns on both sides following the Sino-Soviet border clashes.

Nevertheless, Soviet observations on protracted war in a nuclear age are particularly timely. "It is absurd to suppose that a war of attrition will favor the weak and harm the strong. In such a war the weak will be exhausted before the strong." The result of a protracted war would be defeat for the former (if the strong is not defeated at home!) This is the Soviet conclusion which labels Chinese military science "pure adventurism." The Chinese are accused of flirting with genocide because of their readiness to plunge into nuclear war. Lin preaches "reliance on one's own strength." This principle is castigated as "anti-Leninist, anti-Marxist and nationalist," aimed at separating the developing continents from the Soviet camp.

In a subsequent critique, the Soviets say of Mao's military reasoning: "The Maoists intend to force what is obsolete into a new era. This is not only funny but extremely dangerous. Leaders who uphold this strange military doctrine will be sending patriotic people into white-hot flames. The latter can never achieve victory this way."[19] Were not the Vietcong 1968 Tet attacks on cities and towns a horrifying example of this?

General Petrochevsky, chief Soviet military adviser in China from 1953 to 1957, exposed the danger of Mao's defeatist war tactics in a broadcast to China:

With the appearance of rocket weaponry, attacks play an even more decisive role in combat ... Mao Tse-tung is opposed to this indisputable principle of modern military theory. Instead, he propagates his so-called military doctrine which is basically erroneous, negative and defensive in nature and, in fact, points to defeatism ... As early as between 1955 and 1958 Mao used all means to obstruct the establishment of regular armed forces with strict organization and good training ... He needs his army for other purposes ... to defend his own kingdom and suppress the people. He is turning the army into a tool of autocracy.[20]

This is exactly what happened during the pharisaically-named cultural revolution, say the Russians.

Furthermore, the frenzy at home in implementing the cultural revolution had its counterpart in foreign policy with Lin's messianic claim to Chinese hegemony in the world revolutionary process.[21] General Griffith, an expert on PLA problems, suggested at the hearings of the U.S. House of Representatives Sub-Committee on the Far East and Pacific, that Lin unwittingly may have given the West a psychological weapon by revealing the Chinese leaders to be enemies of international peace and creators of chaos. In their not Aesopian language the "fall of imperialism" means the destruction of the majority of mankind and its cultures. The Soviets accuse them bluntly of "descending the path of extreme racist chauvinism" in their quest for world domination by people of the yellow race, bringing "indescribable calamities for all peoples, including the Chinese."

Mao Tse-tung underscored the role of war in the most pointed terms:

Every communist must grasp the truth: 'Political power grows out of the barrel of a gun.' Our principle is that the Party commands the gun, and the gun will never be allowed to command the Party ... (*sic!*)

The seizure of power by armed force, the settlement of the issue by war, is the central task and the highest form of revolution. This Marxist-Leninist principle of revolution holds good universally, for China and for all other countries.

According to the Marxist theory of the state, the army is the main component of state power. Whoever wants to seize and retain state power must have a strong army.

Some people ridicule us as advocates of the 'omnipotence of war.' Yes, we are advocates of the omnipotence of revolutionary war; that is good, not bad, it is Marxist. In this sense we may say that only with guns can the whole world be transformed.[22]

The Soviet leaders believe just the opposite. When Lin Piao, however, says: "They have completely betrayed the Marxist-Leninist revolutionary theory of war and have become betrayers of people's war," he is wrong.

Lenin erred when he prophesied that the collapse of Western colonialism would greatly weaken the former colonial powers—just the opposite happened. The communists have admitted that the *per capita* growth of the industrial countries in the fifties was twice the prewar rate despite the breakup of the colonial empires.[23]

According to Lin Piao, the newly independent countries should now set about conquering their former West European masters, and in addition the North American colossus which is accused of neo-colonialism. But the truth is that the nationalist leaders in these countries do not wish to see movements emerge that might develop into communist revolutions that would topple them. Such was the pattern Chou En-lai explicitly predicted for Africa. Time has not been kind to Chou's vision. The apostles of revolution whom Peking backs make up a motley crew of small refugee groups from a number of countries. Nor is the Chinese timetable being adhered to in the few developing countries with a left orientation. Guinea is an instructive example. After years of unrelenting hostility toward "neo-colonialism," its president, Sékou Touré, is beginning to show a more friendly attitude toward the West.

Red China preaches self-reliance to communists in the developing countries, to fight to the last man when engaged in an internal people's war. But communist Parties in such countries are generally weak, without the peasant base specified by the Chinese blueprint. And even in those situations where the communist Parties hold power, as in North Korea and North Vietnam, they cannot sustain a war without external help from Red China and Russia. They would both have suffered defeat had they relied only on themselves.

By and large the first nationalist phase of Mao's revolution is over in the Third World. The communists should be successfully creating a broad popular front under their leadership and with their own separate power base. There are no signs that this is occurring in left-oriented countries. In consequence, the more realistic Soviets have adopted a different approach: to have their followers infiltrate the ranks of the top nationalist leadership. And while Chinese rhetoric continues to be revolutionary, they seem to have bowed somewhat to the facts of life. The Russians no longer demand legalization of the local CP from the "national democracies" to prove their progressive character as stipulated in the 1960 Moscow Statement.

Peking's plans have also been frustrated by the actions of the Western governments, particularly the United States. The Maoists advise the developing countries to form a coalition and fight the West and its spearhead, the U.S. But these same nations turn to the West for much-needed aid in developing their economies. Material help is one obstacle to Chinese hopes, armed might another. The U.S. Congress has given notice, for example, that any new communist subversion in the Western Hemisphere will be met by American power.

The Chinese communists won at home because of conditions created by Japanese aggression, just as Nazi aggression plus Western blunders enabled the Soviet Union to install miniscule communist Parties in Central and Eastern Europe and start its march toward becoming a super-power. At present no such ill-starred constellations loom on the horizon. Mao's and Lin Piao's blueprint will prove as wrong as Lenin's.[24]

In the Chinese communist diagnosis the peoples of the global countryside should first overthrow their respective governments in a national-liberation war, a formula for guerrilla warfare "supported by the people." After victory communist regimes should take over. The

Red tactic should be like the one used in the Chinese revolution: "fight-fight-talk-talk, talk-talk-stop-stop, stop-stop-fight-fight, fight-while-talking, talk-while-fighting." The Soviets ridicule Mao's "magic means for victory in revolutionary wars" as a "Delphic oracle, spouting truths and tolerating no objections." The Maoists are leading Asia and Africa down "a catastrophic path."[25]

Lin Piao's "Liberation Manifesto" has been mistakenly compared to Hitler's *Mein Kampf,* or viewed as a blunt invitation to another "Hundred Years' War" in its statement of Red China's historic goals. Other interpretations have read into it implied Red Chinese support for so-called wars of national liberation. But this rehash of Maoist dogma did not say what China intends to do, instead it prescribed what communist Parties in developing countries should do.

American experts have tended to discount the significance of Lin Piao's document. Prof. Benjamin Schwartz stated: "To allow our whole analysis of the world to be governed by the potency of Lin Piao's magic formulas is not sobriety but folly."[26]

Professor Zagoria pointed out that "ironically, there are two—and only two—countries in the world in which Lin Piao's revolutionary *smoergasbord* is regarded as some kind of magic weapon: one is China, the other is the United States."[27]

At U.S. Senate hearings, Professor Hans Morgenthau testified that taking "these geopolitical metaphors as a program for political and military action is to completely misunderstand their ethnocentric source."[28]

During the great China debate at the Senate Foreign Relations Committee hearings Professor Fairbank said that the article was simply "a re-assertion of faith" that the "parochial example of rural-based revolution" in China was a model for developing countries.

Professor Rostow, in the course of a lecture at the University of Leeds, asserted that the concept of wars of national liberation is old-fashioned. He expressed the hope that the war in Vietnam "might be the last great confrontation in the postwar era." The passing of Mao would be the end of aggressive, romantic-revolutionary communism.[29]

Generally speaking, Lin Piao's treatise leans more on the subjective factor, as envisaged by Maoism, and relies less on the objective forces of "history" that, according to the teaching of Marxism-

Leninism, should preeminently operate.

Nuclear Warmongering

Mao had flung down the gauntlet at the 1957 Moscow Conference of Communist Parties, saying: "Let us first have a test of strength." He spoke on the possibility of global nuclear war with an astonishing and blood-chilling point of view as reported in the edited Chinese version:

> I debated this question with a foreign statesman. He believed that if an atomic war was fought, the whole of mankind would be annihilated. I said that if the worse came to the worst and half of mankind died, the other half would remain, while imperialism would be razed to the ground and the whole world would become socialist; in a number of years there would be 2,700 million people again and definitely more.[30]

There had been a Soviet accusation in the Government Statement of August 21, 1963 on the partial nuclear test ban treaty charging that China favored the destruction of half mankind or 300 million Chinese in a nuclear war as the price of advancing communism. The genuine text of Mao's remarks, this *locus classicus*, appeared in the second Soviet Government Statement a month after the first. What Mao had actually said according to the text was:

> Is it possible to surmise how many human victims a future war will take? Perhaps one-third of the world's 2,700,000,000 inhabitants, that is, only 900,000,000 people. I consider this estimate to be even low, if atomic bombs actually fall. Of course it is terrible. But even a half would not be so bad. Why? Because they wanted it, not we. It is they who are imposing war on us. If we fight, atomic and hydrogen weapons will be used. Personally I think that in the entire world there will be such suffering that a half of humanity, and perhaps even more than a half will perish. I argued about this with Nehru. He is more pessimistic in this respect than I am. I said to him: If half of mankind is destroyed half will still be left, but imperialism will be completely destroyed, and socialism alone will be left in the world, and within half a century, or a whole century, the population will increase by even more than half.[31]

In fact, Tito had revealed the substance of this Chinese perspective in a public speech five years earlier, stating: "The Chinese like to boast that their population of 600 million is a guarantee of victory in an atomic war. Peking calculates that if 300 million Chinese were killed there would still remain 300 million Chinese."[32] He repeated the same facts in his speech at the 7th Congress of the communist-sponsored People's Youth of Yugoslavia, accusing Communist China of following a "Genghis Khan policy", notably its plans to push the whole world into an abyss.[33]

Marvin L. Kalb, a diplomatic correspondent for C.B.S. News in Washington, was convinced in his analysis of the Sino-Soviet relationship that Moscow was worried lest "Mao's truculence may accidentally or deliberately touch off an atomic war—one that could destroy Russia's abundance and communism's hope.[34]

In February 1957, Mao discussed the favorable consequences of World War I and II for the spread of communism, stating: "If the imperialists insist on launching a third world war, it is certain that several hundred million more will turn to socialism."[35]

The Chinese communists have repeated many times that nuclear destruction would decidedly not mean the annihilation of mankind. In fact,

> Should the imperialists impose such sacrifices on the peoples of various countries, we believe that, just as the experience of the Russian revolution and the Chinese revolution shows, those sacrifices would be rewarded. On the debris of imperialism, the victorious people would create very swiftly a civilization thousands of times higher than the capitalist system and a truly beautiful future for themselves.[36]

Since Mao's works and official pronouncements are the source of all earthly wisdom, Chinese propaganda has played many variations in the last years on the theme that war is the only solution to present world problems. An editorial on the subject in the Liberation Army Daily, which was also carried in the People's Daily, received a great deal of attention. Reviewing the historically "progressive" function of war in society's development, it again asserted that the consequences of a nuclear world war would not be as frightful as the rest of the world believes. Communism would flower on the ruins of civilization.[37]

The Maoists certainly believe their own words and are not merely trying to terrorize the world with propaganda. After several successful nuclear tests, the Red Chinese made a propaganda film about them that demonstrated survival is possible if the necessary precautions are taken.

The Soviets, on the other hand, have continued to repeat that war is unnecessary for the victory of communism. They have argued sometimes that nuclear war would be just as destructive to the communist commonwealth as to its opponents. The construction of a new society on the rubble of the present one would be exceedingly difficult. One of the exceptions of the rule was Marshal Nikolay Krylov, commander of the Soviet strategic missile units, who stirred worries when he predicted that the Soviet Union would win in a nuclear war because of "objective laws of history," of course.[38]

For all the adulation of Mao Tse-tung's teachings, Peking has never claimed that the idea of propelling society into the communist stage through warfare originated in China. The communist classics have been abundantly cited to this effect. There was a more moderate young Marx, and a much more radical older one. There is a Lenin of peaceful co-existence, and another who recognizes that war shakes and awakens the masses.

Lin Piao in his speech had all the proper quotations by heart, first Marx: "In the last analysis, the Marxist-Leninist theory of proletarian revolution is the theory of the seizure of state power by revolutionary violence, the theory of countering war against the people by people's war. As Marx so aptly put it, 'Force is the midwife of every old society pregnant with a new one.' "[39]

Then it is the turn of the victorious Lenin in 1918 who said: "The war, as a tremendous historical process, has accelerated social development to an unheard of degree . . . War has given history momentum and is now flying with locomotive speed."[40]

This idea found another champion in Molotov, "the extinguished star," who considered it the essence of neo-Stalinist doctrine. In his letter to the CPSU Central Committee in 1961 he stated: "Without serious conflict, without war, advance toward communism is impossible."[41] Premier Chou En-lai, supposedly a moderate, said it more specifically at the Albanian Embassy reception in Peking in honor of the National Day celebration in November 1965: "Imperialism cannot be overthrown without waging a war against it."[42]

Vietnam and the Power Struggle

American escalation of the Vietnam war in 1965 compelled the Red Chinese leadership to determine how much support it would extend to North Vietnam. This thorny problem aggravated existing factional rifts. New light has been thrown in particular on the conflict between Defense Minister Lin Piao and his then deputy, Chief of General Staff Lo Jui-ch'ing, in an important paper by the Rand Corporation.[43] The analysis has been carried further by many other specialists.

Lo, a four-star general, supported the Soviet proposal for a united front, and for good reason. He expected China's direct involvement in Vietnam to provoke Washington into enlarging the Vietnam war and striking at China herself. In this tense situation, which contained the seeds of a confrontation with the United States, Lo and other realistic PLA professionals harbored serious doubts about Mao's infallibility in opposing the Soviet Union.

What was required, Lo argued, was limited cooperation with Moscow in order, among other things, to modernize the Chinese army. It is significant that he praised the performance and strategy of the Soviet army during World War II in an article in May 1965.[44] He did not believe in a Vietcong victory and was prepared to apply the strategy of "active defense." This for one thing meant moving into Vietnam and required some sort of *rapprochement* with the Soviet leadership if the enemy was to be destroyed "in his nest." He expressed "full confidence in the great Soviet people and the great Soviet army." But just a few days later, People's Daily itself expressed a diametrically opposite view.

For years Lo had been the real commander of the armed forces since Lin Piao's health was not of the best. The former was a member of the "in-group" both in the Party and the armed forces, a secretary of the CC, secretary-general of the Military Affairs Committee, vice-chairman of the National Defense Council, 14th vice-premier of the State Council. He was a former minister of public security since 1949 and commander of the public security forces.

Lo's views were shared by Liu Shao-ch'i, Party Secretary-General Teng Hsiao-p'ing, Peking's Mayor P'eng Chen, T'ao Chu, the strongest man in South China, and even by Marshal Ch'en Yi who later changed his mind. They favored a united front with the Soviet Union in view of the danger to China herself. They comprised the wing of the leadership which wanted to prepare for possible American "aggression" against China.

As the Vietnam war intensified so did the debate between Lo and Lin. In the given situation, Lin's speech acquired particular importance. He recommended self-reliance to the Vietnamese in accordance with Mao's dictum: "In the fight for complete liberation the oppressed people rely first of all on their own struggle and then, and only then, on international assistance."[45] But this was merely the formal side of the matter. In the concrete circumstances it meant China had opted for a lower-risk policy of indirect conflict.[46] There would be no direct intervention, just conditional support to the North Vietnamese. By indirection it also rebutted a major argument on the need for unity with the Soviets.

On the same day that the People's Daily carried Lin's treatise it also published a speech by Lo in which he reiterated his stand on the united front and the "powerful socialist camp" in case of an "Asian war."[47] P'eng Chen played a special role in this debate. In the first stage he adumbrated Lin's thesis, most notably during his visit to Djakarta in May 1965. Later he switched to Lo's side.

The Maoists adopted a passive defense, a war by proxy, a much less militant stance than that of their opponents. This reflected their total lack of belief in Soviet support for "active defense" on China's part; they were not prepared to risk a war abroad under such conditions.

It is not surprising then that muted differences in the leadership sharpened to the point of open antagonisms. Lo early became the highest-ranking victim of the great purge, this before the cultural revolution really started. Two other factors may have contributed to the Maoist decision. A Japanese source revealed that at the American-Chinese Warsaw talks of February 1966 the United States allegedly threatened to use tactical nuclear weapons should China intervene directly in Vietnam.[48] In addition, Peking was unable to persuade North Korea to enter the war.

Lo was dismissed and detained in November 1965 on the charge of being a "counter-revolutionary revisionist," an anti-Party, anti-

Mao and anti-Lin man, ambitious to "usurp military power," and a
"leader of the Pen-Lu-Lo-Yang counter-revolutionary revisionist
faction." (The question of the faction will be taken up at a later
point.) His speeches and articles were denounced as "leaning toward
Moscow." He was accused of having gone so far as to absolve the
Soviets of having provoked riots in the Ili area of Sinkiang in 1962.
Yugoslav and Swiss sources revealed that he was also punished in
connection with the unsuccessful military coup in Indonesia and the
subsequent catastrophe.[49] He was publicly humiliated during the
cultural revolution, attempted suicide, breaking a leg in the process,
and allegedly took his life.[50]

Edgar Snow, the famous American writer on Red China, is
perhaps the best direct interpreter of Mao's thought in the West.
The Soviets claim he has acted as an intermediary for behind-the-scene
exchanges between Washington and Peking.[51] He wrote in a Paris
left-wing weekly "that for Mao to accept Soviet policy would mean
to accept a compromise in Vietnam. Capitulation to Soviet pressure
would be the equivalent to him of capitulation to the United States:
[it would mean] sacrificing the revolution and China's national
interests simultaneously; in short, the suicide of the CPC."[52]

Refusing to yield, Mao counter-attacked instead and disgraced
his Party and military opponents, "who would have been the contact
group in establishing a new Sino-Soviet partnership." So concludes
Prof. Franz Michael. The Vietnam war precipitated the latent
power struggle in the Peking leadership, threw it into complete dis-
array, was a crucial factor in the cultural revolution, and exacerbated
the Sino-Soviet rift. But the reality of the Vietnam war also acted as
a restraining influence on the struggle and prevented it from reaching
the breaking point.[53] In an article for *Paris-Match*[54] Snow expressed
the opinion that the enormity of China's domestic and foreign policy
problems caused by the Vietnam war quickly brought her internal
contradictions to the surface and led to a resounding political explosion.

The rapidly widening Sino-Soviet rift with its ensuing tensions
had an impact on Soviet aid delivered to Vietnam across China. A
Chinese government memorandum condemning Soviet rumors concerning Chinese obstruction of Vietnam aid was returned in January
1966 by the Soviet Embassy in Peking and then by the Soviet Foreign

Ministry as well. However, Moscow found it impossible to convene a conference of Warsaw Pact members and ruling Asian Parties devoted exclusively to coordinating such aid. The accusation of obstruction was repeated in the anti-Chinese document of the CPSU's CC of February 1966.

For its part the North Vietnamese regime has maintained strict neutrality in the Sino-Soviet conflict. Prime Minister Pham Van Dong thanked China for her assistance and for the transit of Soviet and other East European material "on schedule," in a speech to the National Assembly, thus refuting the Soviet charge. Peking's Foreign Ministry spokesman subsequently called the Soviet Defense Minister, the late R. Y. Malinowsky, "a liar" because he repeated the accusation in a speech in Hungary.[55]

Once the Chinese government had rejected Moscow's request for an air corridor or landing fields in South China, everything depended on Peking's good will, a sentiment conspicuous by its absence. The Maoists delayed and endangered Soviet air transports refueling for flights to North Vietnam with Soviet technicians aboard.[56] Soviet expert Nikolay Fyodorov declared to *Novosti,* the Moscow press agency, that Soviet shipments were being delayed several weeks, weapons were inspected and often dismantled and could not be put into operation later on or simply disappeared. Supersonic fighter aircraft were being replaced with used, obsolete Chinese army models. Soviet factory trademarks were replaced by Chinese markings. A member of the Supreme Soviet, Viktor Yermilov, confirmed this.[57]

Peking was using obstruction of Soviet aid as a means of applying pressure on Hanoi. For obvious reasons Hanoi denied it, as did Peking itself. By its actions China was virtually giving the United States a free hand in Vietnam; in response the United States adopted an almost benign attitude toward Peking. Then, sometimes in March 1967, Peking allegedly changed its stand. An agreement to speed transit of war supplies was said to have been reached, most certainly at North Vietnam's insistence because of American escalation;[58] North Vietnamese officers began taking over Soviet cargos at the Chinese border. Nonetheless, Peking continued to denounce the Soviet leaders as "a pack of rank traitors" in the Vietnam war, rejected their "hackneyed phrases on united action" and listed the "united action" taken "by Brezhnev and Kosygin with U.S. imperialism" from January

1965 through March 1967 to bring the war to an end through negotiation.[59]

Peking exerted continuous pressure on Hanoi to choose between China and the Soviet Union. It publicized a statement by former Foreign Minister Ch'en Yi: "The struggle between the two lines on the Vietnam question is the concentrated expression of the acuteness of the international class struggle. To oppose imperialism, it is imperative to oppose the counter-revolutionary line of the Soviet revisionist ruling group. There is no middle road in the struggle between the two lines."[60]

During the visit of Japan's then Foreign Minister Miki to Kosygin, the latter stated that he would risk ties with Peking for a Vietnam peace, if conditions were favorable to the Soviet Union.[61] Because of the schism, Moscow could exercise less pressure over North Vietnam and the Vietcong's hard position.

The disorder created by the cultural revolution was another complicating factor. When Premier Chou spoke to the committee in charge of preparations for the 1967 anniversary celebration of the victory, he complained that warring factions were ambushing trains carrying military aid to Vietnam; others were looting military stores with the same destination.

Communist and Western sources reported that China's military and economic aid to Vietnam came to a temporary halt in the spring of 1968 due to the repeated flare-up of large-scale internecine strife in the provinces adjacent to North Vietnam and the chaotic economic situation. Weapons and ammunition were not arriving on schedule, hospitals had not received their medicines nor the population its food supplies. As an example, 500 freight cars loaded with Vietnam supplies were detained in Canton for 4 months, stated the chairman of the Danish CP.[62]

A speech made by Chou En-lai at a nation-wide conference of transport workers in mid-May 1968, and reported by a Canton red guard publication, was quite revealing. He complained of traffic tie-ups at three railroad junctions, important for the transit of Soviet material from the Russian border through East China to Hanoi. They are Shenyang (Mukden) in southern Manchuria, Chengchow in central, and Liuchow in south China. Thugs in the port of Dairen boarded ships to seize arms and hampered their regular operations. So serious was the situation that a Peking directive dated June 13, 1968, had to be issued in the name of the four leading Maoist bodies, the Central Committee, the Military Affairs Committee, the State Council and the central cultural revolution group, offering an amnesty to organizations who returned Vietnam-bound supplies they had looted.[63]

Peking did not desist from its own delaying tactics. One example was the detention of the Soviet tanker, *Komsomolets Ukrainy,* headed for North Vietnam, in Whampoa port near Canton for twelve days. The second mate was accused of espionage and the captain of violating port regulations. Chinese soldiers used force against the crew. Both men were deported following Soviet representations and the ship permitted to leave under armed Chinese escort.

In retaliation, Soviet authorities deported a member of a Chinese aircraft inspection team under the Sino-Soviet agreement, who was accused of taking pictures at Tashkent airport.[64]

After the border clashes of March 1969 the transit of Soviet weapons through China came again to a halt, which was called by *Humanité,* French Communist Party main daily, a "crime".

A note from the Chinese Foreign Ministry to the Soviet Embassy in Peking revealed there had been several "Pueblo affairs" between the two countries, stating: "In July 1967 alone (*sic!*), the Soviet reconnaissance vessels *Gidrolog* and *Gidrograf* made six intrusions into east China coastal waters to engage in espionage activities, flagrantly violating the sovereignty of the People's Republic of China and menacing its security. The Soviet side continued such criminal activities despite repeated Chinese protests."[65]

The mainland press remained silent during the initial phase of American-North Vietnamese negotiations in Paris, stressing instead Mao's admonition to persevere in protracted war until the victorious end.[66] Premier Chou told a senior North Vietnamese delegate passing through Peking that to enter talks "was a major tactical and diplomatic mistake," and that Hanoi "lends a readier ear to the advice of the Soviet Union than to that of China." Mao rejected a request from the same delegate for a meeting.[67]

Because of the new situation, the North Vietnamese consul in Nanning, capital of Kwangsi-Chuang province, was subjected to abuse by red guards, who asked him to condemn the Paris talks. In addition, hostile red guard demonstrations took place outside North Viet-

namese consulates in Kunming, capital of Yunnan and in Canton.[68]
The Russians accused Peking of opposing a peaceful settlement in
Vietnam since "Mao Tse-tung would lose his pretext for interfering
in the domestic affairs of Burma, Cambodia, Nepal, Laos, Vietnam,
and other Southeast Asian countries should the war end."[69]

According to Pentagon estimates, North Vietnamese air force
and other units were trained in China and up to 50,000
Chinese labor battalion troops worked on rail and road repair
until the halt of the bombing. Chinese anti-aircraft units
participated in the battles, and Vietnamese wounded were treated
in Chinese hospitals, which were overcrowded with them. Communist
aid to Hanoi amounted perhaps to a billion dollars in 1968. President
Nixon stated at his Guam press conference that three years ago
(1966) Red China was furnishing over 50 percent of the military
equipment for the North Vietnamese. Later it was approx. 80 to
20 the other way around, namely the Soviet Union is the main supplier. Vice-President Spiro Agnew defined the Vietnam war as a
"calculated aggression by outside forces, heavily supported by major
powers," on the way to his 1969 Asian tour.[70]

According to a Polish source, several Vietnamese combatants
who had been sent to Yunnan from the front were murdered in the
Chinese factional struggle. Anti-communists in Chingtung county of
Yunnan distributed leaflets reading: "We are opposed to the campaign
in support of the Vietnam war! We must fight for freedom and the
overthrow of Mao Tse-tung's autocratic regime!"[71]

Hard upon the heels of the Czechoslovakian events Premier Chou
stated the Soviet Union would betray the war and concede Vietnam
and Southeast Asia as a sphere of American influence in return for
recognition of Soviet domination in Eastern Europe. The Chinese
premier chose a North Vietnamese National Day reception given by
its embassy in Peking as his forum.[72]

A chronology of Peking's utterances reveals divided counsels
and even confusion in Mao's entourage. Peking reprinted an editorial
from Nhan Dan (The People) in which Hanoi stated its readiness to
work for a political solution of the war after Peking scored the Paris
talks as a "plot and fraud." And President Johnson's announcement
of the bombing halt was reprinted in toto in five columns, an act
without precedent since the communists came to power on the

mainland.

The North Vietnamese press occasionally compares the strategy of its country's historical leaders against the Chinese emperors with Mao's military thought and finds the former more appropriate in the present situation. The North Vietnamese theoretical magazine *Hoc Tap* (Studies) frankly condemned the personality cult: "Deifying leaders means to humble the role of the popular masses and, at the same time, to diminish that of the leaders. To achieve a correct leadership, to prevent and limit errors, Marxist-Leninist Parties emphasize the principle of collective leadership," as applied in the Soviet Union. "If a leader commits errors and refuses to correct them, stubbornly sticks to them, he can no longer keep his role as a leader."

What a trenchant condemnation of Maoism from Hanoi in the midst of the Vietnam war!

A Hungarian communist newspaperman who wrote a series of five articles on Sino-Soviet relations, came to the conclusion that "in Southeast Asia, one of the main areas of Chinese foreign policy, Peking tries to discredit and supersede the Soviet Union on the one hand, and to prove that the United States should resolve its Asian problems primarily with China as its partner on the other."[73]

"The Final Solution" for Developing Countries

The rulers of some developing countries prefer one-party dictatorship and state capitalism—centralized management of the economy called "socialism"—which guarantee them secure personal power and relieve them of the burden of dealing with the complicated and risky democratic multi-party system. The dangers inherent in democracy make the "socialist" pattern more appealing to them.

The Chinese prefer armed struggle by the local communist Parties against the dominant nationalist movements; on the other hand, the Soviets seek to subordinate local Parties to the leadership of those movements which have already acquired state power—at least for the time being. The leadership of such non-aligned countries are "natural allies" for Russia, less so for Red China.

Discreetly silent on the fate of the captive nations of Eastern Europe, the Soviet Party program promises that the Soviet Union will not support the export of revolutions(?), nor will it permit the export of counter-revolution—in other words, it bars the self-determination of the captive nations. In *Pravda's* opinion, the export of revolution, "all the more with the help of arms," is allegedly contrary to communism.[74]

In the Soviet view, wars of national liberation are inevitable, "just wars." All the new nations in Africa and Asia are "national democracies," say the Moscow ideologists, and their rulers, members of the "national bourgeoisie," must sooner or later step down and make way for the rule of the Marxist-Leninist Party which is the only one capable of carrying out a socialist revolution and installing the "dictatorship of the proletariat," i.e. a communist government system defined by Lenin as "unrestricted by law and based on force"[75] and, in Stalin's words at the 16th Party Congress (1930), "the most powerful, the mightiest of all governing powers that have ever existed."

The Lenin-Bukharin program of 1919, faithfully echoing Marx, regarded this dictatorship with its denial of human rights as a temporary measure which would inexorably "wither away."[76] Yet Lenin institutionalized it, thereby becoming a revisionist at the antipodes of Marxism with respect to the theory and practice of seizing and holding power. For Mao, too, it is no prelude to the perfect society but an inherently "good society" with proletarian virtues.

In the process of taking power Mao Tse-tung applied Stalin's concentric circle formula of a four-class bloc, calling his governmental system a people's democratic dictatorship, a *contradictio in adjecto* (i.e. in the essence of things) as are so many notions in communist theory. These revolutionary classes included the workers, peasantry, petty-bourgeoisie (formerly colonial or semi-colonial) and the revolutionary segment of the national (middle) bourgeoisie; the latter two groups with the status of junior associates under the dictatorship of the CPC, of course. This system was allegedly more appropriate to the developing countries than the "coalition of the proletariat and peasantry" alone. The native bourgeoisie was tolerated only temporarily. The Red Chinese declared at the time that there was no difference between a dictatorship of the proletariat in the classical sense and a people's democratic dictatorship, except in form.[77] Mao defined it as "a powerful weapon for safeguarding the victory of people's revolution and for opposing domestic and foreign enemy conspiracies to bring about a restoration."

At a session of the Polish C. P. Central Committee in 1961, Wladyslaw Gomulka presented a new explanation of the dictatorship of the proletariat. Stalin's excesses have been explained by the allegedly inevitable aggravation of class warfare in the transition period. Gomulka posed the question as to whether terror is inherent in the communist system of government. His thesis emphasizes the need to limit communist repression of the opposition—the limits depending, of course, on the opposition's strength. He believes that Stalin overstepped these limits and, by initiating the great purges, created a kind of communist inquisition.[78]

In his 1954 Oslo lecture aimed at social-democrats, Kardelj said that the dictatorship of the proletariat is not a necessary condition for the transition to socialism,[79] meaning that socialism can also be achieved without communist Party dictatorship in some countries.

There is nothing either historical or inevitable about the Soviet idea that communists will sooner or later replace the leaders of "national democracy" in the developing countries. Guinea and Cuba provide good illustrations that mortal men are always ready to help or hinder history. Soon after a delegation from Guinea's ruling party attended the 22nd Soviet Party Congress (October 1961), a conspiracy was uncovered in Conakry directed by the Soviet Ambassador, Daniil S. Solod, a Kremlin African expert. To be sure, he was being faithful to the Soviet Party program, his misfortune was that he had "miscalculated" about the proper time to replace "national democracy."

It is doubtful that Castro's proclamation that he was a communist served the further penetration of communism in Latin America. Obviously he did it expecting stronger support for his regime from the communist countries. Up to then it had been an advantage for communism to be able to operate in Latin-America under the guise of *Fidelismo*. Exposed as naked communism its appeal has become much weaker south of the Rio Grande. Castro took Soviet doctrine too literally and Moscow is compelled to prop up his regime economically. But Moscow waited a year before recognizing that Cuba was "building socialism."

The Soviet Party program envisages only the "socialist camp" or *lager* (a Russified German word) as truly communist, while the

Yugoslav program defines all those forces as *bona fide* socialists that aim at the socialization of the basic means of production. The Yugoslav definition of socialism is thus broader. Socialism in the most varied forms is becoming a world system, they say, embracing all elements directed against private ownership and free enterprise, and against American "imperialism", of course.

According to Yugoslav communist reasoning the development of socialism is also possible outside the "socialist camp," attachment to the "camp" is not the only test of socialism.[80] Some newly-independent nations of Africa and Asia are developing state-managed economies, state ownership of the productive means and are nationalizing private enterprises; they may even by-pass capitalism and enter immediately into the building of socialism.[81] In this way distinct forms of socialism are sprouting in Algeria, Egypt, Iraq, Libya, Somalia, South Yemen, Sudan, and Syria, in Guinea, the People's Republic of Congo and in Tanzania, and also in Burma. They are recognized as such by the Yugoslav communists. The late Indian CP leader, Ajoy Ghosh, once wrote a book entitled *Nehru's Socialism—A Hoax*. For Peking, too, these varieties of socialism are a hoax, whereas Moscow's view had become more flexible.

The Soviets now make a distinction between "intuitive socialism" and "scientific communism." The latter notion as the political science of the Soviet ideology was introduced by Mikhail Suslov at a conference in Moscow at the beginning of 1962.

It is important for them that some developing countries are following a non-capitalist path, although they have neither an industrial proletariat nor a communist Party (or a weak one at best) so that no vehicle exists for what the communists call "proletarian class consciousness." There are no longer conditions for the progression from a "general democratic revolution" to a socialist one. The Soviets seem ready to leave the initiative to the "revolutionary national democrats," who act in these countries "in a way communists would act if they were in power." Moscow's advice to communists inside and outside such countries is to be "flexible and wise," to bring them with "tact and patience" by means of the class struggle to "scientific communism," i.e. to the communist doctrine and a communist assumption of power. Communists and national democrats advance "historically" in the same direction despite present differences.[82]

The Chinese reject this explanation. They cite Engels who repudiated any representation of state ownership or nationalization as "socialism." They oppose the "national democracy" type of government in which power is shared by the bourgeoisie and "proletariat" —pro-communists. They call for a "people's democracy" as in the communist countries. They doubt the viability of the non-capitalist path without a Party dictatorship, labeling it the "colonial road." They are uncertain as to whether communists can play a Trojan-horse role in "revolutionary democratic dictatorships" of one-party states.[83] Chinese propaganda approved of the late Ché Guevara's and Castro's belief in the maximum use of force. Nevertheless, though dogmatists, they sometimes also woo some of the nationalist leaders, although intending to overthrow them at the first opportunity.

While granting respectability to such one-party government systems, the Soviets do not renounce connections with the respective communist Parties of these countries, when they exist, since the "final solution" should be a dictatorship of the communist Party. This situation can be embarrassing for the Soviets, as for example, when the "intuitive" socialists persecute local communists. Delegates of Algeria's ruling party had to leave the 23rd Soviet Party Congress because of the presence of members of the Communist Party of Algeria, which is illegal at home. A graver incident happened at Lenin's centenary celebration in Moscow. The Soviets politely rejected the proposed speech by the Syrian Minister of Interior Mohamed Rabah Tawil. The Syrian communist leader Khaled Baghdash got the floor instead. The Minister was offended and immediately left for home. Afterwards a large number of communists were arrested there and in Iraq.

Both Moscow and Peking tried their luck in Congo-Kinshasa when the situation there was still unstable. Soviet missions were twice expelled from that country for plotting. They finally gave up, returned and normalized their relationship to the government, whereas Peking persists in calling for its overthrow. In Nigeria the Soviets supported the central government against the Biafra rebellion. Simultaneously, they back the local Communist Party which operates under another name, as well as pro-communist trade unions.

It remains Soviet doctrine that socialism and communism can

only be built within the framework of the socialist commonwealth and must necessarily lead to communism. The Yugoslav communists also expect these variant forms of socialism to eventually lead to communism. The Soviet Party program states that: "The dictatorship of the proletariat and the leadership of the Marxist-Leninist Party are *indispensable conditions* for the triumph of the socialist revolution and the building of socialism."[84] (Italics provided).

The Soviets are in disagreement with Peking as well on unlimited nationalization and excessive haste in collectivizing agriculture. The Soviets now say this would be harmful to such countries although they used draconian measures to collectivize at home and in East Europe.

CHAPTER IV

Mao's Doctrine Exposed by Yugoslav Communists

The Weakness of Chinese Communism

Peking did not recognize communist Yugoslavia during Stalin's life-time and even not until more than a year after his death. On the other hand, Belgrade recognized the Chinese communist regime immediately after its take-over. It should be kept in mind that in October 1954 Khrushchev took the initiative and personally persuaded Mao to set up diplomatic relations with Belgrade.

Wu Hsiu-ch'üan was the first Chinese ambassador to Belgrade. An 8th CC member, Wu is known as an expert on Eastern Europe. He was the Chinese chief delegate at many East European communist Party congresses. Later he held the delicate post of director of the Central Committee's international liaison department with foreign Parties, and was purged during the cultural revolution.

In the years of the thaw rather friendly relations were established. A Yugoslav Party delegation attended the 8th congress of the CPC in August 1956, and other high representatives from Belgrade visited Peking.

It is interesting that on November 1, 1956 the Chinese government condemned the "way in which the Yugoslav situation was treated during the 1948-49 period" by the Cominform. This statement was issued in connection with the declaration of the Soviet Union made a day before, which was erroneously interpreted as allowing "separate roads" to other communist countries in addition to Yugoslavia.

During the short period of the "hundred flowers", Yugoslav

communists even looked toward the emergence of a Chinese "Tito-ism." In a TV interview with the late Edward R. Murrow, Tito declared that his views on the different paths to socialism (com-munism) were largely identical with those of Mao Tse-tung.[1] After the Chinese communist victory, Stalin for a while suspected Mao of Titoism. The Chairman rejected any rightist deviation in his speech to the 10th CC plenary session in September 1962.

China's revulsion against Khrushchev's pragmatism came in the fall of 1957. It was particularly after the second session of the 8th congress in April 1958 that Peking swung to the left. Nevertheless, the program of the League of Communists of Yugo-slavia was published in its entirely in the People's Daily. It also appeared as a pamphlet to be used as a "negative example." Yugoslavia then came under heavy attack, and the Chinese soon began proclaiming the Cominform resolution of 1948 as correct.[2] Ever since that time until the invasion of Czechoslovakia the Red Chinese have been giving that middle-seized country an unusual importance by labeling it as the leader of the de-Stalinization drive with all its revisionistic implications in the communist world. Be-fore they attacked the Russians directly, they used to attack them by proxy through the Yugoslavs. This was later acknowledged in a Peking pamphlet entitled *Long Live Leninism*.

The Yugoslav communists were compelled to answer the Chinese attacks through their communication media, and it was in this way that the West was able to learn many new facts about the Red Chinese from the communist sources. In the first critical period for Russo-Chinese relations, between the Bucharest (June 1960) and Moscow (November 1960) conferences, there appeared a remarkable book. Its author was Edvard Kardelj, and its title, *Socialism and War, a Survey of Chinese Criticism of the Policy of Coexistence*.[3] This was the culmination and summing-up of Yugoslav criticism of Red China. It afforded a unique opportunity to see clearly the basic problems of war and peace in the com-munist world. Surprisingly, it did not receive its deserved attention in the United States, which is otherwise keenly interested in the problems of China.

Kardelj's book reveals the intimate thoughts of Peking's and

Moscow's masters. It helps one to understand a lot more about the issues on which so much depends. After the exposure of the Russo-Chinese rift, Kardelj sets out to explain frankly what Red China attempted to conceal. This particularly raises the value of his book. The Reuters correspondent in Belgrade went so far as to compare it with Lenin's *Imperialism, the Highest Stage of Capitalism.*

The book offered a unique view of the Sino-Soviet dispute as seen from Belgrade.[4] Yugoslavia did not stand on the side-lines in this affair, but was vitally concerned. Since the League of Yugoslav Communists in its revised program "codified" Titoism, the Red Chinese became the main critics of their Yugoslav comrades, and thereby indirectly of Soviet revisionism as well. Characteristically, when Moscow for the first time mobilised its satellites and Communist Parties against the Chinese dogmatists, Belgrade rose to reply in principle to Chinese attacks. In the main it sided with the Kremlin, and in the Yugoslav counter-attacks against the Chinese critics this book played a key role. It is therefore a document of considerable importance.

. Kardelj does not draw only on the speeches of the leading Chinese statesmen and on articles written by Party theoreticians, but on many other sources which were available to him in his capacity of a ranking official of a socialist state. He circumstantially elaborates on the two theses, revamped by Peking: on the inevitability of war as a form of world revolution, and on the inevitability of armed revolution or civil war.

The Chinese communists are convinced that a third world war between the East and West is inevitable. They reason that it must take place because of "antagonistic contradictions" between communism and "imperialism." According to Chinese leadership the future world war will inevitably turn into a world revolution,[5] and eventually end in a communist victory throughout the world. Therefore the people should not be afraid of war. In the end there will be a great reward: at least half of mankind will survive and then live in "a state of well-being never seen before."

Why was communist China so bellicose in comparison with apparently less militant Soviet policies? Certainly it is economically very weak. The Chinese people are poorer than they ever were before. The regime created through the people's communes a sort of war communism, which started as a collective way of life, organized along military lines. Since workers were paid theoretically "according to their needs," rather than according to their output, the communes had to be a short cut to communism. In fact, they very much exasperated the Soviets, since this would appear to be a communism of misery, rather than a communism of abundant consumer goods.

Kardelj confirmed that the communes caused grave economic and political disturbances to the point of sapping the Chinese revolution. "The internal forces of Chinese socialism are weak," he asserted. It seemed then that the despicable system was about to fall. The economic backwardness of the country, compounded by the extremism of the communes, became the main source of danger threatening with a revival of "internal reactionary forces."

To justify the tremendous sacrifices borne by the Chinese people in the establishment of such a system, the communist leaders, according to the Yugoslav writer, invented a completely new ideology, in which humanism was proclaimed "petty bourgeois hypocrisy," the desire for personal happiness "anti-socialist individualism," democracy "ridiculous philistine prejudices," and criticism of bureaucracy and state monopoly "the worst kind of revisionism."

Faced by immense internal difficulties, politically isolated and economically blockaded by the United States, the Chinese leaders were seeking a solution to their problems in an aggressive foreign policy which may even lead to another world war. The cold war and the threat of a hot one may not be unwelcome to the Chinese leaders, since they believe that it may actually help them in their internal efforts. In mainland China, the Titoist theoretician asserts, an infantile disease of ultra-leftist radicalism prevails.[6] In this way the Chinese communists elaborated their thesis on the inevitability of war, based on Lenin's teaching at the time the young Bolshevik regime was endangered by interventionist powers. Both the Yugoslav and Soviet Parties sharply disagree with this thesis.

The nuclear stalemate established a specific equilibrium between East and West. Here the Soviets again agree with Kardelj. The dogmatists overestimate the forces of imperialism and underrate the forces of socialism. This should in turn be interpreted to mean that "forces of socialism" are so strong that they may conquer the world without an all-out war. By contrast, the Chinese used the same reproach against the revisionists. In their own version this means that the "forces of imperialism" are so weak that they may be defeated in a major war, should this be necessary.

In his polemics with the Chinese, Kardelj insists that no country can be allowed to impose socialism or communism on other countries through aggression. In a total war, he says, with its mounting casualties and devastations, it is quite impossible to bring "happiness" to other people in the name of communism. Lenin rose against the illusion of a "victorious march" of the Red Army through Europe, he reminds. Robespierre uttered the dictum that no nation loves "armed missionaries" (witness Czechoslovakia), and Napoleon saw the whole of Europe united against him when he tried to impose certain principles of the French Revolution upon other nations.

In the opinion of the Yugoslav, the working class both in communist and capitalist countries would never accept any war of conquest waged by the "camp of socialism" against the "camp of capitalism." Aside from being aggressive, such a war would even be reactionary, that is, contrary to communism. It would be, in fact, a true imperialist war against the working class of other countries.[7] The working class attacked in this way would defend their ruling bourgeoisie in the name of national independence. This would result in the set back of the cause of socialism or communism. The working class in the capitalist countries would be at a loss regarding how to seize power in a world war waged by foreign armies—a hard lesson for the Chinese warmongers.

The classics of Marxism-Leninism rejected in particular, as absurd, the mere thought of an international war for the purpose of spreading socialism and communism. Such a war would be "a sort of socialist Bonapartist adventurism." In a future world war both victory and defeat would have almost identical socio-political and material consequences—and the leading Titoist theoretician does not even rule out a defeat for the communist bloc.[8]

Red China's aggressiveness gave new strength to the policy of blockade. Through her megalomaniac trends and chauvinism, her

imperialistic policy has openly and brutally destroyed the unity of
the socialist (communist) world, the author emphasizes. In the
same way Professor Wittfogel ascribed it to the growing megalomania of the aging autocrat.

In Kardelj's view there are only three kinds of a "just war":
1) An internal revolutionary or civil war; 2) A war for national
liberation; and 3) Any defensive war. He finds an extraordinary
similarity between the Chinese communists and the Trotskyists. This
lays them open to the indictment of "high treason" in the communist world. In fact the Trotskyite central organ has praised
China's policy when it stated that the "Chinese standpoints are
sharply distinct from the honey-sweet official Russian statements on
the possibility of peaceful coexistence."[9]

Kardelj is convinced that only a time of peace warrants socialism's (communism's) growth in the world, while a new world war
would put such a prospect in doubt. There is no force in the Soviet
Union which would be able to change the policy of peaceful coexistence, which is not the result of good will, but of Soviet domestic
developments. It also operates as a break on China's adventurist
tendencies. The Soviet leaders are well aware that in the event of
another world war, it would be their industrially developed country
that would suffer more than others.

In fact, sometimes the Chinese leaders, too, speak about coexistence, as was the case in the 1960 Moscow Statement and more
recently. They do this however only casually, for normally they
consider it a hindrance. Teng Hsiao-p'ing, the now disgraced
Secretary-General of the CPC, then said that coexistence should be
nothing more than a tactical weapon to deceive the enemy, as the
British author Edward Crankshaw argued.

In the opinion of the Yugoslav communist leaders, Moscow's
brand of coexistence is not good enough to secure mankind a lasting and stable peace. "Of course," commented Kardelj, "the policy
of peaceful coexistence is not and should not be a policy of defense
of the *status quo* in international relations, and, still less so, in
internal social relations."

For Moscow, coexistence is applicable between ideological and
military blocs, while for the Yugoslav communists active coexistence

is best practiced among single nations without regard to bloc commitments. As far as the Yugoslavs are concerned, the bloc barriers should be gradually removed by the most intensive bilateral and multilateral cooperation among nations belonging to both sociopolitical systems.

In the Soviet view, the transition to socialism will be effected by means of an armed revolution or in a relatively peaceful or evolutionary way. According to Kardelj, there are better prospects for a peaceful road to socialism in highly developed countries, and a sudden communist take-over in a country with well-established democratic traditions might result in complete isolation of "revolutionary forces" from the people. At the 5th congress of the Yugoslav Socialist Alliance, a branch of the League of Communists, Tito among others spoke of the "painless process of social changes in various countries."[10]

As Kardelj sees it, the world socialist revolution will be a "never-ceasing process of internal social developments in every country and their merging on the international, world-wide scene." He reproaches the Chinese for holding the opposite view, saying that "... as soon as anybody ... begins to confuse international war and revolution, he is inevitably in danger of identifying one form of war of conquest with world revolution."

Actually Moscow, for tactical reasons, preaches peaceful coexistence, which would exclude a general nuclear war, in the firm belief that time is working for the spreading of communism through infiltration and subversion as well as through local national-liberation wars.

Communist China, on the other hand, was looking forward to the solution of her enormous internal difficulties by means of a new world war, with communism eventually emerging as the victor. By thus aggravating international relations, Peking is putting permanent pressure on Moscow, forcing it to adopt a more aggressive foreign policy.

Tito's leading ideologist believes, as do all communists, that the capitalist world is disintegrating, and that sooner or later it will die, provided the cold war disappears from the international scene. However, even after the transition to socialism has been effected, the world will still be far from happy. Uneven remuneration will then be necessary for a long time, the quality of work performed as well as the degree of responsibility in the process of production serving as yardsticks. This will result not only in the persistence of inequality in material conditions among people, but also in the retention by some countries of definite elements of state-capitalist relations. Dictatorships will then be the order of the day for quite a long time in order to defend socialism against attempts to restore capitalism.[11]

Polemics With "The Apostle of Yugoslav Revisionism"

Kardelj's book had been extensively criticized by Moscow's *Pravda* and by the Prague magazine Problems of Peace and Socialism, the theoretical and information journal of the Soviet-oriented Parties, *World Maxist Review* in its Canadian edition.[12] Professor Aleksey Rumyantsev of the Academy of Sciences of the Soviet Union, writing about Kardelj's "verbal dialectics," called him an anarcho-syndicalist, and his teaching "national Marxism." However, these two notions are in contradiction according to scientific Marxism-Leninism. His analysis as to whether Kardelj's assertions are Marxist or not, resembled a theological dispute about "the sex of the angels." More important was the conclusion of this Marxist academician about Kardelj's book in general, which reads:

> Experience has made it clear that any pseudo-Marxist effusion is always approved by the defenders of the moribund capitalist system. There is no need to go into bourgeois press comments on the present book. Suffice it to say that this press has welcomed it. If Kardelj really wanted to champion Marxism-Leninism, really wanted to serve the interests of socialism, he would think over what August Bebel once said: "When the enemy praises you, stop and think where you have blundered." But Kardelj has not stopped to think. Things like this, obviously, do not worry him.[13]

War is unavoidable while imperialism prevails—this was an old teaching of Lenin. But the balance of power has changed fundamentally since World War II, the Russians say. The *grandeur* of the 20th Congress of the CPSU according to *Pravda,* lies in the fact that it "creatively assessed" this new balance of power in the world, which calls for a revision of Lenin's previous teaching. War is not fatally inevitable, says the Soviet Party program. And Khrushchev accused the Chinese in one of his Supreme Soviet speeches that for them "war is the only way to the triumph of communism. But this precisely could alienate many people from communism."

Pravda's answer to Kardelj's treaties stated in essence: "War is a categorical imperative of history. It is bound up with antagonistic contradictions among classes and nations." In another place the authors of the article stated that: "The founders of Marxism-Leninism linked the liquidation of wars to the destruction of antagonistic classes and the creation of socialism." They reproached the Yugoslav communist leader for not having established "a link between wars and the struggle of classes within a country," as pointed out by Lenin.[14]

Actually, Kardelj came out in favor of internal revolutionary wars as being just. He merely condemned wars among nations launched in the name of communism.

The authors of the answer are especially enraged because the "apostle of Yugoslav revisionism" dared to admit that a communist nation could wage a predatory war and that the striving to rule over other countries is inherent in the communist bloc as well.

In its reply, Belgrade's *Borba* realized that the Soviet leaders, in criticizing the "dogmatists" (the Chinese Reds, of course), use arguments similar to Kardelj's, that is, revisionistic arguments.[15]

Kardelj's position had also been criticized at length by the Albanian communists, the bitter foes of Yugoslav revisionism, in their Party organ *Zeri i Popullit*. The Albanian communists stated that the CPC maintains a correct ideological position. Kardelj's allegation that wars obstruct the development of communism is for the Albanians, in solidarity with the Chinese thesis, an "obscure idea." War, they say, will be eliminated only after capitalism has been overthrown throughout the world. Furthermore, the Albanian communists accuse the Yugoslavs of spreading "peaceful bourgeois illusions," similar to those of Kautsky, the social democratic principal theoretician. In the opinion of Tirana, coexistence does not mean an ideological and political cease-fire between the two blocs and even less a social peace. It also rejected the "reformist theory of the peaceful integration of capitalism and socialism."[16]

Before the rift came into the open, the Chinese constantly strictured the Yugoslavs, aiming mainly at Moscow. By contrast, the Soviets blasted the Albanians, aiming at the Chinese. Then and now the Chinese press has published Albanian attacks on Moscow *in toto*.

The rift between the communist Big Two has also had repercussions in relation to the Albanian challenge, which goes back to the turning point—Khrushchev's posthumous trial of Stalin at the 20th Soviet Party Congress. The position of Yugoslavia has played here a significant role. Albanians have always feared a reconciliation between Moscow and Belgrade after Stalin's proposal to Yugoslavia to absorb their neighbor into the federation. The recalcitrant Albanian Party leaders, banished by the 22nd Soviet Party Congress with its continuing de-Stalinization, are convinced that they can rule the country only in a Stalinist, ruthless way. Any de-Stalinization and softening of the grip, not to speak of modern revisionism in a Yugoslav, and even in a Russian style, would prove fatal for the regime. Thus, they have become natural allies of the intransigent Red Chinese.

The Albanians got from the Chinese only one fifth of the aid for their third five-year plan which the Soviet Union previously had given them over such a period. When the plan was terminated it was far from being fulfilled. For this reason there was a reorientation to rely on one's own resources, and an opening to the foreign world, expanding economic and tourist relations. For the first time, the fourth five-year plan has been based on agriculture with modest industrial plans.[17]

Tirana has emulated the Chinese cultural revolution by its own "educational revolution and working class supervision."

A commentary from Peking by Wu Chiang came much later, together with a series of articles in the *Red Flag*, directed against the old and the new revisionists (on February 10, 1962 against Bernstein; on March 1, against Kardelj, and on April 25, against Kautsky), aiming as usual at Moscow.[18]

To all that one may add that in a way it is strange to interpret Kardelj in connection with the old revisionists, who laid the
foundation for West European democratic socialism and for the
democratic interpretation of Marxism. Tito's CPY was reorganized
as a Stalinist Party and as such fought the Yugoslav civil war and the
communist revolution in the classic pattern of Leninism and even of
Mao Tse-tung. Its take-over and perpetuation in power is typically
communist, and has nothing to do with Kautsky or Bernstein.

In the context of *Red Flag's* broader goal, the commentary was
much more than a book review of *Socialism and War*. It was a
philosophical polemic with the program of the League of Yugoslav
Communists and with Kardelj's report on that program. The
Chinese author voiced the same slanders as Rumyantsev in quoting
Lenin, as if the Yugoslav leader were "pleasing the bourgeoisie by
shamelessly distorting dialectics."

Criticising the attainment of changes of "qualitative correlation" through changes of "quantitative correlation," namely the socialist trends in capitalist countries, which would through a comparatively peaceful process—a "unity of revolution and evolution,"
according to Kardelj's report—lead to the transition from capitalism
to socialism, Wu Chiang stressed that this (in Kardelj's opinion)
"promising" evolution is nothing but state monopoly capitalism. He
does not agree with the Yugoslav's assertion that "the typical capitalist social system is a thing of the past," and that, because of the
existence of the communist commonwealth, the capitalist society will
surrender its position willingly, which for the "oppressed peoples"
should be a reason for liquidating their revolutionary struggle.

The Chinese author does not agree with the Yugoslav idea
of "different forms and methods of struggle for socialism," nor
with the idea of a "diversified socialist road." This road seems to
him a Kautsky road, contrary to the October revolution, because
for Kautsky, Lenin's idea and tactics were "vulgarization of the
materialistic conception of history."

Kautsky's view was that proletarian dictatorship only "implies
that some individuals exercise unlimited authority over the masses"
("Terrorism and Communism"), and Bernstein added: "Proletarian
dictatorship has become in pratice the enslavement of the pro-

letariat." ("Socialism—Its Past and Present").

Of course, Kardelj was attacked for denouncing "viciously" the militancy of the Red Chinese because of their "policy of conquering the world by socialism through the means of war." At the same time, the Chinese author repeats the "international obligations to give support to the people's revolutions in various countries."

For the Chinese, the "East wind prevails over the West wind," according to Mao's remarks in his speech to Chinese students in Moscow,[19] but nevertheless there exists a danger of war, as long as there are "imperialist forces" in the world, a contention repeated by the reviewer.

The Soviets reproached the Chinese for maintaining that coexistence is only "transitional and temporary," although both sides stress that it is a form of class struggle. Yugoslav active coexistence is interpreted by the Chinese author as an exclusion of class struggle and revolution.

Under criticism also was Tito's 1958 New Year message, according to which dividing the world into the "socialist camp" and the "imperialist camp" destroys the unified world-wide process of socialist revolutionary transformation; this will not be any coexistence; it will be only some kind of a truce pregnant with the dangers of new conflicts of all description.

In Kardelj's definition of international aid from the West for the developing countries, without exploitation, the Chinese author again sees Kautsky's super-imperialism.

Finally, Wu Chiang states that the two salient features of the revisionist's idea are his "pragmatist political morality" in Yugoslav's own words, and his eclectic game.

The Yugoslav Revolution: A Copy of the Chinese

Predrag Vranicki, a Zagreb University professor who belongs to the circle of the wayward Marxist philosophical magazine *Praxis,* is known for his theoretical Marxist-Titoist studies, and is the author of the first *History of Marxism,* written by a Marxist. This is a unique book in the communist world, an anti-Stalinist work written against Marxist "scholasticism, which invented its saints and its heretics," with some of its ideas strikingly similar to those of Djilas.

A whole chapter is dedicated to Chinese communism. He advocated pluralism of Marxist philosophy at the 1968 international congress of philosophers in Vienna, rejected by the Soviets as propagating poly-Marxism, that is, different types of it.

Vranicki presents a short history of Chinese communist theory and practice through the prism of Titoism, highly praising Mao Tse-tung as "an excellent dialectician, a peerless practitioner and strategist of the revolution." Trotsky was right, rather than Stalin, in advocating independent action by the CPC outside of the *Kuomintang*. Without regards to Comintern orders, Mao chose this way back in 1927 in order to organize the peasantry as the main force of the Chinese revolution, and to fight a guerrilla war with a separate Red army by creating the so-called liberated territories. Mao then paid for his innovations, which were labeled as "adventurism." Later on, allied with Chu Teh, he was again in action, the territories under communist control spreading meanwhile like waves following the agrarian revolution and the military and political organization of those territories. Dangerously encircled by the Nationalists, he managed to break through with the Red armed forces and cadres, and the Long March brought him a definite leadership.[20] The common danger favored the anti-Japanese war coalition with the Nationalists. Then Mao promised for the whole of China "a people's republic, neither Soviet nor socialist."

At that time Mao developed his thesis of a new type of a bourgeois-democratic revolution, preceding the advent of a socialist revolution. Such a revolution in two stages has to be a transition from a colonial, semi-colonial and semi-feudal society to a socialist society.[21] He believed that such revolutions would arise in all colonial and semi-colonial countries. To deceive the peasantry, the communists at that time accepted temporarily Sun Yat-sen's slogan "land for those that work it," as well as his Three Principles: nationalism, democracy and well-being. Mao was then against the dogmatists who imported Stalinism, as he was also against the extreme leftists.

The author also highly praises Mao's thesis of contradictions as being in harmony with Titoism. By this he understands the non-administrative (non-oppressive) solution of different non-antagon-

istic contradictions found among the people (though not among
hostile classes!), especially ideological.

Professor Vranicki deplored the negative conceptions of mili-
taristic psychology in Chinese politics during the last years, and
particularly the concept of "a radical conflict between the worlds
of socialism and imperialism through a just war."

From the analysis of this treatise the conclusion may be drawn
that the Yugoslav communist revolution was a copy—*mutatis
mutandis*—of the Chinese revolution. Tito, himself, in fact confirmed this in his political report to the 5th congress of the CPY,
and so did also the former labor union leader Svetozar Vukmanovic-
Tempo in his book on the civil war in Greece, where he stated that
Yugoslav communist fighters followed the pattern of the Chinese
comrades.

In connection with that civil war it was Djilas who disclosed
that Stalin himself advised Yugoslav and Bulgarian delegates who
met him to discontinue helping the Greek communists lest the
United States be provoked into action.[22] This first-hand testimony
notwithstanding, the legend still persists that the Greek collapse was
due to a new policy of the Tito's regime which he pursued when
Yugoslavia was expelled from the Cominform.

During World War II towns and the system of transportation
in Yugoslavia were held by the Axis armies, while the communists
created in the woods and mountains of the countryside their own
so-called liberated territories, held by their own authorities (people's
committees-soviets). They carried with their guerrilla forces
(partisans) a merciless struggle against the occupiers and their aides,
as well as against the forces of national resistance. The Axis
forces had launched seven offensives against Tito, and so did the
Chinese nationalist government in its five encirclement campaigns
against the Chinese communists before the outbreak of the anti-
Japanese war. After the Long March, when there appeared to be
the best chance to annihilate them, the Japanese struck all-out.
Generalissimo Chiang Kai-shek has been compared with General
Draza Mihailovic, the Serbian nationalist resistance leader.

The Soviets produced evidence from the Comintern archives
that Mao was passive, sabotaged their efforts and evaded the answer

to Moscow's inquiry concerning coordination with the Chinese Red Army in case the Japanese should attack the Soviet Union. In 1941-1942 the Chinese communists restricted their participation in the struggle against Japan, and in 1943 an order was issued to stop operations, retire in case of a Japanese offensive and, should there be a chance, conclude an armistice. That was what the Chinese communists understood as their "victory" over Japan.[23]

This was exactly the nature of Mao's tactic of passive temporizing: "70 percent of involvement (of the communists, of course), 20 percent of compromise (with the Nationalists), and 10 percent of fighting the Japanese."[24] In the same way Yugoslav communists were eager to preserve their military power for the settlement of accounts with the nationalist forces. Like Mao, so also Tito made a promise not to install a communist regime, and as in China so also in Yugoslavia, until their expulsion from the Cominform, Stalinism was held up as a model of communism.

Sonja Dapcevic-Orescanin, a member of the Belgrade Institute of International Policy and Economy, has published two books entitled, *The People's Republic of China* and, *The Soviet-Chinese Controversy and the Problems of the Development of Socialism,* both doubtlessly officially approved. She is the spouse of the new Yugoslav ambassador to Peking Lt-General Bogdan Orescanin, one of the originators of the Yugoslav people's defense concept, a warning against the further application of the Brezhnev doctrine.

Presenting a Titoist criticism of Red China's ideology and politics, the author sees in the dogmatic and conservative conceptions a big obstacle for the growth of the world revolutionary movement. She holds that the positive experience of the Chinese revolution has become a weapon for the defense of negative attitudes which have emerged in changed internal and external conditions. Another reason for this development is that the CPC has been one-sided in the revolutionary practice of Marxism, whereas in the theoretical field and philosophical meditations it resorted to clichés. It lacks a scientific Marxist analysis of the contemporary world situation that would help in discerning the needs and next steps in the building of socialism. For these reasons the author's opinion of Maoism is very low, indeed.

China's attitudes have evolved in the course of years from her original backward and undeveloped stage. This objective situation has strangely created a subjective illusion of her role as a great power. The aggressive conceptions of the Chinese general line run counter to the progressive trends in the Soviet Union and in East European countries as well as in the other communist Parties. Basing her policy on Stalinism, China has relied exclusively on administrative measures that would enable her to solve all her problems by force. According to the Yugoslav author she is attempting to build a socialist society on subjective, non-Marxist and non-scientific principles.

The Chinese hold that the basic contradictions in the world are not between socialism and capitalism, but between an allegedly integrated revolutionary national-liberation movement and imperialism. Moreover, the world revolutionary movement was transferred from Europe to the three continents, where the Chinese are looking for their sphere of influence. The author sees in the problem of the bellicose China subjective weaknesses, mistakes and deformations, in other words, subjective lagging behind the objective reality.

The Sino-Soviet theoretical differences are expressing themselves through an inter-governmental conflict. Socialist theory and practice are now so dovetailed that the time of "pure" ideological and theoretical conflicts has passed. This has become a conflict of ruling Parties and socialist governments, that is, a conflict of two nations, each defending its own position. The national aspect is reflected in China's ambition to become a great world power.[25]

The Yugoslav author believes that the main controversial problems are the contradictions between developed and underdeveloped socialist nations, the method how to build a socialist and communist society, the Chinese defense of Stalin and Stalinism, war and peace and peaceful coexistence, the strategy to be adopted in the struggle against capitalism and imperialism, different roads to socialism, the possibilities of a peaceful transition from capitalism, and differences regarding the policy to be pursued toward developing countries into which the Chinese infuse their racial hatred.

The same author regards the ways and methods used by Peking in its struggle with Moscow as inadmissible even "according to contemporary bourgeois normatives applied in relations among nations." It should be noted that these views were expressed already before the cultural revolution. The Chinese methods are listed as follows:

—Illegal distribution of printed material, letters and proclamations written in native languages and disseminated in large quantities in the main cities and other places of socialist nations, all with the purpose or betraying the government and Party leaders of those countries.

—Making use of embassies and diplomatic representatives for subversive activities, provocations and other actions, as well as employment of Chinese students for propaganda purposes on the territory of socialist countries with which China is in conflict. (Since that time these students have been expelled from Moscow and other East-European countries).

—Pompous reception of Chinese representatives returning home from communist countries, identification of the government with the conduct of these employees, and giving the conflict an inter-governmental character.

—Making use of conferences of pro-communist international organizations for subversive activities.

—Giving support to anti-Party groups in countries in which the communist Party is in power, and creating factions in communist Parties of other countries and then financing such factions.

—Subversive activities in the communist Parties of Asia, Africa and Latin America.

—Striving to separate the national leaders from the people, and organizing subversive activities with the aim of changing the leadership of other countries, and

—Violation of territorial integrity of other countries.

Obren Milicevic, an editor of the Belgrade daily *Borba* wrote a booklet entitled Chinese Policies-Background of a Campaign Against Yugoslavia. He deals with such topics as the victory of the Stalinist course in China, the defense of Stalinism for the sake of the defense of their own dogmatism, the glorification of Mao, that is, his personality cult, the argument against peaceful coexistence and disarmament, the Chinese attempt to tutor liberation movements and the already liberated countries, and the imposition of Chinese practices on communist countries and Parties.

Red China's policy is described as contradictory, unprincipled and ambiguous. The anti-Yugoslav campaign organized in China was so vigorous that, for instance, within a period of six months, 367 anti-Yugoslav articles appeared in the Chinese central papers only. It is necessary, says the author, to use cryptography to determine which part is directed against whom, and to discern the real Chinese intentions. Yugoslavia had been chosen to settle account with the "progressive forces" (Khrushchev) in the communist movement. This took place already at the time Yugoslavia was used as a substitute in attacking Russia. The CPC came to life and took its shape when it was an armed political movement which introduced military principles into internal Party life. According to the Yugoslav author, the Chinese Stalinist principles have emerged at a time when they were inevitably doomed as an anti-socialist and reactionary social phenomenon. The Chinese are imitating Stalinism despite the fact that in their revolutionary period they received hard blows from the same Stalin. Mao himself was punished by the Party when he was expelled from the Politburo and the Central Committee, and Liu Shao-ch'i was divested of all his Party functions.

In fact, up to 1935, Mao was expelled three times from the CC and put in prison at the order of the Politburo. He took his revenge in the cultural revolution. Red guards forced their way into the cemetery of revolutionary martyrs near Peking and wantonly desecrated Ch'ü Ch'iu-pai's grave. This man was the CPC Secretary General in 1927 when Mao was expelled from the Politburo for his left-wing petty-bourgeois opportunism in the autumn harvest uprising in Hunan. Mao was severely rebuked by the Party leadership. Ch'ü in his book *The Disputed Issues of the Chinese Revolution* took issue with Mao's ideas. Later he became commissar for education in Soviet China as well as a member of the Comintern Presidium. He happened to be caught by the Nationalists and then executed.[26]

Recording the relations between Stalin and the CPC, the author quotes a "Letter to the Comrades of the Revolution," written by Ch'en Tu-hsiu (1929), then Secretary General of the CPC: "I...

sincerely carried out the opportunist policy of the Comintern, and became an instrument of the narrow Stalinist faction.   I could save neither the CPC nor the revolution... We should recognize... that all opportunist policies at present and in the past originated with the Comintern, which should bear the responsibility." Ch'en Tu-hsiu was later identified as belonging to the Trotskyists in China.[27]

In the communist strategy this dogmatism appears to be similar to the Trotskyist idea of the permanent revolution, giving it in the contemporary conditions the mark of adventurism.   The Chinese hegemonism is very aggressive, and has as its base the misconception that there must be one center of world revolution.   The Chinese leadership holds that with Stalin's death this center was transferred from Moscow to Peking, which gives that new center the corresponding right to determine the strategy and tactics of the entire international communist movement.   This includes all revolutionary forces in the world, as well as "strategic reserves", represented by the anti-colonial and liberation movements.   According to this reasoning of the Yugoslav author, the deterioration of relations between the Big Two stems from the Chinese challenge to Russian leadership and policies.   The general foreign policy of the Red Chinese leadership is practically oriented toward the creation of crises in the world.

The author asserts that in the opinion of Peking's masters, whoever stands for disarmament is helping American "imperialism." At the Peking conference of the World Federation of Trade Unions, in June 1960, the Chinese delegate labeled as an illusion the belief in disarmament as long as imperialism exists.   Disarmament was also attacked by the Chinese delegate at the Stockholm conference of the World Council for Peace in December 1961.   This delegate set the arming of the still colonial and dependent peoples in contrast to disarmament.   The same attitude was upheld by Chinese delegates on all following congresses of international front organizations.

A year after Hiroshima, Mao told Anna Louis Strong, the late associate of the Chinese leadership: "The atom bomb is a paper tiger which the U.S. reactionaries use to scare the people. It looks terrible, but in fact it isn't. Of course, the atom bomb is a weapon of mass slaughter, but the outcome of a war is decided by the people, not by one or two new types of weapon." As Russians see it, this is "an underestimation of the forces of imperialism." In his address made at the celebration of the 50th anniversary of the Soviet Red Army, Defense Minister Marshal Andrey Grechko held that "contemporary imperialism is far from being a 'paper tiger!' " On a later recurrence, he called for defenses in the East as strong as those in the West. And his colleague Marshal Ivan Yakubowsky, the Warsaw pact commander, warned its members that China is preparing for war.[28]

While the Chinese authors declare themselves opposed to an atomic war, they actually envision a paradise which would follow it. This, the Yugoslav author notes, is deeply inhuman. The Chinese juggling with the idea of peaceful coexistence is nothing but tactics. He concludes: "Chinese policy is the anti-pode of peaceful coexistence. In their opinion, imperialism will not surrender, it is necessary to destroy it!"

Zlatko Cepo, an assistant of the Institude for the history of Croatia's workers' movement, defined the meaning of socialism in Russia and China as follows: "Whereas in the USSR, the carrying out of socialism is considered impossible without a highly developed material-technical basis and a corresponding system of distribution which will stimulate further increase of production,—in China, on the other hand, socialism is considered to be established in a society whatever degree of development of its productive forces, when the distribution system satisfies the minimal requirements, and where economic incentives to stimulate production are ruled out."[29]

CHAPTER V

The Moscow-Peking-Belgrade Triangle

Ideological Alignment

In the main issues of foreign policy Yugoslavia and the Soviet Union stand closer to each other than they do in internal policies. Yugoslavia's sympathy with Prague in the 1968 crisis should be viewed as an exception. There was no comparison between the heated arguments of Yugoslavia and Stalin over Soviet economic and military pressure twenty years ago, and the polemical tone in the Yugoslav press in condemning, along with the majority of communist Parties, the Soviet-led Warsaw pact countries behavior toward Czechoslovakia. The latter had the appearance of a "family affair," in which communist Parties rather than governments were involved. Inter-state relations were not affected. What mattered was that "the Soviet Union scrupulously respected current economic undertakings with Yugoslavia, including the supply of military materiél with which this country has largerly equipped its armed forces."[1] High Titoism died with Stalin. Although Party relations were temporarily disturbed, messages between the two leaderships continued to be exchanged.

President Tito has displayed his statesmanship in obtaining armaments largely from Russia while continuing to receive financial support from American-dominated institutions. One can understand why he was successful in both cases. Since Yugoslavia carries on trade with Cuba and North Vietnam, she is not eligible for direct American aid.

Tito is very active among the group of nations forming the

third world. His non-alignment policy between the blocs would have its justification, but it is questionable whether a communist leader can legitimately pursue such a policy. It is true that this gave him an opportunity to play an important role in world politics. But at a time of crisis as in 1968, he was not backed by the principal non-aligned countries. Actually, Yugoslavia was not directly endangered. Instead, support came to him from NATO, so much maligned by Yugoslav communists. At the 5th Polish Party congress Gomulka criticized Yugoslavia for conducting "a policy of so-called non-alignment...only under the protection of the unity of the Warsaw Treaty countries."[2]

Revealing for the Soviet-Yugoslav relations was the attitude expressed by Moscow *Kommunist*.[3] The Yugoslav commentators voiced the complaint that for the Russians nothing was good in Yugoslavia any more. The socialism (communism) of Yugoslavia is not questioned, though. Is it a new variant of socialism, called self-managing socialism? This, too, has not yet been clarified. The leading role of the League of Communists, the fragmentation of unified, "all-public" property and other notions should not worry the Russians. Yugoslav propaganda is certainly effective, and one can understand that the West misreads the apologetical nature of their arguments, and regards these people as mavericks, while they in fact have never given up their communism. This writer is convinced that nobody in Yugoslavia would dispute that fact.

There is a plethora of theoretical debates going on in Yugoslavia regarding this subject. Kardelj himself went on record that a new variant does not exist, whatever the Russians say. The Yugoslavs themselves called some of these new ideas and formulations "frivolously improvised."

Generally speaking, the Yugoslav press and radio pour out never-ending streams of vituperation of Western policies without, however, arousing an appropriate reaction. On the other hand these media are very sensitive whenever anything derogatory appears first of all in the Soviet Union, but also in other communist countries. The Soviets, in their turn, frown when the Yugoslavs attribute to their various innovations international significance. They do their best to trim to size Tito's ambitions on the world scene.

After twenty years of experience with workers' self-management in Yugoslavia, influential economic levers still largely remain centralized or partially transferred to the constituent republics. The powers of ownership of the workers' councils, on the other hand, are closely circumscribed. The Russians designated the self-management as anarcho-syndicalism, a sort of abuse of workers' control of the enterprises. They prevented the spreading of such a system to Czechoslovakia. It is an exaggeration to describe it as "the liquidation of the socialist state," paving the way to personalism and capitalist degeneration. In fact, Yugoslavia is the best proof of the opposite trends. For the Russians, however, self-management appears as a variant of workers opposition.

The "de-etatization" of the economy is viewed as a permanent return to the New Economic Policy, which was Lenin's temporary retreat dictated by the economic plight. The Russians are afraid of rivalry and parochial outlook of industrial enterprises, which can be always corrected by state intervention.

Of a more serious nature are difficulties arising between the nationalities and minorities, which in the past were simply suppressed by the secret police. Here a new dimension was added by Yugoslav-Bulgarian polemics over Macedonia, the Russian hand being hidden somewhere in the background. Yugoslavia's heavy indebtedness to the West, hundreds of thousands workers toiling in capitalist countries or jobless at home, all these weak points are ascribed by the Russians to the economic reform and to the "market anarchy." A Soviet magazine, which usually reflects the views of the Foreign Ministry, reproached Tito for undermining the unity of the communist world. A similar dressing down was given to the Yugoslavs by other Soviet learned magazines.

These synchronized polemics were followed by occasional gestures of confidence. While the Yugoslavs carefully registered Soviet criticism, they did not indulge in theoretical argumentation. They disclaimed any anti-Sovietism and occasionally gave praise to the first country of socialism. Yet a learned Soviet magazine conceded that "there is, of course, a great deal that is interesting and positive about the very idea of public self-management and about the Yugoslav practice of implementing this idea."[4]

One may wonder what the purpose of these polemics are when Kardelj, less than a month after the invasion of Czechoslovakia, declared that the Yugoslavs certainly did not behave in that way because they opted for an anti-Soviet policy or decided to enter NATO. He went on stating: "We were always aware of the great international role of the Soviet Union in the world. For that reason we were always ready to support its every move and policy... This we will do also in the future."[5]

Yet the polemics continued. A Soviet commentator, however, was eager to express his sorrow over the "shortcomings of a friendly country" and "difficulties of our fraternal people." What he wrote should be regarded as a "perfectly understandable anxiety of a friend," since the Soviet press "bars attacks on Yugoslav leaders and on the League of Communists." Yet the Yugoslav press was "poisoning the atmosphere of friendship and cooperation."

The Soviet claim as Gomulka did, that "the security of Yugoslavia is not ensured by its own armed forces, but by the existence, in the present circumstances, of such a powerful anti-imperialist force as is the Warsaw Pact." The Russians scowl when the Yugoslavs speak of the occupation of Czechoslovakia or disseminated the *Hsinhua* version of the border conflict. Nor do they like to see the Yugoslavs advertizing their model as a "pattern of an all-round stimulus," or introducing satirical remarks in the travelogues of the Soviet Union or publishing Solzhenitsyn's "The First Circle." These are regarded as anti-Soviet ideological diversions.[6]

Meanwhile the international communist conference gave a tacit endorsement to Moscow. Consequently the Yugoslav leadership reaffirmed the desire and readiness to maintain "relations and cooperation with the Soviet Union and other socialist countries to be developed in conformity with the principle expressed in the Belgrade and Moscow declarations of 1955 and 1956."

At a press conference following the celebration of the 25th anniversary of communist Yugoslavia, Tito confirmed that his country was building socialism just like the other countries of the Soviet bloc, and that ideologically it belonged to that bloc, though not to the commonwealth, *sodruzhestvo,* as it is called in Russian, of socialist countries where Moscow imposed limited sovereignty. He went on saying that it was now desirable that Yugoslavia should stop dramatizing the matter but rather "work to calm things down and insure that the best possible cooperation should obtain in the international workers movement." He expressed his view regarding the invasion psychosis by stating that there was no reason for the Soviet Union to undertake such an action in Yugoslavia, nor did he believe in such a possibility. At the same time he descried the wishful thinking as if Yugoslavia belonged to some "grey zone" laying outside the socialist world.[7]

Tito was sincere in June 1956 when on his arrival in Stalingrad he made a declaration in the presence of Khrushchev to the effect that "In peace as in war, Yugoslavia must march shoulder-to-shoulder with the Soviet people toward the common goal, the goal of the victory of socialism."[8]

According to press reports, Marshall G. D. Zhukov, then minister of defense, went a step further and gave the impression that an obligation of mutual assistance was reestablished. Speaking in the presence of Tito he said that Yugoslavia and the Soviet Union would fight shoulder-to-shoulder in any future war.[9]

Some years later, at the Party conference in Zagreb in December 1959 Tito stated that in all main problems of foreign policy Yugoslavia "sided with the Soviet Union and supported Khrushchev's initiatives."[10]

As regards Russia, Soviet Foreign Minister Gromyko stated at the session of the Supreme Soviet in December 1960 that the Russians noted with satisfaction that the points of view of the Soviet Union and Yugoslavia regarding basic questions of the contemporary international situation coincided, and added that "the Soviet government hopes that the co-operation between the Soviet Union and Yugoslavia will be further strengthened."[11]

In another part of the world Tito was quoted in *Asahi Shimbun,* Tokyo, as having said that there were no differences between Yugoslavia and the Soviet Union as regards the final goals in the building of socialism: differences existed only with regard to the methods and in their attitude to what he called the communist *lager* (military camp).[12]

In July 1962, when a high-level Yugoslav parliamentary delegation visited Moscow, the Yugoslav communists were given official acknowledgment of their orthodoxy. The Chairman of the Soviet of Deputies, Ivan V. Spiridonov, declared that the Yugoslav people, directed by the League of Communists were "constructing a socialist society with a communist society as their goal."[13] This was confirmed four years later by E. Kardelj leading once more such a delegation to Moscow. Speaking on the Soviet-Yugoslav relations he said that the basic goals of the peoples of Yugoslavia and the Soviet Union were identical, namely the building of socialism or communism, which meant that there was a broad platform of common interests and needs for cooperation and common action.[14]

At the same time for the Red Chinese, "Yugoslavia has ceased to be a socialist country."[15] Peking's delegate Chao Yi-ming at the 10th Italian CP congress in September 1962 even pretended that "capitalism was re-established in Yugoslavia," a statement which provoked roars of laughter among the participants, who apparently knew otherwise. The Russo-Chinese conflict has also come to the open in this regard.

The resurrection of the Belgrade declaration of 1955 (signed during Khrushchev's Canossa trip) was from the ideological point of view an important event for the final joint communiqué issued at the conclusion of the state visit in Belgrade by then Supreme Soviet Presidium's Chairman L. I. Brezhnev.[16] The declaration stressed non-interference in internal affairs "for whatever reason, whether of an economic, political or ideological nature, considering that questions of internal organization of different social systems, and *different forms of socialist development are solely the concern of the individual countries*"[17] (emphasis supplied).

These principles were again confirmed in the Moscow declaration of 1956 on the occasion of Tito's state visit to the Soviet Union in a more specific manner:

> Believing that the ways of socialist development vary with different countries and conditions, that the wealth of the forms of socialist development contributes to its strength, and proceeding from the fact that *any tendency to impose their views as regards the ways and forms of socialist devel-*

opment is alien to both sides, the two sides have agreed that the aforementioned cooperation should be based on complete voluntariness and equality, on friendly criticism, and on comradely exchange of views on contentious issues between our Parties.[18] (Italics provided).

Both declarations were limited to Yugoslavia only, and were not a pattern for other socialist countries, for which the Soviet model of socialism was obligatory.

Later on, following the October 1956 upheavals in Eastern Europe, Moscow went back on this agreement. Addressing the 7th Congress of the Bulgarian Communist Party in June 1958, Khrushchev endorsed the 1948 first Cominform resolution, condemning the Yugoslavs as national deviationists. He added, however, that it would be good to preserve some spark of hope.

Moscow recognized more than once the validity of the thesis of various roads leading to socialism and communism. Yet, this was formally in contradiction to both the 1960 Moscow Statement —the last Sino-Soviet compromise—and the Soviet Party program, which condemned such separate roads. Seen from this point of view, the occupation of Czechoslovakia should not be surprising. It was at first justified, however, because of the danger of counter-revolution, rather than on the ground that the Czechoslovak Party was taking a separate road, as expressed in the action program.

Professor Josip Korbel, Colorado University, a former Czechoslovak Ambassador to Yugoslavia argued that Yugoslavia had influence on Soviet relations with its satellites considering that Moscow accepted equality and many roads to socialism. He expressed this view in his lecture at the symposium of Western scholars on communism, organized by the Hoover Institution on War, Revolution and Peace at Stanford University, California, on the occasion of "One Hundred Years of Revolutionary Internationals" in October 1964. The developments in Czechoslovakia denied that view.

At the same time the Red Chinese were stressing also the 1949 second Cominform resolution, labeling the Yugoslavs "imperialist agents" as against the Soviet retraction of that resolution after Stalin's death.

Speaking of Soviet-Yugoslav relations, Khrushchev in his

Supreme Soviet speech[19] ignored the anti-Yugoslav 1957 Declaration and the 1960 Statement. Instead, he took the line that those
relations were to be based on the policies laid down by the 20th
and 22nd Soviet Party congresses, and continued: "I must say that
the steps which have been taken recently by the Yugoslav communists and their leaders both in internal and foreign policy have
removed certain things which were regarded as erroneous and harmful to the cause of building socialism in Yugoslavia." He foresaw
rapprochement and unity with the whole international communist
movement.

In the same speech Khrushchev explained the separate roads
to socialism and communism in these words:

It is understandable that between us there can be no complete understanding of all the problems confronting communist and workers' Parties in their struggle for the reconstruction of a new society. Different interpretations of
concrete questions of socialist construction, a different
approach to various problems are not ruled out...Com-
munists of that kind must not be regarded as schismatics.

This evidence should suffice to prove that Tito never was a
real heretic, who has abjured his secular faith. Moscow proclaimed *urbi et orbi* that he should not be considered anymore
even as a schismatic, and these attitudes were fully shared under
the Brezhnev-Kosygin leadership.

There was hardly ever a good reason for designating Yugoslav
communism as heresy. The terms heresy and heretic are in this
case both historically and etymologically inappropriate. There exists
an identity of the "dogma" and of the materialist creed between
the Yugoslav and Russian communism. They also have a common
goal. The difference exists only regarding the means. Contrary
to the Russians the Yugoslav communists do not recognize the existence of "one road to paradise" as preached by the "third Rome."[20]
Having been expelled from the Cominform, they made a virtue
out of this fact, and created a small, transient schism, which was
subsequently healed. Consequently Khrushchev and his successors
acknowledged Yugoslavia as a socialist country, and the League of
Communists as a fraternal Party.

The French government for one took a realistic view after all these manifestations and in his 1964 New Year's message President de Gaulle included Yugoslavia among the "communist totalitarian regimes that still constrain the captive peoples."

The new situation was revealed at the 23rd Soviet Party Congress (spring 1966) where the League of Yugoslav Communists was represented for the first time officially by the Vice President of the Republic, Aleksandar Rankovic (who was later ousted). No difference was made among the eleven ruling Parties present. This becomes even more significant when we realize that there was no Yugoslav delegation at the 22nd and 21st congresses, whereas at the 20th congress Tito's message was only read. The same privileged position was reserved to the Yugoslav communists at the solemn Kremlin meeting on occasion of Lenin's centenary four years later, when Chairman of the Supreme Soviet Presidium Nikolay Podgorny greeted Dr. Vladimir Bakaric among the representatives of the ruling CP. This was repeated at the 24th congress.

The Yugoslav communists scored the third revised edition of the History of the CPSU, whose statements have an authoritarian ring, where a new account of the past Soviet-Yugoslav relations was given. The authors, headed by Academician Boris Ponomaryov, a CC secretary, said that the different concept of the CPY and (disturbed) inter-state relations deeply worried the community of socialist countries then, although certain mistakes were admitted. The Cominform resolutions were not mentioned any more, neither the League's program once disputed.

However, the Yugoslavs claimed that the Belgrade and Moscow delarations exonerated the Titoists of any responsibility for the conflict with the Cominform, a view not shared in this text-book. Actually, the new evaluation was milder than that of the previous two editions under Khrushchev's rule. The Yugoslav communists have the satisfaction that most of the signatories of the Cominform resolutions had been either executed or purged.

As anticipated, a virtual halt of Soviet-Yugoslav polemics came in the spring of 1969. The relations improved again, since for the Soviets the struggle against Chinese dogmatism was much more important. Nevertheless, sporadic generalized Soviet criticism on revisionism and right-opportunism followed, interpreted by the Yugoslavs as directed against them. As an exception to the rule, *Planovoye khozyaistvo,* the magazine of Soviet Union's central planning commission (gosplan), scored the whole Yugoslav market socialism as revising the essence of Marxist-Leninist political economy. In turn Belgrade from time to time censured the Brezhnev doctrine of limited sovereignty.

The Lenin centenary theses had the intention, as explained by the Yugoslav communists, "to define the Soviet model of socialism as the only correct one," and implicitely to reject different roads to socialism. Putting thus Lenin and Leninism on the Procrustean bed of the Soviet system, they claim that even Vladimir Ilyich was already opposed to the self-management system and the free play of market laws.[21]

Soviet-Yugoslav Identical or Close Views

When he was given the honor of addressing the Supreme Soviet as a foreign guest five years after his "arch-enemy" Mao Tsetung, Tito pledged that "Yugoslavia and the Soviet Union are going to improve relations as much as possible... Our view-points are identical or very close to each other... Inasmuch as there are still certain disagreements, we shall jointly remove them through constructive cooperation." He added that he was "basically in agreement with Comrade Khrushchev's remarks on Soviet-Yugoslav relations."[22]

It must have been a gratification for the Yugoslav President to have been given the privilege to formulate his brand of communism to the Soviet audience in a speech to tractor plant workers at Volgograd (former Stalingrad).[23] This was his hallmark of legitimacy.

Veljko Vlahovic, representing the League of Yugoslav Communists at the Sixth German Socialist Unity Party congress, received a tremendous ovation during his speech, the first such manifestation since 1948.[24] Condemning the attacks of the Chinese delegate, congress chairman Paul Verner remarked that Yugoslavia was faithfully serving the cause of socialism. It was assumed that the League had definitely re-established inter-Party relations with the Soviet

Party.[25]

It should be noted that in his speech at the same congress Khrushchev accepted the Kardelj's thesis that the socialist or communist system need not be equated with the Soviet military bloc. Hence Yugoslavia can remain a respectable member of the communist world without participating in the Warsaw Pact. According to the Yugoslav program this pact should be regarded as a "natural defensive reaction to the creation of the Atlantic Pact." In fact, NATO was a "natural defensive reaction" to Stalin's conquests, his iron curtain and his aggressive policy. In his speech to factory workers near Belgrade Tito said that the Soviets were carrying the burden of heavy sacrifices for defense, not only for themselves, but for the defense of socialism in general that is, for communist Yugoslavia as well.

For many years an illusion was current in the West according to which Tito's communism was maverick compared with that of the Soviet bloc. The Yugoslav President himself rejected such an interpretation by stating in the same speech:

Other people's flatteries which we hear from various sides to the effect that we have a special kind of socialism with nationalist characteristics, which is acceptable and congenial even for non-socialist countries, should leave us cool. For us such expressions of sympathy are worthless. We want a truly socialist society and are anxious to establish relations which are proper to socialist countries.[26]

Foreign Secretary Koca Popovic at that time stressed cooperation with other socialist countries as the principal objective of his country's foreign policy. According to him common ideology with these countries entailed similar views regarding co-existence and foreign policy in general. Two months later, at the fifth plenary session of the Central Committee, Tito declared that Yugoslavia's foreign policy

cannot harm the cause of the socialist countries and of the workers' movement in general. We must be aware that we are a part of this movement and do not stand outside of it... When I have said that we are siding with the anti-dogmatist forces in the international communist movement

I have defined in that way our place, our duties, and the international duties of the League of Communists of Yugoslavia in the international workers' movement.[27]

The bi-monthly *Medjunarodna Politika* expressed the view that, unlike NATO, the Warsaw Pact is regional and defensive. "The process of dissolution of the Atlantic Pact is irreversible. The real purpose for maintaining the American presence has become completely obvious for everybody. Emancipation of Europe from American influence is under way." That process could be advanced with the disappearance of the Warsaw Pact.[28]

Some dictators in the Third World were Tito's closest friends. After their downfall for purely internal reasons, Tito attacked at the Yugoslav League's CC the "imperialist forces" particularly the U.S., for allegedly endangering Yugoslavia's independence, although it was known that just the opposite was true. Using this as a reason for his pro-Soviet trips to Moscow and Budapest in support of the cause of the Arabs, Tito gave new formulations for the policy of non-alignment, which is said to have been saved by the alignment with Moscow. He then called the policy of active and peaceful co-existence a struggle against "imperialism." Similar views were expressed by several members of the CC who went on record that the policy of non-alignment could be victorious only if the non-aligned countries became aligned with the Soviet bloc.[29]

Tito's stance before the invasion of Czechoslovakia was assessed authoritatively by Professor Mosely in an article in which he said: "Tito's growing tendency to come down more and more often on the side of Soviet policy is in part a reflection of his declining value both to the Kremlin and to leaders of the Third World."[30]

In formulating her foreign policy, Romania, a member of the Warsaw Pact, assumed an independent posture. However, in case of war, Party leader President Ceausescu stated that Romania would fight alongside of the other socialist countries regardless of whether the Warsaw Treaty existed or not. There is little doubt that the same applies to Yugoslavia.

Dr. Viktor Meier, a former East European correspondent of *Neue Zürcher Zeitung*, may be regarded as a recognized authority in this field. According to him, Yugoslavia is relying on the power

of the Soviet Union as well as other countries of the Soviet commonwealth. His view of the Warsaw Pact is more flexible. It was
a Cuban confrontation without Cuba belonging to that Pact. Albania formally withdrew from it protesting that it was directed
against its members. Meier believes that all the specialists are in
agreement while only some official circles have retained "a schematic
way of looking at it", ignoring all hard facts. He is formulating
the questions as follows:

> Why, if the once prevailing system of Communist unity is
> in the process of a new formation, should Communist Yugo-
> slavia not be assigned a firm place within the new system
> of socialist unity, one that probably only later will receive
> a name? And why should the Soviet Union engage herself
> politically and militarily any less in a European country
> of nineteen million inhabitants that is situated in a strategical-
> ly important position, and in spite of everything has a certain
> influence abroad, in order to retain its Communist character
> than, for example, she tried to do in Cuba?[31]

Is not the Soviet "class" approach to sovereignty a confirmation of this?

In the old Tsarist design to spread Russia's influence to the
warm Mediterranean Sea, and in the great Soviet design to squeeze
out the American Six Fleet, Moscow counted with Yugoslav support. Belgrade, indeed, has linked its radar system to the Warsaw
Pact.[32]

The Yugoslav communists have rejected what they call the
"so-called theory of equidistance," and consequently are not meas-
uring American and Soviet presence in the Mediterranean by the
same yardstick. Instead they came out with the idea of the de-
Atlantization of its shores because "Soviet military presence in this
zone is today useful and necessary in the face of the aggressive
activity of imperialism."[33] Yet during the Czechoslovak crisis they
mitigated this point a bit.

The organ of the Soviet armed forces foresaw a promising
development of cooperation between the two armies in 1967:

> The Yugoslav People's Army and the Soviet Army fighting
> shoulder to shoulder against the common enemy during

World War II are preserving close cooperation and friendship even in peacetime.   Thus, a Yugoslav military delegation was present at the combined exercises of the armies
and navies of Bulgaria, Rumania and the USSR, which took
place in August, and also at the "Dnepr" exercises in September.   A naval delegation headed by Admiral of the fleet
of the Soviet Union, S. G. Gorshkov, visited Yugoslavia
in 1967. Admiral M. Yerkovich, assistant to the Yugoslav
State Secretary for National Defense, headed the Yugoslav
naval delegation on its return visit to the Soviet Union.   A
detachment of river vessels of the Red Banner Black Sea Fleet
paid a friendly visit to Novi Sad this year.[34]

What about the absurd Chinese view of Yugoslavia's being
"a special detachment of the United States"?   As has been shown,
the rule that in foreign policy the Soviets and Yugoslavs go hand
in hand in all important international problems was repeatedly
expressed, except in the Czechoslovak crisis, by all prominent Soviet and Yugoslav leaders.   "The identity and closeness of views"
found its expression in the joint Soviet-Yugoslav statement of June
30, 1965, issued after the meeting between Tito and the Soviet
leadership,[35] reaffirmed by Brezhnev in September 1971.

When former Secretary for Foreign Affairs Marko Nikezic
visited his opposite number, A.A. Gromyko, a year later, they noted
with satisfaction that "at present all the conditions exist for further
all around development and strengthening of fraternal friendship
and cooperation between the USSR and SFRY."[36]   Meetings of
this kind at the same time appeared as anti-Chinese moves.

Cooperation between the two countries was indisputable.   A
sincere and mutual friendship was established in the last years of
the Khrushchev regime.   Even "cotton balls which hit you but
never hurt you," to use Enver Hoxha's metaphor, were no more
thrown by Moscow, as was the case before by way of a concession
to Red Chinese pressure.   Cotton balls, though, were thrown again
from Moscow during the Czechoslovak crisis.   It had all the hall-
marks of a story with a happy end, "just as a novel in which two
lovers have to surmount many obstacles before they finally fall

into each other's arms, united for ever," in the words of Slobodan S. Stankovic, the Yugoslav chief analyst for Radio Free Europe in Munich. In fact, Yugoslav foreign policy appears like nothing else but "a useful refinement of Soviet foreign policy."[37] There is an agreement between them regarding the "U.S. aggressive actions" as well as in the use of slogans of communist propaganda. A special world mission is reserved for Yugoslavia acting as a communist agent among the non-aligned countries.

As regards the so-called national liberation wars, one may speak of identity of views between Yugoslavia and the other communist Parties. The regime, indeed, owes its existence to this kind of warfare. Yugoslavs lent assistance to such wars either directly or indirectly, like good communists, particularly in the Algerian case. This shows that the Chinese are wrong again.

In communist countries inter-state and inter-Party relations are interlinked and hence strongly influence each other. Inter-Party relations were re-established between the Yugoslav, Soviet and all other ruling Parties. They joined hands in "the struggle against imperialism" and "to support by all means the people's liberation movement", according to the 1965 communiqué of Soviet and Yugoslav leaders. Likewise "the contacts...have been expanding and growing stronger in recent years, and further strengthening of friendship and cooperation" were foreseen. On the other hand, in his report to the 9th congress of the League of Communists, Tito complained about "stagnation and decline of our cooperation in the sphere of political and Party relations" with the five invading communist countries.

By his own statements Tito has identified himself with the world communist conspiracy. In general, the same communist strategy is also valid for the Yugoslav communists, the difference being only in tactics. The President rejected the myth of an unorthodox Yugoslav socialism and pleaded for a truly Marx-Leninist system whose goal is communism.

All the while, there is an awareness in Yugoslavia that the regime depends on the fate of socialism (communism) in the world, since according to their program Yugoslav socialism is a part in the world-wide social transformation.[38] A Yugoslav League's dele- .

gation in the fall of 1965 became thoroughly acquainted with the "experience of the CPSU organizational, Party and ideological activity and with the success of the Soviet people in building the material and technological base of communism."[39] Yet Yugoslavia's special relationship with Russia depends to some extent upon her capability to maintain her Western and non-aligned ties.

In the second half of June 1968 a delegation of the CPSU visited Yugoslavia on the invitation of the CC of the League of Communists. The subsequent communiqué stressed that the representatives of the League and of the CPSU had discussed the problems of the strengthening of cooperation and agreed upon a concrete plan for the future.[40]

Replying indirectly to Yugoslav communists in an article justifying the occupation of Czechoslovakia, *Pravda* stated: "When a socialist country seems to adopt a 'non-affiliated stand', it retains its national independence, in effect, precisely because of the strength of the socialist community, and, above all, of the Soviet Union as the leading power which also includes the might of its armed forces." This is the tenor of Tito's mentioned statement about the Soviet armed forces supporting the whole socialist (communist) commonwealth. In default of the Soviet nuclear umbrella, smaller communist rulers would feel themselves much less secure. Nevertheless, the fact remains that Yugoslavia upheld the traditional conception of sovereignty in contradiction to the Soviet stand.

The 9th congress of the League of Communists of Yugoslavia in March 1969 was not attended by the ruling communist Parties with the exception of the Romanians. This was unlike the 8th congress when all the Soviet bloc countries were present. At the 9th congress foreign Parties were not given floor to forestall trouble due to discordant voices. Another reason for their absence was their different stand on other issues facing the League. Tito expressed the view that these differences were transitory and re-stated his desire to maintain good relations with both the Soviet Union and the other socialist countries. The congress resolution on international relations rejected the idea of international communist headquarters or of ideological monopoly of any Party.

In his address to the Supreme Soviet, Foreign Minister Gromyko stressed the importance of improving relations with Yugoslavia:

It is essential to emphasize that the Soviet Union attaches
great significance to the development of relations with socialist Yugoslavia, though these relations have not always
developed...well. We are convinced that the adherence of
the peoples of the USSR and Yugoslavia to the ideas of
socialism and [to] their mutual interest in expanding contacts, create the prerequisites for the further development of
Soviet-Yugoslav relations. And we are entirely for that.

This policy was endorsed during Gromyko's visit to Belgrade
in early September 1969. A compromise was found: the Soviets
again formally reaffirmed the Belgrade declaration of 1955. This
time the principles of respect for the sovereignty, equality, and non-
interference in internal affairs were given emphasis. In exchange,
the Yugoslavs agreed "to forget the past," and not to raise the
case of Czechoslovakia (Tito's press conference in Kranj). Soviet
and Yugoslav foreign policy coincided as ever. In his speech in
Zagreb a week later, the Yugoslav President spoke of the development of friendly relations and of the high level of cooperation resumed with the Soviet Union and with other East European socialist
countries. An exchange of Party study delegations followed.[41]

Proselytism Through Non-Alignment

In the above mentioned speech in Belgrade, after his return
from Moscow, Tito gave a fuller explanation of the meaning of
Yugoslavia's brand of non-alignment. He said he had told the
leaders in Moscow that Yugoslavia enjoyed a good name among
the peoples of Asia and Africa, and that this came in good stead
not only to the Yugoslavs and to those countries, but also "to the
progressive movement and to the whole peace-loving world." In
communist parlance this means furthering the cause of communists
and fellow-travelers. Kardelj developed the same idea in a statement he made to *Tanyug*.[42] He said that through non-alignment
communism may become victorious in the whole world in a much
quicker way.

The third conference of heads of state and government of
non-aligned countries, held in Lusaka, Zambia, early in September

1970, was greeted by both Chou En-lai and Kosygin. Moscow as well as Peking had to be satisfied with the resolutions adopted in accordance with their policies, notwithstanding their differences.

During their Afro-Asian tours, Tito and Kardelj made a real effort to review the whole policy of non-alignment so as to bring it closer to the Soviet line. Kardelj in Moscow, speaking about the non-alignment policy, used the adjective "so-called," as if to apologize before his Soviet audience. To make this point clear, he said that that policy did not mean neutrality in the current world struggle "of the socialist, progressive, democratic and peace-loving forces," but was "its inseparable and inherent part."[43] There is little doubt what in communist euphemism these forces represent.

After Premier Kosygin's visit to Cairo, *Pravda* wrote that the policy of the non-aligned countries was of great importance in the struggle of the socialist commonwealth.[44] A Yugoslav commentator then stressed that the Soviet Union has identical or very similar views on the main international issues as a large number of non-aligned countries. It was then understandable that the Hungarian Party leader Janos Kadar, after a visit to Tito in a joint communiqué positively assessed this kind of non-alignment.

During the Czechoslovak crisis, the Yugoslav communists stressed that the Soviet leaders praised the non-alignment policy in Egypt as well as in India. They quoted Premier Kosygin saying, after the above mentioned visit, that this movement constituted a great force in the struggle against colonialism and imperialism and served the strengthening of security, peace and cooperation among states. More recently, Soviet Deputy Foreign Minister N.P. Firyubin in New Delhi paid tribute to non-aligned countries, saying that they represented an important factor in the consolidation of the world. For years the Yugoslavs faithfully served the Soviet cause in those countries. As their organ had it: "How much effort has our League, and comrade Tito in particular, spent both in this country and abroad (especially within the so-called 'third world') to remove the misunderstanding and lack of confidence toward socialism in its Soviet version!"[45]

The Yugoslav communists are disseminating ideological proselytism in the developing countries by advising them to "skip capitalism through Titoism." Senator William Proxmire, Democrat from Wisconsin, said that Tito identifies his type of neutralism with the victory of communism over freedom.[46] This was confirmed by Ambassador George F. Kennan, whom *Borba,* the leading Yugoslav daily, described as a friend of communist Yugoslavia. In his NBC-TV interview of July 1962 he said that what the Yugoslavs were saying to the other neutrals did not often please him, and that he "did not find it to be in the interest of this country."

After the Belgrade conference of non-aligned countries the *Reporter* wrote: "The fitting of the Marxist formula onto the natural anti-colonial reaction is the creative service the Yugoslav regime has made to the communist cause." Discussing this subject, Professor Milorad M. Drachkovitch, a senior staff member of the Hoover Institute on War, Revolution and Peace, Stanford University, went on record that the Tito regime, "has done its best on all levels, to weaken Western positions the world over... They are convinced that in such a way, independently, they will help promote the irrepressible march of humanity toward communism."[47]

A practical demonstration of this policy was Yugoslavia's contribution to the fund of African liberation movements in Dar-es-Salaam, Tanzania, as was revealed at the ministers' conference of the Organization of African States, held in Addis Abeba in February 1967.

After most of the former colonies became independent countries, the Yugoslav communists contributed to formulate a new theory, and then preached throughout the world against economic neocolonialism. This is a new weapon of the communist world in their struggle against the Western powers, including the United States. Tito himself declared at the Nairobi University that the protectionist and discriminatory practices of those powers are the essence of neocolonialism on occasion of his trip to East African countries in February 1970. And because of the gap between the developed and developing countries, he coined the new notion of technological colonialism.[48]

In many developing countries there are three separate types of communist infiltration: Soviet and satellite, Red Chinese, and Yugoslav. They serve the same goal, though they may be at times

at loggerheads. There was sometimes a coordination between the
Soviets and the Yugoslavs in their fight against the Chinese. A
Yugoslav comment had it that "in Peking they are especial-
ly active in the 'salvation' of the newly independent countries and
liberation movements in Africa, Asia and Latin America 'from the
Yugoslav intrigues.' "[49]

By preaching socialism in the developing countries and by
spreading communist ideas to all continents, the Yugoslav communists are giving effective help to world communism through their
rallying of the non-committed nations, whether they accept the socialist creed or not, since these nations would presumably be potential allies of the West.

In his introduction to the book entitled *Yugoslav Communism,*
by Dr. Charles Zalar, a former Yugoslav diplomat, Senator Thomas
Dodd wrote that Tito, like an itinerant missionary to non-aligned
or newly independent nations, "has been far more valuable to world
communism in his present posture than he could possibly have been
as a Moscow communist." The Yugoslav communists seem to
have taken to heart Lenin's vision of a mighty alliance between the
communists and the former colonial peoples aimed against the
Western world.

We can speak about export of Titoism to many countries, since
Tito at times offers his advice to some governments not only in
the field of foreign policy, but also in strictly internal affairs. His
experts seem to be everywhere. According to official information,
in the last years more than a thousand Yugoslav delegations traveled all over the world. "Any attempt to present the scope, variety
and particularly the intensity of exchange and cooperation which
the League of Communists, the Socialist Alliance and our other
socio-political organizations have set on foot with the progressive
parties and movements in other countries, is bound to be incom-
plete," was the comment of the League's organ. Tito stated that
Yugoslavia had so far granted credits amounting to 650 million
dollars to the developing countries and that some thousand of Yugoslav experts are now at work in Africa and Asia.[50]

The Yugoslav Party program is explicit regarding the possibility of building socialism outside the communist countries. It

states that: "The conception that Communist Parties have a mono-poly on every respect of the movement toward socialism, and that socialism is expressed only in them and through them, is theoretical-ly incorrect and in practice very harmful."[51] This is in fact the teaching of Djilas. In one of his famous 19 articles, with which he had confused the Titoists in 1953, he singled out for refutation "the dogmatic and bureaucratic theory that only communists are the life force of socialism." He saw in this slogan a theory of Stalin which transforms communists into "priests and policemen of socialism."[52]

The communist Parties have, of course, a political monopoly in all countries where they rule. This is the essence of the dictatorship of the proletariat. According to Yugoslav opinion, however, such monopoly in the countries not subjected to communist rule, where the movement toward socialism is headed by a non-communist left-ist party or by a coalition of leftist parties, is not feasible at the time being. The ruling parties in such cases, however, must be anti-capitalistic and anti-imperialistic, that is anti-Western. The Yugo-slavs held the old, orthodox Soviet view as harmful to the growth of socialist forces in non-communist countries.

Meanwhile the Russians have modified their views by filling the gap between the theory and practice. Even to a greater degree than Khrushchev the Soviet leadership of our days accepts the non-orthodox Arab, African and Asian socialism, sometimes call-ed "Leninism minus class struggle." Dr. Meier is rather skeptical regarding the outlook of Yugoslav proselytism in the developing countries even though these doctrines have been accepted by some leftist regimes as a model to be followed.[53]

The growing deterioration of relations between Moscow and Peking has certainly contributed to the improvement of relations between Moscow and Belgrade. Since a return to goodwill between Moscow and Peking seems to be out of the question, the danger threatening Russia exercises influence on the Moscow-Belgrade rela-tions. The Chinese indeed have reproached the Soviet leadership for having made an about-turn of 180 degrees in their attitude to Yugoslav revisionism. Moreover, they hold that this is a well-con-sidered attempt to create a split in the international communist

movement. Up until then Red China had a good pretext to attack
Yugoslavia's ideology and policies before addressing itself directly
to the revisionist trends in Moscow, checked by neo-Stalinism.

As things now stand, the provisions of the Soviet Party program bearing on Yugoslavia's "right opportunism" and "bourgeois
nationalist tendencies" are kept for record. Also Yugoslav Com-
informist lectures in Moscow are ominous.

Replying to the Soviet "open letter" the Chinese have turned
their comment to the old question: "Is Yugoslavia a socialist country?"[54] The Soviets, as well as the other communist Parties, the
Chinese "camp" excepted, answered in the affirmative. This is
certainly more convincing than the controversial view of some Western circles. If they honestly believe that Yugoslavia is restoring
free enterprise economy, they have not grasped the nature of Yugoslav communism.

The official Chinese view is that a degeneration of communist
Party power has taken place in Yugoslavia, which has allegedly
renounced the dictatorship of the proletariat and deprived the Party
of its vanguard role. They speak of a "comprador bourgeoisie"
which has taken over the control of the country, as they used to
speak of an old Chinese caste which was accused of having sold
the country's interests to foreigners.

The Leading Role of the League of Communists

Even after their expulsion from the Cominform the Yugoslav
leaders kept on regarding themselves as the best communists. They
felt themselves superior to all the other comrades, including the Soviets, not to speak of the Chinese "leftist adventurers."

At the Marxist symposium at Stanford, Professor Adam Ulam,
author of *Titoism and Cominform,* expressed the view that Titoism
is not a specific ideology, but a particular historical moment. In
his official biography Dedijer quoted Tito himself saying in 1952
that Titoism did not exist as a separate ideology, and that Yugoslav
communists had added nothing to Marxism-Leninism.[55] Later on,
however, they changed their minds and claimed to have enriched that
theory.

In the opinion of Dr. Jan Librach, a former Polish diplomat, author of a book on Soviet foreign policy, there are no basic differences of doctrine between the Yugoslavs and the other communists, and to emphasize it appears to him like a Byzantine dialectical trick. He reminds that Tito concluded the fifth Party congress three weeks after the first Cominform resolution by exclaiming "Long live Stalin." Had Stalin wanted a compromise, he could have had it for a low price even a year after the resolution.[56]

According to the League of Communists' program and all evidence available, Yugoslavia is building socialism as the first stage of communism. To that end the country has established public ownership of all basic means of production, distribution and exchange, except the land of small-holders, and the property of a part of small craftsmen, inkeepers, shopkeepers, and truck owners, partially accepted as being ideologically tenable.

The country is under the rule of the dictatorship of the proletariat. In practice this means the dictatorship of the League of Communists, or to be more exact, of its Executive Bureau and Presidency. In other words, this is a case of a Communist Party monopoly, a totalitarian rule of the Party and state bureaucracy with a self-perpetuating leadership, horizontal rotation notwithstanding. As in other communist countries, this system of government strikes the student of politics like a *perpetuum mobile*. A witty speaker at the last congress of the trade unions federation broached the idea of vertical rotation of leadership—for a change.

Here the Ghanaians gave the communists a good lesson: "People in power should not try to perpetuate themselves in it as if it were their property," declared Brigadier Akwasi Afrifa, one of the presidential commissioners, when they returned the country to parliamentary democracy.

The League plays the role of vanguard and is ever present in all political decisions. In reality, the Yugoslav communist leadership is the master of the state as well as of society, controlling practically everything. The Party program plainly states that communists will hold key positions of state authority in their firm revolutionary hands.

The Program is clear and outspoken about Yugoslavia's internal situation and problems. It acknowledges that "the enemy of

socialism" is "still an important force in the social life" of the country and that "antagonistic forces [that is, 'the class enemy'] are not
yet sufficiently weakened so as to cease being a danger," to the
regime. For that reason the Yugoslav communists "cannot give up
the weapon of the class struggle, the dictatorship of the proletariat
and the leading role of the League of Communists." In their struggle against the forces which "still exert pressure ... in the sense
of capitalist restoration or bureaucratic state capitalism" Yugoslav
communists "relentlessly fight against any undermining of their political power by the bourgeois counter-revolution."[57]

The Communist Party's dictatorship and the rule of the state
by the Party are due to the Party's power monopoly and, as long
as this monopoly exists, no essential change can be expected in the
nature of communist government, for all rotations of the *apparatchiki*
are managed from above and only reflect the will of the leadership.

The guidelines which were issued to serve for the reorganization of the League changed anything on these basic principles. They
emphasized that "The character itself and the socio-political class
contents of the state power remain in essence unchanged: As long
as the state remains an indispensable instrument for the realization
and protection of the social needs of the working class and of socialism by means of organized political force and coercion, the dictatorship of the proletariat remains the state's essence. It becomes
a system of power which guarantees the social domination of the
working class and of its long-term interests in the socialist transformation of society." It is for this reason that the dictatorship of
the proletariat that is, of the League's leadership was retained unimpaired. In general, this document was more specific in exposing
the errors of the past than in describing the way how to overcome
errors in the future.

The self-management system "does not mean that Yugoslav
communists relinquish responsibility for the state policy." The
League retains its leading role as "the ideological-political vanguard
of the class."[58]

On a number of occasions Tito confirmed this attitude in his
speeches. He said that the role of the League was not being curtail-
ed; on the contrary its role would be still growing for a long time.

Again he repeated that the League had not abdicated its "leading role," adding that it was a mistake not to expel those who held that the Party has withered away. He then continued: "Communists are with us in the [Federal] Assembly and in all other organizations; they formulate foreign and domestic policy...Democratic centralism even today is very important and indispensable in the present phase." On another occasion Tito expressed the view that his country had not yet finished with the class enemy.[59]

The Western press reported that Brezhnev wrote a letter to Tito in which he tried to influence him regarding some points in the guidelines. *Pravda*[60] obliquely warned twice that socialism cannot thrive without the leadership of the communist Party. Some theoreticians in Yugoslavia contested this, but they lacked support among the leading circles. Anyway, if a Soviet intervention was needed at all, the resistance was less than minimal. As a Yugoslav saying has it: "It is not difficult to drive a frog into the pond."

Following the student demonstrations in Belgrade and other universities in June 1968, the Presidium and the Executive Committee of the League of Communists issued new guidelines for society without changing its standpoint. The demand for political pluralism that is, for the multiparty system was outright rejected. More resolutely than ever before the requirement was stressed to prevent the restoration of private enterprise.

In a letter addressed to Tito Belgrade students stated that they were embittered by the existence of "enormous social and economic divergences" in Yugoslav society. Leaflets signed by United Student Youth of Yugoslavia called on the citizens "to replace and abolish the autocracy of the League of Communists, and its monopoly over the entire political, cultural and economic life of our country and people."[61]

The League's Statute and the Constitution of Yugoslavia have set up a rotation system of so-called elected organs of authority. A similar system was abandoned by the Russians at their 23rd congress. The system provided for changes in the Party dictatorship through a periodical turnover of both Party and government organs at all levels. This, however, did not affect the stability and the oligarchic control of the top Party ideocratic leadership, vested with the exclusive power of promotion and demotion. The famous "transmission belt" of the Party's line is doing good work. The top leadership of the Party is formally authorized to undertake permanent purges of the *apparatchiki*.

There has been always some rotation among office-holders in communist countries, leaving the system unimpaired. Those who have had some experience with communist rule, however, have never met a case where statutory provisions of this or any other kind would lead step by step to the liberalization or democratization of the regime.

All activities and political doings of the Yugoslav communists are based on what is called scientific Marxism-Leninism. In their Program this is defined as the teachings of the basic laws of development of nature, society and thought (dialectical and historical materialism). The Titoists have added to their practice of Marxism-Leninism some elements derived from the pre-Marxist, Utopian, "non-scientific" socialism, borrowed from the teachings of Proudhon, Saint-Simon and Sorel. To bulwark their position they quoted Lenin: "We do not pretend that Marx and Marxists know the road to socialism in all its concrete aspects." Yet they refused to be regarded as national communists, a label which they received on account of their criticism of great power conceptions, political hegemony and inequality existing among the socialist countries. "In reality, national communism is communism in decline," said Djilas.[62] On the other hand President Nicolae Ceausescu once said that there is no national communism and no international communism. Communism, according to him, is at the same time national and international.[63]

The Yugoslav communists also have rules for governing the mutual relations between the individual communist Parties. According to them, such relations should be based on complete equality, barring imposition of a foreign doctrine or practice, and interference in internal affairs of the Parties. Curiously enough, similar principles were advanced by Chou En-lai at the 22nd Soviet Party congress. This might be dialectically explained as the unity of opposites...

The Yugoslavs describe the partnership among the communist Parties as "an entirely new qualitative factor in the formation of political and ideological unity."[64]   At the Soviet-Mongolian summit in January 1966, the need was stressed for "rigorous observance" of autonomy and non-interference in the affairs of other Parties. At the 23rd Soviet Party congress, Secretary General Brezhnev again emphasized the principles of autonomy and equality in the inter-Party relations.   And at Tito's visit in Bucharest in April 1966, both sides strongly supported the "inalienable right" of all peoples to determine their own destiny and to safeguard the principles of national sovereignty, non-interference and equality.   This was a challenge to Moscow's domination, but after the Czechoslovak events its value may be doubted.

In the opinion of Djilas there are no essential differences between individual communist countries. As he has put it: "The form of government or property as well as ideas differ very little or not at all in communist states. It cannot differ markedly since it has an identical nature—total authority."[65] For this authority in Yugoslavia "there is likelihood of a dictatorship *over* the proletariat on the horizon" asserted the organ of the maverick Marxist philosophers in Zagreb.[66]

The Socialist Self-Management System

The Chinese assert that between 1945 and 1968 Yugoslavia received six billion dollars in aid from "the imperialist powers."[67] There are two opposite schools of thought regarding the justification of assistance to communist countries. Bismarck's saying that one cannot buy one's enemies seems to apply particularly to cases like this one.

Dr. Meier, now representing a number of West German newspapers in Washington, D.C., questioned the wisdom of this policy which strikes one as if the West accepted the Marxist doctrine that the economic base determines the political superstructure. The Zagreb group of Marxist thinkers claim that that maxim could be applied only to developments within the capitalist society, but not to socialism.

The Soviets were at first suspicious of Western economic, technical and military aid to Yugoslavia. They were, however, soon assured that that aid was used for "building socialism" and that the Yugoslavs were not making any concessions to the United States "political or other." On that occasion Tito cunningly remarked: "Comrade Khrushchev keeps on repeating that one cannot build socialism on American wheat: I believe that those who know how to do it, can do it, but those who don't know, will not be able to build socialism even on their own wheat."[68]

According to the estimate of Dr. Zalar, the assistance Yugoslavia at that time received from the West, chiefly from the United States, amounted to approximately 200 to 250 million dollars a year. This sum was equal roughly to one half or even two-thirds of the Yugoslav budget.[69]

The dual nature of the problem of assistance to a communist country was reflected in an answer given by Senator Dodd: "I am not able to understand how we would help people to get free by making their tyrant masters stronger."[70] Aid-without-strings, according to Ernest Halperin, another Swiss authority on East European affairs, now with the Massachusetts Institute of Technology, was harmful: First it delayed Yugoslavia's transition to the West, and then it rendered impossible such a contingency. Lenin once cynically observed that in helping the Bolsheviks the capitalists were making a rope to hang themselves. However, despite the huge sums of money spent in this way, the rope is still loose.

The Yugoslavs hold, and have stated so on many occasions, that the United States are under an "obligation" to help them. The reason they give are their heavy losses incurred during the common war against Hitler. Yugoslav losses during the war were very great indeed. Yet it should be kept in mind that much of it was due to the ravages of the civil war, in which the communists, faithfully followed Lenin's precept that a foreign war should be turned into a civil war and revolution, preceding the communist take-over.

In the opinion of Jan Librach, the Yugoslav regime, despite its economic reforms, could hardly have survived its economic troubles but for the massive American assistance, which was regarded in Belgrade as a miracle. Librach believes that without that assistance the communist regime would not survive.[71] The Yugoslav case confirms the view of George Sokolsky of the old *Journal-American,* when he wrote that contemporary communism is more a technique how to hold power, than an ideal of life. There is some logic in the view of another former East European diplomat, George Damien, who holds that Yugoslav communism is supported by the money of American taxpayers.

Charles Tayer, a former head of the American mission to Yugoslav partisans, advocated economic support for Yugoslavia on the ground that any move away from Marxism by Yugoslav communists had influence on the East European countries. Belgrade's reaction to this view was that "should Americans trust Tayer, they would come to grief ... Congressmen who believed in Tayer, will be deceived ..."[72]

The Chinese are rebuking the Yugoslavs for their revisionism in the economic field, for their attempt to rationalize the communist economic system. This is being done now in the Soviet Union as well as in some other communist countries, but the Yugoslavs have gone further in this direction than others. The purpose of these economic reforms in Eastern Europe is to give some autonomy to individual enterprises and to establish a function to the market mechanism. This is the way the problem was formulated by Luigi Longo at the 11th congress of the Italian Party. To save their own skins the communist countries willy-nilly are taking a leaf from capitalism.

Librach defined the Yugoslav economy as a strange mixture of government planning, Party control and semi-free enterprises. The Yugoslav Party program defines the country's somewhat liberalized economic policy as follows: "The present social plan of Yugoslavia establishes the basic proportions of social production and distribution, assuming within these proportions free initiative of economic enterprises under market conditions and some regulative measures of the state."[73] The Yugoslav market, as the Program claims, is not ruled "by anarchy," as it is supposed to be in capitalist countries. Yet the laws of supply and demand and competition are allowed to operate subject to many restrictions. With considerable industrialization already accomplished, Yugoslavia calls herself a "middle-developed country."

Marxism-Leninism is an economic doctrine of the 19th century. It lost vitality in the communist countries when Stalinist terror was discontinued. Economic revisionism is a stage of experimentation, and nobody knows how the partial abandonment of centralized economic planning, the introduction of the profit motive, competition and decentralization of foreign trade—all these Yugoslav sins in Chinese eyes—will adapt themselves to communist economy. All these measures, departures from the communist economy as they are, can by no means be regarded as radical innovations. The Chinese in fact accuse even the Russians of having gone over to capitalism, just as they have been accusing the Yugoslavs for the same sin.

During the twenty five years of communist rule in Yugoslavia that country or rather its new class have been living beyond their means thanks to megalomania and bounteous subsidies coming from the West. This was admitted by the late Boris Krajgher, vice-president of the federal executive council (government) in his address to the Federal Assembly. He said that in relation to other forms of consumption, the volume of public expenditure (43 percent of the national income) was larger in Yugoslavia than in highly developed countries and urged its restriction.[74] He admitted that the government was facing "an almost superhuman task" of changing the faulty structure of the entire economy.

Following the introduction of the economic and social reform in July 1965 all citizens and the whole nation were urged to tighten their belts in order to establish a workable socialist market economy.

The Organization for Economic Cooperation and Development, of which Yugoslavia is an associate member, in its fifth annual report (1966) spoke about the problems connected with the transition from a centralized "command" economy to a sound economy. Among these it mentioned the distorted price structure, inadequate stocks in some industries, an adverse balance of trade and consequent shortage of hard currency, and a lack of economic institutions such as a well developed system of monetary and credit controls. Is it possible to combine a completely free determination of wages and prices at the enterprise level and maintenance of price stability? Most important was the shift of investments from politics to economics. To cope with all these problems required a long time. Yugoslavia as well as other east European countries have suffered from dogmatic application of outmoded Marxist theory and the resultant mismanagement of the economy.

The Chinese are attributing an exaggerated importance to the workers' council system. They call it "an extremely reactionary slogan" with which Yugoslavia chose to identify itself.[75] They charge the Yugoslavs that their economy is in the hands of bureaucrats, who appear somehow in their eyes as something different than *apparatchiki*. When the Yugoslavs introduced these councils in the so-called socially-owned factories as the basis of their socio-political order, they believed they were true to their socialist creed. Kardelj told an American scholar that Leninism is merely a set of ideas and methods derived from the Russian experience. The Yugoslav experience according to him was different.[76]

Experts on the Institute of Political Science at Belgrade University made an effort to compile a selection of fundamental thoughts of Marx and Engels on public property and the rights of producers. Professor Vranicki quoted Lenin, Bukharin, Rosa Luxemburg and the Italian communist theoretician Antonio Gramsci as being in favor of workers' self-management. One of the historical evidences the Yugoslavs had dug out went back to the Paris Commune which, they found, established an economic-political link between the direct producers and the means of production.[77] Marx hailed the self-management of those producers, while Lenin in his regulation of the workers' control, issued in November 1917, saw every factory and village as a production-consumption commune settling the problems of production and distribution by direct management of the working people. The socialist state for him, in Yugoslav interpretation, was a net sum of production-consumption communes.

That was then the Russian theory. But when the "liberated" Russian workers in 1920 strove to retain control over the factories, Lenin personally ordered the massacre of the workers and sailors of Kronstadt. This was the end of the idea of workers' council in Soviet factories.

When this idea was resurrected by the Yugoslav communists, Russian Marxists raised a protest against the Titoist theory that workers' self-management was a dogma in the Marxist sense, binding for all socialist countries (*obyazatelnoi dlya vseh stran zakonomernostyu*). It was objected that the Yugoslavs through the makeshifts to which they resorted during the transition period were questioning the international validity of socialism's experience in the Soviet Union. This struck the Russians as a kind of national communism, and they reproached the Titoists for "galvanizing some anarcho-syndicalist ideas."[78] Yet the industrial reform of 1962 established in each Soviet factory a permanent production conference with the participation of the workers' collective.

In fact, the Soviet Party program vaguely promises extensive participation of workers' collectives in the factory management, as well as extension of independence and initiative of the management, all underpinned by national production targets. At the same time the role and responsibility of local bodies in economic management are to be gradually increased.[79] This should be implemented by the economic reform.

Workers' self-management was hailed by Khrushchev. He regarded it as "a progressive phenomenon," if it is coordinated with the Leninist principle of single command (*yedinonachalie*),[80] that is, if the factory director is supervised by the Party and by the Party-controlled union, the so-called triangle system. Gomulka, speaking for the Polish experience, stated that workers' councils were a form of workers' democracy inside the system of the dictatorship of the proletariat. But he denied them the character of organs of the working class.[81]

The system prevailing in China before the cultural revolution was called "factory manager responsibility under collective leadership of the Party Committee." The main decision-maker was the Party secretary, while the director of the factory was responsible for the fulfillment of plans and the execution of decisions. This helped the Chinese to avoid the Soviet dichotomy between the Party and the managerial class. Now factories in China are under military control.

In the basic principles (III) of the Yugoslav Constitution there is a provision that "within the framework [of the social plan for Yugoslavia], and within the unified economic system the working people in the working organizations [enterprises] and socio-political communities autonomously plan and develop the material basis for their activities."

Yet Yugoslav workers' councils are not different from those in other communist institutions. They all display dialectical contradictions, that is, are at loggerheads with the reality. In theory the councils are supposed to work freely. In practice, however, they are controlled by the League, which substantially curtails the freedom of self-management. For this reason many observers regard the workers' councils as a mere rubber-stamp organ, although there is some evidence to the contrary. One Yugoslav theoretician wrote that "in some enterprises self-management and democratic practice have been made to appear like a façade behind which self-management's role has been reduced to a formality."[82]

"Democratic centralism" that is, Party rule from top to bottom, weakens any self-government as well as self-management in the factories. There are even too many directives issued by the political authorities, so that the above mentioned Chinese fears are not justified. The districts have a virtual control over important decisions of an enterprise. Moreover, there is a strong pressure on the self-management by associations belonging to the same production line, the governments of the member republics and, finally, by the federal government itself.

Regarding the principal communist charge against the free enterprise system, the exploitation of man by man, a Yugoslav theoretician came to the following conclusion: "The exploitation of man by man is abolished by the junction of direct producers with the means of production, which become "their" means. This takes place when they decide about the distribution of the social product after having eliminated the intermediaries."[83] In the Marxist definition the social product comprises the full amount of the newly created value, the gross national product, less government salaries, and professional and personal services. Unfortunately, there are too many new intermediaries.

Another Yugoslav theoretician holds that exploitation is not abolished by the successful socialist revolution, followed by the communist take-over. He maintains that the product of the surplus value of labor that is, according to Marx, the part of the capital's accumulation, earned by the worker, but not paid to him, is appropriated by a particular social group (the "new class"), which does not participate at all in the working process. This appropriation occurs without the express consent of the workers, creators of the national income. This means that exploitation goes on in the communist countries. There is a "persisting necessity to distribute the largest part of the surplus of work for definite common national interests."[84] Djilas knows by his own experience that the communists invented the 20th century's most modern technique for man's exploitation by man.

Dr. Vladimir Bakaric, the Croatian communist leader in a speech to the Zagreb City Council Committee expressed the view that workers in Yugoslavia work directly for themselves one hour out of every three hours. The two remaining working hours are the surplus value of labor, a part of which they get back indirectly. The ratio is thus 1:2, the same ratio, he reminded, when the Spaniards arrived to the land of the Mayas. He added that some archaeologists were astonished at this development for a revolution would presumably break out whenever this ratio would appear. The surplus value of the means in operation amounted up to 25 percent.[85] This state of things has not improved after the introduction of the reform. The share of enterprises in the surplus value of labor was just one third in 1966, and during the next years dropped.[86]

Dr. Bakaric returned to this subject in a speech at a plenary session of the League of Communists of Croatia's CC. He said:

Now or up to this day ... surplus value is disposed of by a group of people who did not belong to the worker-producers. They hold the surplus value and prevent its transformation into use value. Similarly Stalin, the guardian of the surplus value, asserted that there was no surplus value at all ... Today self-management is defective in just this particular field. The task is a more resolute and rapid transformation of surplus value into use value.[87]

The guidelines on the reorganization of the League conceded that only the economic reform would become a significant step in the overcoming of the extortion of the surplus of work from those who created it. And it went on declaring that "there are monopolistic tendencies in the administration of some sections of social property, leading to the allocation of the surplus of work for objectives not approved by the associated worker-producers, to the division of society into an independent stratum of professional administrators of economic and political activities ... and to the perpetuation of privileges."

This shows that exploitation of workers in Yugoslavia exists even under the system of self-management, because that system has never been fully applied.

The resolution of the 9th Congress of the League dealing with socio-economic relations stated that a considerable part of the surplus product wast still purloined from the producers. This was done not only by the state, but also by "emancipated economic forces in the fields of banking, foreign trade, etc." For this reason it is desirable that "the administrative escape of surplus value" be restricted.[88] Tito himself expressed this in his final speech at the congress when he said that "we should gradually give our self-managers more money, considering that they themselves give more money to us."

In the Yugoslav opinion the condition of the workers in other communist countries is much worse. In the words of Prof. Svetozar Stojanovic of Belgrade University: "In such a (socialist state) system the working class has undergone the worst kind of subjugation and exploitation. Not only has it no final word in the management of production, but *it does not even possess those rights which the working class in the developed bourgeois-democratic system has wrested for itself* [emphasis supplied]. Under state socialism members of the working class are not free to change their jobs nor to bargain collectively." The socialist revolution of those countries has then degenerated into a new "exploitating, class society."[89] These are of course the ideas of Djilas, who is not a prophet in his own country.

To be effective, the sweeping reform should mean nothing less than reduction of administrative interference and increased strength of workers' councils. All preceding reform resulted in the administrative tightening and deterioration of economic condition. Professor Ulam compared all these changes in Yugoslavia to a dog chasing his own tail. Desimir Tochitch, a member of the London Study Centre for Yugoslav Affairs, after analyzing all evidence available summed up the influence of the reform on the workers' management in these words: "There is still no real workers' participation in management and no real influence by the workers on the Yugoslav economy. Nor is there likely to be so long as the principle of 'democratic centralism' that is, communist dictatorship prevails in Yugoslav society."[90]

This opinion of one of the opposition leaders in exile was corroborated in the decisions of the sixth plenary session of the Central Committee of the League of Communists. According to that judgment: "Along with statements in favor of the decisions and attitudes of the Brioni plenum, an effort is made in some organizations of the League of Communists to act from old positions. This may be seen in the attempts to intervene in the internal relations of enterprises in order to take over the business and authority of organs of self-management and of representative bodies."[91]

Mijalko Todorovic, a member of the top Executive Bureau, said in an interview that the League was ridding itself of communists who were transforming the self-management into a "pure façade." In the same sense spoke Bakaric in an address to military leaders in Zagreb. According to him: "The role of the state is still very big, immense, decisive, and for that reason there was hardly any significant progress in self-management." Tito himself presented a disappointing picture speaking to Zagreb political activists: "Our self-management has made no progress, but is stagnating, and in (some) places . . . has also regressed."

A full-fledged movement against self-management developed in 1969 by setting up business committees to run the factories on the basis of a new amendment to the Constitution. Kardelj intervened to prevent the introduction of the Soviet managerial system of one-man leadership. The workers were willing to sacrifice self-management to better economic results for the factories and themselves.

Workers, who are members of the workers' councils, are by no means participating in the self-management, which was meant to be a panacea. They are getting reports before the session, but throw them away without looking on them. This was reported by a Zagreb weekly having the largest circulation in the country. The weekly then went on: "We ask them to speak up, but they are silent. What then is self-management? It looks like something you cannot catch. Perhaps a modern mirage?"[92]

The guidelines unwittingly threw light on the state of things when they complained that the conservative forces in the Party lacked belief in self-management when they said that the workers were not capable of running their enterprises and suggested instead a vigorous administrative centralism. According to them the self-management bodies should be nothing more than a transmission apparatus. The progressive part of the League should lead the workers in their struggle with the resistance to self-management which seeks to achieve totalitarian powers in economic and political spheres by bureaucratic usurpation.

The Central Committee report to the 9th Party congress voiced complaints that the self-management was lagging behind, that the influence of the executive administrative apparatus was still considerable, the conservative, bureaucratic forces were ruthless, and the League of Communists itself was operating autocratically. The situation was summarized by a headline of the country's biggest daily which reporting the congress discussion plainly stated: "We should not allow that the first steps in self-management be petrified."[93]

The suggestion made by some communist theoreticians that the self-management principle be introduced in Party life was rejected as another attempt to introduce the multi-party system through the back door.[94] The streamlining of the League is the task lying ahead. The guidelines vaguely speak of "a fuller integration of the League of Communists with the self-management system." This is as far as went the latest congress proclaiming the "Party of a new type."

An attempt had been made to introduce workers' councils in Czechoslovakia, and a pale version of them was imitated in Poland and Hungary. If they were allowed to live and develop, they might soften the dictatorial grip of the totalitarian communist Party-style and eventually lead to the emancipation of workers. Experience, however, teaches that communist Party monopoly implies both exploitation of workers and atrophy of labor unions, defenders of working people's interests.

Contrary to the Chinese "Third Comment"

The Chinese also reproach the Yugoslavs for their grievous sin of giving up the collectivization of agriculture. This charge could be addressed to communist Poland, too. Gomulka saw in the Soviet collectivization the roots of Stalin's lawlessness, the effect of which was the destruction of millions of peasants in Soviet Russia.[95] The collectivization drive in Yugoslavia came to grief following a resolute resistance of the peasantry representing then more than three quarters of the population. The regime was eventually compelled to dissolve most of the collective farms, called peasant-work-cooperatives. As in Poland, now about 85 percent of arable land in Yugoslavia is in the hands of individual farmers. The industrialization has greatly reduced farming population, but even now about half of the population is engaged in agriculture.

The Yugoslav Party program contains a promise that no further measures of expropriation will be taken. Although socialization of private land holdings remains the aim, this has to be achieved by persuasion.[96]   After the communist take-over a radical agrarian reform was carried out, limiting individual holdings to 25 acres of arable land. Subsequently many peasants joined the general agricultural cooperatives. As these cooperatives are restricted to grant credits to individual peasants, an important incentive to join disappeared. The peasants often take advantage of the cooperatives for their own personal benefit, and even the legal maximal limit of holdings is sometimes disregarded.

At the beginning a huge increase of the socialist sector in agriculture was foreseen. Tito went on record that between 1.2 and 1.7 million acres of arable land would be needed for this privileged sector. He expressed his impatience by saying that no time must be lost by individual farmers in joining cooperatives and forming large land estates. Two years later he promised a further consolidation and expansion of socialist relations in agriculture and in the village.[97] The policy of the regime is to expand the socialist sector and reduce the private one. Individual peasant land holding is then regarded as a temporary expedient. The 1969 farm census revealed that the arable land of the socialist farms increased by around two million acres acquired from the private sector over the last ten years.

Private peasants have not an easy lot in Yugoslavia. In the years of the industrialization drive tens of thousands of peasants, chiefly young people, left the countryside. Higher taxes and price discrimination as well as other measures were taken to induce those who remained to join the socialist sector. Only the resulting chaos and decline of production compelled the regime to moderate its methods. Addressing the representatives of large socialist estates, Tito said: "Of course, we never denied, and we are not denying even now, that we intend to socialize agricultural production ... The socialist transformation of the countryside may take ten or more years; what is important is that we keep on moving in that direction."[98]

The U.S. agricultural attaché in Belgrade reported that the Yugoslav government "is attempting to socialize agriculture by suppressing private farming rather than forbidding it."[99] Economic measures are taken to insure gradual collectivization by making it harder for the private farmer to compete. Lacking modern agricultural machinery and short of credit facilities, they have an inducement to join collective farms. The regime's objective is socialization of 50 percent of the arable land. Assistance to private farmers would upset the plan of the government in this respect. This should set the Chinese fears at rest.

Rebutting the Chinese view, Moscow *Kommunist* held that the Polish gradual way of socialist transformation of agriculture is "valid." This applies to Yugoslavia, too. After having foisted almost complete collectivization in all but two communist countries, Moscow came to the conclusion that experience urged to take into account the deep attachment of the peasantry to private land ownership. Consequently farm collectivization is now looked upon as a project extending over a long period.

According to the Chinese information there are some 115,000 independent craftsmen in Yugoslavia. They were allowed to exist because the public services which were supposed to take over their role were inadequate. Later they were forced to close down and as a result the old shortages reappeared. In the end they were given a new lease on life, but the districts and unions were hostile to them.

According to the Yugoslav Party program, private craftsmen, still about one half of the total, have little chance of survival. Their gradual liquidation by economic and administrative measures is foreseen. This view, too, seems to be now given up or modified. The economic reform has brought about unforeseen developments. Many workers lost their jobs. The more lucky ones among them received severance pay which enabled them to establish their own workshops.[100]

In their "third comment" the Chinese do not object to other features of the Yugoslav system, which is at least in form different from that of other communist countries. This has its own reason. In spite of the very complicated bi-cameral system at the district level, and the pentacameral system at the constituent republic and federal level, with few exceptions the election appears like a one horse race with approved Party candidates, although, like in Poland, there are more candidates than seats. In both countries the so-called parliamentary elections took place in 1965. In Yugoslavia, there were 64 candidates for 60 vacant seats in the Federal Chamber, and 452 candidates for 327 seats in six Republican Chambers. In Poland, out of 617 candidates 459 were elected. The most important thing to keep in mind is that the Party bosses never lose, that is, are always elected. In 1967 in Yugoslavia 81 candidates applied for 60 seats in the Federal Chamber (now called Socio-Political Chamber), and 428 candidates ran for 325 seats in the constituent republics. In compliance with the guidelines the League takes care to insure "the best possible cadre composition" of the assemblies, as confirmed in the 1969 elections.

Nationality and minority problems were always somewhere in the background. Before the ouster of Rankovic, then Vice President of Yugoslavia, they were hushed up. National contradictions, antagonistic or not, to use the Maoist language, appear in their disguised form as rival economic interests of constituent republics and of nationalities. One of the purposes of the reform and of the weakening of the centralists is to insure equitable distribution and allocation of economic resources.

Unlike the Russian and Chinese communist practice, where the road to communism implies for the non-Russian and non-Han nationalities Russification and Sinification respectively, opposite tendencies characterize Yugoslavia. However, in spite of their professions, the Yugoslav rulers were not successful in satisfying the aspirations of the nationalities and minorities in harmony with their slogan of brotherhood and unity. The existing contradictions were then sometimes presented by leading communists as class struggle, and the people claiming equal rights were labeled as class enemies, which is a very serious charge in a communist country.

Donald Brook of Radio Free Europe in Munich summed up, at the Marxist symposium at Stanford, the contradictions, that is, basic economic and political problems, into four categories: 1. Those involving the main nationalities; 2. The problems of developed and underdeveloped republics; 3. Antagonisms between the technocrats and the *apparatchiki,* and 4. antagonism between the former partisans and the younger generation. According to Dr. Bakaric these contradictions are so serious that, unless they are removed, there is the danger of the "end of socialism, end of Yugoslavia and end of us all."[101]

A big contradiction, however, was within the Party itself. Its source was the "Party in the Party," represented by the Rankovic factional group of the secret political police. As described by the

League's Presidium in a proclamation to the membership, its existence spelt "ideological dissolution, disunity and disintegration of the socialist community."[102]

This group had its headquarters in Serbia. It stood for a policy of the strong hand and Serbian domination over other nationalities. Absolute power, which it wielded over two decades, resulted in absolute corruption. It spread its activities of eavesdropping on the highest Party leaders all over the country and over its representations abroad. Systematic liquidation of hundreds of thousands of anti-communists after the end of the war was never mentioned in public criticisms as inconsistent with the Party policy. Of all these misdeeds only the persecutions of the Albanian minority in the Kosovo autonomous region were later revealed.

In the future the activity of the secret police was to be limited to the suppression of internal and external "class enemies." Following a purge, its influence was to be reduced in the Party's and country's life, and, moreover, the secret police was put under government control. These were the decisions of the Brioni session of the Central Committee of 1966. Another Brioni Presidium session deliberated about Yugoslavia's grave political and economic crisis in 1971.

The responsibilities for the previous sad state of things, however, could not be laid at the door of the factional group alone. This was confirmed not only by Tito himself, but particularly by Maks Bace, a Croatian communist leader, a former member of the cabinet and ambassador, who made the following statement:

Simultaneously with the self-management, there appeared on the scene a tight organization of a police state, backed by the Party and its organizations ... We all now wonder how all this could happen. It was not only Rankovic who rose above the society and law. We have all somehow got used to the injustices which he and others inflicted on the people. The rule of law is not yet firmly rooted in this country. The ministry of internal affairs has its share of responsibility. For years they used to hold investigations, although the law prescribes that this is the function of courts. Even after twenty years our lawyers are not allowed to see the documents of the investigation judge. It is a sad fact that institutions and people who preach legality, *de facto* made legality impossible.

We have been aware of all this, but in time became used to it. There was a discrepancy between our words and our deeds.[103]

Of late, there was some improvement in the judicial procedure in Yugoslavia. The country was freed from the pressure of the secret police, which is now carrying out its investigations only in exceptional cases. However, this is still a case of "socialist legality", where the rule of law is limited by the Party monopoly, like most other things. The secret police has permeated the Party to such a degree that a thorough reorganization had to be undertaken to purge it of all ingredients inconsistent with the self-management system.

Amendments to the Constitution have been made to enhance the statehood of the republics. This is a new development emphasizing the federal character of the multi-national country through an extensive decentralization. The Leagues of Communists of the constituent republics have in practice provided a fair degree of autonomy, as the guidelines stated. In the Soviet Union, however, diametrically opposite tendencies assert themselves.

The amendments increase the rights of the republics and nationalities, of autonomous provinces and minorities. They insure their equality in making decisions in the fields of foreign policy, national defense and internal security, and set limits to the authority of the federation in legislation and appropriation of funds for investment purposes. A common market throughout the country provides for a homogenous economic policy, excluding any monopolistic position.[104]

In the Soviet Union the ambivalence of the new Party program has led to a lengthy debate among Soviet academicians for and against real federalism. Many local leaders in six Union republics have been purged in the last years. Through the Sino-Soviet schism centrifugal forces were released. It is also significant that this conflict induced the Soviet regime to give priority to the economic development of the eastern regions. At the 23rd Party congress some sort of togetherness (*sblizhenie*) was advocated. Here the problem is to find the proper balance between the natives and the Russians in the top republican leadership.[105]

The Party monopoly notwithstanding, Yugoslavia (and Czechoslovakia) are becoming federations to a higher degree than the Soviet Union ever was. The six republics of Yugoslavia are recognized as states based on the sovereignty of the people. The third revision of the constitution created a collective State Presidency, and tried to harmonize disparate political views among the nationalities. Deficiencies in the workers' self-management system were made formally responsible for the reorganization. Yet a Croatian nationalist movement including the communists was of importance in conceiving the momentum for it as well as Tito's succession. The State Presidency is not responsible to the Federal Assembly and more powerful of it. The federal government and the governments of the republics and autonomous provinces have to concord their work. The Yugoslav government, however, composed of an equal number of members of the constituent units, can proceed with the implementation of important measures, if a decision could not be reached with them. No one has the right to sign or recognize the capitulation or occupation of Yugoslavia or parts of it. The provision of the Croatian national defense law that no one has the right to invite foreign troops to enter the country, was not mentioned in the amendments though. Djilas, himself, expressed the view that by 1984 Yugoslavia might become a real confederation.

The Chinese in their "Third Comment" do not mention the Federal Assembly which in some cases went so far as to refuse to pass the bills of the government. The establishment of a Constitutional Court is certainly a novelty in a communist country, but this court had no effect on the system. An undeserved importance is often attributed in the West to statements and writings of some Marxist professors and theoreticians, who often share Djilas' ideas, but whose words have otherwise no weight.

No political opposition is tolerated outside the pale of the Party and its subsidiary, the Socialist Alliance. Doctrinal conformity is strictly enforced.

On the other hand cases of wild strikes, called work-stoppages, were tolerated. Naturally no union controlled by the Party could authorize them. Moreover, unemployment has reached such a degree that the regime was compelled to agree to large-scale emigration to the West. No other communist state has followed its example.

There would have been probably no particular Chinese-Yugoslav verbal battle, had not Red China first chosen the Yugoslav revisionists as whipping boys rather than attacking directly "the Khrushchev clique" and its successors. In spite of it, the Yugoslavs opposed excommunication of China from the world communist movement as planned by Khrushchev. They as well as other communist Parties are well aware that such a decision would weaken their strength in dealing with Moscow, which in fact was obliged to replace its directives by consultations.

The Yugoslav communists have judged Red China's policies realistically. This may be seen from the following quotation from the Belgrade leading daily: "Asia and the whole world are confronted with dreams of hegemony which in the long run may prove harmful for China itself. In an attempt to impose its will on all, China could find itself alone, isolated and compromised. One should not forget," the paper went on "that Asia does not fight Western imperialism in order to become a prey of China or any other great state."[107]

Yugoslav reporting on the "great leap" is discussed in Chapter X, and its reaction to the Chinese cultural revolution in Chapter XII. After the invasion of Czechoslovakia, Yugoslavia began to play a neutral role in the Sino-Soviet conflict. Yet the Ussuri River clashes were viewed as "a grave tragedy, for this was for the first time that an armed conflict arose between two socialist countries."

Although ambassadors replaced chargés d'affaires in Peking and Belgrade and a new trade agreement was signed after ten years, the relationship between the two socialist countries remained guarded. Meanwhile a message from a Yugoslav Marxist-Leninist organization was sent to the CC of the CPC on occasion of the 20th anniversary of the PRC's founding. In that message Tito's rule was called that of "renegades and hidden traitors," and the Marshal was labeled the "Liu Shao-ch'i of Yugoslavia." The organization accused the League of Communists of national inequality, mass unemployment, steady lowering of the living standard, and economic and political(?) dependence on the "imperialist" countries, first and foremost, on the United States. Therefore in Yugoslavia a new Marxist-Leninist Party must be built "so as to overthrow the revisionist renegade clique with violence."

The Belgrade reaction was vehement. The message was rejected as a flagrant attempt at interference in the country's internal affairs. It was compared with the Cominform resolutions, and termed as a "heavy blow" to future relations[108] which improved on the state-level though. Peking even promised "firm support" against-aggression.

CHAPTER VI

The Unequal Treaties and Historical Borders

Major Territorial Issues Rejected

"In the years between 1840 and 1945 one coun'ry or another has taken bites out of China," Arnold Toynbee wrote once. "That's why China is so grim.   When they recover their frontiers, China may calm down, I think."

Toynbee's diagnosis was shared by one of the leading American experts on China's military power and strategy, Samuel B. Griffith 2nd, a retired Marine brigadier-general who wrote: "China wishes to regain her ancient position in Asia. She considers this aspiration to be justified by propinquity, by his'ory, by cultural affiliation, and by economic fact".[1]

The Chinese territorial claims against the Soviet initially appeared in a somewhat veiled form.   The problem of the readjustment of boundaries was first raised by the former Head of State, Liu Shao-ch'i, while he was attending the 1960 interna'ional communist conference in Moscow, but Krushchev simply ignored it.

To the surprise of many, Peking managed to settle boundary disputes satisfactorily with Outer Mongolia, Burma, Nepal, Pakistan and Afghanistan.   Yet the Sino-Indian and Sino-Soviet boundaries have remained unsettled.   High on the list of the disputed areas loom the Pamirs, a mountainous region secretly divided between Britain and Russia in the last cen'ury, the tract around Manchuoli, and some spots in the Amur Valley as well as islands at the confluence of the Amur and Ussuri Rivers.   In the Pamir plateau, ranging over thirty thousand square miles, only one of the eight Pamirs is left in Chinese hands.   The disputed border area of the

Amur and Ussuri was purposely left undefined on the new maps
of A Concise Geography of China, published in Peking late in
1965—a new threat of at least cartographic expansion.

Much more has been at stake here than plots of land. The
Sino-Soviet dispute has, for one, exposed the fallaciousness of the
habitual communist contention that "imperialist" territorial disputes and the ensuing wars were the result of capitalism and that
such belligerent confrontations would simply not occur among communist states. A compromise settlement seems more and more
unlikely as the Chinese territorial demands become increasingly
strident.

When in September 1963 Khrushchev scored those who referred
to "the frontiers of the Old Testament", he was reacting to the
Chinese reminders of "unequal treaties", imposed on weak Imperial China by various powers, but above all by the Russian imperialists. All that happened during the "old revolutionary era",
as the communists call it between the first Opium War of 1839-42
and the May 4th Movement of 1919, which protested against the
Versailles Peace Treaty for having handed over to Japan the former
German possesions in Shantung.

The existence of the Chinese claims was officially confirmed
on November 29, 1963 in the letter of the CPSU's Central Committee to its Chinese counterpart.[2] The former stated that during
the last years "the situation created at different points of the Sino-
Soviet frontier cannot be viewed as normal. Recently, declarations
were made in China on the aggressive policy of the Tsarist government, and on the unjust treaties imposed upon China. Certainly
we will not take up the defense of the Tsars, but we cannot neglect
the fact that there are historic borders between states." They were
so unrealistic as to stress that "Our common aim is communism,
under which state borders will gradually lose their former significance."

Politburo member Suslov went further in accusing the Chinese
leaders of being "blinded by nationalistic arrogance", as he repeated
the same theme in his Central Committee speech, emphasizing that
the border was formed historically and that the Soviet Union was not
prepared to discuss major territorial issues, but only minor border
adjustments.

Meanwhile, the seriousness of the Sino-Soviet border dispute was being fully realized abroad. "While these border regions constitute a type of secondary problem, over long periods of tension," Professor Scalapino told the Subcommittee on the Far East and the Pacific, U.S. House of Representatives, it is the problem that can touch off an explosion."

Soviet government protests on the Chinese border violations and the setting up of a joint commission that began discussions on February 25, 1964, were first confirmed by the Chairman of the Supreme Soviet of Deputies, V. Spiridonov during his visit to India. These discussions, according to later informations, were conducted in Peking on the embassy level and collapsed after three months without any conclusive results. The Soviet side expressed readiness to continue the consultations on the very day of Khrushchev's downfall.

In the alleged circular letter of the CPSU CC to "fraternal Parties", dated February 1966, it was charged that when the border-delineation talks were about to collapse, Peking had threatened to use "other means" than negotiations to restore her "historical rights"; thereupon the Chinese refused to resume suspended negotiations.

"But the Chinese People's Republic has no 'historical rights'," the Soviet confidential letter continued. "The territories which the CPC leadership now talks of have never belonged to China. The current Soviet-Chinese border has a firm international basis; it is stipulated in treaties signed by the governments of the countries."

Early in 1963 the Chinese spoke of eventual peaceful renewal, when the time was "ripe", of their claim to south-east Siberia and parts of Soviet Central Asia, taken from China by the "unbridled aggression" of the Tsars.[3] Yet when Khrushchev in 1964 proposed in a message to the heads of state all over the world a joint renunciation of the use of force for settling of territorial disputes or boundary issues, Premier Chou En-lai denounced it as a "new fraud".[4] At about the same time the Chinese delegate to the congress of International Association of Democratic Lawyers, a left-wing body, in Budapest declared that their government rejected to "undertake any commitment not to resort to force in order to change existing

state frontiers". Thereupon, in September 1964 the Soviet Foreign
Minister Gromyko reactivated Khrushchev's proposal in his letter
to the Secretary General of the United Nations, thus angling for a
confirmation of the territorial status quo of the Soviet Union.

Among the nine treaties mentioned as unequal, three concern
the Soviet Union. However, the enumeration of the unequal treaties
ends with "etc.", which indicates that other treaties might also be
questioned in the future as it really happened.

The May 1858 Treaty of Aigun, imposed upon the
Chinese authorities in Manchuria by the Tsarist armed
forces, ceded to Russia the entire north bank of the
Amur (Heilung Kiang, Black Dragon River in Chinese)
from its tributary Argun to the estuary of the Amur and south of
the outer Stanovoy Mountains, Khingan in Chinese. The territory
east of the Ussuri River (Wusuli) and east of the Amur after its
junction with the Ussuri was temporarily put under a joint administration until the definitive determination of the frontier. Actually the new frontier had been established previously as a result
of conquest. Citizens of both countries were allowed to navigate
the Amur, Ussuri and Sungari Rivers.

The Chinese scholar Ch'eng T'ien-fong, however, branded the
Treaty a bluff and deceit. According to him, the Chinese pleni-
potentiary had overstepped his authority and was dismissed. The
Treaty was never ratified by the Emperor of China. Yet, Russia
went on to acquire 231,600 square miles, or, as Chinese nationalists
claim, even 246,200 miles. As Friedrich Engels pointed out, Russia
had despoiled "China of a country as large as France and Germany
put together".[5]

Some Sinologists remind us that the territories dealt with in
the Aigun and Peking treaties were inhabited neither by Chinese,
Manchus or Russians, nor effectively ruled from Peking. However,
the Manchu Imperial House regarded them and the tribal peoples as
their private domain.[6]

The Great Soviet Encyclopedia does not mention the sixty-
four Manchu settlements on the left bank of the Amur which, under
the treaty, were to retain Chinese jurisdiction "forever" and were
not to be exposed to any "injustice" on the part of the Russians.[7]
In 1900, following the Boxer rebellion and the ensuing Chinese-

Russian hostilities, the Russians drove all the Manchus of the Settlement as well as the Chinese merchants in Blagoveshchensk into the Amur River. Almost seven thousand perished. This is how Russian authority was established in the area.[8]

The November 1860 Treaty of Peking, ending the British-French-Chinese second Opium War, was imposed on China as a result of the mediation of the Russian Ambassador and under the impact of the *T'ai-p'ing t'ien kuo* (Peaceful Heavenly Kingdom) rebellion which claimed forty million victims. It completed the Aigun Treaty and secured to Russia the Ussuriysky and Amursky *Krai* (territory), embracing today the Primorsky *Krai* and large parts of Khabarovsky *Krai* and the Amurskaya *Oblast* (region). The eastern borders between Russia and China were delineated from the junction of the Shilka and Argun Rivers along the Amur, Ussuri and Sungacha Rivers, and further over the lake Khanka (Hanka), and the upper mountain range to the Tuminczyan (Tumen) River (art. 1), and to the Korean frontier. The western borders streched from the pass Shabin-Dabag in the Sayan Mountain Range to the lake Czay-San (Zaysan), and along the Tyan-Shan (Tienshan) Mountains to the Khanate of Kokand (at that time still independent).[9] A formal frontier was established between Western Turkestan and Sinkiang for the first time, but not on the whole 1,150 mile border. The border between Kashgar and what is now Tadzhikstan remained undefined (435 miles). It was delineated by the Anglo-Russian agreement of 1895, but never formally accepted by China.

In the east, China lost again 154,400 square milies,[10] altogether a half of the "historical Manchuria." In addition to the conquest in the Far East, Russia annexed a vast, ill-defined area of nearly 169,840 square miles in Central Asia by the same Peking Treaty and the Tarbagatai (Chuguchak, Tacheng) Treaty of October 1864. Cheng's estimate was much higher, 400,000 square miles.

Finally, the February 1881 St. Peterburg, or Ili, Treaty, provided for the Russian occupation in a part of West Sinkiang, for which Russia was compensated with large commercial advantages. It was signed after a serious crisis between the two powers because the Chinese had not ratified the Livadia Treaty. The upper Ili River Valley had been occupied by the Russians with Chinese consent, in order to put down a rebellion of the native Chinese

Moslems and Uighurs. According to the Ili Treaty, merely a western strip of Ili was annexed to Russia. The citizens had the right
to take Chinese or Russian citizenship. The duty free trade was
extended for the Russians to the vast territory north-west of the
Great Wall.[11] As a result of the Treaty, Russian influence in Sinkiang was strengthened. But that was not all. China had to give up
27,020 square miles in the following four boundary treaties.

The Russians admitted that Peking's claim to their territory
amounted to more than one-and-a-half million square kilometers
and was equal to an attempt to recarve the map of the world.[12]
This figure was again confirmed in the Chinese Government Statement of May 24, 1969, an area three times that of France or twelve
times that of Czechoslovakia. Summing up all these amounts to 582,-
860 square miles. The population involved was approximately
more than ten million.

In that way Russia became an arch-imperialist and colonialist
power at the expense of the weak Manchu China. The unequal
treaties, continued the aforementioned article in People's Daily,
"will be accepted or revoked, reviewed or renewed according to
their content." Furthermore, as stated at the time when the conflict had not yet come into the open, the Chinese policy "toward the
socialist countries is basically different." It was in this manner and
spirit that the Chinese-Russian border problems and the entire conflict were discussed at meetings of governmental and educational
institutions all over China.[13]

Former Foreign Minister Ch'en Yi confirmed the Soviet estimate
of these vast "lost lands" in a conversation with the Japanese Liberal-
Democratic Member of Parliament Utsunomiya visiting Peking.
He added it is necessary to admit this historical fact. And in written answers to a group of Scandinavian journalists, he mentioned
1,540,000 square kilometers of Chinese territory annexed by Tsarist
Russia (reduced to 1,510,000 square kilometers in the Chinese Government Statement).

He maintained that "Tsarist Russia and the Soviet Union have
crossed the boundary defined under unequal treaties and occupied
many more places in China" and that the Soviet claims regarding
them were "preposterous and unreasonable".

Ch'en Yi also accused the Soviets of carrying out "unbribled subversive activities" in China's border areas: "They have deployed their troops on the Sino-Soviet border and carried out continual military maneuvres on the border, which presupposes China as the enemy".[14]

When a group of Chinese students were expelled from Russia in retaliation, they were greeted in Peking by the Chinese Deputy Minister of Education, Tuan Lo-fu, in November 1966, with the following thunderous message: "Chairman Mao has taught us that the Chinese nation has the spirit to fight the enemy to the last drop of our blood, the determination to recover our lost territory by our own efforts."[15]

The Russians would not be outdone in saber rattling. In February 1967 for instance, the "month of mass defense work" in the Soviet Union was particularly stressed by the voluntary society for cooperation with the amy, air force and navy along the Chinese border, where Komsomol operational detachments are helping the border guards to counter any "provocation". Marshal Nikolay Krylov underlined the occasion by inspecting the Trans-Bailkal military area.

During the 1969 border clashes, Col.-General Vladimir Tolubko, a former deputy commander-in-chief of the Soviet missile forces, was named commander of the Far Eastern military region bordering on China in Khabarovsk as a most technically qualified to command a threatened front. Actually he dropped a hint that the Soviet Union was ready to use tactical nuclear weapons. Then Vitaly Titov, secretary of the Party Central Committee of Kazakhstan, called in *Pravda* for an all-people's defense system. A new Central Asian military region was created in the fall facing Sinkiang, and embracing Kazakhstan, Kirghizia and Tadzhikistan. This region was truncated from the Turkestan military region to which now Turkmenistan and Uzbekistan were left.[16]

The Most Dramatic Aspect of the Schism

In connection with the border clashes on the Ussuri island, the information department of the Chinese Foreign Ministry in Peking stated in March 1969 that at first China had proposed to Russia that "any side [the Russian side only, of course] that occupies the territory of the other side in violation of the treaties must, in principle, return it wholly and unconditionally to the other side, but this does not preclude necessary readjustments". The Soviet side however, refused to recognize the treaties concluded between Imperial Russia and China as inequal in order to perpetuate "its occupation of the Chinese territory that it seized by crossing the boundary line defined by the inequal treaties." If the Soviets "refuse to mend its ways, the Chinese side will have to reconsider its position as regards the Chinese-Soviet boundary as a whole." Meanwhile, the statement continues, the Soviets "have sent large reinforcements to the Chinese-Soviet border, stepped up disruption of the status quo of the boundary, occupied still more Chinese territories, carried out armed provocations and created incidents of bloodshed."

The Soviets explained all this away as "advancing extravagant territorial claims and even demands for a 'revision of the Sino-Soviet border' ". The Soviet Foreign Ministry, in its note proposing the resumption of border negotiations, also mentioned the Tientsin *traktat* which had merely specified that not delimited boundaries would be settled in a later convention, in addition to unequal provisions obsolete a long time ago.[17]

A long Chinese government statement gave a thoroughly stern reply late in May 1969 to the Soviet government note rejecting the Soviet proposal as merely "flaunting the signboard of consultations."[18]

The note was positive as to Peking's willingness to negotiate and on maintaining the status quo pending a settlement, Peking being against resort to the use of force. Red China stood ready to take the unequal treaties as a basis for determining the alignment of the entire boundary. The Soviet people, it claimed, bear no responsibility for these treaties, and large numbers of them have lived there for a long time. Moreover, Peking still professed a desire to "safeguard the revolutionary friendship between Chinese and Soviet people" —a myth still retained on both sides, all evidence to the contrary notwithstanding.

Peking nevertheless rigorously insisted on negotiations with the aim of an *"over-all settlement of the Sino-Soviet boundary problem and the conclusion of a new, equal treaty"* (italics supplied) to replace the old unequal ones, rather than "consultation" for "clarification on individual sectors of the Soviet-Chinese state borderline."

The Chinese note reminded the Soviets that Lenin's government renounced all treaties (the Karakhan declarations of 1919 and 1920) imposed on China by Tsarist Russia and promised to replace them and remap their national boundaries, a promise that failed to come true. Lenin termed the Tsarist policy on China a "criminal" one and, before the October Revolution, even considered a Chinese war on Russia as "just."[19] Yet, Peking charged, today's Soviet rulers were employing "a gangster logic in defense of Tsarist Russias' imperialist aggression." It scored Moscow's "truculent attitude": "What the Tsars occupied is yours, and what you want to occupy is yours, too."

The Chinese government listed just "for instance" two territories as occupied by the Soviet Union in violation even of the unequal treaties: the first, 7,720 square miles in the Pamir region contrary to the Protocol of 1884 on the Sino-Soviet boundary in the Kashgar area; and the second, 600 of the more than 700 islands in the Amur and Ussuri rivers, Chenpao (Damansky) included, or 386 square miles, thus pushing the boundary back almost entirely along the Chinese bank—contrary to international law. These territories must in principle be returned, the Chinese note insisted, adding that this demand "brooks no ambiguity".

In a pessimistic admission clearly reflecting the utter gravity of the situation, the Peking government denounced Moscow's policy of "war clamors" and of brandishing the threat of "nuclear weapons on China" to realize its territorial claims, then bluntly declared: *"Neither a small war, nor a big war nor a nuclear war can ever intimidate the Chinese people"*(italics supplied).

Finally, the Chinese government proposed that no futher incursions should take place, that frontier guards should not open fire under any circumstances and that border inhabitants should continue their normal productive activities. The Chinese complained about Soviet provocations on the boundaries, quoting a Soviet border representative who read threateningly from a prepared text on April 3 that "the Soviet Union will not cease fire unless the Chinese government holds negotiations with the Soviet government, nor will it cease fire unless the Chinese withdraw from Damansky Island."

The mainland press published the note together with the Soviet note of March 29, 1969, calling on the Soviet government to publish the Chinese note. The first Soviet reaction came from Colonel-General Pavel I. Zyryanov, commander of the Soviet frontier troops, under the KGB (Committee of State Security), repeating the offical stand that the boundaries with China were legally and historically fixed.

The Soviet government was disinclined to publish the Chinese note, probably since it wanted to conceal from its public the most dramatic aspect of the schism. It soon replied to Peking with a correspondingly long note, in which it attempted to refute the Chinese claims with many historical facts. The Soviets generally rejected these claims as "absolutely groundless," as due to "misrepresentation and deliberate distortion" and as "slanderous concoctions" of history.

While any consideration of territorial problems is out of the question, the Soviets are ready to discuss without preconditions the borderline at some particular disputed stretches—but only to define it more precisely. What the Chinese are claiming "justly belongs to the Soviet Union" (the territories involved extending the length and breadth of five European countries: France, the two Germanies, Poland and Yugoslavia).

These lands "the Chinese conquerors entered or planned to enter in the remote past." At that time, Russia and China were separated by vast, sparsely populated or uninhabited expanses of semidesert or taiga. The northern state boundary of China was the Great Wall, lying more than 640 miles southwest of the Amur and Ussuri. Manchuria then, and up to the end of the last century, was a fief of the Ch'ing (Manchu) dynasty.

As an adminicle that the Chinese were not the traditional masters of the Amur and Ussuri, Moscow quoted a report dispatched by Manchu military leaders at the end of the 17th century after launching campaigns against the early Russian settlemen's. They wrote back of their success, saying that lands "that never belonged to China became part of your [the emperor's] domain." Later, the Manchu rulers conquered Mongolia and the Dzungaria Khanate of Oirats—what is now Sinkiang. They also conquered Kokand and several Kirghiz khanates, now Soviet territory, but the Soviet note makes no mention of this. The Great Ch'ing emperors (their empire was called *Tai Ch'ing Kuo*) conducted, according to the Soviet note, a predatory, colonialist policy of enforced assimilation of oppressed nationalities.

As for the Aigun Treaty, the Soviets affirm that it was approved by decree of the Chinese emperor. In the Tientsin Treaty of June 1858, "indisputable documents on the border" were envisaged. The Peking treaty was supplemented by the 1861 protocol on the exchange of maps and delimitative descriptions of the Ussuri territory. The red line on the maps was drawn along the Chinese bank of the Ussuri in the Damansky area, and it is not true that the maps were drawn up unilaterally, say the Russians.

The Manchu population lived at a distance of at least 512 miles from the Amur and the Ussuri. The northern boundary of the Manchus was the fortified "willow palisade" that passed near Mukden, the capital of northern Manchuria. The Ussuri was never for them an "interior river." The Soviets do not recognize the border passing through the middle of the river's mainstream as a relevant application of international law. The Sino-Soviet communist agreement of 1951 on navigation in border rivers, their tributaries, and lakes, a navigable distance of 3,598 miles, applies "irrespective of where the line of the state border passes." Nevertheless, the Soviet side is willing to accept mutual concessions to the benefit of the two rivers' border population.

The Soviets also affirm that the Sino-Russian Protocol of 1884 dealt with the Tienshan Mountains' delimitations and not with the Pamirs, where the Russians allegedly occupied a large territory in the Kashgar area in excess of the treaties. Instead, the two countries formalized the Pamirs' delimitations ten years later by an exchange of notes.

The Soviet note rejects as absurd the Chinese contention that the western border of China passed through Lake Balkhash in Soviet Asia. It passed, in fact, a few hundred miles away. There never was a Chinese administration or population in what is now Kazakhstan or the Soviet Central Asian republics.

Lenin's decrees cancelled all unequal and secret treaties with China such as those on extraterritoriality and economic concessions, but there was no question of annulling or revising the borders. Mao himself confirmed this on two separate occasions.

The Chinese lack a class approach to the conquests of Genghis

Khan, Kang Hsi and other feudal rulers, complain the Russians. What Peking is claiming now from Russia would be similar to Great Britain claiming the United States, Spain Latin America and Greece the conquests of Alexander the Great. (We would add that, in turn, Mongolia may present a demand for China and Russia, because the Mongolian Yüan dynasty ruled over both).

The Soviets regret that the Chinese continue provocations on the borders, which are inviolable. They reject "the absurdity" that the Soviet Union plans to attack China. The Soviet collective leadership twice proposed to normalize relations before the cultural revolution. The Soviets accept the Chinese proposal that present treaties be taken as the basis for talks and suggest the resumption of consultations.

The exchange of these two diplomatic notes did not conduce toward creating an atmosphere favorable for negotiations. The Soviets were unwilling to concede that the disputed territories claimed by China were gained illegally.

Nevertheless, negotiations were resumed in Peking in the second half of October 1969 on the level of Deputy Ministers of Foreign Affairs. This was the outgrowth of a meeting solicited by Moscow when Kosygin and Chou En-lai, on their return from funeral for Ho Chi-Minh, had talks at Peking airport. It was reported that Kosygin, in addition to urging border negotiations, proposed mutual withdrawal of frontier forces, a "cease-fire," increase of trade, reinstatement of ambassadors, and an accord allowing Soviet planes to fly through China to Vietnam. The Russians tried to show good will to the anxious world communist movement by attempting some accommodation. The motive of the Chinese to meet was clearly expressed in the Peking government's statement of October 7, citing "war maniacs" who would "dare to raid China's strategic sites," stating: "There is no reason whatsoever for China and the Soviet Union to fight a war over the boundary question," confirming ugly Soviet hints of frightening Peking to negotiations.

Hung Ch'i called, in this respect, for a better strategic translocation of the Chinese industry. There were reports of moving nuclear installations from the vulnerable border regions to more protected sites in Tibet. In the opinion of their Lilliputian allies, the Albanians, the Chinese, faced by this *force majeur,* "lost their nerve" since they could expect nothing because of Soviet "treachery."

Following the border incidents there were rumors of the possibility of a nuclear preemptive strike against the Lop Nor atomic center in the remote Takla Makan desert of southern Sinkiang. Harrison Salisbury and Roderick MacFarquhar reported on both sides of the Atlantic on a Soviet circular letter to East European governments and foreign communist Parties sounding out their reaction should such a confrontation occur. The Moscow correspondent of the London *Evening News,* with strong connections to the Kremlin, in a startling report went so far as to envisage the Brezhnev doctrine to be applied to China with the help of anti-Maoist forces asking for "fraternal help," threatening with the "scorched earth" policy in the case of future border incidents.[20]

In the Chinese government note mentioned above two things were stressed: 1) irreconcilable differences of principles, and 2) maintaining normal state relations on the basis of peaceful coexistence. The Chinese see no response in the Soviet government statement of June 13 to their statement of May 24. They are not demanding the return of the territories annexed by the unequal treaties. In lieu of the "root cause of tension" are "many disputed areas" occupied in excess of the treaties as indicated by the exchange of maps in 1964 (which were never published.)

Border negotiations should be of a technical nature namely reaching an agreement on provisional measures, a *modus vivendi* for maintaining the status quo by withdrawing their armed forces, or refraining from entering these disputed areas.

Whereas Peking accepted the negotiations under dangerous threats, the Chinese Ministry of Foreign Affairs issued the very next day again a long document, this time refuting the Soviet government statement of June 13 as a "forgery of history" making the negotiations extremely difficult. The Soviet government was accused of defending "Tsarist Russian imperialist crimes of aggression against China." Contrary to Moscow's view, Peking stressed that China was a unified multi-national country "never confined to the Han-inhabited regions" of over two thousand years ago. It rejected the "reactionary" doctrine that state boundaries should be determined by nationality. Peking claimed that its jurisdiction over the Heilung (Amur) River basin was asserted centuries before

Russia became a unified country. In the latter half of the 17th century China launched wars of resistance against the Russian colonialist invaders. The willow pale in northern Manchuria marked the internal limits of forbidden areas built up by the Ch'ing dynasty covering a very small portion of that vast region. The Soviets are repeating the last Tsar's theory marking the Great Wall as the northern frontier of China, as part of "grandiose plans" for carving her up.

Regarding China's western borders, the Han dynasty before the Christian era set up administrative organs east and south of the Balkhash Lake lasting up to the 19th century. This was even confirmed in the Soviet historical atlas of 1958.

In the Sino-Soviet agreement of 1924, art. VII, there was explicitly stipulated that the two countries are "to re-demarcate their national boundaries." In the Soviet diplomatic dictionary of 1961, edited by Gromyko and others, it was unequivocably admitted that the Treaty of Peking was an unequal treaty.

Finally Peking rejected the Soviet-proposed Asian collective security system as an anti-China ring of encirclement to control Asian countries.

The most irksome problem is determining the status quo—by taking the treaties as basis, the Soviets hold more territory than they should have. Thus in the Pamir area Russian troops occupied more territory and in 1894 China was forced to agree to this new "temporary" demarcation line. This line of military occupation should now be recognized as the status quo.

According to the Chinese, a further example of the violation of the unequal treaties was the maps drawn up for the Peking treaty, and the red line. They do not define the precise location of the boundary line for the rivers. In 1861 only the land boundary at a point south of the Khanka Lake (Hsingkai) was surveyed and marked.

The Chinese note quotes a Soviet document, art. 5 of the regulations on the safeguarding of the Soviet state frontier of 1960, recognizing the center of the main channel of the navigable boundary rivers or the *Thalweg* as the state boundary. Therefore the Chinese reject the new Soviet territorial claim that for the most part the Chinese river bank should be the border.

Before the negotiations started, Politburo ideologist Suslov again condemned the Peking leaders in *Kommunist,* and called for an intensified struggle against those who are trying to split the ranks of the international revolutionary movement. In this connection, communists throughout the world view with indignation and profound concern the adventurist and chauvinistic policy of the present CPC leaders who have broken with Marxism-Leninism and the principles of proletarian internationalism.

Actually the Chinese were not sure if the Soviets who were forcing a verbal confrontation at the conference table did not have in mind a time-gaining strategem, starting from the position of force and seeking to create the impression that they had tried to find a solution. The Chinese suspicions were expressed in two Nanking broadcasts accusing the Russians of "counterrevolutionary dual tactics" of negotiating while preparing for war. Social imperialism, as Soviet foreign policy is called, said one of them, "often uses peaceful negotiations as a cover to launch surprise and large-scale aggressive wars. We must face this with high vigilance. . . ." During the Khabarovsk navigation conference, the Soviets talked "sweetly but acted evilly,", the Chinese complained. Because of the possibility of a Soviet political hoax and military adventure China must make full preparation for the worst. There were speculations that some of the Peking leaders were prepared to compromise with the Russians, while others were opposed to it and saw the negotiations as a loss of face for China, according to a Hungarian editor who visited Peking.

The strategic arms limitations talks between the superpowers were assaulted by Peking as a further development of the American-Soviet "nuclear military alliance," a nuclear blackmail to intensify their collusion against China. While the Soviets avoided polemics for a while, Peking continued attacks on Soviet policy calling again the Soviet leaders a revisionist renegade clique.

The protracted border negotiations were stalemated for a long time. The Soviet delegation encountered a social cold shoulder as expected, and there were reports of derogatory wall posters. Armed clashes were eschewed, whereas the negotiators could not agree on the status quo, the frontier demarcation, nor on the withdrawal of troops.[20a]

The Soviet leadership tried to make an imposture in this connection with the new third, twice revised edition of the History of the CPSU. This edition first went on sale in eary fall 1969 denouncing Maoism in the usual way. After the Kosygin-Chou En-lai meeting, it was suddenly withdrawn. A few months later a rewritten edition appeared softening the stricture of Communist China, and dropping assaults on the Chairman. Yet this was no more than a hoax, since from the beginning of 1970 the Soviets resumed their full-scale castigation of the Peking regime.

The "Chinese" Great Northwest and Northeast

The Chinese communists laid down their cartographic documentary evidence most completely in the text book A Brief History of Modern China, by Liu Pei-hua, circulating in Mainland China for a number of years, and reissued in 1960. Attached to it was an intriguing map captioned, "The Seizure of Chinese Territory by the Imperialists in 1840-1919". The map was first noticed by the Nepalese who passed it on to India.

The book and map divides the Chinese claims into three groups in respect to their historical relationship to China. The first includes the state of Assam and the Andaman Islands (India) as well as Malaya and Thailand which were never under Chinese rule. The second group embraces the former Chinese tributaries, the Ryukyu (Japan) and the Sulu Islands (Philippines), whereas the third one consists of Burma, Nepal, Annam (now the three Indo-Chinese states), Korea, Bhutan and Sikkim which were considered former Chinese vassals. A belated Russian comment on the book and map asserts that it is a distortion of history to speak of "seizure", since these countries had never been part of China.[21] As for the alleged Chinese protection of them, the Russian writer calls it "brigand savage incursions" with the sole aim of plunder and slaughter. (The problem of Outer Mongolia is discussed in the next chapter.)

The controversial book was at one time disallowed by Peking because of the many contemporary independent countries listed as parts of China, but the disavowal did not extend to the Russian territorial acquisitions. The greatest surprise of the map is a "Chinese" Great North-West and Great North-East in what is actually

Soviet territory. The latter covers a huge area extending in a
semicircle from the junction of the Shilka and Amur Rivers to the
vicinity of Chumukan on the Sea of Okhotsk. This revised Russian-
Chinese "border" runs along the Stanovoy Mountain Range, cutting
off the Soviet Far East from the Soviet Union, and leaving the
entire Amur-Ussuri basin to China. The Great North-West, according to the text on the map, was seized by Imperial Russia under the
1864 boundary Treaty of Tarbagatai.

The lost Chinese territory in Soviet Central Asia, Ch'eng T'ien-
fong says, had extended to the Balkash Lake, some 200 miles west
of the present frontier, including east Kazakhstan, Kirghizia, most
of Tadzhikistan, and east Uzbekistan with such cities as Pavlodar,
Semipalatinsk, Alma Ata, Tashkent and Frunze. The "boundary"
runs from the northern tip of Lake Balkhash to the Altai Mountains, and from the southern tip to the present border. The book
also claims the whole of Sakhalin "illegally occupied" by the Russians.

The Chinese nationalists are in full agreement with this cartographic expansionism and echo the claims against the Soviet Union
for territories "feloniously grabbed" by Tsarist Russia. The
new Foreign Minister Chow Shu-k'ai added up both the Far Eastern
and Central Asian claims to what amounted to some 900,000 square
miles.[22]

Some Chinese nationalist and Russian émigré writers had suggested that Liu Pei-hua's book was merely a historical account and
should not be taken as an actual presentation of Chinese claims.
But Far Eastern history abounds in strange parallels. Thus, in
1934 U.S. naval intelligence came upon a children's book in Japan,
outlining the Japanese warlords' ambitions in the Pacific; in the
early forties this chauvinistic juvenilia turned into frightening
reality.[23]

The Chinese communists themselves have repeatedly indicated
that A Brief History of Modern China is serious business. At the
end of 1963 a booklet was distributed at the Chinese Trade
Fair in Mexico City, showing Vladivostok and the Maritime Ter-
ri‘ory as parts of China. The Chinese Embassy in London has
been recently distributing a map issued by the Foreign Ministry
in Peking, featuring eastern parts of the Soviet Union as belonging

to China and Khabarovsk and Vladivostok bearing Chinese names,
Poli and Haishengwei.[24]   And a Hungarian youth weekly published
a map distributed by the Chinese depicting the Soviet territories
claimed by Peking—the south-eastern part of Central Asia, the
southern part of the Soviet Far East, Sakhalin, the People's Republic of Mongolia, and the Tuvinian Autonomous Republic of the
Russian Federation.[25]

It was only in 1964 that the Soviet public was finally informed
about the Chinese textbook in connection with Mao's interview
given to a group of Japanese socialist members of parliament, published in a Tokyo magazine.[26]   The revelation that vast territories
of Russia were claimed by the Chinese as theirs "by right" came
as a shock to many Russians.[27]

Ideological questions were not even mentioned in Mao Tse-
tung's talk.   Instead, these were the main highlights:

...We are prepared to continue this war [on paper with the
Soviet Union] 25 years more... There are too many places
occupied by the Soviet Union...The Soviet Union actually
placed this country [the Republic of Mongolia] under its
domination...In 1954, when Khrushchev and Bulganin came
to China, we raised this question, but they refused to discuss
it...They detached everything that could be detached.
Some people said that the province of Sinkiang and the
northern part of Heilungkiang should be incorporated in the
Soviet Union. The USSR is concentrating troops on its
frontier. The Soviet Union has an area of 22 million square
kilometers, and its population is only 220 million. It is
about time to put an end to this allotment...About a hundred
years ago, the area to the east of [Lake] Baikal became
Russian territory and since then, Vladivostok, Khabarovsk,
Kamchatka and other areas have been Soviet territory. We
have not yet presented our account for this list.

The Soviets responded to the Chinese claims by intensifying
their military preparations. As early as in 1964 Soviet war games
had already assumed a Chinese invasion of the Primorsky Krai.[28]
On the governmental level, Secretary General Brezhnev set
the tone with a pilgrimage to Vladivostok, where he awarded the
Order of Lenin to the Maritime territory. His visit was linked

with the build-up of Soviet troops along the Chinese border.

In Brezhnev's footsteps, the President of the Supreme Soviet, Nikolay V. Podgorny hurled a veiled warning at Peking by emphasizing that the Amur border was well defended against "any invader", as he awarded the same Order to the Khabarovsk territory for its achievements. Khabarovsk itself, according to an early eyewitness, presents a decidedly martial aspect: soldiers everywhere, guarded bridges, border sections cleared of brush and trees, ploughed up and rigged with alarm signals. No direct connections exist between the city and Manchuria.

At least forty combat-ready Soviet divisions, including motorized, tank, and airborne divisions, long range and tactical air force, nuclear missile units, confronted even more Chinese divisions including paramilitary formations along the former "friendship boundary." The ratio of Soviet and Chinese troops there was to the disadvantage of the Russians according to the annual survey of the Institute for Strategic Studies in London covering information up to the end of 1970. Moscow revealed a 12 percent increase in allocations for the defense of border areas in the military budget for 1970.

The Chinese nationalists held that along the border the strength of the Chinese communist forces doubled that of the Soviets, not including the Production and Construction Corps which was extended from Sinkiang to Kansu, Inner Mongolia and Manchuria.[29] Japanese estimates are considerably lower.

No wonder then that the head of the central cultural revolution group, Ch'en Po-ta told a military rally: "Our enemy is the Soviet Union, and we shall have to fight this enemy sooner or later."[30]

A Czechoslovak source revealed that it was common knowledge that the Soviet army had taken a whole series of measures to prepare for the event that Peking should decide to widen the so far occasional border skirmishes into a broader armed conflict. The emphasis on the importance of conventional weapons and of land forces in the Soviet military doctrine is also an expression of a serious assessment of the potential danger which has developed in China.[31]

The border rivers are the site of many Russo-Chinese confrontations. The new unilateral Chinese navigation code for foreign

ships voyaging along the Amur and its tributaries is very stringent—
all weapons and ammunition on such ships must be turned over
to Chinese authorities, use of any kind of signal equipment is prohibited, except in emergencies.

The Soviet Foreign Ministry charged the Chinese with the disruption of the 1967 annual conference of the joint Soviet-Chinese
commission for navigation on the border rivers of the Amur basin
in Harbin. The Chinese tried to force the Soviet delegation to deal
with questions of the origin of the boundary, an issue not in the
commission's competence. No conference was held in 1968. At
the 1969 conference in Khabarovsk, the Chinese side tried to bring
up the same issue, but was again rebuffed by the Russians. Surprisingly, this time the Chinese did not insist and the commission reached an agreement on traffic maintenance work and
on the new wording of shipping rules on the Amur, Ussuri,
Argun, Sungacha rivers and on Lake Khanka.[32] No agreement was
reached on the questions discussed at the 1970 conference.

The Chinese nationalists are in complete agreement with Mao's
contention that the regions "east of Baikal", i.e. "south of Yablonovy
Khrebet (west of the Stanovoy Mts.), east of Ussuri River up to the
Pacific, including Sakhalin island, Vladivostok, Khabarovsk, and
Kamchatka peninsula, and the regions west of Erkhuna River
(Argun), up to the area, surrounding the Baikal Lake," were Chinese
territories, according to historical records.[33] This means a return
to the Treaty of Nerchinsk (1689), the first correct agreement with
Russia in the eyes of Chinese historians, violated by the advance
of the Cossacks to the Pacific.

To bolster his position in Asia, Mao was busy stirring unrest
in the Soviet sphere of influence in Europe with his references to
Soviet seizures of Polish, Rumanian, and East German territories.[34]
The Rumanians alone picked up the ball. They republished an
old article by Marx on the "Eastern Question", condemning Tsarist
Russia for the seizure of Bessarabia, and published a map of the
province replacing all Russian or Russified place names with the
original Rumanian names.

For their answer, the Russians chose Ivan Bodyul, secretary of
the Moldavian communist Party, who at the Party Congress in
April, 1966, accused unnamed people of "laying claims to the ter-

ritory of the Soviet Union". He further implied that some people in Moldavia were speaking of reunification with their co-nationals. Tens of thousands of Romanian-speaking people were exiled from Bessarabia and Bukovina to Soviet Asia.

The Romanians kept up their fire. In a speech marking the 45th anniversary of the native CP, First Secretary Nicolae Ceausescu blamed both the Comintern and the previous domestic Party leadership for having failed to defend the country's territorial integrity at three interwar congresses. His statement was interpreted as reasserting Romania's claim to Bessarabia and Bukovina, two regions ceded to the Soviet Union in 1940. The President Party leader referred to the present rule there as "ruin, plunder and distruction", without of course, mentioning Moscow directly.[35]

Several months later Ceausescu reiterated Romania's determination to resist Soviet pressure, by stating at a plenary session of the Communist Party's Central Committee: "The old practices of imposing points of view from the outside, of interfering in internal affairs of other Parties has not yet been renounced...There have been insinuations, exertion of pressure and accusations of all kinds, there was a repetition of the well-known tendency of condemning some Parties by proxy."[36]

Premier Chou En-lai revealed that he had raised the territorial issues concerning the East European countries, as well as China, Japan, and the Middle East, during his visit with Khrushchev in January 1957. In an interview published by the Japanese daily *Asahi Shimbun*, Chou En-lai asserted that he had requested that the USSR "make proper arrangements" concerning these territories, since "the Soviet Union had taken too much land". To nobody's surprise, he did not get a satisfactory answer.[37]

A French correspondent, who visited China in 1959, was shown by military authorities that the best unities of the PLA were facing Russia at the outer fringes of the country, along the great arch from Manchuria to the Pamir—a defensive deployment of troops on the "underbelly" of the Soviet empire. Yet he failed to draw the correct conclusions at that time.

While Soviet imperialism is of an apparently static nature and tries in a way to consolidate the status quo, Chinese imperialism, instead, is dynamic. China—the historical Central Kingdom (*Chung Kuo*), which after the democratic revolution of "Double 10th" (1911) may be called the Central Realm—has always regarded adjacent peoples as "barbarians", who once lived in dependent, vassal states, which owed tribute to the Heavenly Emperor. In this regard Sun Yat-sen was of the opinion that many states "wanted to bring tribute and adopt Chinese culture. . .[and] considered it a great favor for China to annex them." He listed Tibet, Thailand, Burma, Nepal and Bhutan as having belonged to China.[38]   Mao in his early writings has enumerated the following "Chinese dependent states and a part of her territory" taken "by the imperialist powers": Taiwan with the Pescadores, Port Arthur, Hong Kong, Macao, Korea, Annam, Burma, Nepal, Bhutan and the Ryukyu islands. Professor Schram analysed the original text of his writings and found out that Mao as an adolescent was deeply affected by a pamphlet deploring the loss of Indochina, Korea and Burma.[39]   That article was included in his *Selected Works*, where all these by now independent nations are described as "many neighboring countries formerly under her protection."[40]

In this respect at least, there is not much difference between Sun Yat-sen, Chiang Kai-shek[41] and Mao Tse-tung. All three subscribe to the Chinese historical slogan: "Once China, always China". Similarly the Red Chinese outlining their trans-Himalayan aspirations, have been largely copied from those of the *Kuomintang*.

In one of their most blistering attacks on Chinese designs, the Russians constructed their own "domino theory" about "Mao's strategic plan" which is often mentioned in the Peking media without further explanation. Mao's plan of conquest, the Russians assert, is much larger than Tanaka's, which was limited to East Asia. In the first stage China will include

Korea, the Mongolian People's Republic, Vietnam, Cambodia, Laos, Indonesia, Malaysia, Burma, and several other countries in that region. In the second stage of the 'storm from the East' it is planned to expand in the direction of the Indian sub-continent, Soviet Central Asia and the Soviet Far East. What is planned on paper for the third stage is not entirely clear yet. But the plan does not limit itself to Maoization of Asia. 'We shall gaze proudly on five continents", says one of Mao Tse-tung's supporters.

Only a nuclear third world war could clear the way for Mao's plan which seems "like the ravings of a madman or a phantasmagoria". To the socialist Genghis Khan "communism is the dictatorship of Mao plus radiation". The adventurist military autocrats in Peking who are supporting Mao's plan are dreaming of a greater Chinese Empire.[42]

This frightful picture of a distinguished Russian journalist looking at China "from the Pamirs" was revived in the barrage of anti-Maoist vituperation in connection with President Nixon's invitation to Peking wheeling out their biggest guns previously recorded throughout this book.

In a spate of articles Red China was depicted as a center of planning for aggression and world domination. The Soviet army daily *Krasnaya zvezda* portrayed China as "the maniacal great power chauvinistic line of the Mao group." The government organ *Izvestia* explained why the Chinese communists have rejected all reasonable proposals in the border negotiations. Its acceptance would "tie their hands, prevent them from playing on international differences and from making China into a 'central power' in the world."

Moscow designated Peking's moves as anti-Soviet collusion, and their mutual slanging match reached new hights. In Professor Possony's opinion, expressed in *Politische Studien* (192-198/1970-71) historical records show that they are irreconcilable antagonisms between Russia and China, whose aim is to partition of each other. Their respective CP leaderships intend to overthrow each other, and grasp the command of the international communist movement. The same irreconcilable antagonism applies to their ethnic minorities as well as to their struggle for influence in the third world. Since both communist giants are aggressive and committed to fight for control, the worst is not excluded, in Possony's and Harrison Salisbury's opinion.

CHAPTER VII

The Great White Colonial Power in Asia

The Confrontation is Delayed

"Vladivostok is far away, but it is ours, nonetheless," Lenin once remarked.[1] On another occasion he said: "We shall never give up a single conquest we have won."[2]

With the creation of a multinational Soviet country and establishment of Russian as the dominant language on the pretext of economic necessity, the demands of building communism, the Soviet Party program officially proclaimed the denationalization of its non-Russian peoples. The thrust of education and the entire economic policy must serve the aim of submerging other nationalities by exposing them to an intensified Russification. According to the program's pronouncement, the concept of the "boundaries between the Union republics of the U.S.S.R. are increasingly losing their former significance . . . until complete unity is achieved." The Chinese commented that "the Soviet revisionist new Tsars" restored the policy of non-Russian oppression and turned the Soviet Union back into their prison.

In point of fact, the republics never were allowed genuine local government, and the deliberate fusion of their cultures is developing an international culture common to all the Soviet nationalities. Manifestations idealizing the national past are rejected as narrow-minded. Their national language and cultures are unscrupulously suppressed. This Professor Wittfogel called total colonialism.

Yet the high birth rate of Soviet Asia's native population worked against these tendencies notwithstanding heavy Russian coloniza-

151

tion in connection with the border tension.   In many regards, however, the conflict with China has impeded the Soviet policy of as-
similating other nationalities, and the Soviets have had to defend
themselves against the criticism of Great Russian chauvinism.   By
putting the Soviets on the spot, the Chinese also manage to damage the
Soviet image among the developing countries, blaming Moscow in
addition of pursuing there an economic policy of "draining
the pond to catch the fish."[3]

Whereas other nationalities of the Soviet Union accounted for
46.6 percent of the total population under the Great Russian yoke
in 1970 and are on the increase to outnumber the ethnic Russians,
only a quarter of the Soviet Union's peoples inhabit Soviet
Asia.   In the last few decades, the Soviet Union has been settling
the peoples of its Asian regions mainly in the territories adjacent to
the borders of China and the Mongolian Republic.   Reacting to
Chinese accusations on this score, *Pravda* in a full-page reply acknowledged Russia's territorial larceny by saying that "the borders
of Tsarist Russia were determined by the policy of imperialist
predators."   At the same time, it alleged, the Soviet Union's identical borders were formed in accordance with a "self-determination
of peoples"—something that never took place.[4]

What really happened was that the former Khanate of Khiva
and Emirate of Bukhara became Russian protectorates after the
19th century Tsars had annexed all of the surrounding territories.
St. Peterburg thwarted all attempts to restore the Kokand Khanate
and to place it under the protection of the Sublime Porte.   The
native peoples of these regions certainly did not choose communism;
the Red Army and Bolshevist state imposed it on them.   Kazakhstan
and Soviet Central Asia became five union republics.

According to a British scholar, "The ostensible purpose [of
Soviet policy] was to remake frontiers on lines of ethnic division.
The real aim was to exalt dialect into languages and tribes into
nations, in order to divide the Central Asian Moslems against each
other, and link the divided lands separately to Moscow."   And, on
another occasion: "The Russian communists have steadily opposed
the notion of a single Turkestani or Turko-Tatar nation, conceding
only separate Turkic- or Iranian-speaking nations."[5]

When their own interests were involved, the Soviets and Chinese alike, both false anticolonialists, suppressed the Pan-Turkic movement. C.L. Sulzberger rightly observed: "It is a sardonic joke that Russia and China, each of which muffles its large Islamic minority, should now carry the Moslem standard in ideological warfare."

Through collectivization or forced resttlement to the Urals and Siberia for industrialization purposes, the Soviets sharply reduced the population of Kazakhstan and Soviet Central Asia. The actual decrease of about 1.5 million Kazakhs was the consequence of starvation. Besides, Russian immigration persisted continuously; the native communist authorities could not limit it, being under pressure both from Moscow and from Russian communists locally. According to the 1970 Soviet census, the dominant native population accounted for only 32.4 percent of the total in Kazakhstan, 43.8 in Kirghizia, 56.2 in Tadzhikistan, 64.7 in Uzbekistan and 65.6 percent in Turkmenistan.[6] There are in the Soviet Union 9.2 million Uzbeks, 5.3 million Kazakhs, 2.1 million Tadzhiks, 1.5 million Turkmen, 1.4 million Kirghiz, and 173,000 Uighurs, half of them refugees from China. The ratio of European Russians and Ukrainians to natives is 10 to 23 million, respectively.[7]

Soviet theoreticians first explained the association of all these naionalities with Russia as a "lesser evil," and later, as an "absolute good" in view of the concomitant sociopolitical transformation. The "alphabet of Lenin" (Latin), first introduced by the Soviets, was replaced by Cyrillic in the late 1930s. While the Soviets, too, hail wars of national liberation, they now present the rebellions of some of these peoples against Russian rule as "reactionary."

Is Soviet colonialism, then, a success story when compared with disappearing Western colonialism? In the opinion of Robert Conquest, an authority in the field, the Soviet Union has succeeded merely in delaying this confrontation. However, he continues, "It would seem that, despite the success claimed for the nationalities policy, Soviet Russia could not in the final analysis depend on the loyalty of these nationalities any more than could the Russia of the Tsars."[8]

The underground *samizdat* (self-publishing) paper *Khronika tekushchikh sobitii* (Chronicle of Current Affairs) smuggled out of the Soviet Union reported, in its 8th issue, an outburst of anti-Russian feeling in May 1969 when a number of mass meetings of Uzbek nationalists took place under the slogan "Russians, get out of Uzbekistan!" Tashkent was surrounded by troops, and many were arrested getting mild sentences. The paper is dedicated to the "human rights year in the USSR."

Soviet Moslem now number over 36 million and are linked to one another by spiritual, cultural and social ties. Why, then, should Moscow's own anticolonialist propaganda—that directed, for example, to the Arab world—not influence its own nationalities? From all available data, it seems clear that the Soviets support such ideals as nationalism, self-determination and independence only outside their own state and consistently combat them within it.

While the population from 1959 to 1970 increased in Kazakhstan and Soviet Central Asia by 44 percent—also through the influx of Russians and Ukrainians, the vastness of Siberia still suffers from demographic stagnation in addition to economic weakness. The Soviet Union is making extraordinary efforts to populate Siberia, but, because of the very difficult living conditions, some resettle, other quit it altogether (about 50,000 persons every year)—and thus the entire population does not exceed 20 million. Just 10.5 percent of the total Soviet population lives in Siberia and the Soviet Far East. The tempting open spaces of Eastern Siberia and the Far East, with respective population densities of just 2.6 and 3.4 persons per square mile, invite constant pressure from the most populous nation on earth. The Soviet Far East of 1.2 million square miles is inhabited by less than six million people.[9]

Capital investment in Soviet Asia reached 30 percent of the Soviet total. The percentage of Soviet armed forces there today is probably higher than this. The Soviets have strengthened this presence with medium-range rockets from Omsk to Khabarovsk—all of them trained on Chinese targets. In July 1967, the Soviet Government adopted an extraordinary nine-year regional economic plan for top-priority development of the Soviet Far East providing for an infusion of vast amounts of capital and envisaging big settlements. Large chemical, metallurgical, and machine-building areas, and unique power stations have been created there.

The Soviets are calling the North Siberian rail trunkline now being built "the construction project of the century." The new line, cutting by 620 miles the distance from the Urals to the Far East, will pass from 248 to 434 miles to the north of the Trans-Siberian railway's course. This will facilitate exploitation of the great oil, iron ore, copper and other mineral deposits and development of an iron-and-steel center south of Yakutia. Meanwhile the Turk-Sib's railroad younger sister was built, shortening the distance from Soviet Central Asia to European Russia by 468 miles, and for those who had to travel by way of Tashkent, the path to Moscow between the Aral to the Caspian Seas will be 936 miles shorter.[10]

For the Siberian and Far Eastern regions, a resettlement drive has been revived. According to a decision of the Soviet government and Party Central Committee, most attention goes to populating the Far Eastern areas of Chita, Amur, Khabarovsk and Primorye in the coming years up to 1975. Thousands of volunteers from European Russia are ready to go and thousands more are submitting applications, lured by the state's favorable assistance provisions.[11]

A Russian émigré scholar has described the general Siberian situation with regard to China in the following illuminating way:

Military bases without populated rear areas, highly developed means of communication, firm economic support and elaborate sources of supply do not indefinitely guarantee the possession of territory. However, military might, actual as well as potential, wins time, which is important not only for ensuring the systematic development of Siberia and the Far East, necessary for self-sufficiency in the event of a large-scale war, but also for ensuring the ability to conduct an offensive in order to effect a realignment of forces in Asia.[12]

In so unexpected an event, the Soviets would like to be able to justify the Tsars' grabs of vast territories from the Ch'ing (Manchu) dynasty's control—to pretend as if those territories, particularly the Amur Basin and the Maritime Territory, never belonged either to the Manchus or China but rather, that indigenous local tribes, neither Manchurian nor Chinese, populated them. According to this claim, the Russians later took possession of the northern part of the Basin and the Chinese, of the southern part.[13]

Siberian archeologists are quoted to the effect that the original cultures of Siberia and the Far East were not brought there by Chinese tribes, as the "latter-day Peking expansionists" claim. Instead, it is argued, the Amur tribe of the Juchen conquered half of China under the Sung dynasty in the Middle Ages.[14]   The Academician V. M. Khvostov has invented a new theory for this purpose. He asserts that, in the oldest agreement between Russia and China, the Tsars allegedly ceded to Peking the entire Amur because China then was militarily stronger.   This was the Treaty of Nerchinsk.

In the Aigun and Peking treaties, therefore, "Russia took back only part of the territory [the left shore of the Amur] that the Chinese had grabbed by the Nerchinsk agreement."   The only explanation for Chinese territorial claims in Kazakhstan and Soviet Central Asia is the general one that the Ch'ing dynasty sometimes occupied the regions around the lakes of Zaisan, Balkhash and Issyk-Kul.[15]   As for the recent suggestions of Red Chinese historiography that the Manchus need not be considered from the Han point of view as invaders at all and that the Ch'ing period means a further development of "a united, multinational state," as the 1954 Constitution called China, Soviet historians cite this as the sign of a trend toward Chinese "bourgeois nationalism."[16]

The Siberian and history branches of the Soviet Academy of Sciences jointly compiled a five-volume book, History of Siberia From Ancient To Modern Times, trying to historically refute Peking's claims to vast territories.

There were few reports in the Soviet press and none in the communist Chinese press about various clashes on the Russo-Chinese border before 1969.   Occasional Soviet allusions to prior incidents include a vague report from Khabarovsk by the poet Konstantin Simonov.   He wrote that Soviet border guards had displayed "truly iron steadfastness and tenacity although no real military clashes are taking place" as Chinese villagers—a yelling crowd of several hundreds, or possibly thousands, drove trucks over the ice on the Usuri River into a chain of Soviet border guards barring their way.   Some of them appealed to the Soviet soldiers not to obey their officers.   This kept up for several days as military organizers across the river egged the crowds on.[17]

A much more tragic report came from a Viennese editor, Hugo Portisch, who visited China and then Siberia and wrote revealing books on China.[18]   In Irkutsk he met Pavel Silinsky, head of the regional State Planning Commission, who blandly declared:

"Of course, the Chinese want Siberia.   They are also greedy for Central Asia [Kazakhstan and Uzbekistan] and our Far Eastern provinces [Amur and Ussuri]. But nothing that they claim has ever belonged to China."

Then he repeated the Russian thesis explained above. Silinsky also told Portisch of many incidents in 1966 and thereafter. One of the most serious occurred in the Chita district near the triangle of Soviet, Chinese and Mongolian territory. Under cover of night, the Chinese drove in about 30,000 men, women and children, old and sick persons among them, having already inculcated them with hatred telling them that the Soviet territory was Chinese and that they had a right to settle there. The Chinese authorities also told them that they would be fired on if they tried to return. The Chinese commander did not yield until the Soviet threatened to shell the Chinese garrison town. Soviet commanders on the Chinese borders had received a free hand, and could have carried out such a threat.

Even more serious incidents occurred almost daily on the Amur in the winter of 1966. Red guards dragged out prisoners accused of being friends of the Soviet Union and beheaded them in the middle of the frozen river. The heads and corpses were left until spring, when the river carried them downstream, where they were displayed to Chinese inhabitants as victims of Russian atrocities. The Chinese brought a great number of their own people to these executions. When they marched 20,000 persons out on November 7, 1966, to witness another decapitation, the Russians threatened to bombard the Chinese side of the frozen river and the Chinese withdrew. They continued to demonstrate close to shore.

Why then was the Soviet press silent over all these grave incidents while reporting extensively on the excesses of the cultural revolution? Silinsky explained that the Soviet people is kept informed about what is happening on the eastern frontiers at meetings and lectures, but not through publications. Why? So as not to scare the people with notions of how serious relations with China were?

The minimum in Chinese provocations was a constant stream of loudspeaker propaganda appealing to the Soviet side to overthrow their Party and government leadership and repeating Chinese territorial claims. Sporadic armed clashes have occurred continually along the Sino-Soviet boundary, but not on a large scale, said Colonel-General P. R. Zyryanov.[19]

Claim to Outer Mongolia

The particular situation of Outer Mongolia in the framework of Soviet colonialism has been unique. The Bolshevists installed a communist regime there and the country remained a Russian satellite. On the other hand, Moscow prevented it from falling back into its former status as a province of China, from which it had escaped at the overthrow of the Manchus through a Tsarist engineered *coup d'état*. Yet, Moscow recognized in the 1924 Agreement that "Outer Mongolia is an integral part of the Republic of China."

On all maps but the Chinese, Outer Mongolia looks like a great gusset cut from the pattern of China. On all Chinese maps in Peking, however, including that already mentioned, the People's Republic of Mongolia is shown as part of China—despite its recognition as an independent state by Peking in the 1950 Sino-Soviet Treaty and in the Boundary Treaty of 1962. TASS has related the story told by a Mongolian youth who studied in a Chinese history class in Peking: "We saw a political map of the world printed in the People's Republic of China, and it failed to represent our independent country, the Mongolian People's Republic."

The Boundary Treaty with Mongolia was mentioned in the Chinese reply to Moscow on their border claims. Yet Radio Urumchi disputed it because it was signed by "opponents of Mao Tse-tung", and "the Chinese people cannot recognize its validity." The transmission claimed as Chinese territory the area around three lakes in the farthest west of Mongolia, 77 square miles in all.[20]

While China denies Outer Mongolia's right to statehood, the Soviet Union, which sustained its formal independence at the Yalta conference, has continued to control it. The Soviets have confirmed that the Chinese leaders in 1954 proposed an agreement to deprive Mongolia of formal independence and make it a Chinese province again, when Khrushchev visited Peking on the fifth anniversary of the communist take-over there. The Soviets have also pointed out that this was a novel proposal.

Bazaryn Shirendyb, president of the Mongolian Academy of Sciences and a Mongolian Party Central Committee member, recalled that the All-Chinese Congress of Soviets in November 1931 asserted in its resolution on the nationalities question that the projected constitution must point out that "the Chinese Soviet Republic completely and unconditionally recognizes the independence of the Mongolian People's Republic." He remarked that it was senseless to claim a neighbor's territory "on the basis that the Mongol conquerors had once established their dynasty in China, or because Chinese militarists had occupied part of Mongolia in 1919 and 1920."[21]

The Chinese have attempted to stir up unrest in Mongolia by propaganda pressure. Earlier in the 1960's, with Peking's full support, some members of the highest Mongolian leadership tried to overthrow the pro-Soviet leaders in Ulan Bator. The attempt was thwarted in time, but anxiety over a possible repetition of such efforts has not been completely removed. This is surprising, given the only alternative open to Outer Mongolia—that of becoming an "autonomous region" of China.

The Central Committee of the Mongolian People's Revolutionary Party condemned the plotters,[22] and the Mongolian Foreign Ministry protested to the Chinese ambassador four times in the summer of 1963 and the spring of 1964 against Peking's "direct interference in [Mongolia's] internal affairs."[23] Purges continued for five years. Of 147 members of the Central and Auditing Committees, 83 suffered purge as insufficiently pro-Soviet.

The Mongolian news agency *Montsame* issued a long statement after Mao's interview with the Japanese socialists in 1964, giving a new interpretation to the Chinese leader's noted dictum: "The wind from the East [Peking] prevails over the wind from the West [Moscow]." *Montsame* maintained that communist China's great-power policies were a legacy of the Manchu conquerors. The statement stressed that Mongolia's "friendship with the Soviet people stands as an insurmountable barrier to the realization of the Peking leaders' dream of making Mongolia part of China." Finally, it remarked that "Our people would have shared the fate of the Inner Mongolians and other national minorities of China, toward whom a policy of great-Han chauvinism is being pursued."[24]

Relations between China and Mongolia worsened considerably during the cultural revolution, when Peking identified the Mongolian leadership with Soviet revisionism. There were several, periodically recurrent incidents. When Mongolian authorities deported three Chinese teachers from Ulan Bator for disseminating Maoist propaganda, the Chinese embassy personnel present at their departure demonstrated. This resulted in the arrest of more than 20 Chinese nationals. Red guards several times afterwards besieged the Mongolian embassy in Peking and finally forced their way onto the grounds, causing heavy damage to property and subjecting officials there to violence. They also set the ambassador's car afire.[25] The Maoists coupled these outrages with a campaign of slander. *Jenmin Jih-pao* called for the overthrow of the Mongolian leadership, which retaliated by scrapping cultural cooperation with Peking, ordering Mao's writings and portraits destroyed and prohibiting the import of Chinese books and publications.[26]

A Western military expert predicting trouble in Sino-Soviet relations has observed: "Outer Mongolia strategically . . . is an area of the utmost importance as a rally-point for potential attacks on key industrial centers in northern China and Manchuria."[27] It also protects Siberia's key industrial area, the Irkutsk-Angara rayon.

Before the Soviet-Mongolian military alliance of 1946 had lapsed, the two sides signed a new 20-year treaty of friendship, cooperation and mutual assistance on January 15, 1966, in the presence of Leonid Brezhnev, secretary general of the Soviet Party. The Treaty contained a clause automatically extending its life in 1986 for another ten years. Most important, however, was the provision of article 5 that both sides "will render mutual assistance in ensuring the defense potential of both countries" and "will jointly take all necessary measures, including military ones, with the aim of ensuring the security, independence and territorial integrity of both countries."[28] They obviously had China in mind as the most likely source of menace.

Thereafter, the Kremlin reportedly posted Soviet troops to Mongolia's Chinese border. Units of Soviet military engineers replaced the 6,000 Chinese technicians and workers expelled from Mongolia in 1964 as a result of Peking's intrigues in that country.[29] A Chinese diplomatic note to the Mongolian embassy in Peking later protested against intrusions into the Inner Mongolian region by soldiers for intelligence purposes. In turn, Chinese frontier guards were probing along the southeastern border of Mongolia in the Gobi desert area.[30]

Tuva, the size of South Vietnam and inhabited by a Turkic race, was part of northwestern Mongolia under Chinese rule. Urged on by Tsarist Russia, it won nominal independence after the proclamation of the Chinese Republic. In fact, it became a Russian protectorate and has remained such under Soviet rule. Between the two world wars it was known as the Tannu People's Republic. Thus, the "first coun'ry of socialism" actually had two satellites.

The Soviets secretly annexed Tannu Tuva in 1944, and in 1961 it became an autonomous socialist republic of the Russian SFSR. Its population comprises Tuvinians and Rusians in a proportion of 57 percent to 40 percent, respectively.[31] Mao's claims on territory "east of Baikal" seems not to embrace that part of the Buriat Au'onomous Republic (no longer called Buriat Mongolia) annexed to Russia by the Nerchinsk and Kiakhta (1727) treaties with China. The latter treaty, called the second and last *equal* one between Russia and China, recognized Chinese sovereignty over Tannu Tuva.

Death of the Sino-Soviet Alliance

Red China's propaganda apparatus has been busy exposing Russian imperialism to the world at large. Peking has proclaimed the Soviet Union to be a non-Asian country intruding at the expense of the Chinese and other Asian peoples. China has launched the racist slogan, "Asia belongs to the Asians," in this regard.

The partial nuclear test ban, initiated in July 1963 after three "earnest counsels" from Peking failed to deter Moscow, added a new dimension to the rift. Professor Griffith even saw this as the very birth of the schism, since the heavy open polemics between Moscow and Peking started around the same time. Asked why China sought "with or without trousers" to develop nuclear weapons when the Soviet Union had said it would defend China against outside attack, former Foreign Minister Ch'en Yi replied: "In the first place, what is this Soviet assurance worth? If tomorrow we say that we will make ourselves responsible for the defense of Australia, what value would you place on it? This sort of promise is easy to make, but . . . worthless. Soviet protection is worth nothing to us."[32]

The late Marshal Rodion Malinovsky asserted as Soviet defense minister even before the rift came into the open that Soviet military power would be used only to defend "those socialist states friendly to us."[33]   The organ of the CPSU's Central Committee also betrayed doubts about Soviet support for China.   "Why," *Pravda* wondered, "did the Chinese newspapers ... carry articles about incredible territorial claims against the USSR? ... The Peking leaders from time to time still utter high-sounding hypocritical phrases that 'in the stern hour of trial' the CPR and the USSR will always be together ... How do you intend to ensure this when a filthy anti-Soviet propaganda [campaign] is going on in China?"[34]

The main organ of the Soviet government went even further, admitting that the Sino-Soviet alliance had practically dissolved. The Chinese had withdrawn their observers from the Warsaw Pact organization, completely halted deliveries of strategic materials and stopped forwarding altogether foreign-policy information in accordance with the 1950 Treaty from Peking to Moscow, *Izvestia* noted. Then it declared:

> Casting doubts on the efficacy of the Soviet-Chinese treaty of friendship, alliance and mutual aid, CPR Minister of Foreign Affairs Ch'en Yi alleged in December 1963 that Soviet assurances as to the defense of China in the event of imperialist aggression are of no value ... He said, cynically: 'Soviet protection is worth nothing to us!'   Marshal Ch'en Yi declares that China is a 'nonaligned' country.   In political language this means in fact that he does not consider China a part of the world socialist camp.[35]

Two years later, Ch'en Yi repeated that China did not expect Soviet aid in the event of a war with the Americans.   Premier Chou En-lai said afterwards that "to become prepared for war is one of the goals of China's cultural revolution," but "we will not try to have the Soviet Union side with us."[36]   Harrison Salisbury, after visiting the countries bordering communist China, said that "there is mounting evidence that the Chinese-Soviet treaty ... signed in Moscow on February 14, 1950, is dead.   Each has violated its terms and each is conducting itself as if the treaty no longer had any force."[37]   Professor Donald Zagoria had already termed this agreement the last of the unequal treaties signed by China.

Former U.S. Defense Secretary Robert McNamara doubted Soviet support for China early in 1964. "As a result of the Sino-Soviet split," he thought, "the Chinese must certainly feel considerably less confident of Soviet support in the event of a military clash with some other major power." Three years later, he said in his annual report to the Senate Armed Services Committee of this conflict that "the tension on the borders is likely to continue, while an outbreak of hostilities between China and the Soviet Union does not appear probable at this time."[38]

In retrospect, Stalin seems to have signed the Sino-Soviet alliance treaty with limited objectives in view—one of them, as a deterrent to the United States before launching the Korean war. Later, with the broadening of the conflict, the meaning of the alliance declined. While the war did not yet involve Peking, Moscow served notice that China could expect no more from the Soviet Union in the event of its involvement than arms and "volunteer" pilots and technicians. Khrushchev rejected Mao's confrontation strategy towards the United States when Mao, relying on a Soviet nuclear umbrella, asked him to "provoke the Americans" and offered "100, 200 or 1,000 divisions."[39]

True, the Soviet Union did deliver to China a nuclear research reactor and a gaseous diffusion plant, besides training Chinese physicists at Dubno and elsewhere. However, the Russians repudiated the secret agreement of October 1957 on new technology for national defense when in June 1959 they refused the Chinese a sample atomic bomb and technical data on its manufacture. The Chinese, in turn, rejected an interim Soviet request for integration of China's armed forces with theirs and refused in particular to put the use of nuclear weapons under strictly Soviet control.

A Yugoslav source explained Khrushchev's downfall in connection with China's development of the nuclear bomb. The fallen Soviet leader was scored in the Politburo for promising Mao support for the Chinese nuclear program. Khrushchev could honor his promise only after ousting of the so-called Molotov anti-Party group. After the aggravation of the schism, when the Soviets stopped all support, it was too late. The Chinese already had the essential data. The Soviet government was informed in October 1964 that the Chinese were preparing their first test. Khrushchev was again attacked in the Politburo and soon after dismissed. Two days later the first Chinese atom bomb was exploded.

Mao revealed at the tenth Central Committee meeting in 1962 that "Khrushchev brought up a plan for a Sino-Soviet joint fleet, thereby attempting to place the coasts of China under Soviet control and to blockade China."[40]   Peking also rejected any Soviet military control and the stationing of Soviet troops in China. Thereafter, Moscow terminated its military aid in 1959-60 and the alliance lost all of its meaning.

When Khrushchev proposed that the Chinese take Hong Kong and Macao instead of showing interest in Soviet territories, the Chines leaders declined and Ch'en Yi called it a "revolutionary compromise." They also rejected the two-China solution advanced by the then Soviet Chairman, leaving that matter for the time being where it is today. Judging from Mao's own statement to some Latin American communist leaders, it may last another hundred years.[41]

In point of fact, the Russians had announced while the Sino-Soviet dispute was still dormant that they would not intervene in what they called China's civil war with the Nationalists.[42]   When the Soviets accepted the Republic of China's adherence to the 1963 partial nuclear test ban treaty, Peking interpreted this as indicative of Soviet acquiescence in two Chinas.[43]   And, in early 1968, the Chinese Foreign Ministry protested in a note to the Soviet embassy in Peking against showing the Chinese nationalist flag in an inside cover picture of Olympic games in a Soviet publication.[44]

The Peking leadership early disabused itself of the illusion that it could count on Soviet support in any likely military crisis. The captured Chinese secret military papers of 1961 contained frank admissions to this effect. Again, according to K. S. Karol, an author on Red China who won the trust of Peking's leadership, Premier Kosygin, homeward bound from Hanoi, talked to Mao in January 1965, and when Mao asked him if he would regard an attack on China as an attack on Russia, Kosygin gave no reply.[45] Mao himself was seemingly unenthusiastic about the possibility of a Soviet intervention, as his interview to a Japanese Communist Party delegation shows. He revealed worries he had in the spring of 1966 that America would attack China, giving the Soviets "a pretext" to occupy China, and noted that in any such event, "The result will be a confrontation across the Yangtse of the Chinese Liberation Army and the Russian Army."

Chou En-lai openly and officially declared in a speech that the socialist camp as such no longer exists at all and that there cannot even be talk of common interest of the socialist commonwealth, as recorded by the Russians.[46]

The Soviets themselves seem quite conscious of what any such confrontation would involve. As Morton Halperin, an expert in this dispute, has cautioned: "Russian intervention would come only when perceived as necessary for the *narrow Russian national interest* [emphasis supplied] and would almost certainly be confined to defense of North China and Manchuria."[47]

Aleksey Adzhubei, Khrushchev's son-in-law and the former editor-in-chief of *Izvestia*, spoke in Tsarist style of the Soviet Union's frontiers being backed by their armed forces in the east as well as in the west, confirming again that much more than border adjustments are involved in the conflict with China.[48] Khrushchev himself repeated the same view in his talk to Japanese parliamentarians, emphasizing any attempt at changing these borders by force would mean war.

Not just the Khrushchev family but all Russians, generally, share these anxieties. The outstanding writer Andrey Voznesensky sounded the alarm in a poem warning of the "Mongol Hordes," saying: "I hear: 'Give us Baikal!'" He stressed Russia's historic mission ("Russia the savior!") to defend European and Western civilization against the menace from the East—as represented by Mao Tse-tungism, as the Russians call it. "Shall Shakespeare be forced to make public confessions of ignorance of 'isms'? Will Stravinsky be dragged through warring streets with a garbage pail on his gray head?" Voznesensky compared Mao Tse-tungism to Kuchumism as representative of vulture-like chauvinism and warmongering. (Kuchum, a descendant of Genghis Khan, was the ruler of Sibir when it was conquered by the Cossack Yermak. Interestingly, he was blind).

One of the best known Russian poets Yevgeny Yevtushenko in a patriotic poem "On the Red Snow of the Ussuri" after comparing Mao with "a monster ... the tragic farce of the arrogant

pseudo-communist" and his quotations with "bloodspots", conluded:
"The new Mongol Khans have bombs in their quivers. — But if
they attack the warning bells will peal—And we shall have enough
warriors—For the new battle of Kulikovo." (This battle in 1380
ended the Mongol domination over Russia.)[49]

The "aggressive character of imperialism" (Lenin's notion)
has been much misused by the communists with regard to the dying
Western colonialism and in disregard of the flourishing communist
imperialism—both the Russian form in east Europe and in Asia
and the Red Chinese imperialism in Tibet (coupled with genocide),
Sinkiang and Inner Mongolia. The question is thus raised, will
the Afro-Asian countries in the United Nations finally abandon
their double standard on colonialism and support the genuine cause
of the captive nations under communism?

In his discussions on the Sino-Soviet conflict for Radio Free
Europe, Professor Hugh Seton-Watson of London University, a
name already famous to East Europeans because of his late father's
merits as a historian, asserted:

> It is a grim and astonishing, not to say shaming, irony that
> the West has never made any effective protest, at the United
> Nations, against the fact that the Soviet Union exploits tens
> of millions of Central Asiatic Turks—Uzbeks, Kazakhs, etc.
> — in a colonial regime, not to mention Eastern Europe.
> And I have no doubt that it is going to fall to the Chinese of
> all people to pillory the Russians with no inhibitions at all
> —the Chinese, who have a colonial empire of their own,
> including Turks and all.[50]

Sure enough, the Red Chinese leader, assigning to non-Euro-
pean peoples the greatest importance in the revolutionary struggle,
reminds the world as well as these that there is no distinction between Western and Soviet colonialism. Yet, the Russo-Chinese
conflict has revealed nationalities due for liberation in both countries. Both sides accuse each other of colonialism, largely for the
edification of African and other Asian peoples and their rulers.
What conclusions should these peoples draw from this polemic
if they are honestly opposed to colonialism everywhere? Again,
are national-liberation wars "just" ones only outside the communist
orbit?

Certainly, power politics is the chief factor involved in the Sino-Soviet conflict. The Soviets conclusively revealed their essential standpoint before the Russian public in a panel discussion on Chinese splitting activities not long before Khrushchev's fall from power: "It is now evident that it is not any ideological, theoretical argument, nor struggle for the Marxist-Leninist doctrine, but an undisguised, open course of expansion and hegemony, a great-power, chauvinist course."[51] China's course, then, is but the latest version of sinocentricity in the several thousand-year-old tradition of the Middle Kingdom reestablished by Mao Tse-tung. For Peking's part, in the polemic around the "second Bandung" conference, postponed *ad calendas graecas,* the Chinese communists have rejected the Soviet Union as an Asian power on the ground that "three-fourths of its population lives in Europe." Actually, the Soviet Union extends over about two-fifths of the Asian continent—more than the combined areas of China, India, and all the biggest Asian countries together. Moreover, the Soviet press has emphasized the individualities of the Asian Soviet republics as ethnic entities—although all have been subjected to a high degree of Russification.

The "Bandung II" conference's postponement was a great failure for Peking's aim of championing the underdeveloped Afro-Asian countries. Only six of these endorsed Mainland China's views, and the overwhelming majority of them stood prepared to invite the Soviet Union and, in practice, isolate China. They rejected the Chinese thrust as fostering discord between white and colored peoples and preaching racial hatred. The Algerian press ascribed the responsibility for the conference's postponement in the main to China, and a gloomy shadow has descended on relations between Peking and many of the Afro-Asian nations. Attempting to save what credit he could, Chou En-lai "sternly condemned" the Soviet government as the culprit, scoring its "sabotaging activities"[52] as the real cause of the failure of the conference to take place.

Yugoslavia, however, China's rival for championship of the Afro-Asian non-aligned countries, did not allow the Chinese premier to escape through this recriminatory smoke screen. The Yugoslav communists criticized what they termed China's impermissible great-power *Diktat* ignoring the will of 50-odd small countries. In their opinion, China had experienced one of its biggest defeats in a generally aggressive policy which, — they added, violated the principles of the first Bandung conference.[53]

For their part, the Afro-Asian countries have neither accepted the Chinese point of view that Rusia is a white and European country nor endorsed any effort at the political expulsion of the Soviet Union from Asia. As the leading American daily saw matters, however, Russia's diplomatic interests among these countries were not its chief stake in the ongoing Sino-Soviet dispute:

> As the latest Soviet note comments, the Chinese position is that the Russians are merely another group of white colonialists in Asia. And this in turn implies they are enslavers who must be made to give up their ill-gotten gains in Siberia and Central Asia. For the time being Moscow certainly has the military power to defend these Tsarist conquests. But the planners in the Kremlin cannot mistake the long-range blow to their position in Novosibirsk, Vladivostok and Tashkent.[54]

It was a timely observation. A Soviet Party Central Committee memorandum, circulated to and discussed by domestic Party committees at their meetings beforehand, went out to foreign communist Parties. This was the first disclosure meant for serious consideration abroad that the Chinese side had been provoking border conflict long before the Ussuri clashes. It revealed that the Chinese side was creating trouble along the frontiers from Central Asia through Mongolia and to the Far East. Most of this took the form of illegal border crossings. Besides complaining about these encroachments, the Soviets further accused the Chinese of attempting to subvert Soviet citizens living in border areas and of flooding these territories with anti-Soviet literature. Mao himself, they noted, exhorted his armed forces to be ready to defend the long frontier with the Soviet Union.[55]

CHAPTER VIII

The Sinification of Minorities

Armed Revolts and Mass Escapes

While national minorities comprise only six percent of mainland China's population, they cover 50-60 percent of its territory. Their total number, given as 35 million by the 1953 census, was listed as 38.5 million by Peking's 1964 statistics and has reached 45 million according to recent estimates. The Russians claim the Chinese have almost twice as many. According to the Chinese census they may be divided into the following groups: Uighur, concentrated in Sinkiang with the related Uzbeks (13,000 in Ili) 3.64 million (now five million, say the Russians); Mongols, a minority in their Inner Mongolia, small groups in Sinkiang and Manchuria, 1.46 million. In addition there were some 470,000 Kazakhs, 80,000 Kirghiz, 15,000 Iranian Tadzhik, 5,000-10,000 Orochen, Solon, and several smaller tribes. There are also Chinese Moslems (*Hwei* or *Hui* in Chinese, *Dungan* in Russian), in Sinkiang and in China proper, 3.6 million (now 4.5 million).[1]

The Turkic peoples in the "New Dominion" (Sinkiang) are ethnically the same as on the other side of the border in the Soviet Union. These minorities may be relatively small in numbers, but since they occupy huge territories, they are important for our considerations.

Back in 1931, the Constitution of the Kiangsi Soviet Republic, with Mao as its Chairman, had proclaimed: "The Soviet Government of China recognizes the right of self-determination of the national minorities in China, their right to complete separation from China and to the formation of an independent state for each

169

national minority." But the 1954 Constitution stipulates in sharp contrast: "Acts which undermine the unity of the nationalities are prohibited." The official prospect for the minority peoples today is gradual compulsory assimilation with the Han people, the "elder brethren", and a metamorphosis into "genuine" Chinese.

Instead of acknowledging the national minority problem, the Chinese communists call it a "class issue". They claim that in the "socialist transformation" the Han people has reached a more advanced stage of "socialist construction", while the national minorities are not merely lagging in this forward march along the "socialist road", but even opposing it. Modernization should therefore ultimately lead to their fusion with the Han people and their final disappearance as distinct nationality groups. As future "socialist nationalities", Peking maintains, they should prepare themselves for a loss of identity in the larger entity of the Chinese people. Consequently, their Sinification is more important than their ideological remolding.[2]

The Russians, pressed as they are by their own restive minorities, have tried to capitalize on the Chinese nationalities' problem in their anti-Maoist campaign. The Vice President of the Soviet Academy of Sciences, A. Rumyantsev, utilized the Academy's festive session on the occasion of the 50th anniversary of the October Revolution to spring the revelation that it was Mao Tse-tung who, at the international conference of communist Party representatives in 1957, had insisted that minority nationalities be denied the right of self-determination. The assimilation of the non-Han nationalities and the harassment of people observing national customs under the pretext of a struggle against "feudal culture"—these are the Russians' favorite targets. The Soviet press gave a wide coverage to the maltreatment of China's national minorities during the cultural revolution, with a special emphasis on closing non-Chinese language schools and abolition of newspapers, magazines, publishing houses and radio stations in native languages. Russian journalists have been making continuous reference to a statement in *Hung Ch'i* that the ultimate goal of China's nationality policy is "the complete liquidation of national characteristics and distinctions."[3]

The idea of compulsory assimilation has found vocal support in mainland China's academic community as well. Since amalgamation of nationalities in China is a historical fact, argued the noted historian Chien Po-tsan, it should be accomplished by force. (His radicalism, however, did not save him from being purged during the cultural revolution.) In Professor Tang's view, "the famous [Stalin's] catchword: national in form, socialist in content, actually permits little in the way of real autonomy and nothing in the way of self-determination".[4]

The ferment amoung China's minorities has been repeatedly confirmed by Chinese authorities. Liu Ch'un, deputy chairman of the Nationalities Affairs Commission of the State Council, charged that "nationalist elements", fired by "anti-Han, independence and no reforms" slogans, have been "very rampant" in recent years "under the influence of imperialists, foreign reactionaries and re-visionists, as well as reactionary elements inside China", who "try their best to provoke contradictions between nationalities".[5] The same thesis was repeated by Premier Chou En-lai in his major report to the third National People's Congress in Peking. According to him, national minorities were "ganging up" with all foreign and domestic enemies of China in order to split up the country.

In their efforts to solve the minority problem, the Chinese have borrowed a leaf from the Russians and have resorted to large-scale population resettlement, inundating the minority territories with Chinese. Millions were moved into Manchuria, Inner Mongolia, Sinkiang and Tibet. The compulsory migration, especially to the north-west, reached its peak during the "great leap" and has con-tinued ever since.

One of the outstanding expressions of minority resistance was the attempt of Mongol nomads, admitted by Chinese communists, to establish an independent republic in Inner Mongolia in 1957. The pro-Soviet newspaper *Unen*, published in Ulan Bator, quoted a Mon-gol living in the so-called Inner-Mongolian autonomous region as saying that his compatriots there "live without freedom under the surveillance of a Chinese supervisor". Chinese outnumbered Mon-gols there by ten to one before the dismemberment of the region, in the opinion of Dennis Bloodworth, author of *The Chinese Look-ing Glass*.[6]

The Chinese emperors conquered the Sinkiang (Chinese Tur-kestan) nationalities in the 18th century and deprived them of their independence—a "forcible enslavement" and "subjugation to the most severe colonial yoke", according to a newspaper in Alma Ata, capital of Kazakhstan. Since then, Eastern Turkestan has overthrown Chinese rule four times. The last pro-Soviet republic quasi-independent from China lasted there from 1944 to December 1949, when most of its leadership perished in a mysterious plane crash.

Khrushchev questioned China's right to Sinkiang in an interview with a Japanese parliamentary delegation stating: "Let us take Sinkiang for example. Have the Chinese been living there from time immemorial? The Sinkiang indigenous population differs sharply from the Chinese ethnically, linguistically, and in other respects. They are Uighur, Kazakh, Kirghiz, and other peoples."[7]

Just as before the Red Chinese take-over, the steady worsening of Moscow-Peking relations was nowhere felt as keenly as in the Sinkiang border area. A purge of pro-Soviet elements affected mainly natives in prominent positions. They were sent to "re-education camps" (a euphemism for plain concentration camps), where, according to testimony of a Sinkiang-born Kazakh poet, Bukhar Tyshkanbayev, many died of scurvy or froze to death. A discrimination campaign against Uighur intellectuals was launched in 1957; many Uighur and other nationalities schools were closed and books in native languages, including those received from Soviet Asia, were burned.

The Uighur backlash culminated in an attempt by local nationalists in 1958 to separate the province from China, according to Red Chinese offical reports. Uighur refugees in Hong Kong revealed that over sixty thousand partisans (guerrillas), half of these trained and armed by the Soviet, were involved in the unrest. Peking's reply was swift and clear: arrests, convictions, persecution, and a new purge of local nationalists. Hundreds of important cadres of national minorities were killed, some fifty thousand cadres were demoted. Use of native languages in public places is being openly discouraged.

Sporadic armed revolts were also reported in 1959, 1960, 1962, and 1963. They were all suppressed by Chinese troops. Not surprisingly, the whole region is closed to non-communist observers. In the opinion of their Chinese overlords, the residents of Sinkiang have two hearts: a Russian heart that must be trampled, and a proper red Chinese heart.

The vice-chairman of the regional revolutionary committee Azizi Saifudin complained in a speech that "national secessionists" and others "lurking within our ranks" were trying to sever the Ili-Kazakh autonomous district "and the whole of Sinkiang" from China. More than a year later, the regional revolutionary committee complained about the "large amount of poison spread by social imperialism," that is, the Soviet Union. "Class enemies" were attacked for "counterrevolutionary crimes in undermining national unity and splitting the unification of the fatherland," according to Radio Urumchi.[8]

The 1960's have seen an endless stream of Chinese protests, charging the Soviets with the incitement of national minorities in China. In 1963 Peking revealed that during April-May 1962 the Soviet Communist Party had used its organs and personnel in the Ili district (western part of the Uighur region) to entice a mass escape of refugees, mostly to Kazakhstan, and then refused to repatriate these citizens of China on the pretext of the "sense of Soviet legality" and "humanitarianism". (The incident remains unsettled to this very day.) They had to leave, said the Russians, under the extreme circumstances resulting from intolerable exploitation, poverty, suppression, and discrimination.[9] Soviet personnel at the consulates of Kuldja[10] (Ining), Chuguchak (Tacheng), and Urumchi (Tihwa) were accused of handing out thousands of Soviet passports to natives who had never held Soviet citizenship previously.

The Russians have retaliated by accusing the Chinese of attempts to stir up national discontent and separatist ambitions among the native people of Soviet Central Asia and Kazakhstan. According to Moscow, systematic Chinese infringements of the Soviet frontier began in 1960, with over five thousand violations registered in 1962 alone. (Ch'en Yi mentioned the same figure of "Soviet-instigated" incidents for a longer period, from July 1960 to the end of 1965.) In addressing the Central Committee of the CPSU at the beginning of 1964, M.A. Suslov said that Chinese border violations "became a constant occurrence in 1962 and 1963, sometimes assuming the form of gross provocation". An exchange of fire was reported when Chinese units entered Soviet territory in pursuit of Uighur refugees.

The Peking's government note of May 24, 1969 offered somewhat more exact figures stating: "From October 15, 1964 to March
15, this year, the Soviet side provoked as many as 4,189 border
incidents, two and a half times the number of those it provoked
from 1960 to 1964 (this would be around 1,047 cases) with its
tactics getting even more vicious and its behavior even more unbridled. Soviet troops intruded into Chinese territory, indulging
in murder and arson, killing barehanded Chinese fishermen and
peasants by beating and running armoured cars over them or even
throwing them alive into the river."[11]

The Soviet accusations regarding the border incidents were
answered by the CPC's Central Committee in a letter dated February 29, 1964, stating that the differences could be settled by negotiations, but at the same time asserting, in reference to 1962:

The Soviet side has made frequent breaches of the status
quo on the border, occupied Chinese territory and provoked
border incidents. Still more serious, the Soviet side has
flagrantly carried out large-scale subversive activities in Chinese frontier areas, trying to sow discord among Chinese
nationalities by means of press and wireless, inciting China's
minority nationalities to break away from their motherland,
and coercing tens of thousands of Chinese citizens into going
to the Soviet Union.

Chou En-lai emphasized again the role of the Soviet Union in
those disorders without mentioning her by name (this was after
Khrushchev's ouster) in his previously mentioned report, adding
that "protagonists of local nationalism staged a traitorous counter-
revolutionary armed rebellion in Ining, . . . under the instigation and
direct command of forces from abroad".[12]

Italian and Yugoslav communist sources have confirmed Western reports from Moscow about incidents on the Sinkiang-Kazakh-
stan border in May 1969, where Chinese troops in regimental strength
occupied fifteen square miles of Soviet territory in the mountainous
area of Druzhba (meaning friendship), the Soviet border station on
the unfinished Soviet-Sinkiang railway line, southeast of Semipalatinsk. This territory is shaped like a small curve protruding into
Sinkiang. At the same time *Hsinhua* reported that peasants of the
Ili River area were loyal to Chairman Mao. Soviet leniency in this

case was explained by the forthcoming communist international conference. French sources also reported incidents in the Ili River valley between the Soviet town of Panfilov and the Chinese Kuldja area. Further incidents are commented on in chapter XV.[13]

Soviet Agitation in China's Far West

The situation in the Uighur-Sinkiang Autonomous Region had grown so tense even before the cultural revolution that Chinese military reinforcements along the Soviet border were bolstered to a point where any flight across the border would be much more difficult than in the previous decade. A similar activity proceeded on the other side of the border.

Despite deportations of natives of Sinkiang into China proper, several of China's minority nationalities constitute a majority, at least for the time being, in that officially "autonomous" region, covering one-sixth of the country's territory. Peking economists claim that Sinkiang could sustain 50-60 million people, but today its population is composed of 4.2 million Uighurs, farmers with their oasis civilization, and probably three million Chinese.[14] The rest are nomadic Kazakhs, shepherd Kirghiz, Tadzhiks, Uzbeks, Mongols, and Cossacks. The Chinese colonialists are composed of the top officialdom, members of the armed forces, soldier-farmers on the public estates, workers in the oil and uranium mines, and youths, including the students in the labor brigades. Shanghai alone has sent 200 thousand youths to Sinkiang for permanent settlement in 1963 as members of the military Production and Construction Corps; another 100 thousand were added in 1964. It was disclosed in the fall of 1966 that more than 1.1 million Chinese youths had been sent to Sinkiang. In the spring of 1969 the China watcher Robert Elegant calculated that two million of them were compelled to settle in Sinkiang. Some headed home in the turmoil of the cultural revolution, but the mainland press published appeals to get them to move back again.

A five percent minority back in 1953, the Chinese "colons" constitute probably less than a third of Sinkiang's population. The density of population in the region is the same as in neighboring Kazakhstan, about ten per square mile. The non-Chinese minorities of Sinkiang were first compelled to adopt the phonetic signs of the Latin alphabet, experimentally for the Peking dialect, and to discard the Arabic script best suited to the phonetic peculiarities of the Turkic languages. The next step was the imposition of the Chinese characters, completely alien and unsuitable for their languages.

The number of refugees increased in direct ratio to the vigor of Chinese repressions. In the spring of 1962 an estimated 60 thousand, or six thousand Kazakh families, had fled from Sinkiang, according to a Chinese government statement. (*Pravda's* figure was 50 to 60 thousand, while Professor Kapitsa reduced it to 45 thousand in his book Left of Common Sense.) This mass flight was followed by a massacre on May 29, 1962 covered in the Soviet press considerably later. Kazakhs who had gathered at the seat of the Ili Communist Province Committee to protest against the withholding of permission for around forty people wishing to return to the Soviet Union, were machine-gunned. Eighty-five Kazakhs, mostly women and children, were killed and hundreds were wounded. Several incidents in the Ili area were again reported in mid-1967 by Japanese and Hong Kong sources. To justify their measures, the Chinese have subsequently displayed in Urumchi Soviet weapons allegedly taken from Kazakhs and other Turkic rebels and have accused the Russians of large-scale subversion.[15]

The Chinese accusation were not completely unfounded. Kazakhstan Radio played an active part in urging mass flights with its blunt declarations that Sinkiang would be "liberated" from the Peking regime and attached to the Soviet Union with a "real" autonomous status. The press and radio of Alma-Ata, Tashkent and Frunze were fully utilized in a concerted series of attacks against the Chinese regime in Sinkiang.

To stem the flood of Turkic escapees from Sinkiang to the Soviet Union, numbering some 300 thousand since 1952, the civilian population of the region was evacuated 25 miles away from the Soviet border and the newly established "border security zone" was settled by veterans and soldiers. And yet Moslem refugees were still crossing the border into the Soviet Asian republics. The leak was partly plugged for a while with the erection of many new Chinese frontier posts and minefields, and with the Soviet hands-off policy during the period of "non-polemics", when, to avoid further incidents, the Russians were sending refugees back for a while. But this situation changed with fresh Chinese provocations coinciding with the cultural revolution. In turn the Chinese reproached the Soviets for creating a no man's land along the border.

Ex-officers of the Chinese communist army now play an important role on the Soviet side of the tense border region. An Uighur, Zumun Taipov, former major-general in the Red Chinese army, once a colonel of the Moslem national army in the pro-Soviet East Turkestan Republic and, the former deputy chief of the general staff of the Sinkiang-Uighur military region, now allegedly commands a 60 thousand strong army from Alma Ata. In 1963 he described the massacre of the Kazakhs by the Chinese "as proof of the collapse of the nationalities policy of the Chinese leaders, a reproach to their unclean conscience".[16] Deserters from Peking's armed forces also include Balkhash Bafin, a Kazakh and a former lieutenant-colonel, who fled to the Soviet Union.

Isa Yusuf Alptekin, chairman of the National Center for the Liberation of Turkestan in Istanbul, composed of Turkic refugees from China and Russia, claimed that at least 40 thousand well-armed Turkic partisans are now operating in Sinkiang.[17]

Chinese reprisals have exacted an especially severe toll from Sinkiang's intellectuals. The former president of Sinkiang's writers' association, Ziya Samedi, an Uighur poet, was sent to a concentration camp together with numerous Uighur and Kazakh intellectuals. It is to him that we owe the report of the talented Kazakh writer, Kazhykumar Shabdanov, who could not suffer the Chinese "re-education" any longer. Samedi managed to escape to Kazakhstan, where he is now a leading member of the Uighur section of the Kazakh writers union, and chairman of the Committee for the liberation of East Turkestan. He has frequently complained about the suppression of Uighur literature in Sinkiang. In a similair vein, Adbulkhai Ruzi, an Uighur poet and former member of the writers association in Urumchi, called Sinkiang "a prison for the small nationalities", subjected to heavy Sinification.[18] These exile writers have denied Chinese charges that the Kazakh national intelligentsia is trying to establish a Kazakh khanate of their countrymen in China, Mongolia, and the Soviet Union.

The status of formal autonomy, accorded to Sinkiang under

communist China's constitution, was completely abolished during
the cultural revolution. The same is true for China's other "autonomous regions". Enforced assimilation is now the law in Sinkiang. Kazakh, Uighur and Kirghiz girls are taken away from
their parents and are forced to marry Chinese under penalty of
death, as revealed by a former citizen of China who fled to his
relatives in Kazakhstan. During the cultural revolution, red guards
were cutting off the tresses of Turkic women and forbade them to
wear national costumes.

Small-scale raiding and fighting had become a routine occurrence
along the Soviet-Chinese border long before the recent revelations.
At the People's Congress of the Ili-Kazakh autonomous chou, held
in August 1963, the Kazakh Chairman Irhali accused the Russians
of "constantly creating border incidents and attempting to disrupt
production in the border areas". He asserted that subversive and
sabotaging activities were carried out in "trying to poison relations
among the various nationalities in order to undermine our national
unity".

The next occasion to lambast the Russians was the meeting
of the Provincial People's Congress in the capital city of Urumchi
to elect deputies to the National People's Congress in Peking. A
warning was issued in the second half of 1964 that "we will never
allow others to invade and occupy an inch of our land . . . a sacred
inalienable part of China".[19] Charges of subversive and sabotage
activities were raised subsequently by the former vice governor of
Sinkiang, Iminov, at the festivities of an autonomous chou on the
border of Kirghizia and Tadzhikistan. And Governor Saifudin
again mentioned the danger of foreign (i.e. Soviet) subversion in
his speech to the National People's Congress in Peking.[20]

The border tension was again stressed in all official messages
and speeches in September 1965, on the occasion of the 10th anniversary of the founding of the Sinkiang-Uighur Autonomous Region. The State Council of Red China "called on the people of
Sinkiang to maintain high vigilance, be ready at all times to smash
further sabotage by the modern revisionists (i.e. Soviets) . . . to
safeguard the frontiers and to consolidate the nation's defenses."

Vice Premier Marshal Ho Lung, then member of the Politburo
and head of the central delegation to the celebration (subsequently

purged in the cultural revolution), praised the suppression of "the counterrevolutionary armed riots masterminded by the modern revisionists and their subversive and undermining activities ... Khrushchev's revisionists will not stop their attempts to sow dissension between our nationalities and undermine our national unity and the unification of our fatherland. They will continue to carry out subversive activities and sabotage. We must ... resolutely carry on to the end the struggle against them".[21]

The first secretary of the CPC regional committee in Sinkiang, Wang En-mao, a Han-Chinese like the highest Party functionaries in the region, with the exception of the governor, said at the celebration: "The local nationalists and other reactionaries had demanded the disintegration of the fatherland's unification. The Khrushchev revisionist clique had worked hard to instigate the independence of Sinkiang and had unscrupulously carried out a series of malicious, subversive activities against Sinkiang. Their aim had been to separate the people of all nationalities in Sinkiang from the great family of our fatherland".[22]

Radio Peking, in a Russian-language broadcast, accused the Soviet Union of trying to separate Sinkiang from the rest of China, calling the province a Chinese colony, and inciting its people to oppose the CPC.

After the 9th CPC congress Red Flag complained that "Soviet revisionism ... constantly conducted subversive and sabotage activities in Sinkiang and has always regarded Sinkiang as a target of annexation." And in the 1969 National Day editorial Moscow was generally castigated for its "futile attempts to organize rebellions in our border areas."[23]

The geopolitical situation on the Kazakstan-Sinkiang border has not changed because of new weapons, which might never be applied. The last Tsarist Governor-General of Turkestan, Adj.-General A.N. Kuropatkin, made this clear in his comprehensive report to the Tsar on February 1, 1917:

As far as China is concerned, the future danger for Russia from this Empire of 400 million people is beyond all doubt. The most vulnerable part of the Russian frontier, as 800 years ago, remains the great gateway of peoples through which the hordes of Ghengis Khan poured into Europe. So long as Kuldja rests in the hands of the Chinese, the protection of Turkestan from China will remain very difficult, or will demand a great number of troops.

This gateway must not be left in the hands of the Chinese.

A change in our border with China is urgently necessary. By drawing the border line from the Khan-Tengri Range and the Tienshan in a direct line to Vladivostok it will be shortened by 4,000 versts [2,652 miles], and Kuldja, northern Mongolia, and northern Manchuria will become a part of the Russian Empire.[24]

Significantly, the Soviets accepted the Kuropatkin line along the 43rd parallel, thus keeping not only Outer Mongolia but also Manchuria and Sinkiang under their potential influence—that is, until Mao conquered the mainland and frustrated their plans.

CHAPTER IX

Against Khrushchevism and Its Successors

The "Three Peacefuls" Epitomize Revisionism

In the post-Khrushchev era, the Soviet oligarchs at first tried to calm the *furor theologicus* that resulted in the conflict. But since the Russian words were not backed by deeds, the Chinese did not yield. In an article published both in their leading daily and their theoretical magazine, the Chinese stated that they would not stop the public polemic "for a single day, for a month, a year, a hundred years, a thousand years, or ten thousand years."

They reproached the Soviet leaders with having taken over Khrushchev's revisionism and "splittism" lock, stock and barrel. A return to some neo-Stalinism in the Soviet Union could not placate the Maoists. The Soviets are continuously attacked for their three "peacefuls"—peaceful coexistence, peaceful competition and peaceful transition—and their two "entires"—the State and the Party of the entire people as proclaimed in the Soviet Party program. These five reproaches are part of the Chinese general line laid down in the Central Committee letter of the 14th June, 1963, in points 11, 13, 16, 18 and 19 of the 25-point program. They were repeated in the ninth Chinese reply to the Soviet "open letter" in which misgivings were expressed regarding declining morals in the CPC.[1] Professor Loewenthal therefore called this reply Mao's political testament and the beginning of the cultural revolution. The replies were seemingly drawn up by Mao personally or by his ghost-writers Ch'en Po-ta and Wang Li (who were later purged).

The nine replies appeared both in the People's Daily and the Red Flag from September 6, 1963, to July 4, 1964, and were concluded on November 21st of that year with an explanation of Khrushchev's downfall. They dealt with the origin of the conflict, Stalin, Yugoslavia, neo-colonialism, war and peace, peaceful co-existence, and with Khrushchev's "splittism" and revisionism. The drawnout exchange of polemics began earlier, however, with eight theoretical attacks on Soviet revisionism that were published in People's Daily between December 15, 1962, and March 9, 1963.

Added to the above three Soviet "peacefuls" are, in the opinion of the Chinese communists, "three shams and three realities: sham anti-imperialism but real capitulation, sham revolution but real betrayal, sham unity but a real split." And to make it absolutely clear to everybody, they accused Moscow of "selling horsemeat as beefsteak."[2]

In considering the Soviet "peacefuls," however, sight must not be lost of the Berlin provocations, the Cuban confrontation, the Soviet engagement in the Vietnam war, not to mention the aggression in Hungary and Czechoslovakia or the Soviet naval buildup, and most recently the Soviet-Egyptian missile cheating and the Soviet complicity in Syria's tank invasion of Jordan. The question then arises: what is peaceful coexistence to the Soviets? Is it strategy or tactics?

The CPSU theses on Lenin's birth centenary (April 1970) quoted the founding father on the subject: "Peaceful coexistence of states with differing social system presupposes an acute political, economic and ideological struggle between socialism and capitalism, between the working class and the bourgeoisie. Peaceful coexistence has nothing in common with class peace and does not in the least query the sacred rights of the oppressed people to use all means, even armed struggle, to achieve liberation."

Peaceful coexistence was proclaimed as a Leninist principle, although Stalin used it at his own convenience; it is a general line of the Soviet Union's foreign policy; it was included as an axiom in the program of the CPSU; and it was stressed at the Soviet Party's 20th congress, in the Moscow Declaration of the ruling communist Parties as well as in the Peace Manifesto of all communist Parties of 1957, in the Moscow Statement of 1960, in the main document of the 1969 international communist conference, and at the 24th congress.

But the communist Chinese have given the documents of 1957 and 1960 a more "revolutionary spirit" than the Muscovites.[3] What was really thought about this "illusion" was best described by Senator Jean Terfve, theoretician and Politburo member of the Belgian CP, who declared: "Peaceful coexistence is for the Chinese but a timely limited method of struggle and a temporarily applicable tool for the attainment of a definitive objective. This is a policy serving a purpose and not an end in itself ... We believe that our Chinese comrades, in spite of certain slighting remarks about the imperialists ... overestimate their own strength."[4]

Coexistence as an end in itself was advocated by the former Chinese Deputy-Minister of Foreign Affairs, Chang Wen-t'ien, a candidate member of the Politburo who was purged as a rightist and revisionist in 1959. This was three years after coexistence was recorded in the CPC statutes adopted at the 8th Party congress.

Khrushchev's idea of coexistence was formally approved by Mao Tse-tung in the Moscow Declaration and three years later by Liu Shao-ch'i in the Moscow Statement. But the question of the sincerity arises.

More sincere perhaps was Ch'en Yi, who said in his speech on the occasion of the 13th anniversary of the communists' take-over in China that capitalism and communism could not coexist.[5] Lin Piao, Mao's heir apparent, took the same line in his speech at the sixth Peking rally of the red guards in the presence of the "great supreme commander" in declaring the proletarian revolutionary line and the bourgeois reactionary line as "incompatible as fire is to water," a meaning directed at both the Chinese opposition and the Soviet revisionists,[6] which are equated with "capitalism."

Khrushchev himself made many statements on the subject, and even provided a definition of peaceful coexistence. "It means," he said, "mutual respect for each other's territorial integrity and sovereignty, nonaggression, noninterference in internal affairs, for economic, political or ideological reasons, equality and mutual advantage".[7]

But the definition is not his invention. It was mentioned in the five principles (*Panch Sheel*) of the Red Chinese formula for coexistence contained in the preamble of the Non-Aggression Pact concluded with India four years before in their agreement on Tibet.[8] Ironically, that Pact was mentioned in the Moscow Statement issued after the Red Chinese had invaded territory on the frontier with India.

Red China's five principles, however, had proved to be but a string of empty phrases. Yet, Chou En-lai revived them in a speech made on the eve of the 20th anniversary of CPR's founding and on other occasions.

In November 1968, the Peking Foreign Ministry called on the United States to join in "an agreement on the five principles of peaceful coexistence," linking it to an impossible condition—American withdrawal from Taiwan.[9]   Nevertheless, Moscow immediately accused Peking of "collusion" with Washington, a mirror image of what China denounced as Soviet-American "collaboration."

Khrushchev elaborated further on peaceful coexistence in a speech he made at Novosibirsk. "Coexistence," he said, "means the continuation of the struggle between the two social systems, but by peaceful means, without war, and without intervention by one nation in the internal affairs of another. We consider it to be an economic, political and ideological struggle, but not a military one."[10]

However, in a later speech on the same subject, he said:
Peaceful coexistence does not imply conciliation between socialist and bourgeois ideologies . . . The peaceful coexistence of states with different social systems presupposes an unremitting ideological, political and economic struggle of the working people inside the countries of the capitalist system, including armed struggle when they find that necessary *(sic!)*, and the steady advance of the national liberation movement among the peoples of the colonial and dependent countries.[11]

He explicitly denied that coexistence means status-quo: "No Marxist-Leninist ever interpreted peaceful coexistence of countries with different social systems as preservation of the status quo, as a sort of truce with imperialism, as a 'safe conduct' against revolutionary processes of national and social liberation. No one applies this principle to the relations between imperialism and oppressed peoples, since the principle of coexistence by no means places a 'veto' on the struggle of these peoples."[12]

At the 22nd congress of the CPSU Khrushchev said: "In contemporary conditions the perspective was discovered to obtain peaceful coexistence in the whole period, during which all the social and political problems, now dividing the world, should be solved."

The Soviet Central Committee's journal saw this as a historical necessity, dictated by the conditions of the present era, but not meaning a coexistence of ideas, since the ideological struggle will not be weakened.[13]

Therefore, peaceful coexistence is not actually a lasting condition of the free world's survival but rather it means an active world revolution. This is the substance of Khrushchev's speech to top Party theoreticians in which he said peaceful coexistence is a tactic that "promotes the growth of the forces of progress, of the forces fighting for socialism; in the capitalist countries it facilitates the work of the communist Parties and the other progressive organizations of the working class; makes it easier for the peoples to combat the aggressive war blocs and foreign military bases; and contributes to the success of the national liberation movement."[14]

An official Soviet definition of peaceful coexistence is: "This is a dialectical process which organically combines the sharpest class struggle between capitalism and socialism and the cooperation of nations with two opposing systems on behalf of the preservation of peace."[15]

And a Russian "scientific" definition of this tenet says:

Peaceful coexistence means ensuring sovereignty, territorial inviolability, political independence and equality of all peoples and countries, respect for systems chosen by the peoples, and recognition of the right of every people to choose, in conformity with its sovereign will, one or another form of government, as well as a new socio-economic system without interference in one another's internal affairs and without export of revolution and counterrevolution.[16]

However, following the Cuban missile crisis, the Russians took a much softer line: "Mutual concessions and sensible compromise . . . This is precisely the policy of peaceful coexistence in action."[17]

The present Soviet leadership calling itself a Leninist collectivity (*kollektivnost rukovodstva*), is "consistently defending the principles of peaceful coexistence in relationships between nations with different socio-political systems," although "supporting national liberation and revolutionary movements." But, the leadership adds, "the governments of certain Western powers should realize that the principle of peaceful coexistence is indivisible."[18]

This was later explained by Edvard Kardelj in a speech he made in Moscow: "[This does not mean] peace between the oppressed and oppressors. It is clear to everybody that world peace cannot be preserved at the price of conciliation with the oppressors' practice in whatever part of the world."[19]

The Soviet peaceful coexistence between military blocs is, according to the Yugoslav Party program, only "a temporary truce, concealing the danger of new conflicts." This was admitted by Warsaw Pact members in a statement issued in Bucharest in July, 1966, which declared that coexistence between military blocs is impossible.[20]

While the Soviet Central Committee's plenary session in April, 1968, claimed a "sharp aggravation of the ideological struggle between capitalism and socialism", the Soviets deny that peaceful coexistence is a temporary communist ploy and a tactical maneuver since, in their opinion, "history's objective laws" will lead to the victory of socialism and communism anyway. Professor Brzezinski has called this a "limited coexistence" with ideological rigidity and hostility toward the West.

At the same time the Soviets reject bridge-building as a kind of peaceful coexistence. They call such an endeavor a selective, discriminating coexistence, to be found toward some socialist countries. Under such a cover, they say, more advantageous conditions will be created for ideological diversion and subversive activity to undermine the Party's leading role and the socialist system internally, making way for the liberation of antisocialist elements. Individual socialist countries will then be wrested from the world communist system and, the Soviets fear, such activities will support the "splitting" intrigues of the Maoists. Soviet Party secretary Konstantin Katushev called bridge-building "a perfidious tactics ... aimed at undermining the cohesion of the socialist countries and causing friction between them", speaking at the 10th Rumanian Party congress, a few days after President's Nixon's conspicuously warm welcome in Bucharest. Therefore cooperative approaches to all east European states are advised by Professor Brzezinski, thus avoiding Soviet paranoia. He then elaborated: "We must adopt a position of peaceful concern toward the changes in the communist world, which is aimed at assisting changes in the Soviet orbit and in the Soviet Union; not peaceful coexistence, which is a static concept excluding the mutual penetration of ideas."

The third international communist conference proclaimed that peaceful coexistence

demands observance of the principles of sovereignty, equality, and territorial inviolability of every state, big and small, and noninterference in the internal affairs of other countries, respect of the rights of every people freely to decide their social, economic, and political system, and the insurance of a political settlement of outstanding international issues through negotiation. The policy of peaceful coexistence facilitates the positive solution of economic and social problems of the developing countries, [and] ... does not contradict the right of any oppressed people to fight for its liberation by any means it considers necessary—armed or peaceful. This policy in no way signifies support for reactionary regimes. It is equally indisputable that every people has the inalienable right to take up arms in defense against encroachments by imperialist aggressors and to avail itself of the help of other peoples in its just cause.[21]

The doctrine of peaceful coexistence was received skeptically in the West and the sincerity of the Soviet rulers questioned—although it did offer an alternative to the cold war and could possibly avoid a world holocaust.

The British foreign minister, the Earl of Home, said in an address to the United Nations General Assembly that the most dangerous cause of conflict "is the communist effort to impose their system on the rest of the world by that type of political warfare backed by force they call 'peaceful coexistence.' "[22]

The late West German Chancellor Konrad Adenauer said at a Washington Press Club luncheon that "in the future, when I hear peaceful coexistence mentioned again, I will think of Cuba."[23]

However, former Secretary of State Dean Rusk was more optimistic when he said: "We can take seriously the discussion of peaceful coexistence by the Soviet Union."[24]

The Japanese press considers the Soviet-American peaceful coexistence as a form of power politics.

Professor W. W. Kulski of Syracuse University, a former Polish envoy to Britain, said in his book *Peaceful Coexistence: An Analysis of Soviet Foreign Policy,* that the Soviet viewpoint during the period of nuclear stalemate was "To avoid an all out nuclear war . . .; to defend, at any price the Soviet part of the present international status quo; and to change, piecemeal and without an all out war, preferably by political, economic and ideological means, the status quo in the non-Communist world to the detriment of the West."[25]

Coexistence is not a communist invention, but an old pacifist idea. A book about its true meaning, entitled *Collision Course,* by Professor Henry Pachter of the New School of Social Research in New York City, examines the coexistence idea from Lenin to Khrushchev. Pachter concludes:

> Coexistence is not a durable relationship among good neighbors; it is not a durable guarantee of mutual security. Rather, it describes the conditions under which the two camps may compete for domination and world power. It is a form of conflict, not of reconciliation. It has become less cooperative and more antagonistic as its protective aspects have yielded to its aggressive potentialities. Its strategy is no longer the shield of a fledgling communist state, but the weapon of a strong power bent on conquest.[26]

In Professor Wolfgang Leonhard's opinion, coexistence is no more as a by-product of foreign policy objectives for the collective Soviet leadership because of its fragmentation of the decision making under neo-Stalinist pressure.[26a] This was before Brezhnev's ascendancy.

Ernst Kux, in his neutral Swiss view on coexistence, said: "Marxist theory and Soviet foreign policy prove that the policy of coexistence is a calculated manoeuvre to deceive the opponent, applicable and effective only within a particular constellation of power."[27]

Communist theoreticians have discussed the possibility of a peaceful transition from capitalism to socialism, but also such a transition would be, according to the Soviet Party program, a revolution, destroying the old state apparatus and leading to a dictatorship by the communist leaders.

Engels wrote in his book *Second International* that, ". . . any means that leads to the aim suits me as a revolutionary, whether it is the most violent or that which looks the most peaceful."[28]   Marx, and later Lenin, also spoke of a peaceful revolution involving fewer sacrifices.

The same dichotomy has been expressed in the Soviet Party program: "The success of the struggle of the working class for the victory of revolution will depend on the extent to which it and its Party learn to employ all forms of struggle, peaceful and nonpeaceful, legal and illegal, and on whether they are prepared for the swiftest and most surprising replacement of one form of struggle with another."

The essence of a peaceful transition is explained as dialectics of evolution and revolution by Soviet Professor M. Rozental:

The concept of the peaceful transition to socialism pertains to the form and not the content, not to the essence of the process. The content of this transition cannot vary.

Its essence always remains revolutionary: It is a revolution, a revolutionary leap, since it is accompanied by a radical change in the conditions of people's lives and the replacement of one social system by another diametrically opposed system. The critics 'on the left' [i.e. the Chinese], who canonize only the form of armed rebellion, also allege that to consider a peaceful form of the revolutionary leap from capitalism to socialism, possible under present conditions, is a betrayal of Marxism.

The essence of the matter here is to compel the bourgeoisie to surrender without armed resistance . . . and topple the monopolists [monopoly capital] from their commanding heights of economic and political positions.

These new features of development [after the communist takeover] however, affect neither the fundamentals of the dialectic law of the transformation of quantitative into qualitative changes nor the dialectical premise regarding the two stages of any process—the quantitative 'evolutional' and qualitative 'revolutionary.'[29]

This particular idea was accepted by Marxists and communists a long time ago. In 1920 the well-known Hungarian economist, Eugene Varga, alluding to a speech made by Marx in The Hague, wrote in his book *La dictature du prolétariat,* about the possibility of parliamentarianism in a period of socialist dictatorship without terrorism.[30]

The Stalinist dictator of Hungary Matyas Rakosi called such a way "salami tactic" in a lecture at their Higher Party School, meaning the destruction of leaders and political parties of which the communists had requested cooperation using most contemptuous means.[31] This is the bitter experience of "coalition" governments with communist participation in East Europe.

Khrushchev himself, in a speech at a congress of the Socialist Unity Party of East Germany, revealed that Stalin had inspired the 1946 British communist platform based on a peaceful road to socialism.[32]

This road was followed particularly by the Italian Communist Party. As a result of the heavy government intervention in Italy's economy, production was nationalized to a high level, and an "Italian way to socialism" was worked out with certain structural reforms, dealt with in a paper to the tenth Party congress.[33] The Italian communists also accepted the "state of the whole people" as a starting point for highly developed nations replacing the dictatorship of the Party. In such a socialist society there would be different political parties. The Secretary General of the Italian Communist Party Luigi Longo pointed out that the Soviet society could not serve as a model for others.

"A peaceful transition from capitalism to socialism along conditions of a multi-party system" was also considered at the 18th Congress of the French Communist Party.[34] Yet the communist maverick philosopher Roger Garaudy remarked that such a road was not tolerated either by the Chinese or by the Soviet leaders.

Such resolutions were criticized by the Chinese as a betrayal of the socialist revolution with all its violent implications.[35] On the contrary, the Chinese said, a peaceful transition, in Lenin's words, is an extraordinarily rare opportunity in the history of world revolutions. Therefore, in their opinion, the overthrow of the old regime is best achieved through an armed revolution. The Soviet magazine *Voennaya istoriya* (Military History) has claimed that "the oppressed peoples of the world" could carry out a socialist revolution through various forms of class struggle "under the condition of maintaining peace." But this idea has been attacked by People's Daily, which stressed the point that revolution means "the seizure of power by armed force and the settlement of the issue by war."[36]

Some form of "peaceful transition" has happened in Eastern Europe with Soviet intervention.

Peaceful competition is being used by all major powers, even by the Chinese themselves where they are trying to compete with the Soviet Union and the West. But the race of supremacy in armaments could thwart the ideals of peaceful competition if not checked in time.

The Motive Forces of U.S. Foreign Policy, edited and published by the Institute of World Economy and International Relations of the Soviet Academy of Sciences in 1965, asserts that provided there is "peaceful coexistence" between the Soviet Union and the United States, "the competition between the socio-economic systems and the ideological struggle between the two main antagonisms in the international arena will proceed within the confines of broad economic, diplomatic, scientific and cultural competition and cooperation, without bloody collisions and wars."

The book declares that "Soviet-American relations, the relations between the greatest powers in the world, constitute the axis of world politics, the main foundation of international peace."[37]

Khrushchev, in a report to the 21st Soviet Party congress used similar words: "The normalization of the international situation could be helped to a decisive degree by an improvement in relations between the Soviet Union and the United States of America, as the two great powers which shoulder special responsibility for the fate of general peace."

This "central issue" was again endorsed by President Nixon in his address to the United Nations General Assembly celebrating its 25th anniversary: "Their strength (of the great nuclear powers) imposes on them special responsibilities of restraint and wisdom. The issue of war and peace cannot be solved unless we in the United States and the Soviet Union demonstrate both the will and the capacity to put our relationship on a basis consistent with the aspirations of mankind."

On the other hand, the Chinese communists refer to Russia's three formal "peacefuls" collectively as peaceful evolution and regard it as a symbol of revisionism. But the concept is nonexistent in dialectics, and therefore a "metaphysical abstraction."[38]

The Meaningless "Two Entires"

As in the case of the three "peacefuls," the Chinese tend to exaggerate when referring to the Soviet's two "entires"—that of the State and the Party of the entire people. In fact, they accuse the Soviets of enforcing "a dictatorship of the privileged bourgeois stratum,"[39] replacing the dictatorship of the proletariat.

By way of contrast, the Soviet blueprint says that Party dictatorship will no longer be necessary, since the construction of socialism has been carried out in the Soviet Union.

However, the Soviet program declares that even "the period of full scale communist construction—that is, up to 1980—"will be characterized by a further enhancement of the role and importance of the Party as the leading and guiding force of Soviet society."[40] Thus, the Party-state will remain as it is.

At Moscow's 22nd congress Khrushchev said: "Those who are counting upon a softening of the general order in our state are destined for a bitter disappointment," and his successors have certainly not changed this view. Professor Robert Tucker of Indiana University is correct then when he termed the Soviet blueprint "a credo of conservatism."[41]

The real question is: how can a dictatorship wither away, during the construction of communism, when the essential element of the communist government system, the Party monopoly, remains, in substance, unchanged? This in fact means that the Soviet Union retains the weapon of class struggle in an allegedly classless society, as do other communist countries, where the socialist construction has not yet been completed.

The Chinese maintain that in the Soviet Union there are irreconcilable antagonistic class contradictions between the ruling "bourgeois stratum" and the people (the exploiters and the exploited), i.e. a class struggle is in fact going on. The Soviets reject such a contention which would justify the domination of administrative methods of violence in politics and economics,[42]—a euphemism for Stalinism.

In this polemic it is important to realize that the CPSU remains what it was, a dictatorship of the Politburo, and that "the Party and the state of the entire people" are again just Khrushchev's over-optimistic and boastful expressions without any deeper meaning. And since in practice this is so, Chinese ideological objections make no sense at all.

The two "entires" were not even mentioned at the 23rd Party congress, and in general, Khrushchev's Party program today is less often mentioned, particularly its optimistic predictions. The Soviet Union is now, of course, a developed socialist society. A gradual transition to communism belongs to the future.

Soviet Party leader Leonid Brezhnev made, in theory, a perceptible retreat when explaining the all people's state in his speech to the expanded plenary session of the CC on the occasion of the 50th anniversary of the October Revolution.[43] He recalled with approval the state of the dictatorship of the proletariat which "can exist and does exist in various forms." The CP remains "a necessary prerequisite for the building of socialism." The Soviet Union "has become" an all people's state. This is only, in fact, a heavily disguised form. He reaffirmed the continued validity of the dictatorship, contending that it is realizing a new form. Khrushchev probably believed the new form was replacing the old one. Brezhnev, however, said the all people's state is "continuing the cause of the dictatorship of the proletariat."[44] In this respect anarchists rightly held that the Marxist state is a more vicious slavery practiced in the name "of the people."

Identical views were expressed in the CC theses for the centenary of Lenin's birth, stressing that "the main instrument of building socialism is the dictatorship of the proletariat," while "the socialist state of the whole people" is serving for the construction of communism.

Brezhnev contradicted the Maoists much more with his contention that "social and national antagonisms have departed forever from the life of our society," leading it towards social homogenity in the words of the theses.

Regarding the running polemics with Peking he gave full approval to the policies of the 8th congress of the CPC, particularly to its "line for eternal and unbreakable friendship with the great USSR and all the peoples' democracies." He then excluded China and Albania from the peoples "under the banner of socialism" while including Yugoslavia.

The main problem of developing countries, Brezhnev pointed out, is social progress, and not turmoil as the Maoists continue to preach. About the same time the Chinese communists accused the Soviets of distorting the road to the October Revolution. They rejected the multifarious processess in the transition from capitalism to socialism, believing only in that of violent revolution, and backing this belief with quotations from Mao Tse-tung and Lin Piao.

The teaching of Marxism-Leninism is indivisible, said the theses, rejecting leftist and rightist distortions. Maoism was called a reactionary Utopian regimented socialism, brainwashing the people with militant anti-Sovietism, and with a pharisaical philosophy of poverty as a benefit.[44]

In the words of Lin Piao, the "great new development" of the Chinese revolution's road, as indicated by the October Revolution, was

the way the Chinese people seized political power by force of arms under Chairman Mao's leadership and may be summarized as follows: under the leadership of the political Party of the proletariat, to arouse the peasant masses in the countryside to wage guerrilla war, unfold an agrarian revolution, build rural base areas, use the countryside to encircle the cities, and finally capture the cities.[45]

The CPSU was accused of being a "bourgeois" political party with one-third of her membership made up of experts, with almost all her secretaries of regional organizations having a higher education, while the members with worker and peasant background were declining. They criticized even the big changes in the composition of the CC membership from the 19th congress of the CPSU while Stalin was still alive, up to the latest congress. This is the conclusion of the Maoist about the present Soviet leaders: "A mighty storm of proletariat revolution that is sure to sweep the Soviet land some day will undoubtedly overthrow the Soviet revisionist renegades and tear to shreds their black banner of 'the party of the entire people.' "[46]

The dictatorship of the proletariat (of one class) was theoretically transformed into an "all people's state." A similar idea of German socialist leader Ferdinand Lassalle was rejected by both Marx and Engels. Yet the self-imposed Soviet rulers remain the same, of course. They ("the working class") will have "completed" their role of leaders of society after communism has been built. A classless state should wither away, predicted the classics. The Soviet Party program promises that the organs of state power will gradually be transformed into organs of social self-administration.

It is true that in the Party program there is some indication that certain government-controlled bodies will become organs of public self-government. The blueprint goes so far as to envisage the gradual fusion of all mass organizations, such as the soviets on various levels, trade unions, *kolkhozes* and others, into one unified form of communist self-government. There is, however, no indication as to how this will work in the absence of any tradition of self-government under Soviet communist rule.[47]

In terms of Marxism there can be no state without antagonistic classes. The proclaimed "Party of the whole Soviet people" is nonsense, because, according to Marxism, the Party is the organized part of a class. Moreover, a cadre Party cannot be a mass Party. The statute of the Yugoslav Communist League defines the Party as "the organized political force of the working class and the working people."

According to the Soviet Party program state and law is closely linked, and Soviet law should express the will of the "all people's state." In fact, "law" should no longer exist in a classless society as an expression of the will of a nonexisting ruling class, according to the teachings of the communist classics. Arbitrariness in the Soviet Union was justified by the immunity of the state apparatus from legal regulations.

Thus, Yugoslav legal theorist R. D. Lukic believes that Soviet theory divorced itself from the sociological-class elements of Marxism, and accepted Kelsen's positivism-normativism. However, the main Soviet legal magazine, Soviet State and Law, said in 1959: "Every legal act, every legal norm in the socialist society, is dictated by the policy laid down by the Communist Party of the Soviet Union."

On the other hand, Soviet rulers (and similarly other communist rulers) are not restrained by the same law which they themselves created. Some legal functions in the Soviet Union, for instance, have been transferred to the "voluntary people's militia" and to the "comrades' courts," both Party controlled, opening the way to new arbitrariness. Socialist legality is proclaimed but there are no guarantees and no remedies for the protection of citizens, particularly shown in the indeterminate isolation of political dissenters in prison-psychiatric hospitals.[47a]

In spite of Khrushchev's de-Stalinization, Stalin's living spirit has remained in Soviet society, strengthened under the new leadership by the deceleration of that process.

The Dialectics of Strengthening the Socialist State

Significantly, no section of the Soviet program deals with the complicated problems of an allegedly classless society, a cause of headaches for the theoretical magazines *Voprosy filosofii, Kommunist* and *Oktyabr*. On the other hand, the program containes a chapter dedicated to the "Elimination of the Survival of Capitalism in the Minds and Behavior of the People."

However, the illusory withering away of the socialist state envisaged by Marx and Engels has been promised only after the building of a developed communist society, and the victory and consolidation of communism throughout the world. According to Khrushchev in his speech at the 22nd congress, this transition will encompass an entire historical epoch. In fact, no modern complex state can ever wither away, least of all a totalitarian state. In contemporary communism there exist many anachronistic Utopian formulas derived from the naive 19th century view of human perfectibility which found shelter in the pseudo-scientific secular faith of Marx (Leopold Labedz.) There are contradictions between an Utopian doctrine and the power needs of communist countries to fit the state into the Marxism mold by crippling or even directly falsifying it.

The Russians did not like Kardelj's preaching on the withering away of the state. The Soviet Party Central Committee organ commented: "In passing, one may ask the question: Is Kardelj really as ardent a protagonist of the withering away of the state and as strong an opponent of dictatorship as he proclaims himself to be? One has not heard so far that the army has withered away in Yugoslavia, or that tribunals and the police have vanished!"[48]

In this matter, the Chinese and the Russians do not quite agree. Mao himself writes:

Don't you want to abolish state power? Yes, we do, but not right now; we cannot do it yet. Why? Because imperialism still exists, because domestic reaction still exists, because classes still exist in our country. Our present task is to strengthen the people's state apparatus—mainly the people's army, the people's police and the people's courts—in order to consolidate national defense and protect the people's interests.[49]

In their program, the Yugoslav communists blame Stalin, saying: "This Marxist-Leninist theory was transformed into Stalin's theory of the state which is not withering away, and which has to grow even stronger in all areas of social life."

According to Marxism, the state had to wither away following the victorious socialist revolution and at the start of the transition period between capitalism and communism.

But Lenin's dictatorship of the proletariat relied directly upon force, and was not bound by any laws, while Engels believed there had to be a parliamentary republic, even an administration of things replacing the traditional government of persons. Such a contradiction of the strengthening and dying of the state was explained by Stalin as reflecting Marxist dialectics, while Kardelj called it the "eternalizing" of tht state. This dictatorship, Kardelj said, was a murky bureaucratic despotism, exploiting the mass of the workers, supported by the bureaucratic caste as a remnant of the capitalist class. He admitted that bureaucracy in a socialist country is the final and strongest fortress of the remnant of a class system, i.e. a class in itself. The late Boris Kidric, head of the Yugoslav State Planning Commission at that time, completely identified the socio-economic role of the Soviet bureaucratic caste to the role of the capitalist class. That was the time of "high Titoism."[50] Here Lenin can be quoted against himself: The *apparatchiki* "tower over the voiceless people like a dark forest."

Yet after the Soviet-Yugoslav reconciliation, Kardelj expressed a more positive attitude on the preservation of a socialist state. In Yugoslavia, he said, the state has had to remain because of the existing antagonism in its international relations, and the class antagonism within the country. However, the "withering away" process will be limited to social self-management of functions, in the areas of economy, culture, education and social services, which are never completely in the hands of a democratic state, but are a matter for free activities. Yet behind decentralization of state administration and economy stands the monopolist Communist League.

Kardelj even stood up in defense of socialist bureaucratism. It

makes no sense, he said, that the working class fights its own bureaucracy, although this was just what Marx advised. Kardelj denied the
class character of such a bureaucracy in a socialist state which is now
transforming into a self-management system.[51]

The Soviet conception of the state has not changed. The
standard book, Foundations of the Soviet State and Laws, says that
"the strengthening of the Soviet socialist state is the most important
condition for the construction of a communist society in USSR."

The strengthening of the state was justified by the necessity to
crush the remnants of the dying classes. The end of these classes was
officially announced by P. N. Pospelov, Party secretary, in April,
1958. Furthermore, The History of the Communist Party of the
Soviet Union, says "all exploiting classes have been liquidated," and
therefore, a classless state now persists. The Soviet state must grow
stronger, nevertheless, Khrushchev declared a year later, "so long as
there exist aggressive military blocs of Western states." In the collective work, Theory of State and Law, Soviet Marxists conclude that
the state will be preserved under communism, too, (i.e. after its
full-scale construction) if the danger of military attack from without
is not removed.

In Marxist dogmatic thinking, the state is an instrument of
coercion, of the ruling class and of class warfare. Hence, when there
are no more classes, the state, too, loses its *raison d'être*. This was
directed against any autocracy which had to disappear to make way
for a society, without classes, state and law, phenomena of superstructure, as a result of the changes in the production forces and
relations.

In reality, however, communists who came to power as professional revolutionaries and militant cadres, are builders of a new caste,
with great caste interests and a highly developed caste solidarity. As
Djilas says *they form a new class of owners and exploiters whose
power over men is the most complete known to history.*[52] The
original caste developed into a class.

One must recall the words of the Russian Marxist philosopher,
G. V. Plekhanov, who worked abroad with Lenin for many years and
died as an opponent of the Bolsheviks. He warned Lenin against
setting up a new "Inca ruling caste of the Sons of the Sun." Today
these "Sons of the Sun" rule over the communist empire; they are not

the rank-and-file communists, but the *apparatchiki,* Djilas' privileged "new class." Their totalitarian state is an instrument of the new ruling class (to apply Marx) against the whole people, who are more oppressed than ever before.

Trotsky first realized this phenomenon in the 1930's and called it a caste, whereas for Djilas in the 1950's, it was just a new absolutist class separated from the people, a means of suppression without precedence.

In the course of a secret service purge and reorganization of the League of Yugoslav Communists, the struggle against bureaucratic deformation of the system, called self-management, was particularly stressed. The Yugoslav Party program also closely watched Soviet bureaucratism which, in its interpretation, consists mainly of the merging of the Party and the state apparatus, which has become master of Soviet society. The Moscow *Kommunist,* in answer to this charge, quoted Lenin as saying: "Anyone who proposes to you to put an end to bureaucratism is a demagogue. We will fight bureaucratism for many years."

Professor Jovan Djordjevic of Belgrade University was linked both to Trotsky and the Maoists by a Soviet journal because he wrote that socialism was certain to overthrow its own army of bureaucratic exploiters,[53] and the Macedonian leader Krste Crvenkovski was quoted as saying the "working class," after the take-over of power, "must seriously defend itself against its own bureaucracy," which is not in agreement with Kardelj.

In Red China the bureaucracy was much the same as Russia's before the cultural revolution. Professor Doak Barnett of Columbia University listed 24 ranks in the Chinese bureaucratic stratification, depending on when the individual members joined the Party.[54]

But is a divorce of Party and state functions possible at all in a communist country? It was carried out in Yugoslavia ·in the ruling bodies of the League of Communists. But the problems mostly remain as they were in the past, and despite all endeavors to eradicate bureaucratism in Yugoslavia, the League's program is valid in recognizing such rampant tendencies:

In the arbitrariness of certain organs; in under-estimation of
the need to coordinate general and personal interests; in opposing the would-be higher goals of socialism to the care for

every day needs of the working man; in neglecting to build
institutions of socialist democracy; in bureaucratic centralism,
selfish particularism and nationalism and in attempts to weaken
and dismantle workers' self-management.[55]

The guidelines on the reorganization of the League of Communists have this to say about bureaucratism: "As Marx pointed out,
the working class is endangered through the possibility of independence of action by the administrative—social stratum entrusted
with administrative functions, — that is, by the bureaucratization of
its own political vanguard which begins to coalesce with the state
apparatus."

The ninth congress of the League rejected (in the sense of
Djilas) a "class-ridden bureaucratic élite" in the ideological-political
resolution. It was said that the congress finally broke with the Stalinist
concept after twenty years of de-Stalinization. Two Yugoslav theoreticians hold that socialist bureaucratism, an etatist class, is a collective
owner of the means of production (in the Soviet bloc) in contradiction with a quasi-ownership of self-managing enterprises in Yugoslavia. Therefore this class is more dangerous than attempts to restore
capitalist relations.[56]

One must admit that all these "deformations," (to use an expression much in vogue in Yugoslavia) were candidly recognized.
The reorganization and decentralization should help to remove these
tendencies of bureaucratism.

It was Lenin himself who created the Party "from top to
bottom," and from the professional revolutionaries developed the
Party bureaucratic caste. Rosa Luxemburg expressed considerable
concern early, in the piece about monopoly of power in the Party,
Jacobinism and absolutism of the Central Committee and the power
concentrated in the Politburo, and finally in the single dictator, *Vozhd*.
(This word has the same meaning as *Führer*.)

The same idea was expressed at a conference of scholars on
"Fifty Years of Communism in Russia," sponsored by Stanford University's Hoover Institution on War, Revolution and Peace. Bertram
D. Wolfe, a former communist and the author of *Three Who Made a
Revolution: Lenin, Trotsky, Stalin,* said that "Lenin had begun the
process that led to a totalitarian 'ideology of structure' by confusing
the people with the proletariat, the proletariat with the Party, the

Party with the Party machine and the Party machine with himself."[57]

In the Party of a "new type," unparalleled by any other political party in the methods used to fight for power and to keep it, lies the root of Stalinism, now covered up by the "personality cult." A full analysis of Stalinism has never been carried out by the Soviet Union or by other Parties because it would mean a complete unmasking of the true oppressive nature of communism. The Soviet press pointed out that such "honest people" as some Western communists accepted the "bourgeois thesis" of a Stalinist degeneration of the Soviet system. (Stalin himself called them—"honest fools"). The Chinese, by criticizing the Soviet idea of the state and the Party "of the whole people," see the degeneration in just the opposite terms.

Khrushchev made "two steps forward" unmasking Stalin's crimes. But the Soviet joint leadership later could not make one full "step back," (as it had been suggested before the 23rd Congress) to save the face of Soviet communism and to give the 50th anniversary of the Soviet Union a more distinguished façade separating the achievements from the former long dark years of terror. Yet the abatement of de-Stalinization continues.

Three Soviet historians have proposed that "the personality cult period" be eliminated as "unscientific" and "un-Marxist."

Another five Soviet historians condemned those collegues who critically wrote of Stalin's policy. It is not opportune "to slander" the historic experience of the CPSU at a time of sharp ideological struggle, they argue.[58]

The Soviet leadership's view on this thorny problem is given in the eighth volume of the Soviet Historical Encyclopedia: "An artificial overmagnification and glorification of the role of the personality of J. V. Stalin which is alien to the principles of Marxism-Leninism and which emerged early in the thirties: The practice of Stalin's personality cult produced the violation of the norms of Party and social life and of socialist legality." It further says Stalin violated Lenin's will (to shift him from his position of secretary general because of his negative qualities) and placed himself above the Central Committee, dodged its control, and fenced himself off from criticism, claiming for himself extraordinary achievements. The formulation was coordinated with the decision of the Soviet Party Central Committee of June 30, 1956.

In the third, revised edition of the History of the CPSU already mentioned, a balanced appraisal of Stalin portrayed him as the great wartime leader. This was understandable because Stalin betrayed his allies, defeated them politically, created the cold war lasting a quarter of a century, and made of the Soviet Union a superpower with pretensions equal to the United States although with less than half of the latter's resources. Marking the 90th anniversary of Stalin's birthday, *Pravda* praised him as a "foremost theoretician and organizer" notwithstanding his unwarranted repressions and theoretical and political mistakes.[59]

Even with this official explanation, however, Bolshevism and Stalinism, the root of all evil, cannot be excused for the *magnum crimen* in modern Russian and East European history.

Socialist Economic Efficiency and Public Ownership

In order to disguise the real motivation behind the Sino-Soviet rift, and to slander Russia in the best communist tradition, the Maoist propaganda constantly accuses the Soviet leadership of taking the "capitalist way." Similar distortions and falsifications were repeated by the Chinese in their own formidable purge and struggle directed against a majority of the communist veterans.

It might be predicted that the economy of mainland China after Mao's demise, or later, at the time of de-Maoism, will be approximately the same, if not worse, as the Soviet economy was after the death of Stalin. The communist compulsory economy has an intrinsic quality of self-destruction. Liu Shao-ch'i admitted as much when he said: "Our economy is approaching the verge of bankruptcy."[60] In the Soviet Union there was a form of non-admitted state bankruptcy. She suspended the payment of internal public debts for twenty years to avert inflation. The whole Soviet economy was chaotic with astronomical deficits, while the industry wasted resources at a phenomenal rate just to keep to the tenets of orthodox Marxism-Leninism. The accumulation of unwanted merchandise was worth several billion rubles.

This happened without the disastrous "great leap" and a second revolution which brought disorder to the economic life of mainland China, and these destructive effects were more fatal and far-reaching. During their economic convulsion the Soviets had to resort to several forcible internal loans, to devalue the ruble, to increase the price of main food stuffs, to allow black markets, and all the while trying desparately to get foreign loans at long term rates. All kinds of malpractices were necessary to keep the economy going at all. Meanwhile the rate of growth in production and the effectiveness of investments dropped much more than was admitted by Soviet official data.[61]

Khrushchev's idea was to balance the income and the expenses at any price, to put the Soviet economy again on a sound basis. He allowed criticism of the Stalinist system, of the *Gosplan* (the total economic plan for the whole country—*val*) with its over-centralization, and promised the introduction of scientific methods of econometrics and cybernetics. He decentralized the Soviet economy in regional units (*sovnarkhozes*) and allowed Professor Libermam of Kharkov in September 1962 to start his plan to improve industrial management by giving certain autonomy to single enterprises and to make profit, as an economic category of socialism, the criterion for their profitability.[62] This socialist profit should reflect "the usefulness" of one type of labor or another to society as a whole. In Soviet euphemism profitability means the rate of return on capital.[63]

Khrushchev prepared a radical economic reform, and was ousted for just this primary reason, according to one leading Sovietologist.[64]

His successors presented a more modest set of "technical-organizational measures" to the CC in September 1965, and later to the 23rd Party Congress, materializing what Khrushchev put forward at the previous congress. It included economic accountability (*khozraschet*), the raising of productivity (30 per cent of the American standard up to now), profitability, eliminating waste and rationalizing the price system, thus creating economic efficiency. The introduction of these measures was explained reluctantly and cautiously by the propaganda media, because a new economic theory has still to be worked out, and many *apparatchiki* are against the reform.

Kosygin's report to the CC was entitled: "On Improving Industrial Management, Perfecting Planning, and Enhancing Economic Incentives in Industrial Production." He said, essentially that economic problems can be solved only when "centralized planning is combined with the economic initiative of enterprises and collectives, with the increased application of economic levers [profit, price, bonus and credits], and material stimuli, and with sound business principles."

The Liberman experiment which finally got underway in 1966-67 now embraces many of the best Soviet enterprises, comprising 72 percent of the nation's gross industrial output and 80 percent of aggregate profit. The independence of enterprises has been increased and the material incentives for workers has been raised in accordance with the profit made.[65] The use of market-type controls is far from a socialist market economy in Yugoslav terms. Liberman claims that the manager who is getting only the key goals from the above, drawing up his own plan, working with the broad participation of the workers and whose wages and bonuses have substantially increased will get much better results. The performance of the enterprises is judged by the output sold and by the profit level, a better yardstick for guiding the work in a factory. In principle, Liberman says: "Central planning is entirely compatible with the initiative of enterprises in managing the economic profitability. This is as far from 'private enterprise' as the latter is from feudalism. The law of value is not a law of capitalism, but of any form of production for the market, including planned commodity production, which is what socialism is."

The hallowed communist principle of democratic centralism in the management of the Soviet economy was maintained. Liberman, stressing this point, said: "To strengthen and intensify central planning of production by combining it with the initiative and full economic accountability of enterprises is to realize the principle of democratic centralism."[66] The number of indices given by the *Gosplan* to the enterprise was considerably reduced, but the improper encroachment of superior agencies on the enterprise continues.

In another article, Liberman criticized what he called the dubious socialist theory of "full capacity," meaning that demand must exceed supply. The result, he said, are the lines that are part of the daily life of the Soviet Union. His theory is just the opposite: supply must exceed demand, and only then will the lines disappear,[67] resulting still in a fantastic weekly loss of around one billion rubles.

Another outstanding Soviet economist, the Academician Stanislav G. Strumilin, is critical of the "acute question": what is the permissible limit of the use of profit as a criterion for the effectiveness of production? He admits that in comparing the present reform with the New Economic Policy (NEP) of the twenties, they were compelled in both cases to "reckon with the dictates of the market in price formation, i.e. with the forgotten law of value." (Stalin executed the *Grosplan's* chairman N. Voznesensky for his "undue deference" to that law.)

Strumilin scores Liberman, "now a very celebrated Soviet economist in the West," for having proclaimed the need of high rates of profits, "ignoring the dialectics of social accumulation and consumption." Strumilin claims that this can be obtained only through higher prices that are advantageous to the enterprise, and disadvantageous to the consumer, reducing the real value of their earnings. High profit means expanding production through postponement of the workers' needs, and this is what the plan is allegedly balancing. Besides, the Soviet Party program does not call for maximizing profits, but for price reduction. Strumilin is afraid of localized tendencies because what is good for the individual enterprise is by no means always good for the country as a whole. He sees the key to economic reform in the closest combination of nationwide interests of planning and the most concrete down-to-earth interests in optimum fulfillment of the plan by all concerned. He also scores Liberman for being pledged to a "bourgeois ideal" and for negating socialist planning.[68]

Afterwards, Liberman published a book in which he retracted some of his theories. Now he contends that profit in socialism is not the main criterion of success. Market socialism and self-management of enterprises are for him a kind of cooperative socialism with anarcho-syndicalist ideas condemned by Lenin.

The Hungarian Marxist philosopher Gyoergy Lukacs, a rehabilitated maverick, critically analyzed the trend for economic reforms in the Soviet Union and in communist countries in general, concluding:

The most important thing ideologically is that this Stalinist transformation of the Marxist-Leninist method still persists... In this way, one successfully hinders a truly modern Marxist analysis of changes in the world economy. One also hampers the discovery of new economic traits; on the other hand, one introduces into Marxism a non-critical acceptance of certain Western 'discoveries.' Instead of self-criticism and a true reform of principle, what often develops is a link between bureaucratic and dogmatic conservatism and certain new slogans coming from the West.

Let us mention, for example, the proposals aimed at creating a theoretical—and purely bureaucratic—base for the planned economy. These seek their goal not through a return to purified Marxism—a non-dogmatic Marxism based on existing facts—but through a conservative bureaucracy armed with cybernetic machines.

It is increasingly clear that the mere overthrow of the absolute rule of the political police and the removal of the most exposed and expendable old Stalinists is insufficient if a properly functioning socialist economy is to be brought into being. The compelling influence of economic factors is therefore producing a real reform movement which is trying —regardless of theoretical considerations—to set free the real forces straining for economic renewal.[69]

In an interview with Radio Moscow, Liberman said that in capitalism as well as socialism surplus value in production is reflected in profit. These profits cannot be acquired by a private individual or by an enterprise. To the simplified view made by some Western economists that this is "capitalism without capitalists," Liberman ingeniously replied that this then is like a disease without a patient, in which case, there is no disease.[70] There is, in the Soviet Union, neither private ownership of the means of production nor the holding of stocks, since stock markets are nonexistent.

The abolition of the *sovnarkhozy* was neither a retrogression nor a strengthening of centralization over decentralization. The industry was again placed under separate Union and Republican ministries.

The economic reform did not, and could not, change the basic tenet of the Soviet Party program: "Communism is a class social system with one form of public ownership of the means of production." For the time being there is still a separate *kolkhoz* (collective ownership). The industrial enterprises are state-owned and the market is strictly controlled by the state.

Because of the principle of "one form of ownership," no special effective rights are granted to enterprises regarding the means of production they operate or their product. This undivided public ownership is a very important source of the Party's autocratic power and certainly prevents resurgence of capitalism with its multi-party system. The central *apparatchiki* surrendered only some of their power to the managers. Liberman complained about the enterprise director's limitations. "In political economy this means that the Party claims on the leader's authority, sovereign 'natural' rights of ownership over a country's economy,"[71] as was so clearly explained by Djilas. The Polish people are calling the communist rulers "the owners of Poland." How unlimited are the powers of those owners in comparison to Western capitalists! Factory administration by workers' self-management as applied in Yugoslavia is opposed to the Russian principle. Public ownership is divided.

The reform was called a new economic policy at a higher level. The former Moscow municipal Party leader Nikolay Yegorichev said that communism could be reached with the help of commercialism under Party supervision.[72] The reform, he said, should also serve the policy of peaceful competition with the West.

The alarming Soviet agricultural situation was thoroughly discussed at the CC plenary session in March, 1965. It took two years to start a cost accounting system in a number of *sovkhozy* on an experimental basis, and by January 1, 1969, 3,679 were using the system. In some *kolkhozy* a small team system was established working on parcels of land given to them for their free use. The new model charter omitted it. Private sectors in agriculture are no longer hampered, but private plots constitute no more than 3.3 percent of the total cultivated land. Even so, they provide one-third of the total production of meat and milk, and half the production of vegetables, evidently proving the superiority of private enterprise over collective and state enterprises. The new *kolkhoz* charter brought no improvement. However, the new system could not work well without a substantial increase of capital investment in agriculture (25 percent of the total) which was promised at the CC session in July 1970 providing new incentives by raising prices for meat and dairy products paid by the state.[73]

Both Russia and China had to import massive quantities of wheat (more than 33 million tons) from the West. Both the *kolkhoz* and rural markets in China were allowed as a concession to the peasant's resistance. To call these modest measures a "new *kulak* economy," as the Chinese are indeed calling it, is sheer nonsense.

The Russian answer to the Chinese[74] critics on economic revisionism is also valid for the Yugoslavs:

Implementation of the reform will strengthen centralized planning and the management of public property. At the same time, the enterprises are given broad scope for displaying initiative aimed at fulfilling the national economic plan...A reduction in directive plan indices, the strengthening of the economic autonomy of enterprises, and more consistent implementation of the principle of economic advantage in the development of production—all these substantially raise the personal responsibility of the executive and of each worker to the collective and of each production collective to society for the results of their economic activities.

Profits under socialism are explained as a cost-accounting category, one of the forms of surplus value which goes allegedly to the people. As opposed to the Chinese ascetic self-denial on poverty during the complete period of the construction of socialism, the Russians "call for paving the way to a better future for their descendants by doing everything to make life happier and richer *today* for their contemporaries." Defending the commodity-money relationship, taken over from capitalism, the Russians claim it has acquired under socialism a qualitatively new content, which is important in solving the task of communist construction.[75]

In answering the critics of the reform, Professor A. Rumyantsev and two colleagues of his told orthodox Marxists not to submit "as proof only quotations which contradict the creative spirit of scientific communism." Surprisingly, the three professors presented the labor collectives as socialistic co-owners, closer to the Yugoslav form, meaning that labor should not be a hired commodity.

Market socialism is rejected in the over-all plan because "the market, trade, and the economic instrument of the law of value do not command under socialism, they are themselves subordinate to the planning principle." The problem remains, however, of "how to improve the mechanism of operation of the law of value within the framework of a planned economy and democratic centralism in the economy. This mechanism consists above all in planned price formation."[76] It is manifest that market socialism embarrasses Soviet theoreticians because it tests the planners.

At the All-Union conference assessing the economic reform in mid-May, 1968, many shortcomings were reported, although the national income was 25 percent higher in the enterprises embraced by the reform over the last two years than in the five year period before the reform. The central plan still imposes essential elements which go into the making of an enterprise plan. The Party planners have their preferences but the consumer influence is not yet sufficiently taken into account. The procurement of supplies and the sale of products are hampered by bureaucratism, the material stimulation is not satisfactory, and the authority of factory directors is whittling away. The Central Planning Committee still directs the production of two thousand important articles, and the Union ministries of 38,000. The conclusion can be drawn that the transfer of the new system to less successful enterprises will be done with much more caution.[77]

The Joint Economic Committee of the U.S. Congress, in its analysis of Soviet economic performance after the first two years of reform concluded that "modest reforms have been only partially implemented and they have had little effect so far upon the operation of the enterprises concerned."[78] However, this is only a "first impression" verdict.

A much broader negative picture of the Soviet economy was given by the Yugoslavs in the wake of the Czechoslovak crisis. The economic reform alarmed the bureaucratic-conservative forces who feared that this trend would go even further.

Heavy industry is still favored in the Soviet Union and it grows five times faster than light industry, and thirty times faster than agriculture. On the other hand, 70 percent of the Soviet population has an inadmissively low standard of living, since the prices of most important consumer goods are often many times higher than those in Yugoslavia, where the prices are nearing world standards.

Particularly revealing are the diverging interests between the Russian and Ukranian republics. In Moscow the interest lies in developing Siberian industrial power to resist any possible Chinese pressure, while in Kiev, since the Ukraine is the most developed union republic, the interest lies more in developing the consumer goods industry.[79]

The Soviet Union is compelled to carry on its reform because 50 percent of industrial enterprises operate without profit, the majority of agricultural state farms operate at a loss and the majority of collective farms make no profit, according to one Russian émigré scholar.

For the slowdown of the Soviet economy in 1969 there were two explanations. The supporters of the economic reform charged the conservatives of sabotaging it, while the latter complained that evading plans, wage inflation and squandering of resources brought about Brezhnev's discouraging account. However, profits, incentives, and factory independence were again stressed by Brezhnev.[80]

The Maoists, who are the first to denounce Soviet profit-making, are themselves making handsome profits. An *Asahi Shimbun* correspondent who accompanied a Japanese economic mission to Peking, reported that the amount of profit in China is exorbitant due to the communist exploitation of the impoverished Chinese masses. The mainland Chinese even use a translation from Russian, meaning appropriated profit, previously called expropriated profit.[81]

French expert in communist affairs, Lucian Laurat, analyzing the history of the economic transformation in the Soviet Union, commented that they had come only a very short way on the road to profitmaking, and that on the road to capitalism, they had taken not one step. Assertions to the opposite are either Chinese communist distortions, or wishful thinking of Western optimists,[82] the introduction of capital charge on fixed and working capital in enterprises and of operative interest rate on long-term loans notwithstanding.

German author Georg von Wrangel, after examining the economic reforms and their meaning in the Soviet Union and other East European countries, excludes radical change. The political interests of the Party monopoly will always prevail over economic common sense for fear of losing control, he says. He doubts that there will be a convergence of the two systems, and concludes: "To maintain that the introduction of our Western economic methods brings with it a *fundamental* change of structure and economic policy in the national economies of the Eastern bloc is to confuse the means with the ends." And that is the communist nature of their economies.[83]

Irreconcilable Antagonism

Since the "schismatic meeting" (in the words of Peking) in March, 1965, in Moscow of 16 communist Parties to prepare the third world conference of the movement, the activities of the Soviet leaders have become "more diabolical and scheming," pursuing Khrushchevism "with double-faced tactics, more cunning and with more hypocrisy."

The People's Daily particularly blamed Brezhnev and B.N. Ponomaryov, CC secretary, in the form of a thesis and antithesis: "The new Soviet leaders cause a schism while advocating 'unity,' come up with anti-Chinese activities while speaking of 'improving' the Sino-Soviet relations, fabricate rumors, and smear and slander the CPC and other Marxist-Leninist Parties while talking about 'ceasing polemics'... [They] have carried out frequent and numerous anti-Chinese instigations at home and carried out covert anti-Chinese activities in many places abroad."[84] This was during the period between the downfall of Khrushchev and the start of the cultural revolution, when the Soviet leaders formally kept their self-imposed ban on polemics—with a number of exceptions which Peking referred to as "out and out shams."

The Soviet anti-Chinese propaganda was followed by speeches, reports and articles by communist leaders and Party press of East Europe (with the exception of Romania), Italy and France. It was understandable in view of the increasing number of reports of Chinese activities on African and Asian soil aimed at destroying the authority of the USSR and the CPSU.[85]

Peking sent wrecker teams to one leftist international conference after another where they publicly attacked and slandered the Soviets. Making use of confusion and blackmail, the Red Chinese delegates hoped to oppose both white and colored peoples, cultivating a misanthropic ideology of racism. At the Afro-Asian Peoples Solidarity Organization council session in Nicosia, Cyprus, only three out of 52 delegates supported the Peking stand. Previously, at Havana, the delegates of the first conference of the Afro-Asian and Latin American leftists rejected the Red Chinese demand to play a leading role in this three continent movement. They had similar trouble at sessions of the World Peace Council, and in other leftist and procommunist international organizations.

Meanwhile Peking has created a few Afro-Asian "split" front organizations such as the Journalist Association, the Writers' Permanent Bureau, the Lawyers' Conference, and the Peace Liaison Committee for the Asian and Pacific Regions, of which only the first one shows some activity.

These tactics came to an end at the 16th general council meeting of the World Federation of Trade Unions, held in Sofia in early December, 1966. The Chinese asked for the expulsion of the Yugoslavs as observers, and later abused the Soviets. After they had repeatedly disturbed the proceedings, the Chinese were ousted for 1) violating the standing orders, 2) not being representative, 3) the unclear situation in the Chinese Federation of Trade Unions. This was the first time the Chinese had effectively been barred from a meeting of any communist-dominated world organization, and by a majority of fifty nations—as opposed to a minority of eight (China, Albania, Romania, North and South Vietnam, North Korea, Cuba and Venezuela.) As a result, Peking decided to boycott such international meetings which are now dominated by the Russians.

The Soviets, commenting on the Chinese boycott, said: "The Chinese schismatics, after suffering an outright defeat in their solicitations, considered it correct to leave the organization and by this action have isolated themselves from the broad peoples' masses of the two continents."[86]

Both the Party and state relations have deteriorated at the same time. "The Chinese people cannot trust you," was the Chinese reaction, as it was once before during Khrushchev's time, when a Chinese Party Central Committee letter of February 29, 1964, to its Soviet counterpart rejected the offer for returning Soviet ex-

perts to China, saying: "The [Chinese] enterprises have just healed the wounds caused by your withdrawal of experts." Symptomatic of the existing bad state of relations between the two communist giants is the underground war being waged between Soviet
and Chinese intelligence agents around the world.[87]

According to the Soviet Party Central Committee confidential
circular letter of February, 1966, Peking had in April, 1965, repudiated an offer to cooperate with the Soviet Union in construc-
ing industrial projects as provided for in the 1961 trade agreement.
In early July, 1965, the Chinese also withdrew its scientists from
the joint nuclear research institute at Dubno, and refused to cooperate with the socialist countries in space research.

On the one hand, the Chinese press invites the people of the
Soviet Union to overthrow its government, having "no alternative
but to fight them to the end,"[88] and on the other, the Chinese
leadership has propagated the possibility of military confrontation
between China and the Soviet Union. Professor Hans Morgenthau
might be right in saying that the Soviet Union is mortally afraid
of China. The confidential circular letter makes it clear to its re-
cipients of the Soviet Union's growing concern of the military-poli-
tical demands of its Asian defense.

Peking, however, fears encirclement from what it calls the "holy
alliance" against China.

Behind the Sino-Soviet polemics lie the profound differences
regarding the general line of the international communist movement,
the fundamental problems of world revolution in our time, and how
best to promote it by subverting established governments. The
polemics deepened with the letter from the CPSU Central Committee
of March 30, 1963, to the Chinese Central Committee, raising all
the problems which had arisen between Russia and China after
the 20th Soviet Party congress. The CPC Central Committee answered with a letter, already mentioned, particularly stressing that
the ultimate victory of the communists in Asia, Africa and Latin
America will also lead to the conquest of the industrial countries
of the Northern Hemisphere, anticipating Lin Piao's treatise.

Commenting on the second anniversary of that letter, an article
which appeared both in People's Daily and Red Flag said that
there "was not a shade of difference" between the present

leaders Brezhnev and Kosygin, and Khrushchev. At the celebration of the Bolshevik revolution in 1964 the Soviet leaders explicitly told Chou En-lai that "they had not the slightest difference with Khrushchev in their...attitude toward China." But compared with Khrushchev, the Chinese said the present leaders "are practicing a more covert and more dangerous revisionism." The "soul" of their revisionist general line is "Soviet-U.S. cooperation for domination of the world."[89]

For the Chinese the emergence of modern revisionism is not a fortuitous phenomenon but rather the product of a class struggle. This was pointed out in the joint 1957 Declaration: "While the essence of the bourgeois influence is the domestic root cause of revisionism, submission under the pressure of imperialism is the foreign root of revisionism."

The vital ten voluminous articles written by the editorial departments of *Jen-min Jih-pao* and *Hung Ch'i* together with the letter of June 14, 1963, were published in a book called *Polemic on the General Line of the International Communist Movement*. It contains an appendix with the Soviet letter of March 30, 1963, and the "open letter," a rejoinder,—the most important documents of the "irreconcilable great debate." An ideological coexistence with the Soviet leaders was excluded in the book's text.[90]

The contents of the book deal with the main issues of the schism, including the Soviet views on foreign policy which range from their efforts to curry favor with the U.S. to the renunciation of the fight against "imperialism" and their policy of peaceful coexistence. The Chinese views include the glorification of Stalinism, identifying it with communism, splitting activities in communist Parties and depicting Yugoslavia as an allegedly noncommunist country.

Khrushchev's collected speeches and writings were compiled and published in China under the title "Statements by Khrushchev."[91] They were made available to Chinese Marxists as an "encyclopedia of modern revisionism." The collection was intended to run to some 10 million characters in thirty volumes, but was issued in Peking with considerable hacking.

The first two volumes were published at the height of Khrushchev's ideological war with Communist China, covering the period between 1932 and 1953. The third one appeared after his ouster and more followed eventually, dealing with his eleven years as first Soviet Party secretary and premier. In a publisher's note to the third volume, Khrushchev's works were labeled as "truly a flood of putrid verbosity." The collection contains every word the former Soviet chairman ever uttered in public, his speeches, his reports, press interviews, letters, cables, and articles which appeared in the communist press. Only one famous speech was excluded from the collection—that on Stalin, which was never made public in the communist world, but which reached the U.S. through sources in Yugoslavia.

Khrushchev's Chinese editors explain that the fallen Soviet leader's use of the three "peacefuls" and the two "entires" symbolize revisionism as it is inherent in the Soviet political doctrine today. Under new slogans Khrushchev did away with the communist revolution and the dictatorship of the Communist Party. In the editors' view, Russia's present top executives are no better.

The editors upbraid Brezhnev and Kosygin for destroying Khrushchev's works, photographs and portraits. "What is the use of confiscating and burning books? Can it possibly prove that Khrushchev's revisionism has been thrown overboard?" they query. "Khrushchev's revisionism is a vast poisonous weed. When uprooted it can be used as fertilizer... Dialectics cannot develop without the repudiation of metaphysics," they add. Khrushchev's works are providing the communist world "with a mirror in which to distinguish Khrushchevism without Khrushchev"—personified by the present Soviet leaders—"in order to carry the struggle against Khrushchev's revisionism through to the end."[92]

But the cultural revolution changed these views. The publishing of Khrushchev's works was explained as a "perfidious plan" of the toppled CC propaganda department to indirectly discredit Mao's points of view and actions on revisionism. Therefore, not a single new volume from the "negative example" of Khrushchev has been published.[93]

Almost half-a-year after Khrushchev's downfall *Hsin-hua*[94] attacked Moscow for the book The International Revolutionary Movement of the Working Class. The book, labeled anti-Chinese, was a leftover from the previous era. (Generally, after Khrushchev's ouster the Soviet leaders were restrained on the great schism and on Chinese attacks against them.) It was published by the Soviet State Publishing House for Political Literature and gives great play to Khrushchev's revisionism. In the opinion of the Chinese, Khrushchev's ouster has meant only a "change of signboards." Mao Tsetung and other Chinese leaders are rabidly attacked by name in the book, and are given many political labels such as neo-Trotskyism, petty bourgeois nationalism, left-opportunism, ultra-revolutionary, theoretical messianism, adventurism, hegemonyism, nationalism, Chinese dogmatists and "splitters."

The book only intensified the anti-Chinese agitation in the Soviet Union and deepened the split. The Chinese 25-point program for world communism is rejected as "unacceptable and harmful", and the book accuses the Red Chinese of advocating "the path of war as a means of pushing the world revolution" and proposing "to test the durability of the capitalist system by means of war." They are proclaiming the national-liberation movement in Asia, Africa and Latin America as well as the peasantry in general as the prime moving force of world revolution. The newly independent countries should solve the task of economic liberation with "rifles and guns." The revolution should be exported by means of war.

The Chinese, the book adds, are neglecting the principal class contradictions and are advancing "the petty bourgeois and even the national bourgeoisie to the leading role in the world revolutionary process." The editors say that "economic competition between the opposing social systems is the concentrated expression of class struggle on a worldwide scale."

The Chinese are "portraying the future communist society as something between a primitive community and a baracks-like settlement, in which consumption is kept to the barest minimum and where there is no place for personal interests."

However, the Chinese denied the Soviet claim that "the Peking leaders have raised the demand for the redistribution of the national income and national wealth of the Soviet Union and of other economically developed socialist countries among the less developed countries of the socialist community with a view to dragging these countries down to a certain average level."

The Soviets accuse the Chinese "of vituperation against peaceful economic competition, rejection of peaceful coexistence, and staking war." They say it is wrong that China "should impose its own formulas and dogmas upon all Communist Parties."

The ideological differences have extended to interstate relations, and the Chinese have gone so far as to raise the "absurd demand for a reexamination of the international boundary of the Soviet Union in favor of China."

The Red Chinese attacks are, for the Soviets, "intolerable, crude and insulting,"—merely mud slinging tactics. For the sake of revolution the Red Chinese leaders are prepared to pay the price of a world thermonuclear war and to agree to the destruction of half of mankind.

A revised edition of the same book appeared in 1965 and this time the attacks on Chinese views and policies were left out. This was just an exception. However, at the same time, a collection of anti-Chinese papers such as Suslov's report, the "open letter," and other Soviet documents and publications of the same kind were available in book form for Soviet Party agitators entitled *For the Solidarity of the International Communist Movement.* Also, anti-Chinese pamphlets have usually been available in Soviet book booths.

Criticizing Brezhnev and Kosygin by name, the Chinese leading newspaper and theoretical journal declared: "There are things that divide us and nothing that unite us, things that are antagonistic and nothing that is common."[95] It is, they said, "an irreconcilable antagonism," a "class antagonism" between the Marxist-Leninists who represent the proletariat, and the Soviet revisionists representing, in the Chinese opinion, "the bourgeoisie."

The Chinese contradicted themselves by admitting that communists can defeat "imperialism" only through uniting their forces and "uniting with all other forces that can be united," and yet, at the same time, refusing to take "united action" with the Soviet Union.

A year after Khrushchev's downfall the Soviets sporadically answered[96] the Chinese vitriolic abuse, calling the Chinese reply to a Soviet invitation for a "united action" in Vietnam a hostile, provocative slander "in the ferocity of its attack and crudeness of tone," doing "tremendous harm" to the communist cause throughout the world. The Chinese said bluntly that unity of action of the CPC with the CPSU is impossible since the two Parties are "diametrically opposed." They ominously threatened "to draw a clear line of demarcation both politically and organizationally between themselves and the revisionists," and "to discard those decaying old revisionist groups and build new revolutionary Parties."

In its answer *Pravda* took a note from China's own attitude, calling for "an organizational disassociation" from the Soviet Union, pledging themselves to "carry the debate to the end," i.e. to perpetuate the schism. Yet the Soviets refrained from a complete break.

To add fuel to the fire, TASS news agency had to issue corrections to a report delivered by D. S. Polyansky, Soviet Politbureau member, at the celebrations of the 48th anniversary of the October revolution, on two issues which are fundamental in the Sino-Soviet altercation. In the first instance, the following sentence was deleted: "It is not through a world war by nuclear missile weapons but in peaceful economic competition that the question of which system is better, capitalist or socialist, will be decided." Secondly, the eye-catching phrase "Soviet-American cooperation" was left out. Polyansky blundered and the Chinese believe he let the cat out of the bag.[97]

Perhaps the inferred relationship could best be described as a U.S.-USSR condominium or, as Cyrus Sulzberger called it "explicit enemies, implicit allies," a relationship somewhat disturbed by Peking's tactical conciliatory gestures without changing its basic policy.

CHAPTER X

Presages of The Tempest

Cataclysmic Collapse

Mainland China, for its massive land area, has the potential of a medium-sized nation. Although fertile valleys line the big rivers of the east (arable land comprises 12 percent only), it is mostly an arid land of barren mountains and deserts, plagued by recurring natural disaster. The Chinese are irretrievably burdened by their country's underdevelopment. Even Mao has admitted that his country is "very poor" and "economically backward."[1] Ambassador George Ball has called China a "light heavyweight" with a *per capita* daily wage of twenty-five cents, or "the elephant described by blind men."[2]

Under Mao's regime, the Chinese are fenced in against the outside world and the experiences of others. As Dean Rusk has said, the Chinese communist leaders vision of the world is unreal. Their state of mind was a "combination of aggressive arrogance and obsessions of [their] own making." And Secretary of State William Rogers stated in an address to the National Press Club in Canberra, Australia: "Although we are inclined to speak of China as a great power, we should remember that this power is potential more than actual. I believe there is a tendency in many quarters to build up the Chinese communists by equating their capabilities with their rhetoric."

The Chinese communists, under the influence of Mao, have taken measures against the laws of human nature and of natural laws themselves since before the cultural revolution. Reliable reports from the mainland suggest China has become a giant on clay feet because the policies of the regime were not viable in human terms, according to Professor Benjamin Schwartz. The prospects of nuclear war need not be taken too seriously. The regime of Mao Tse-tung, which has called other powers "paper tigers," is itself a weak one.

After the take-over, the Chinese communists were forced to launch five cultural rectification campaigns against anti-communists, anti-Maoist writers and various intellectuals. In the area of ideology, the short-lived (six weeks) campaign called "Let a hundred flowers blossom, let a hundred schools contend" after an old Chinese saying, which took place in the spring of 1957 after a speech by Mao at the supreme state conference, was a failure, a fake interlude. The campaign served merely to flush out Mao's enemies so he could identify and purge them. It was later officially described as a "dark scheme." The CPC however, was bitterly criticized and the Party leadership realized it could not afford to bring such serious criticism upon itself again.

At that time the big character posters, which were to appear later during the cultural revolution, were seen for the first time throughout China criticizing the Chinese communist leadership which was being untiringly praised in the completely controlled media. Roderick MacFarquhar, former editor of *The China Quarterly*, in his book quoted one NCNA journalist who deplored the general lawlessness: "The high-ranking cadres violate law and discipline while the lower echelons have little regard for the law. They do not hesitate to perpetuate any evil save manslaughter and arson . . . the central gavernment should be held responsible for this."[3] It was the moving outcry of the intelligentsia longing for freedom.

The Italian leftist writer Alberto Moravia commented figuratively at the time that a whole bouquet of flowers had been uprooted leaving only one, the "great, immense, aggressive, exclusive flower" of Mao Tse-tung.

Several years later, after the big collapse, the "contention" was revived—with limitations to academic, literary and artistic circles. The Communist leadership expected from the intellectuals a *mea culpa*. They must change or be changed. But they turned out to be anti-Maoist.

Peking's policies in general swung to the left in September-October of 1957 during the Central Committee plenary session when it became clear that the regime could not afford any relaxation of its authority. Peking was dissatisfied with Krushchev's leadership of the international movement—"a hen among the dung-heaps"—he was called—particularly after he made his *fait accompli* speech denouncing Stalin's crimes. It was then that the anti-rightist campaign began, and for three years, from 1957 to 1960 purged those in opposition to the regime. Over 1.8 million people were investigated. Peking claimed to have discovered 100,000 counter-revolutionaries and rightists in the administration—five percent of the apparatus—and 5,000 in the Party, 620 in the highest government bodies.

Abandoning the Soviet economic model followed from 1949 to 1956, Red China embarked on her own policies. The Soviet model was unsuitable to the Chinese communists not only in the economic, but also in political and cultural areas.

According to the view of the Kremlin hierarchy, the construction of socialism in the Soviet Union was almost completed, and the building of communism was approaching. It was then that Mao decided to pass over gradual stages of economic development, and to attempt with "the great leap forward" by means of economic short-cuts and the people's commune system to make hasty communism out of the human sea of China, skipping the necessary economic and technological foundations.

Yugoslav correspondents in Peking have reported—but with some restraint—over the years on the absurdities of Red Chinese policy. They were the first to give notice of the recall of all Soviet technical experts from China in June 1960 under the pretext that the Chinese had tried to influence them and had barred Soviet political instructors from working among them. This was a big blow to progress on the mainland and put excruciating pressure on the Chinese economy. Within one month, 1,390 Soviet experts were withdrawn. At the same time, the Russians scrapped 343 contracts and agreements with the Chinese, and abolished 257 scientific and technological cooperation projects.[4]

The chaos of "the great leap" was described in great detail. Ninety million peasants (Mao's own figure) were taken out of the fields to make cast-iron and steel in backyard furnaces, and to engage in fantastic public works projects. The quality of the produce from these rural furnaces was very poor, and the iron and steel had to be reprocessed in big foundries.   Through the construction of canals and locks in mammoth irrigation and dam-building projects there were spectacular failures in water conservation.

During the resettlement of the embittered peasants, following the breakdown of the campaign, about thirty million persons were transported from urban and industrial centers back to the villages, even though eighty percent of the population of the Chinese main-land lived in the countryside in creeping poverty. The reset-tlement involved mostly people who had come to the cities after 1957, one third of the urban working force, a fact confirmed later by Chou En-lai at the National People's Congress.   Some were ordered to move to specific places in the remote border areas. These displaced and hungry hordes had been of great concern to Peking. On the other hand, many craftsmen and industrial workers were sent back to the towns from the countryside where they participated in the "industrialization" of the communes.[5]

It cannot be doubted that the cataclysmic collapse of the two Red Banners, "the great leap," and the people's communes has damaged the whole Chinese communist triptych, including the first Red Banner, the new general line of building socialism-communism. The 8th Party congress explicitly forbade hasty industrialization. It was a "great leap" into uncertainty and danger.   An ignominious retreat was unavoidable.   An "adjustment" was decreed at the 9th Central Committee plenary session in January 1961, suspending the "great leap" and reducing the power of the communes, to halt a further decline in production.   Professor Wittfogel called Mao's retreat a "controlled madness."

The national economy was completely shattered, the country-side thrown into abysmal confusion.   The "great leap" had wrought havoc. The communes brought with them an unprecedentedly crude rule and miserable suffering. The breakdown had occurred under the strain of the follies and cruelties of Mao's "Caesarian madness", another adequate comparison of Professor Wittfogel. It manifested the extreme discontent of the peasantry, although collectivization had been carried out with vertiginous haste. The experience proved once again that it is impossible, even with ruthless communist coer-cion, to build an industrial power in so short a time, and to consolidate agriculture, so vulnerable to natural calamity, by abusing nature and human beings.[6]

This was the official explanation of the collapse as it was repeated many times: "In 1962 China was encountering temporary economic difficulties as a result of the perfidity of the Krushchev revisionist renegade clique and the three successive years of natural calamities."[7] In addition provincial and district Party secretaries were blamed for the failure. They were charged with not having properly implemented and supervised the instructions and of not having "enough aroused" the masses.

This conception of communism in poverty was again in Peking's declaration of ideological independence from Moscow when Liu Shao-ch'i proclaimed the international significance of the people's communes for the whole communist world in the last Chinese contribution to the *World Marxist Review* made in October 1959. He is now accused of having been against the communes.

The policies governing the communes were a series of vacillations and more retreats.[8] Finally the communes had to be decentralized into production brigades and village teams, reduced to a "*kolkhoz*" in the opinion of Professor Schram. The structural changes have so altered the communes that it can be said they are no longer integrated economic units. However, they remain basic administrative units with responsibility for their own "internal security," local industry, financial, banking and irrigation projects.[9] Following this, the Chinese leadership was forced to withdraw its previous claim that the communes were a short-cut to communism. This was an Utopian dream, they had to admit.

Mao has remained a symbol of victory throughout his life, but experience showed he was an inept ruler. His mistakes compelled him to resign as head of state and retire into the "second line" after bitter wrangling at the 6th Central Committee session in Wuhan in December 1958. This was revealed in a printed eight-page wall newspaper about the national work conference's top leadership meeting held on October 25th, 1966, when Liu Shao-ch'i and Teng Hsiao-p'ing made self-criticism for the first time. Mao was treated by the session at Wuhan "as if," he said, "it were conducting a funeral for a dead parent."[10] At the time, only Chinese nationalist sources gave the correct version of what happened.

Mao claimed that Liu and Teng tried to pigeonhole him for eight years thereafter. However, by the decision of the Central Committee which had removed him, Mao could resume the presidency "in compliance with the opinion of the people and the decision of the Party."

Mao said then: "But I don't want to be treated like a dead father." He evidently lost part of his political power because of internal opposition and external pressure from the Soviet Union.

In spite of Mao's for a long time unopposed leadership of the 25,000 *li* (7,775 mile) Long March survivers, after he was driven out of his Kiangsi Soviet, Red China went through a series of internal crises and large-scale ideological purges following the communist take-over. The top leadership was involved in the "anti-Party" groups of Kao Kang, who was vice chairman of the central government, and Jao Shu-shih, in 1954, of Marshal P'eng Teh-huai, the defense minister, all pro-Soviet, and in the recent great purges, because the policy differences raised by the latter continued to persist. The pro-Soviet elements were defeated at the 8th Central Committee plenary session in Lushan, Kiangsi province, in the first half of August 1959, after they tried to completely unseat Mao with the full knowledge of Krushchev.[11]

Krushchev himself defended the memory of Kao Kang and P'eng Teh-huai, prosecuted for opposing "the incorrect policies of the CPC toward the CPSU", at the June 1960 Bucharest conference of communist leaders assembled for the Rumanian Party Congress.[12] Professor Tang, when he compared all Soviet and Chinese documents at the time, could not find any evidence that Kao Kang was pro-Soviet.[13] Kao was the fifth ranking Red Chinese, a top Party, government and military leader in Manchuria, who committed suicide in prison under mysterious circumstances. Between 1950 and 1954 there was a secret tug of war between Moscow and Peking for the domination of Manchuria. The whole affair was well concealed at the time. Jao Shu-shih, a Party leader from east China, was a Central Committee secretary and director of its organization department. He was expelled from the Party and removed from all his posts. Mao had stood up against them after Stalin was dead.

Marshal P'eng raised the spectre of a military revolt against Mao, a *coup d'état*. He was head of a military goodwill tour to the

Warsaw Pact countries in the spring of 1959. He met Krushchev on the occasion of the latter's visit to Albania in May of the same year and submitted a memorandum to him.

The defense minister opposed the communes and the "great leap," denounced the decline of living standards, and, naturally disapproved of a breach with Moscow, the only supplier of modern military equipment. This was, in fact, the plaform of opposition backed by the newly-elected Head of State Liu Shao-ch'i, as it became clear later during the cultural revolution. A resolution made at the 8th Central Committee plenary session concerning P'eng and his group was disclosed, in partial form, eight years later. In a petition made up of ten thousand characters, he claimed that "if the Chinese workers and peasants were not as good as they are, a Hungarian incident would have occurred in China and it would have been necessary to invite Soviet troops in." P'eng was linked in an anti-Party alliance to Kao and Jao. His "Letter of Opinion" coincided with Khrushchev's anti-commune speech in Poland.[14]

Along with P'eng, all other signers of the petition were dismissed from their positions. They were: Huang K'o-ch'eng, deputy defense minister and chief of the general staff, deputy foreign minister Chang Wen-t'ien, a Politburo candidate member, and altogether about 40 key generals, high ranking Party leaders in national defense, foreign affairs, the provincial Party committee first secretaryship who for the time being kept their full or alternate membership in the Central Committee or the Politburo depending on their "behavior."

Further revelations said htat P'eng called the "leap" an "exaggerated trend" and the commune system "a mess" introduced contrary to the decisions of the 8th Party congress. Mao never admitted the catastrophic failure.

P'eng asserted that Mao's military theory was now obsolete and no longer applicable. This was also the opinion of the Russians as shown before. P'eng was accused of trying to usurp leadership in the Party and the army, of diminishing the leadership of the Party in the army with a system of one-man command, of favoring the abolishment of the militia, of negating the value of the people's war, of giving first place to military technique, of relying on Soviet missile deterrents, and of dependence on the Soviet Union in general. The Marshal was charged of having illicit relations with a "foreign country," the Soviet Union, of course.[15]

It is now evident that there has been a strong—and contagious —revisionist faction in the CPC, which was against Mao's adventurism in domestic and foreign policies, and which favored a *modus vivendi* with the Soviet Union. That faction was symbolized by Marshal P'eng, and was supported by a majority of the Party cadres. Mao's monumental failures and his shattering series of defeats at home and on the international scene have weakened his image with the Party and have strengthened the more moderate and rational wing of the communists who feared that their "helmsman's" policy of making enemies everywhere was heading China towards self-destruction.

Mao threatened at the Lushan plenum that, should the army desert him and should he be defeated in the Central Committee, he would return to the countryside and recruit a new army, and fight all over again. What in 1959 was merely a threat on Mao's part, he actually carried out in the cultural revolution, because in the meantime, the majority of the CPC supported P'eng's platform.

New efforts were made to rehabilitate P'eng by the Head of State in January 1962 and later. He did his best to help him. At that point the Maoists proclaimed: "With powerful support and encouragement from China's Krushchev, P'eng Teh-huai brough out in June 1962 a document running into a full 80,000 words aimed at reversing the edict passed on him."

During the cultural revolution, P'eng was arrested at Chengtu, Szechwan province, where he was relegated to a minor position as third deputy director of the southwest Central Committee Bureau's control commission—though highly respected by the anti-Maoist leadership of that Bureau. He was brought to Peking as a prisoner and nothing was heard about him anymore. No "warmth" was applied to the Chinese supreme commander in the Korean war as had been promised in the 1959 Central Committee resolution.[16]

Popular Disaffection

Under the pressure of popular reaction in China—general demoralization, despair and apathy—some realism seemed to have prevailed temporarily in Peking, summed up in the slogan "Proceed slowly and gradually on firm ground."[17]   At the September 1962, 10th plenary session of the Central Committee, the new policy for the future was described in these words: "With agriculture as the foundation and industry as the leading factor." Professor Alexander Eckstein of Michigan University holds that the "great leap" cost the Chinese economy roughly a decade of growth.[18]

However, at the same plenum, Mao launched his counter offensive—an all-out attack on revisionism, cultural relaxation, and all cover opposition[19] which had accumulated during his failures— of Himalayan proportions—in the words of Marshal Tito. From then on, Mao began to restore his influence.

Meanwhile the old "three flags" of disaster were supplemented with a new three-fold movement: class struggle, the struggle for production and scientific experiment, formulated by Mao in his speech of May 9, 1963.[20]

Even in 1965, the Chinese communists had not yet begun to recover from these disastrous effects, according to both Soviet and Western estimates, which were striking in their similarity.[21]   No economic plans or budgets have been published by the Red Chinese since 1959.

Mainland China "began," in the fateful year of 1966, its third five year plan which had been delayed for three years by the caution of the planners on the basis of the 1962 decision, which involved making no economic changes. The Yugoslav communists objected that it is not known who passed it and when. The goal was now to catch up with advanced countries in "two or three decades." Sources of funds, important figures and indices were never made public. The plan emphasized that "ideological and political work must be given top priority." Mao's thought was placed first, along with revolutionization of the people, including all the later slogans of the cultural revolution.[22]

The situation in the army was not any better.   Secret journals of the Red Chinese army Bulletin of Activities, available for Party members at the regiment commanders level and above which were captured by the Khampa rebels (Tibetan racial group) who overran a Chinese military post, revealed the deep moral crisis which was occurring in the army during 1959-1961 at least.

The Bulletin, of which the first eight months of 1961 are available, was published by the general political department of the Red Chinese army and exposed its political and technical weaknesses. It was translated by the Hoover Institution, edited by Chester Cheng, and published in a bulky volume. It gives the true picture of the commune disaster and the three hard years. This was the time of armed peasant uprisings, called "armed banditry" in the accounts, which culminated in the Honan revolt, the result of chaos, village starvation and general popular disaffection. The army was caught in this unhealthy condition and purged ruthlessly of "corrosive and disintegrating influences." The militia, made up of several million men, is described by the people as "rabid dogs, whippers, bandits, groups of tigers." The army used torture and generally mistreated the populace "to suppress the counterrevolutionaries and pacify the countryside." What happened was described, in theoretical terms, as antagonistic contradictions between the people and the Party which had developed from non-antagonistic ones.[23] After June 1959, the influx of technological innovations from the Soviet Union was stopped. It is significant that Lin Piao wrote in the Bulletin, that enmity with the United States is not necessarily lasting.

The Liberation Army Daily revealed "five tendencies" among the officers and men of the armed forces: "There exist many ideological problems, particularly bourgeois tendencies, paralyzing peace tendencies, individualism tendencies, subjective tendencies, and metaphysical tendencies."[24]

Remarks made at the January 1966 conference on political indoctrination in the Chinese army by three-star General Hsiao Hua, director of the army's general political department, could be interpreted as evidence of serious opposition within the military to Party control. He revealed for the first time the existence of two lines of thought in the Party. Army commanders seemed to have become restive over interference with their command by political commissars, and it was admitted that some senior officers had refused all "ideological reform." Among communist sources, *Tanyug* and *Humanité* have carried reports of dissension between the army and the Party in China. The conference included a call for struggle against modern revisionism in the military, and stressed the principle "that military affairs should be run by the whole Party, that the system of dual leadership by the military command and the local Party committees under unified leadership of the Party's Central Committee must be resolutely enforced, that the army must come under the absolute leadership of the Party ... in order to ensure that the line, principles and policies of the Party are resolutely implemented in the army." This should be the guarantee that the army never turned aside from the principles of the Party. How things were reversed in the cultural revolution!

Hsiao told the politcoms that the People's Liberation Army really feared political degeneration, quoting an ominous statement by Mao that: "If ... [the] class struggle were forgotten ... then it would not take long, perhaps only several years or a decade, or several decades at most, before a counterrevolutionary restoration on a national scale would inevitably occur, the Marxist-Leninist Party would undoubtedly become a revisionist party or a fascist party, and the whole of China would change its color." Without Party authority in military matters, the army would diverge from the Party doctrine, or "go wrong," which is what the Maoists feared most.[25]

Prominence should now be given to Mao's thought as the basis of the revolutionary struggle against revisionists, professionalists and rightists in the armed forces.

One of the most prominent of the Red Chinese commanders, the then Vice Premier Marshal Ho Lung, admitted that some professionals in the armed forces, whom he called "bourgeois military thinkers" advocated the abolition of the Party committee system and its methods which were utterly useless, even harmful to the conducting of modern warfare, in their view.[26] He too, was later disgraced.

Since the communist take-over, the mainland Chinese have staged numerous revolts against their tyrannical rulers. Peking's Minister of Justice Shih Liang reported in January 1961, that there were 8,323, 680 anti-communist incidents amongst the people during the period between 1951 and 1960. Evidently, such incidents during the first year of communist rule were not counted. At the same time, the regime held an exhibition on public security in Peking. This showed that the government discovered 56,000 anti-communist incidents in 1958, 76,900 in 1959, 115,350 in 1960,

and 249,012 in 1961.   As for the years 1962 and 1963, intelligence
reports reaching Taiwan revealed that there were 356, 448 incidents
in 1962 and more than 400,000 in 1963.   The Chinese communists
have not published any statistics on popular uprisings since then.[27]

The monthly journal of the Institute of International Relations
in Taipei, *Issues & Studies*, described six kinds of anti-communist
activities which occurred on the mainland during 1965:   armed
peasant revolts, sabotage in the towns and industrial centers, mass
riots, beating or killing of communist cadres, the dissemination of
anti-communist propaganda, defection and outright armed rebellion
by communist Party members themselves.[28]   This was before the
great purge began.

Such activities continued during the cultural revolution when
the anti-Maoists were joined by anti-communists.[29]

Armed *Kuomintang* forces in south China raided communist
military units and newly-established revolutionary committees in
southern Tibet, Yunnan and Kwangtung provinces.   They were
celebrating the tenth national congress of the *Kuomintang* held
in Taipei in March-April 1969.   Many communist soldiers and
cadres were killed.   Barracks, broadcasting and radar stations, gran-
aries, and bridges were destroyed.   (Among the bridges was the
newly-completed "People's Bridge" across the Pearl River).   Guerrilla
forces of the Chinese National Salvation Army seized communist
weapons and documents and liberated several hundred inmates from
a "reformatory camp."   A Chinese nationalist commando group raided the mainland coast in mid-January 1970, and claimed to have
sunk two cargo vessels.

The subcommittee on foreign commitments of the U.S. Senate
Foreign Relations Committee revealed in heavily censored secret
testimony about Chinese nationalist small-scale military operations
against the mainland.   War games of the Nationalists together with
Americans in the last ten years trained Chinese special forces to
be airdropped behind communist lines to join insurgent forces and
then link up with conventional landing forces, in order to practice
offensive tactics.[30]

The free world's pinning hope in the post-guerrilla generation
seemed justified by the results of the June 1964 congress of the
Chinese Communist Youth League.   Its leadership had been disband-

ed in the upheaval. The League was composed mostly of those who had not been tempered by two decades of terrible civil war.

The League's first secretary Hu Yao-pang (who was later purged) expressed doubts about the nation's youth, saying:

... under the corrupt influence of bourgeois ideology, a certain number of bourgeois elements and revisionists will inevitably crop up among the young people. It is wrong and dangerous to think that youth, born in the new society and brought up under the red flag is 'born red' and can automatically be heirs to the revolutionary cause.

Afterwards he said: "... we are in a position to crush all activities ... aimed at sabotaging and staging a comeback ... to battle the urban and rural capitalist forces and prevent any evolution into capitalism."[31] The League's secretary Hu K'o-shih (also purged) spoke even more bluntly about the ideological deviations of Chinese youth, admitting: "If they are not checked in time, the capitalist force will inundate the whole League and its organization will disintegrate."

At the beginning of August 1964, a nation-wide drive was initiated to foster a new generation of successors to the revolution —for the present leaders were well over 60.[32]

Although revolutionizing was the central theme of this 9th League's congress, Mao himself demonstrated before the outset of the cultural revolution a pathological skepticism towards the younger generation. The course taken by the congress gave some hope that Chinese youth may reject Mao's hard-line, his revolutionary fanaticism, inclining towards moderation as the Soviets have, when they assume the reins of power. In this case, the Maoists would be in the tradition of China's one-emperor dynasties. There has been among them a growing psychological apprehension that there will be a shift in policy by their successors.

The China Youth Daily, also a victim of the purge, reported on deep resentment amongst young people, and young intellectuals who summed up their ambitions in the slogan: "To be passable politically, to be very good professionally, and to be comfortable in daily life." This was in contradictions to the orthodox line that "redness" comes before "expertness." The Party paper acknowledged that "this idea is embraced not only by part of the college students and teachers, but also by some young scientists, technicians and workers in art and literature, as well as other young intellectuals."

They did not mention, of course, the terrible political pressures of the regime, the "voluntary" physical labor in factories, collective farms and reclamation works, the low wages, and the ever-present possibility of compulsory "shipment" to the wilderness, the remotest parts of China—even before the latest intemperate fulminations. It was revealed that over forty million educated urban youth were already sent "up to the mountain and down to the countryside"—one third of them, a very high figure even for China.[33] Letters from parents were printed in the press declaring that the State and the Chairman "own" their children and have the right to do with them as they wish for their "socialist re-education."

However, the CC of the League was "in line" on the eve of the cultural revolution, when the third and latest plenary session was held in April 1966, making the League "a school for creative study and application of Mao's thought" in the class struggle between two paths of thought, promoting the revolutionization of the young. But all this was in vain.

The Maoist leadership set up a provisional secretariat because the old CC built its work on the principles "of the revisionist Soviet *Komsomol*." In the opinion of the Soviets, "an official revision of the basic Leninist priciples of the organizational and political work of the Chinese Communist Youth League was in preparation."[34] In turn, this secretariat was also later disbanded by the "red rebels."

Chou En-lai revealed the weakness of the regime[35] in his report on the work of the Peking government at the third National People's Congress which was mentioned already. He described the aggravation of the class struggle, stressing that a very long time will have to pass before the problem of whether socialism or capitalism will prevail in China, is definitely solved. The Premier said that not only would the dispossessed classes be powerful for a long time, but that the new "bourgeois" elements would constantly grow. Opponents of communism will attempt to find protectors and agents everywhere with the goal of restoring capitalism, he said. "Hostile forces" are advocating liberalization and restoration of individual economy, and in the international field there is Soviet revisionism with all its implications, the Premier declared. At that time, the CPC was not yet overtly split.

Chou was only repeating Mao's declaration that who would be the final victor "is still not really settled," made at the enlarged session of the supreme state conference in February, 1957.[36] Later Mao assured his propagandists that "the new system of socialism will unquestionably be consolidated" though it would take a long time. "Who will win—has been decided," said Liu Shao-ch'i in his report to the 8th Party congress.

This doubt reappeared in the "ninth comment" of the CPC, mentioned previously. It confirmed the fact that the danger of capitalist restoration would continue to exist in China until the achievement of full communism—which could encompass many generations, "anywhere from one to several centuries."[37]

Mao himself expressed his doubts on the future of communist China to Edgar Snow, before the cultural revolution: ". . . youth could negate the revolution, and give a poor performance: make peace with imperialism, bring the remnants of the Chiang Kai-shek clique back to the mainland, and take a stand beside the small percentage (?) of counterrevolutionaries still in the country."[38]

"The Storm Center of the World Revolution"

Communist China, the biggest developing nation, is ambitious to become leader of all the developing countries in three continents, universalist goals abhorred by the Soviets. Yet China's heavy-handed diplomacy, her interference in the internal affairs of a number of other countries, as if she were a rogue elephant, have assiduously turned friends into foes. And her own turmoil, being a nation wracked with convulsions, has cost her the confidence of some of them. Mao and his cronies have even resorted to slogans urging non-whites to unite against whites. In some developing countries, people have asked why is another revolution needed now against national leaders and political parties?

The *coup d'états* in Algeria and Ghana deprived the Red Chinese of their trusted friends Ben Bella and Nkrumah, and the collapse of the Peking-Djakarta axis was followed by Peking's temporary retreat in Asia and Africa. Red Chinese diplomats were expelled from a number of newly-independent African countries. First Peking's aggression in India, and then its provocative stand in the Indian-Pakistani conflict were noted everywhere. China has become a scarecrow throughout the world. The meddling by Red Chinese representatives in the affairs of other nations did not stop even in communist countries like Cuba, where they attempted to subvert the armed forces. All this resulted in a kind of diplomatic bankruptcy for the Red Chinese. In 1967, a year of rebellious diplomacy by the Chinese, Peking quarreled with 32 countries, 10 of them communist states.

Is the Maoist leadership as warlike in deed as it is in word? The biggest catastrophe in Chinese foreign policy occurred in Indonesia, just across the South China Sea. Its results were: destruction of the mightiest Communist Party outside the communist orbit, (once numbering three million with membership cards and 15 million belonging to front organizations), and the persecution of part of the Chinese minority, suspected of sympathizing with the mainland regime. The abortive communist *Putsch*, called *gestapu*, a Malayan acronym, was organized with the help of Peking according to East German Politburo members, although it was generally known to communist leaders. Hermann Matern said at a Central Committee conference that Red China was responsible for the "physical extinction of hundreds of thousands" of Indonesian communists. This was the price that had to be paid for "adopting the Chinese policy." Alternate member Hermann Axen added that as a consequence of the Indonesian disaster, the Chinese suffered defeats and setbacks "and largely isolated themselves."[39]

At the trials of former Indonesian Foreign Minister Subandrio and Vice-Marshal Dhani, it was disclosed that it was Premier Chou's suggestion to create the fifth force communist militia and to supply them with 100,000 small arms from China.[40]

Mao said during an inspection trip in his native province in the summer of 1967: "As a political center of world revolution, China is determined to support the national liberation movements with weapons. They are to be openly given weapons, even engraved with Chinese characters, with the exception of some specific areas. We support openly, in order to make our country an arsenal of the world revolution."[41]

In the Indonesian people's revolt against the attempted communist subversion, a revolt backed by the military, at least 300,000 people were killed, mostly with Soviet weapons. Among those killed were many of Chinese origin. The property of pro-communist Chinese nationals and their organizations were destroyed or seized, and several hundred thousand persons were deprived of their livelihood, (out of a minority population of over three million). Three hundred thousand children of Chinese ancestry were forced to quit minority schools, and 10,000 teachers lost their jobs. The angry Indonesians, sometimes together with Chinese nationalists who pledged their allegiance to the Indonesian government, engaged in more than forty armed raids on Chinese communist diplomatic missions, wrecked the communist embassy together with its consulates, agencies and the living quarters of Chinese diplomats. A total of 68 diplomatic personnel were wounded in the shootings and beatings. Thirteen office buildings and residences were forcibly occupied. The *Res Publica* University in Djakarta, a stronghold of Chinese communists and their Indonesian supporters, was destroyed.

Houses and shops of Chinese nationals were later ransacked and burned, schools were destroyed, Chinese farmers were forcibly evicted from their land on a massive scale. The Indonesians killed and wounded Chinese everywhere. Tens of thousands of Chinese were thrown into concentration camps and prisons. All this was revealed in full detail in the Chinese communist protest notes to the Djakarta government which were largely ineffectual, and were published later in the *Peking Review*. In a style typical of Peking's bombastic diatribes, all this was called simply "a small adverse current in the present excellent world situation" in a Chinese communist government statement.[42] Finally, Indonesia suspended all diplomatic relations with Peking.

Meanwhile fugitives from the *gestapu* have full support of Peking. Communist subversion and guerrilla activities were renewed in Indonesia. Most Chinese nationals there were reluctant to return to the mainland until applications were permitted once again for Indonesian citizenship.

The Indonesian catastrophe was not enough for Peking. The remnants of the Indonesian Communist Party prepared, under the direction of the Chinese communists, a new armed uprising in East and Central Java in the summer of 1968. At the same time, Radio

Peking launched a massive propaganda campaign, listing in detail
the areas of concentration of communist forces on the big island.
The Indonesian army destroyed them in one mop-up operation.

 Indonesia revealed that the remainder of the native communists
in the capital and the surrounding areas were being directed by
"another" Communist Party, the Soviet of course, "acting under
its so-called international obligation." Radio Djakarta added: "The
split in the international communist movement has taught us that a
common enemy does not unite the communist Parties, but rather
worsens the split among them."[43] This group apparently did not
participate in the uprising.

 Afterwards, Moscow accused Peking of undertaking an "ir-
responsible adventure," when the time was not ripe for a communist
take-over, costing the lives of thousands of communists in yet another disaster. The Central Committee of the CPSU, in a statement complained that the President of Indonesia rejected a request
for pardon by a group of native communists, among them two Politburo members.[44]

 Had only a few such incidents happened to some national
minority elsewere, it would have been sufficient for a *casus belli*.
Peking, instead, contented itself with sending one protest note after
another. Actually, the Chinese communist leadership has acted
in the same manner on its doorstep's as did the weak Manchu
emperors before their downfall.

 What was the reaction of the Soviet government to the annihilation of the Indonesian Communist Party? The Chinese communists had a ready reply, accusing the Soviets of continuing to
provide arms to the Suharto-Nasution government during the massacres. They prettified the new rulers, and heaped lavish praise
upon them, the Chinese contended. They invited a number of
military and political leaders to visit the Soviet Union, continued
to train Indonesian military personnel and agreed to defer the repay-
ment of Indonesia's huge military debt to the Soviet Union, which
totaled 1.2 billion U.S. dollars. All these dealings were called
crimes of "the Soviet revisionist renegade group."[45]

 In all these significant events, the strong American commitment
in the Vietnam war played a pivotal role in barring a Chinese
policy of expansion. What China thought of as her best chance

for a "people's war" on the other side of the South China Sea could not be utilized.

The contagion of the cultural revolution, declared an international revolution,[46] spread across China's borders. This was intended by the regime who, in trying to export Maoism, exploited the Chinese minorities in neighboring countries. Burma and Cambodia were neutral border countries, but nevertheless, they had trouble with Peking after they opposed the importation of Maoism. In retaliation, Peking scrapped all economic and technological agreements and 415 Chinese experts were ordered to leave Burma. Nothing less than the overthrow of the government of Burma was proposed, and guerrilla activities of the local Communist Party were revived with the support of Peking. In reprisal, Chinese embassy offices, homes and shops were raided, and more than a thousand destroyed. Four top-ranking communists were executed in the "liberated territory" for opposing a Chinese-style revolution.

When Peking viciously attacked its friend Norodom Sihanouk, then the Cambodian head of state, he declared: "This is a flagrant interference in the internal affairs of a sovereign state." The Phnom Penh paper, *Réalités Cambodgiennes* defined Maoism as the "preaching of armed rebellion and toppling of existing governments." In a letter to *Le Monde*, the Prince said the local rebellion in his country was "launched from outside." Propaganda pamphlets were discovered "printed in Peking and carrying the portrait of Mao." Then he added: "It is perfectly clear that Asian communism, [i.e. Maoism], does not permit us any longer to stay neutral ... Not being able to make of us ... allies supporting it unconditionally, Asian communism strives to overthrow our regime from within."[47] Cambodia was trying then to keep a precarious balance with China.

Much changed with the ouster of the Prince, when an anticommunist government came to power in Cambodia. "With Sihanouk in the hands of Peking," commented Dr. La Dany, "China entered the geographic and political scene that Hanoi claims as its own." The long-awaited chance for assuming political leadership in Indochina arrived. Peking formed an Indochinese coalition of North Vietnam, the Vietcong, Pathet Lao and Khmer Rouge in the tradion of the old Indochinese CP. The old Marshal Yeh Chien-ying was reported as heading a military mission in Hanoi and south-western China to organize assistance to communist forces in the whole area.

What Sihanouk himself predicted in a speech in May 1967, when he acknowledged the support given to North Vietnam, the Vietcong and North Korea, precisely happened. "But," he continued, "we cannot support certain of them in their attempts *to neo-colonize Cambodia* (italics provided), our homeland, or to make a satellite of it by using the Cambodian Reds as their Trojan horse." Sihanouk's role in events after his ouster make this speech ironic.

Moscow was losing influence and its denunciation was harsh: "The Peking leaders, pressing their adventurist tactics on some segments of the communist and national-liberation movements in Southeast Asia, are trying to use them as tools for asserting Chinese domination in Asian countries and to condemn them to defeat and destruction." They claimed that "Chinese interference prompted the rightwing forces in Cambodia to stage a coup and to seek American support." As further examples they mentioned defeats in Indonesia, Malaysia and the Philippines, but did not dare to score the new coalition directly. Traditional Chinese strategy was compared to silkworm eating at a leaf, which means gradual step by step assimilation of neighboring countries. Another good example was a golden seal sent by a Chinese emperor to Laos several centuries ago having the motto: "Disobey and die."

The red guards demonstrated violently in front of twelve foreign diplomatic missions in Peking, six of them belonging to communist countries; in doing so, they trampled under foot all the standards and obligations of international law and of decent behavior. Premier Chou condemned these attacks and issued a six-point statement of instructions prohibiting the manhandling of foreign residents, and the damaging and setting fire of buildings.

The Soviets rapped Peking's diplomatic irresponsibility since all this was done with the complete connivance of the Maoist authorities, and in glaring violation of the 1961 Vienna conference on diplomatic relations and immunities.[48]

The mores and methods of the cultural revolution were discredited in many Afro-Asian countries because the Chinese communists tried to instigate disturbances in some of them, and to fan racial and territorial disputes. These were the best antidotes to communism. The activities of the Chinese communist embassies were provocative. Pressure, blackmail and bribes were utilized whenever possible—highlighted by Peking's overtures to President H. Kamuzu Banda of Malawi, who was offered as much as 18 millions in sterling for his political cooperation.[49] Also remarkable was the discovery of the Chinese communist saboteur "academy" in Ghana which prepared fighters for terror and subversion all over the continent. The Russians could not stay behind, and they too participated separately in preparing subversive activities under the shield of the "Redeemer." It was a ludicrous byplay.

When Hsü Tzu-tsai, a civil engineer, tried to defect in the Hague, he was murdered. More fortunate was Liao Hu-shu, the chargé d'affaires in the Hague who had an intelligence background, and who was the highest ranking communist Chinese diplomat who ever defected.

The Maoists are stepping up the arming of the Nagas in northeast India, instigated openly by *Hsinhua* and pro-Peking communists. They are encouraging the Palestinian guerrillas, the Thai communists and the Philippine *Hukbalahap*. They are calling for the overthrow of the governments of India, Indonesia, Malaysia and Singapore.

Peking's intentions were to create a confederation of Himalayan states under China's aegis, including Sikkim, a protectorate of India, Bhutan, an independent State whose foreign affairs are handled by India, and the northeast areas of India. The proposal was turned down by the King of Bhutan. Large areas of Bhutan were placed within China's frontiers on a mainland map. So were Burma's with which country China concluded a boundary treaty.[50]

No other communist leader could answer the Chinese with language equal to Castro's when Peking violated its rice-sugar cane deal with Cuba. He accused China of:

"dishonesty," "cynicism," "bad faith," "perfidy," "hypocrisy," of being "extremely insidious," of "the most venomous intent," of using a "hidden dagger," of "blackmail and extortion," of "exerting pressure, committing aggression and strangulation," of resorting to "the worst methods of piracy, oppression and filibustering," and of having "committed a

criminal act of economic aggression" against Cuba.
At the end, the bewildered Castro asked: "Will this prevail in the world of tomorrow?"[51]

The Soviets rapped Mao's policy of intensifying troubles in the world, of unceremoniously interfering in the affairs of other countries in disdain of the rights of other nations. The exposure to Maoist propaganda was declared "a sacred and inalienable right of Chinese living abroad" to convert them into a "fifth column." Special rights were asked for them. These were essentially neo-colonialist demands which looked very much like requesting ex-territoriality. A tentative estimate was made of the total capital of the 13 million Chinese emigrants in Southeast Asia, the *hua ch'iao*, at three billion dollars. After the bankruptcy of Peking's assertion of hegemony in the national liberation movement became apparent its subversive activity was drastically intensified according to one Soviet commentator.[52]

Following Mao's inspection of certain provinces, which served as an eye-opener to him, there were signs that Peking was contemplating a change in the pugnacious character of its foreign policy. Chiang Ch'ing, Mao's wife, in her remarkable speech to the red rebels of Anhwei province, called upon the thugs not to commit hostile acts against foreigners in accordance with Chou's instructions. The Soviets commented: "Peking is afraid that the *hung weiping* may turn everything upside down in foreign policy just as they have done at home."[53]

During the cultural revolution, communist Chinese envoys in foreign countries, with one exception, were recalled home for "re-education". After the 9th CPC congress, a partial normalization of Peking's relations with the outside world was taking place. Mao's foreign policy was adequately described in a Soviet book entitled, indicatively, To the Left of Common Sense, by Professor Mikhail S. Kapitsa, an author of several books on China.[54]

CHAPTER XI

The Great Purge: Maoists Fight the "Russian Disease"

Three Harmonies and One Reduction

In the spring of 1964, Yang Hsien-ch'en, a leading CPC ideologist and a Soviet trained Marxist scholar came under fire because of his revisionist views.[1] Yang was a member of the Central Committee, and until August of the same year, president of the Higher Party School, a major ideological institute. In this way he started a philosophical debate over the nature of dialectical materialism. According to his interpretation of the basic law of social development "two combine into one." One here means a single conceptual whole. This was contrary to Mao's teaching of "one divides into two", based on Lenin's *razdvoyeniye yedinovo*. That implied an irreconcilable class struggle at the national as well as international level which found its expression within the CPC itself. Compared to Bukharin, Yang was described as a non-dialectitian.[2]

In this way Yang provided a philosophical basis for the "Soviet line" of three harmonies and one reduction, implying reconciliation with Soviet revisionism, as well as with United States "imperialism", and even with the Chinese nationalists, that is, with the Chinese people. It also called for reduction of assistance to the subversive movements abroad, known as revolutionary struggle of national liberation. Premier Chou charged "some misguided comrades" for advocating such a "capitulationist line" in December of the same year. Occasionally it was called "three surrenders, one extinction" (*san ho i shao*).

Maoists of the North China CC Bureau held that this philosophy originated with Liu Shao-ch'i as its doyen, Yang being only his pawn. In his article "Why Do People Make Mistakes" and in other writings

Liu came out with the theory of "two combine into one." He stressed that "the most fundamental character of a contradiction is its unity. ... Our principle is to make use of the unity of a contradiction rather than to increase its struggle ..." In this view "two opposite things combine to become a new thing." Liu, as well as the Soviets, hold that classes and class struggle have been eliminated in socialist society and that "dialectical opposites and contradictions have changed into differences, and differences then merge into unity." This concept is called metaphysical by the Maoists, and is regarded as contrary to dialectical materialism. Liu and the revisionists deny the absolute character of the struggle between the opposites and arrive at the theory of their harmony, that is, class reconciliation.

This teaching runs counter to Mao's world outlook of "one divides into two." According to him "Marxist philosophy holds that the law of the unity of opposites is the fundamental law of the universe. This law operates universally, whether in the natural world, in human society, or in man's way of thinking." He holds that the unity of opposites is conditional, temporary and transitory and hence relative, whereas the struggle of opposites is absolute. In the Maoist interpretation "unity and struggle in the Party constitute the unity of opposites and are mutually opposed and complementary. The unity and solidarity of the proletarian Party is achieved and consolidated in the course of continuous struggle. The philosophy of the CPC is one of struggle and revolution. Otherwise it would stagnate and degenerate." In their view this means recognition of class contradiction and class struggle in the Party in accordance with dialectical materialism.[3]

The Soviet Academician P. Fedoseyev calls this Maoist theory of a necessary split of any unity into warring parts falsified dialectics. In this way, he says, an attempt is made to justify the splitting activities in the world communist movement and the crushing of the CPC. He broadly rejects the ideas of "some newly hatched Mandarin oracle."[4]

Clinging to dialectical materialism, the communists are convinced of the inevitability of their final world-wide victory. Once the communists have come to power, dialectics that is, everlasting struggle and change, will stop and there will be no more revolutions. An early refugee from the Soviet camp, Yevgeny Zamyatin, a well known Russian novelist, took a critical view of the totalitarian rule saying that "there is no such thing as the last revolution, for the number of revolutions is infinite." He foresaw revolutions which would overthrow the communist rulers in their turn.

Other Chinese mainland authorities in their philosophical studies regarded the application of Mao's works "in a creative way" as philistinism, oversimplification and pragmatism. In the history of philosophy Confucius was again praised, and the ideas of the French revolution "liberty, fraternity and equality" were revived. In economic studies progressive scholars made an effort to restore profit and money economy. In historical studies the "royalists" countered Marxism-Leninism with historicism. In literature and art the opponents of the regime laid stress on realism, truthful writing, human nature. They accepted the literature and art of the whole people, as advocated by anti-Maoist commissars, and rejected the notion that art should be more ideal than life, as well as heroic characters, revolutionary optimism and romanticism. They objected to the "smell of the gunpowder" in Mao's teaching seeking to transform all people into soldiers, ready, like the Red Army, for a "people's war." In their opinion, Mao's blind faith in armed struggle as a sole and universal form for advancing socialism is an aberration. In the field of education, Chinese pedagogues were accused of spreading the theory and system of Soviet revisionism. In journalism the desire to impart knowledge was decried by the Maoists, because for them truth, too, has its class nature.[5]

All this intellectual fermentation in China was an expression of a deep crisis of the regime which might have serious repercussions on further development. It was an expression of a general disaffection of a large section of the population with the conditions under "war communism."

In response, the frightened Mao sounded the clarion of the "great proletarian cultural revolution" in the sense of an "extremely violent, bitter and all-pervading class struggle." A definition of this movement was given later by Yao Wen-yüan, Mao's son-in-law, a member of the group in charge of the Central Committee for the cultural revolution. In a speech commemorating the 30th aniversary of death of the leftist writer Lu Hsun he said:

Today, under the dictatorship of the proletariat, we have

launched the great proletarian cultural revolution, a movement without parallel in history. This great, torrential revolutionary movement was started by Chairman Mao on the basis of a summing up of the experience of the class struggle in China and in the international arena, and of the historical experience of the dictatorship of the proletariat, taking into account the profound aspirations of the revolutionary masses. This is a great innovation in the socialist revolution in our country, a revolutionary movement of the proletariat carried out at a higher stage and after the proletariat already seized power and transformed private ownership. Its aim is remolding the outlook of society and of its ideology. This is an extremely great revolution, far-reaching and deep-going, touching the people to their very souls.[6]

The armed forces paper *Chieh-fang Chün-pao*[7] which started the real campaign in the spring of 1966 with the *Hung Ch'i,* later to be followed by the entire Chinese communist press, admitted that not only the broad masses of the intellectuals were hostile, but that the disaffection with Mao's extreme policy and the preference for a relatively moderate line reached even the high-ranking cadres within the regime itself. In doing so it stated that the People's Liberation Army was the mainstay of the dictatorship of the proletariat.

The regime took the situation very seriously because it saw in the intellectual fermentation the danger of a Chinese variety of the Hungarian revolution. Consequently a struggle against all anti-Mao and counter-revolutionary phenomena in the contemporary Chinese society was proclaimed in order to prevent the "breeding of Petoefi circles." This comparison was made by Mao himself on the occasion of his address to the All-China Federation of Literary and Art Circles in June 1964. The Maoists issued a warning that should this movement succeed, Chiang Kai-shek might come back to the mainland, the Party might disappear(!) and "even our heads might be cut-off."

Furthermore, it was boldly asserted that the counter-revolutionaries were those who agreed with the Soviet Union and hence that the new synthetic revolution from above was at the same time anti-Russian. The anti-Mao elements allegedly went so far as "to stage a counter-revolutionary *coup d'état* similar to that carried out by Khrushchev."[8] It was asserted that these elements penetrated the

Party, government, armed forces and cultural institutions.

The new revolution took at first its biggest toll among higher Party officials, particularly in the propaganda and mass communication fields, among high government functionaries, university presidents and professors, and educators in general, many of the most respected writers, economists and youth leaders. It then gradually spread to the whole Party and state apparatus. The previous anti-rightist campaigns were conducted mainly outside the Party. The so-called cultural revolution, on the other hand, was essentially an intramural Party purge, directed against the men in power in the Party.[9] The new revolution became a "class struggle" of the hard-liners against the higher echelons of the Party. It went from the top to the bottom and vice versa. Public criticism, purges and humiliations were carried out in all provincial, regional and municipal Party committees and demoralized the whole apparatus. Party coherence thereby suffered irreparable damage, and the CPC will in fact never be the same.

Among the communist writers who tried to communicate their real feelings to the people was the well known playwright, poet and film-maker T'ien Han, former chairman of the Association of Chinese Drama Workers, and author of the Chinese communist national anthem "March of the Volunteers." Somebody brought attention to the fact that a number of films portrayed anti-communist feelings, disseminated the idea of overthrowing the communists, expressed sympathy for the *Kuomintang* and called for a rising in response to a nationalist counter-attack.

In a play called Hsieh Yao-huan dealing with the conditions at the court of Empress Wu of the T'ang dynasty, T'ien described the corruption, nepotism, intrigues, persecution of upright officials, and the abuse of people "as much grass" by minor officials. The play was entitled after a lady in waiting who uttered the significant words: "If the annexation of land will not be halted, there will be no peace in the country."

It was not difficult for the watchdogs to realize that T'ien insinuated that Mao was alienated from the Chinese people and no longer represented their interests.[10] It was obvious that he appealed in his works for political and social reform, which eventually led to his arrest.

The nation-wide campaign to purge the intellectual ranks of

"bourgeois and opportunist elements" followed a general "rectifica-tion" drive among the writers and artists. *Hsinhua* reported that 16,000 literary and art workers "repaired" in 18 months to factories, rural areas and armed forces "for physical re-education", to remold their thinking. They lived together, ate together, and worked to-gether with the masses of workers, peasants and soldiers.[11] They were followed by 400,000 "undesirable elements" and "enemies of the people" and their families who were forcibly removed to rural areas to do manual work.

Although the total number of "unreliable" persons banished to the countryside and remote areas for "purification" is kept secret, there was evidence in Japanese and Hong Kong sources to the effect that between the last months of 1966 and the spring of 1968 alone several million people had been deported. These deportees' lot was one of the worst. The peasants were and are hostile to them because they are not used to rural work and are therefore a burden to the rural community which must feed them from its own meager re-sources. There is evidence that some of them were killed or poisoned by the people among whom they lived. When they succeeded in re-turning to urban life, they are not given jobs, nor ration cards. Those urban residents who are lucky enough to be allowed to remain in the cities are required to do physical labor for one month a year.[12]

Hai Jui — Disguised Anti-Maoists

A number of communist and non-Party writers satirized con-temporary affairs through camouflaged old anecdotes or, to use the regime's version, "by using historical events and characters to ridicule, attack and slander the realities of present-day socialism." Prominent figures in contemporary Chinese culture, arts and science from among the middle-aged and older generation of intellectuals were exposed to virulent public criticism and then purged. Some were Marxist intel-lectuals who had long held high posts and had never before been suspected of revisionism, the "Russian disease."

The Liberation Army Daily accused the "black line" in literature as a combination of the capitalist way of thinking, of modern revi-sionism, and of the literature and art in the 1930's. In fact, during the Red regime very few new writers of distinction emerged in China and the sterilizing effect of communist ideology on art makes any comparison invidious.[13]

A striking example of this new trend was the abject self-accusation of Kuo Mo-jo, an old Chinese classicist, poet, politician, and one of the greatest scholars of China. He was a symbol of the highest link of the top intelligentsia of the old Chinese generation with the top leaders of Red China. As the main interpreter of Mao's philosophical poetry, he had been for many years president for life of the Chinese Academy of Sciences, chairman of the All-China Federation of Literary and Art Circles, and deputy chairman of the Standing Committee of the National People's Congress. At a session of the Committee in April 1966 he made a confession and publicly repudiated his own works in order to influence dissident intellectuals. This made it possible for him to resume his functions. His case illustrates the absurdity of the whole campaign. Yet the Japanese press made an effort to downgrade his self-criticism.[14] Later he was exposed by the red guards as a "capitulant and reactionary writer" as well as an enemy of the people, but those posters soon disappeared.

His example found a follower. Hua Lo-keng, director of the Mathematics Institute of the Academia Sinica, top scientist in his field, disavowed 40 years of his work.

Kuo Mo-jo later refused to attend the Moscow session of the Lenin International Peace Prize Committee in April 1967, of which he was a deputy chairman. He stated that he no longer wanted to remain a member.

The campaign against the revisionist intellectuals started at the Party committees of Peking's municipality and university. The highest victim of this struggle was P'eng Chen, the 6th ranking Politburo Standing Committee member and secretary of the Central Committee. His other functions were vice chairman of the CPC and of the National People's Congress Standing Committee, as well as deputy secretary general of the CPC. He happened to be also Mayor of the capital city, and was not a revisionist, but dared to score the Chairman. In spite of it, he first got the title of "comrade-in-arms of Chairman Mao." He had been tarred with the guilt of association, removed from the post of the first secretary of the capital's Party committee, and specifically charged with responsibility for anti-Maoist and anti-socialist activities of his subordinates during the last six years when the first veiled criticism of Mao appeared. It was also rumored that he was incriminated for the disaster in Indonesia as he was in charge of relations with the national liberation movements.

P'eng was accused of endeavoring "to repeat in China the ugly dream of Khrushchev's usurpation of the Party, the army and the administration."   He was arrested in the dark of the night as a conspirator, and humiliated at a mass meeting in the presence of Wu Teh, acting Mayor of Peking.[15] There were rumors that P'eng Chen died in prison.

In previous years P'eng was marked by the Soviet press as particularly hostile to the "united action." His speech at the Soviet embassy in Peking on the occasion of the 1964 October revolution celebration was remembered. He then presented for the first time the conflict with the Soviet Union as a class struggle, and, by implication, the Soviets as class enemies. In the conflict with the Soviets, P'eng Chen, like Liu Shao-ch'i and Teng Hsiao-p'ing, then went hand in hand with Mao. He would have found it hard to believe then that the same false charges would be leveled against him and many other Chinese communist leaders only a year later. Yet he voiced the opinion of those who opposed Mao and Lin and advocated that China must take seriously the grave situation resulting from the escalation of the war in Vietnam.

P'eng played an important role in trying to avoid the coming storm, and to interpret the cultural revolution as a theoretical proposition rather than a blue-print for purge, which it became a year later. In the Central Committee circular of May 16, 1966 it was revealed that his "Outline report on the current academic discussion made by the group of five in charge of the cultural revolution" was first approved and then, three months later, revoked. It formalized Mao's attempt to regain undisputed control of the Party and of the cultural revolution. The approval and subsequent revocation can be explained as a result of the purges which had taken place in the CC as an expression of the cultural revolution. The Chairman had in mind the recapture of the state power which he reluctantly had ceded to Liu Shao-ch'i.

P'eng was accused of having acted arbitrarily against the cultural revolution. That revolution was initiated by Mao in October 1965 at the conference of the Politburo Standing Committee, attended by the leaders of the regional bureaux. It started with a massive propaganda attack on Wu Han, the non-communist vice-mayor of Peking. The "Outline" was meant to turn the movement to the right, and called for a "rectification campaign" against the left, that is, against the emerging Maoists. The circular stressed that there was a considerable number of anti-Party and anti-socialist representatives of the bourgeoisie(?) in the CC and in the Party, in the government, and in departments at the central as well as provincial, municipal, and autonomous regional level, which must be taken to task and repudiated. It went on to say that "people of the Khrushchev brand are still in our midst."

The bone of contention was the dismissal of the "right opportunists" at the Lushan conference in 1959. P'eng tried to stem the tide. He was against the cultural revolution and indeed wanted to launch a counter-attack in retaliation. The circular revealed Mao's battle for survival. It has been called "the clarion call of the cultural revolution."[16] Instead, K'ang Sheng, Politburo Standing Committee member, addressing a rally welcoming the Albanian Party and government delegation in Shanghai, said that it was in the same city that Mao sounded the battle call in March 1966, using the devise: "Overthrow the rulers of hell and set the little devils free." Mao indeed had to stay in Shanghai from November 1965 to July 1966, P'eng Chen having prevented him in Peking from carrying out his plans.

The former Peking Mayor's "crimes" were listed during the summer of 1967 and later. They were picked mostly from his statements and speeches he had made after the communist take-over in China. Like so many Chinese literati, P'eng too chose many examples from Chinese history in order to ridicule the existing situation and in this way "to attack indirectly and maliciously Chairman Mao."[17] Thus in one of his speeches he said that the "good, old emperors, unlike the bad ones, displayed willingness to listen to the council of others." He hailed the emperor Li Shih-min, the first of the T'ang dynasty, who listened to his counselors.

P'eng held that criticism should be accepted and that everybody should be free to criticize what he regarded as wrong. Speaking about the strategist Chu-Ko Liang of the "three kingdoms", P'eng said that the CPC is in danger of resembling an old man who is not only unable to jump, but even to move. This was a clear allusion to Mao. He expressed the view that everybody can make mistakes. To claim that somebody is infallible is tantamount to fooling the people, as the Maoists were doing in the cultural revolution. That only some people should be entitled to criticize, and others be the only object of criticism, should be forbidden. P'eng was also accused of seconding Liu Shao-ch'i, who expressed himself that cadres, Mao included, were nothing more than tools of the Party, and that care should be taken regarding the best use of these "tools." Positive achievements should not be put to the credit of one person only, nor to the credit of the CC. The opinion of the cadres should be independent, nor should they cultivate idolatry of any person. Nobody is irreplaceable. Old and senile persons should not be allowed to hold jobs. It was not difficult to guess against whom all these statements were directed.

P'eng was particularly criticized for advocating the theory of disappearance of the class struggle in socialism. This meant a critical stand against the dictatorship of the proletariat. P'eng held that the repressive role of the latter was overused in China and in that way identified himself with the Soviet tenet of the "state of the whole people." For the Maoists, however, the acceptance of the class struggle in a socialist society is the dividing line between true revolutionaries and revisionists.[18]

The most vilified trio under P'eng included Wu Han, Teng T'o, secretary of the capital's Party committee, and the historian Liao Mo-sha, director of the united front department of the committee. The three were often known under the pseudonym, or acronym, Wu Nan-hsing. They were denounced as the "black inn", a traditional place in China where guests were murdered. Their chief "crime" was their collective work entitled Notes of the Three-Home Hamlet, altogether 67 allegorical essays which appeared after the disaster of the "three red flags" and the deterioration of Peking-Moscow relations. In these Notes the authors obliquely criticized Mao's despotic policy from October 1961 to July 1964, by way of innuendos. Their writings were called a continuation and an elaboration of the Marshal P'eng-Huang anti-Party group opinions.

Wu Han was a noted historian and a prominent literary figure. He was also president of the Peking Television University. In his historical dramas he layed stress on traditional values. He was accused of supporting right opportunists, ousted in the previous purges. His historical drama Hai Jui Dismissed From Office, which appeared in January 1961, amounted to an apology for Marshal P'eng Teh-huai who had the courage to speak up against Mao's follies. His rehabilitation was urged by a part of the armed forces. In fact, the subject of the drama was the overthrow of tyranny and returning of the robbed lands to the peasants as a precondition for lasting peace. This was regarded by the Maoists as an attempt to undermine the people's communes. P'eng Chen tried to save Wu by raising the question of historical accuracy of the story of Hai Jui. (The author later admitted that there were historical errors in his story). On the basis of this evidence the trio was called "the strategists of the *Kuomintang.*"[19]

Many see the formal start of the cultural revolution in Yao Wen-yüan's attack on "Hai Jui" in Shanghai's *Wen-hui Pao,* endorsed by the Liberation Army Daily in the fall of 1965. The article was inspired by the Chairman himself and even supervised by his spouse, as was later revealed. Actually several months passed before the start of the great purges. Five months later the notion of the great socialist cultural revolution, sometimes also called proletarian, was mentioned, however, in the same paper for the first time.[20]

The present plight of the Chinese people on the mainland was compared to that in the first half of the 16th century in Hai Jui's Memorial to the Throne in these words: "Everything was swept up in the individual homes . . . natural and man-made disasters brought the people to poverty . . . people are on the verge of starvation, wandering about aimlessly . . . the government is cursed everywhere."

Later additional details were revealed in the Red Flag regarding the start of the cultural revolution by attacking Wu, the bearer of the "big poisonous weed." As Chairman Mao pointed out: "The crux of Hai Jui Dismissed From Office is the question of dismissal from office. The Emperor Chia Ching (of the Ming Dynasty, 1522-1566) dismissed Hai Jui from office. And P'eng Teh-huai is Hai Jui, too."

This criticism, made by Chairman Mao, hit the mark not only with regard to Hai Jui Dismissed From Office, but also with regard to the whole "bourgeois headquarters".[21] The leading German expert Professor Mehnert, explaining Wu's thought, came to the conclusion that the private-ownership mentality in the present China is still much stronger than in the Soviet Union.[22]

In this connection it was disclosed that in 1962 "the right opportunists attempted to stage a comeback and to launch a counter-attack." This confirmed the existence of a strong revisionist group among the communist intellectuals and Party cadres in general.[23]

Teng T'o, a former editor-in-chief of People's Daily, and a member of the department of philosophy and social sciences of the Chinese Academy of Sciences, was the head of the capital's press, the *Peiching Jih-pao* (Peking Daily), the *Peiching Wan-pao* (Peking Evening News), and the magazine *Chien Hsien* (Front Line), organs of the municipal Party committee. These papers were later shut down and reorganized. It was discovered that Teng was "a big rightist who escaped the net." He was attacked for his 153 essays entitled The Night Talks Around Yenshan, written between March 1961 and September 1962. Among others he described a small but educated official who was wrongly dismissed during the Ch'ing dynasty. Following his dismissal he spent his time in writing poems and painting. In these writings he revealed his character, "refusing to be a slave" and "striving to be his own master in all respects and to tread out a path for himself." This circumstance, as well as other essays in the form of anecdotes and satires, were deemed as sufficient proof of opposition to Mao's dictatorship. In an article entitled "A Big, Empty, Idle Talking" he exposed the emptiness of the slogan "The east wind is our benefactor, and the west wind is our enemy." He compared the Party with a person who swallows his own words, and then becomes hysterical and insane and moreover suffers from amnesia. Mao is here characterized as boastful and conceited.

Teng's writings came under fire. He was accused of piping the same tune as Khrushchev, and prodding the rightists to withdraw from the Party. His pro-Soviet line was disclosed particularly in his essay entitled "How one gets friends and guests entertained." Another accusation was that he was inciting the part-time writers to resist the Party when it was telling them what to write. This is in fact the right for which so many Soviet and East European writers are fighting for.

All these three prominent writers were persecuted for having published a large amount of "poisonous weeds" of the revisionist kind. Obligingly the controlled press recognized that their writings had an influence throughout the country. Following a protracted, vicious persecution, according to wall posters in Canton all three on the same day committed suicide.[24]

At the Peking University the revisionists evidently tried to win over the younger generation. The reshuffled Party municipality committee ordered the removal of Lu P'ing, president of the University and secretary of its Party committee. It also decided to reorganize the whole committee by task force. Under attack also came Chien Po-tsan, vice president of the University. He was inculpated that as a historian he "beautified and eulogized" in his writings kings, emperors and prime ministers of old China. Furthermore, he was accused of ascribing the declining rebellious disposition of the Chinese peasantry in the past to the liberal policy of the ruling class. The charge against him was that he was working for the *Kuomintang*. Lu P'ing and his associates at the University also were taken to task for blindly imitating the Soviet Union and secretly emulating the West. It was said that P'ing transformed Peking University into an institution of the Chinese nationalist type.[25]

Meanwhile the purge went on and among others hit at the top Lu Ting-yi, a leading figure since 1949 and the 13th vice-premier and minister of culture, alternate member of the Politburo and full member of the secretariat, as well as director of the CC's propaganda department. With him were purged his deputies, all vice ministers of culture and propaganda deputy directors.

In March 1957 Lu participated in the phony "100 flowers" campaign with a speech. Three years later he wrote an anti-Soviet pamphlet, entitled *Long Live Leninism*. He was always considered as one of the most faithful of Mao's men. At the beginning of 1965 he succeeded Mao Tun as minister of culture. The latter was dismissed when a film called "Lin's Shop" was made after his novel. The film was described as bourgeois and anti-socialist, since it did not stress class struggle.

In the all-embracing campaign against Liu Shao-ch'i, Lu's name was hardly mentioned. He was regarded as a "scholar-tyrant," a pedant who made professional skill his supreme objective, something for which Mao's China has less taste than any other country. He was taken to task for expressing the view that different opinions on educational policy should be allowed inside the Party and that opposing views should also be tolerated outside the Party. His greatest sin however was that "he praised the educational method, policy, and system of Soviet revisionism and regarded them as a theoretical basis for advancing the counter-revolutionary, revisionist, educational line."[26]

A surprise came in the purge of Chou Yang, vice-minister of culture. Chou Yang was also deputy director of the propaganda department of the Central Committee, and executor of Mao's literary and cultural policies throughout the past thirty years. We may regard him as Red China's Zhdanov. He formulated what amounted to a dialectical justification of factionalism in the international communist movement, and therefore of the Sino-Soviet conflict. Yet he was accused of having "stubbornly adhered to the bourgeois, revisionist line on literature and art,"[27] advocating liberalization and opposing ideological monopoly and dogmatism. His influence extended to literature, art, educational, academic and publishing fields. Another charge raised against him was that he was preparing a revolution of intellectuals after the Hungarian pattern. He halted the further printing of Mao's works, arguing that enough of them were in circulation. After his downfall Maoists called him "No. 1 demon in the kingdom of hell."

Chou opposed the fanatical deification of Mao. He said that "the propagation of Mao Tse-tung's thought and cult of the individual deprive everybody of his initiative and creativeness."[28] Both he and his superior were also accused of having offered resistance to the transformation of the Museum of the Chinese Revolution into Mao Tse-tung Museum.

Peking University was not alone in this witch-hunting. *Hsinhua* listed a number of others: Nanking, Wuhan, Chiaotung (Sian), Kiangsi, Chungking, Chengchow, Yunnan. All these "conspired with the Peking University." As a result many faculty members were purged and these institutions were seriously crippled. Most writings in the provinces condemned by the Maoists reflect the Three Principles of the People by Sun Yat-sen as well as Chinese traditional values.

Not even Li Ta was spared. He was a surviving CPC founding father—one of the twelve persons present. He was president of the Wuhan University in the southern province of Hupeh and head of the Chinese Philosophical Society. He called "the great leap" a "great retreat." The Maoists in turn called him a "sham communist and a genuine nationalist."[29] He was dismissed because he expressed doubt that Mao's doctrine was the last word of Marxism-Leninism. He reacted to this proposition by asking: "Does that mean that Marxism will not develop any further?" According to him the concept of Mao's philosophical works On Practice and On Contradiction is not necessarily correct. He viewed these two booklets to be of low taste and not interesting at all. According to a Canton red guard publication Li Ta was "struggled" to death. Afterwards his family was chased out of their home.[30]

The most prominent among the purged economists was Sun Yeh-fang, a former director of the Economic Research Institute of the Academy of Sciences. His charge was that he had called "the great leap" a great mess. He accepted the ideas of Professor Liberman stressing profit and material incentives in the management of the economy, and was called the "yes man of revisionism." Since he advocated liberalization of enterprises and self-management, his teachings were labeled as modern revisionism of the Titoist, Khrushchevist type and as "Khrushchevism without Khrushchev."[31]

During the period of the economic adjustment following the disastrous "leap" (1961-1964), the Liu-Teng faction's economic policy was based on Sun's pragmatism in which experts and sensible Party people held ground. He scored Mao's economic theory as abstract nihilism, divorced from reality. This was at a meeting called jointly by the Association of Economic Affairs and Peking University in June 1964. Sun emphasized the importance of the law of value, whereas Mao saw in this theory the stepping stone which would transform the socialist economy into a capitalist.[32]

To make life a little bit easier for the unhappy collectivized peasants and small merchants, three freedoms and one undertaking in the commune life were advocated by Sun. These were the extension of individual farm plots for private use (3 to 7 percent of tilled land), and of free markets, the increase of small enterprises with sole responsibility for their own profits and losses, and the fixing of the output quotas for compulsory delivery to the state at the household level. Sun emphasized living standards as the Soviets do.

Among the top leaders Ch'en Yün is China's ranking economist standing for economic rationalization. He was a member of the Politburo's Standing Committee and the second vice-premier of the State Council. He was accused of opposing the three red banners and preaching revisionism. First he was repudiated, but later was allowed to reappear.

The red guard and rebels' newspapers labeled him the "Mikoyan of China." He called agricultural collectivization an "impetuous policy of leftist infantile disorder." He held that farmland should be distributed to peasants "thoroughly and completely." He was said to have quoted a popular satirical piece of peasant wisdom: "The people who under Chiang Kai-shek led a life of privation had steamed rice for meals. The people who now enjoy a life of happiness under Mao have nothing but gruel to heal the pangs of hunger." The charge raised against him was economism.[33] Yet he survived as a full member of the new CC.

Tug-of-War at the Apex

The deep crisis of the regime and the CPC became clearer after the publication of the communiqué and the 16-point decision on the implementation of the cultural revolution. This took place during and following the 11th plenary session of the Central Committee in the first half of August 1966. The communiqué and the 16 points were regarded as the principal documents exposing the regime's own weakness. Mao propelled himself personally as the leader of the all-embracing movement, with Lin Piao as his own deputy, heir apparent and closest comrade-in-arms. Lin was elected a member of the Politburo's Standing Committee and vice-chairman of the Party at the second session of the 8th Party congress. He was a Politburo member since 1956. From the start of 1965 he held the rank of the first vice-premier. The decision itself was anticipated in the Liberation Army Daily two months before.[34]

The most important provision in the decision was directed against the Party powerholders "taking the capitalist road." This militant call was mentioned for the first time at the end of 1964 at a national work conference of the CC. Such conferences usually included the Politburo members, the secretariat and the six regional bureaux. At that time evidently nobody in the Party leadership was aware of the far-reaching significance of this call against "counterrevolutionary revisionists", which eventually led to the biggest purge in the history of the CPC.

The conference endorsed the 23-article document written by Chairman Mao. It dealt with the problems of the socialist education movement in the rural areas, the people's communes, the organization of the poor and lower middle-class peasants, and with the role of the basic cadres below the district level, lacking the revolutionary enthusiasm so much stressed by the Chairman. At the same time it challenged another document, a CC directive called the revised "later 10-points", which had been ascribed to Chairman Liu and advocated the revisionist line based on incentives, private plots and rural markets. What became even more important, the repudiation of this document opened the way for unbridled criticism of *apparatchiki* from the outside. These documents happened to be seized by free China's armed forces during their raids on the mainland coasts.[35]

The Central Committee group in charge of the cultural revolution was headed by Ch'en Po-ta, the chairman's former political secretary and a new member of the Politburo's Standing Committee, as well as deputy chairman of the Chinese Academy of Sciences. The "revolution" was conceived as a continuation of the socialist education movement of 1962 aiming at indoctrination of the Maoist line. The movement had to operate through the four badges of cleanness which came to life in 1965. Its aim was to purify politics, ideology, organization and economy in the cities, and to check in rural areas property, accounts and working points handled by cadres.[36] Evidently these early beginnings of the movement did not work satisfactorily and consequently a new revolution from above had to be launched to supplant it.

It was pointed out that the aim of the "great proletarian, cultural revolution" was to revolutionize people's ideology and thereby "to achieve greater, faster, better and more economical results in all fields of activity." It set a new standard for the whole nation which then became divided into Mao's revolutionaries and their opponents. According to Mao: "A cultural revolution is the ideological reflecttion of the political and economic revolution and places itself in their service."[37] In conformity with Maoism there are now three stages of the revolution in general: the democratic stage, the socialist stage, and the cultural revolution under the dictatorship of the proletariat.

Moravia believes that the cultural revolution is a kind of an autarchic, nationalist Great Wall, a final orthodoxy the aim of which is creation of an absolute and permanent immobility. Professor Ralph Powell of the Research Analysis Corporation of Virginia, and not only the Russians, called it a pseudo-revolution.

In foreign policy the line the cultural revolution took was to denounce the new "Holy Alliance" against Communist China, and to accuse the CPSU of betraying Marxism-Leninism. It called for a clear line of demarcation to deal with "modern revisionist groups led by the CPSU," and banned a united action with the Soviet Union. In opposition to the preceding Party congress decisions, all anti-Soviet pronouncements of the Chinese leadership after 1962 were reaffirmed by the Central Committee. The joint 1957 Declaration and the 1960 Statement were not mentioned any more. In the Maoist vocabulary, revisionism is tantamount to treason. In fact this leftism seems to be a senile illness of communism. There is little doubt that the cultural revolution as allegedly a philosophy of moral transformation has nothing to do with historical materialism.

What the Maoist government rejects more than anything else is peaceful evolution. They regard it as a "subversive plot." China's international defeats in their turn were dismissed as "inevitable zigzags and reversals."

In sum, the goal of the cultural revolution was proclaimed to be liquidation of the old ideology, the old culture, old customs, old habits, and creation of new socialist ideals, transformation of education, literature and art, and of everything in the superstructure that is incompatible with the socialist economic foundation. To this end it was necessary also to discredit and oust the bourgeois academic authorities, and above all to topple any communists in power who follow revisionism as the Russian way.

The decision openly admitted that many Party cadres were not delighted with the prospect of fighting the supposed "monsters and demons." They were described as afraid, more afraid or even extremely afraid.[38] The strategy was suggested that the left elements, a minority, should win the middle of the road elements and thus isolate the rightists. This "dominating faction" (the rightists) was mentioned in the communiqué of the Central Committee which found that the "supporters of this faction can be found both at lower and higher echelons."[39]

Party cadres were divided in four categories: 1) the good ones; 2) the comparatively good ones; 3) those who made serious mistakes but repent; 4) those labeled "three-anti" elements (anti-Party, anti-socialist, anti-Mao's thought) who must be persecuted.

Leaflets distributed by the red guards divided the Party members and all the people in China into ten categories. Only the first category consisted of the bold ones interested in the cultural revolution. The remaining nine categories were "negative," although they included the majority of the Party members. They were labeled as the obstinate ones, who only mechanically carry on their activities. They were described as loyal to the group leader, people who follow the main currents, who do what others do, are in favor of compromise, are timid, without scruples, believe in bargaining or are time-servers. At the end the leaflet raised the question: "Revolutionary comrade, to which of these categories do you belong?"[40]

The decision described the resistance to the new revolution as virulent and stubborn even among responsible men and significant groups. It was recommended to give a chance to these cadres to repent, which appeared to be a concession to the Liu Shao-ch'i faction. Warning was issued not to use violence against the dissident "minority." Students should not be treated severely with the exception of those "who have committed murder or arson, spread poison, did acts of sabotage or stole state secrets."

The organs in charge of the cultural revolution were advised to act like the Paris Commune, adopt an election system, and regularly replace incompetent persons. In this respect we should keep in mind that the Chinese Politburo was expected to convoke the Central Committee at least twice a year for the approval of its work according to the old constitutional requirements. Instead, the Central Committee did not meet for four years, and the Party congress, which should renew the mandate of the high Party organs, had been overdue for eleven years. These were irregularities unusual even in a communist country. They point out that the adventurous Maoist policy lacked support of the leading cadres.

The rubber-stamp plenary session did not mention the purge of Central Committee members. This right belonged to congress.

It was admitted in the decision that the Chinese schools were dominated by the "bourgeois intellectuals." The reform of teaching has to combine education and productive labor, shorten the studies and use the same pattern. It was recommended that in the campaign against bourgeois academic authorities recognized scholars and trained technical personnel should be protected.

This decision was evidently made at a rump session of the Central Committee with supporters of the cultural revolution in the gallery replacing regular members, elected at the 8th Party congress. Notwithstanding the illegal participation of Mao's supporters, there was resistance at the session. Mao was quoted as saying: "I have obtained support from a little over half of the comrades at the plenum. Yet, there were still many comrades who voiced disapproval." When he started the cultural revolution Mao admitted his isolation, saying that a vast majority of people thought that his understanding of the situation was out of date. He said that on several occasions he could not find one single person to agree with his opinion. Later two Hong Kong communist dailies conceded that the session was packed with observers.[41]

At the same time a new leadership was installed, actually handpicked by Mao. According to *Hsinhua* announcements, the new order of precedence was disclosed at the subsequent rallies of the red guards. Mao again violated what is called communist legality. It is estimated that roughly more than two-thirds of the Central Committee's full and alternate members had been disgraced and purged for not supporting any more Mao's policy. The fact that even the number of participants was not mentioned in the communiqué was without precedence. The red guards were mentioned as "revolutionary young people."

The last count of the old Central Committee before the cultural revolution was 94 full and 79 alternate members. Some were in trouble even before the great purge. According to nationalist sources, of 173 members no more than 55 (that is less than 32 percent) have been known as Maoists, the majority being against the "great leader." Other nationalist reports listed 52 for Mao, 106 against him, and 15 neutral or potentially hostile to the Chairman.[42] At the 19th anniversary celebration of the take-over, CC members were not listed by name any more.

Reliable information had it that only 80 full and alternate members attended the 11th plenary session. With so many CC members ostracized or silenced, Mao usurped the name of the CC to fabricate the decision and resolution of the plenary session. They were spurious documents. This rump CC nominated new members to the ruling

Politburo's Standing Committee, whose tenure expired in 1961. In reality then, all the so-called CC decisions, the decisions of the four supreme bodies in conjunction, that is, of the CC, the Military Affairs Committee, the Ch'en Po-ta group and the State Council, promulgated during the cultural revolution, are nothing else than Mao's personal decrees.[43]

Russian, Japanese and Western records agreed that the Chinese Party Central Committee had practically ceased functioning. Of the 17 full and 6 alternate Politburo members elected at the 8th Party congress, 14 have been repudiated and purged. Among the Central Committee secretaries many have been purged and the rest have received other jobs. Of the leaders running the six regional Central Committee Bureaux, most have been disgraced and suspended.

The State Council as the caretaker of administrative affairs has been torn apart. Of the 15 vice-premiers, only a few have been spared humiliation, while nine have been purged. Of 49 ministries and commissions under the State Council, 33 have been placed under military control. Among the cabinet ministers and commission chairmen as well as among vice-ministers and vice-chairmen, altogether 122 have been purged, that is, one third of the members of the State Council. On the other hand the experts and non-Party men escaped unscathed. Chou En-lai with his businessman's acumen succeeded in saving his "economic brains", namely, Li Fu-ch'un, Li Hsien-nien and Ch'en Yün.

Since most of the ministries are under the control of the Military Affairs Committee, the State Council has been reduced to the control of foreign affairs, to finance and trade, internal affairs, agriculture, forestry and several other departments.

Of the National People's Congress Standing Committee members more then one half have been purged.[44] Among these were five deputy chairmen.

The complete isolation of Mao's Central Committee, in reality a minority of Mao's supporters, has been revealed in a statement of the outspoken former Vice-Premier and Foreign Minister Ch'en Yi as reported by a Japanese deported from Peking. According to him Ch'en said bitterly: "It is indeed a shame that in the great CPC there are only six persons—Chairman Mao, Vice-Chairman Lin Piao, Premier Chou En-lai, Ch'en Po-ta, K'ang Sheng, and Chiang Ch'ing—

on whom the rebels can depend."[45]   Eighty percent of the old CPC members were against the Chairman, he asserted.

An alarming assessment of the situation was given by Ch'en Yi, entitled "This Foreign Minister of Mine," published in February 1967 as reported by a Chinese nationalist source:

> Tens of thousands of senior cadres have been liquidated. In the work teams [which Liu Shao-ch'i sent out to suppress the cultural revolution] 400,000 cadres have been tortured and liquidated ... All my department directors have been now thrown out of jobs. What kind of a foreign minister am I anyway? Everybody is scared. Everybody lives in constant fears of being dragged out. It is all power struggle over and over again, and there are Khrushchev-type revisionists everywhere.
>
> We don't believe in the cult of the individual. We don't have any cult of Stalin, of Khrushchev, or of Chairman Mao. Chairman Mao is but an ordinary man. Who has not been opposed to Chairman Mao? There is but a very small handful of them. I believe it is not an easy matter to have 20 percent of the Party members truly supporting Chairman Mao ...
>
> Who of all the comrades standing by the side of Chairman Mao is trustworthy? Do you consider as trustworthy Chairman Mao, Lin Piao, Chiang Ch'ing [Mme Mao], the Premier, Ch'en Po-ta, K'ang Sheng? It is indeed very lenient of you [referring to the red guards] to count in the five vice-premiers, thus raising the number of trustworthy comrades to 11. Are those the only 'clean' men in such a great Party as is ours? I am reluctant to be included in the list of such 'clean' men. You might as well drag me out to face the people.
>
> 'Down with Liu, Teng, Ch'en, Chu, Ho.' Why putting them down into the same pillory? They should be dealt with individually. 'Down with Chu Teh, the big warlord.' Chu Teh worked for the state for several decades. Does it not disgrace the Party to call him a 'big warlord'? Now he has been dragged out for humiliation, and even his ancestors [he belonged to the low gentry] cannot get away from being repudiated. What would people say to this? They would say that you communists can't even tolerate an 81-year old man,

'Down with Ho Lung, the big bandit.' To me this is totally unacceptable. Ho Lung is a Politburo member. He was a marshal. Now you threaten to crush his 'dog's head'. No wonder the people have condemned the Communist Party for being ungrateful to the men who contributed tremendously to the establishment of our political regime.

So many veteran cadres have committed suicide. What has forced them to put an end to their own lives? Many of you here are children of Party cadres. If your own parents had been dragged out and abused, how would you have felt? There are among you children of workers and peasants who have fought for the interests of the working class and of the peasantry, but met with a sad end [in the civil war]. Don't you feel sorry for them? Now you have come all out to put up big-character posters, because somebody behind the stage directed you to do so. What the hell are you doing anyway? Now the students are authorized by the central authorities to behave like lunatics ...

Now you suspect everybody and everything. You say that all stereotypes should be crashed. In my opinion Mao Tse-tung's thought is the biggest stereotype of all.[46]

Ch'en Yi had hard times during 1967. The revolutionary rebels seized control of the Ministry of Foreign Affairs in August for two weeks. Functionaries and guards were beaten, doors and windows were demolished, and confidential papers seized already in May. Even the exhibition of the activities of foreign affairs, approved by Premier Chou, was smashed to pieces by revolutionary rebels of the Foreign Language Institute according to a red guard publication produced for internal circulation, as revealed by Chinese nationalists.[47] Ch'en Po-ta asked them not to drag out the Foreign Minister on the ground that his ministry was led by Premier Chou who called on the red guards to criticize Ch'en Yi. The cultural revolution chief asked them to give him a chance to "correct his mistakes." He was one of the commanders of the Red Armies and Marshal of China. In fact Ch'en Yi had to make two public self-examinations and to give a written confession of his "errors of class attitude," when he had to repudiate a big-character poster signed by 91 ambassadors and department heads of the Foreign Ministry in his defense against the distortion of the extremists.

His biggest 'crime' was the statement he made about the "great leader." He said: "The CC of the Party might as well put up 'big-character' posters to criticize Mao. I had opposed Chairman Mao in the past. Those who oppose him are not necessarily counterrevolutionaries, and those who support him are not definitely revolutionaries." Ch'en Yi resumed his post for a while only, with an undermined authority. Many purged officers of his ministry have been rehabilitated.[48]

The strange procedure of first letting a high functionary to be mobbed and then expressing surprise, is reflected in a Mao statement, quoted in a red guard paper: "How can Ch'en be struck down? He has been with us forty years and has to his credit so many achievements. He has lost 27 pounds in weight. I cannot show him to foreign guests in this condition."[49]

"What Chairman Mao Says, the Hung Weiping Do"

The Maoist leadership tried to arouse the masses with an increasingly primitive propaganda, worse than Stalin's, which could convince no reasonable Chinese. This propaganda was challenged by a significant part of Party members as well as by the anti-communist majority of the people. In the opinion of Chinese nationalists "the purge on the Chinese mainland unmistakably shows that the anti-communist wave of the mainland people has exerted a powerful influence on the communist cadres and intellectuals, on one hand, while the anti-Maoism of the high cadres of the Peiping regime has further intensified the anti-communist sentiments of the mainland people, on the other."[50] The resistance of the cadres served as an inspiration to the Chinese people in their fight against Maoism which threw the country into a convulsion without parallel.

A week after the plenary session of the Party's Central Committee a new extra-Party organization of young executioners appeared in Peking to aid the new "cultural revolution" authorities in their nefarious project. To that end a fierce campaign marked by day and night demonstrations was put on stage with the deafening accompaniment of gong, drum and cymbal beating, red flag waving, while hundreds of thousands of youngsters in the streets carried banners with big letter slogans. The red guards (*hung weiping*) were officially authorized to set no limits on excesses, which were often accompanied with symbolically administered violence and ritualistic acts of desecration, commented Professor Henry Pachter.

Whom would they like to make believe that all this was a genuine movement? Mao's tempestuous storm troopers created an image of public opinion by rioting and threatening to bash the skull of everybody who disagreed with Mao's thought. The result was something which appears like organized mass delinquency. Communist techniques of using fraud and deceipt are no secret, and its Maoist style was true to form. Licensed hooliganism and organized terrorism were set on foot. The main task was to make trouble and create a rebellion, as they openly admitted. They were said to be sons and daughters of workers, peasants and soldiers, of revolutionary cadres, that is Maoists, and of communist martyrs. They had the right to arrest and punish anybody, and to disrupt the regular Party and government administration in order to destroy the "four-old" and to set up the "four-new" as decreed by the decision. Their terror was legalized.[51] "Wherever there is repression of the individual, there can be no greater crime," wrote Mao when he was young.

The para-military olive drab, uniformed shock detachments with red armbands, obviously buttressed by the army, created an atmosphere of complete irresponsibility. They had struck panic, and fear entered into every mainland home. This was a new pogromist organization of high school and college students and some teachers, by-passing the Party organization and superseding the Young Communist League and the China Student Federation. According to the Red Flag they were "youngsters who had not yet rid themselves of their baby smell," prodded and authorized to terrorize, torture prisoners in public and kill them. In their 23 theses program the most important point was "equality in poverty."

The Chinese nationalists described them by these words: "Their immaturity, their love of adventure, their rebellious disposition, and their strong impulse for mischief and destruction could surely be manipulated to serve Mao's pernicious purpose."[52]

Their "rebellion" was patterned on the peasant Red Guards in the civil war. This was a genuine rebellion against the landlords and the established authority. Young peasants then acted spontaneously. Mao made an investigation of this movement in the Hunan province and wrote a report on it.

Forty years later the Maoists used the same methods and even the same terms: terror, hats of infamy, opponents again became diabolic autocrats, the situation was "excellent" and the limits were never exceeded.

These teen-agers and adolescents were easily available. The closing of schools made the youth idle. They were hastily created by Lin and at once institutionalized as a "permanent revolutionary organization," and a "powerful reserve force" for the army. The regular Party organizations were expected to conform. Posters announced that Party committees should stop activity, and the red guards would take over "correcting" their work.[53] A thorough reconstruction of the Party was in the offing. Cultural revolution authorities and the red guards were specifically empowered to assume the functions of local and higher level Party committees.[54]

Before the plenary session of the Central Committee, Chairman Liu and Party Secretary General Teng, then representing the regular Party hierarchy, dispatched operation teams (groups of inspectors) to various parts of the country to surround, discredit, brake and disband the red guards who were starting the cultural revolution. They were called "units of firemen." When Mao regained power, the operation teams were disbanded.

Their secret files against various Maoists were declared void by the Central Committee in order to restore the reputation of the incriminated. Moreover, the Military Affairs Committee declared "invalid" the material bearing on the unruly red guards, which was gathered by the Party organizations. It ordered that it be burned. Party organizations, however, did not surrender this "black material." The result was that the red guards made an attempt to seize the material compromising them. Clashes and bloody encounters took place particularly at many Shanghai higher educational institutions and elsewhere.[55]

The new propaganda chief T'ao Chu, the 15th vice-premier, adviser to the central cultural revolution group, former first Party secretary of the Central-South Regional Bureau of the Central Committee, was propelled from the 86th to the fourth place in the Standing Committee of the Politburo. He was director of the political department in Lin Piao's fourth field army. He accused President Liu and the Party secretary general of having tried to pervert and suppress the cultural revolution, during fifty days between June and July 1966, by the operation teams. In his speech to medical workers he admitted that Liu's views were shared by many people, and followed chiefly by the leadership of provincial and city Party committees. There were public statements, actions and meetings in Peking and throughout the country against Maoist extremism.[56]

Several months later T'ao Chu himself was purged, which drastically revealed the chaotic nature of the struggle. Japanese and free Chinese sources confirmed that the rowdies paraded T'ao and subjected him to a kangaroo court as the "Khrushchev of Central-South China." He was accused of having deplored the "great leap," belittled Mao's thought, advocated reconciliation in the middle of the class struggle, and of being liberal in cultural affairs. Another charge against him was that he was an admirer of the "hundred flowers" by saying that "all doctrines, schools and arguments should be allowed to exist and permitted to 'bloom' and 'contend'."[57] His latest "crime" was that he had carried into effect the Liu-Teng line into Mao's head-quarters. He was also involved in sending out operation teams to suppress the cultural revolution.

A further symptomatic charge against him appeared later on. It concerned his two books, which came out in Chinese only. Their titles were Ideals, Integrity and Spiritual Life and Thinking, Feeling and Literary Talent. T'ao was really an adherent of "goulash" communism, a complete contradiction of Mao's thought, as may be seen from the following paragraph quoted by his accusers:

T'ao Chu says that 'the ideal of communism means comfortable houses.' It is 'to provide every room with electricity at night and enable everybody to be well dressed and ride in motor-cars ...' In short it means 'good food, good clothing and good housekeeping.' It means seeking pleasure. He is ready to sell his very soul, with a cheap 'communist' label thrown in to anybody who gives him good food and good housing. This is indeed the philosophy of the most abject traitors. It is communism in appearance, but ultra-individualism or capitalism in reality. That is the nature of T'ao Chu's 'ideal of communism.' Would it not follow from this goal that the life of the U.S. bourgeoisie is in full agreement with this 'ideal of communism'?[58]

In conformity with the headlines of Peking newspapers which read: "What Chairman Mao Says, the Hung Weiping Do," the red guards' activities reflected the Maoist leadership's "highest instructions."[59] Mao himself confirmed it at a leadership meeting held at the end of October 1966: "I myself had stirred up this big trouble, and I can hardly blame you if you have complaints against me."

Red guards were overtly militarized, legitimate organizations under the dictatorship of the proletariat. Their mission was "to destroy the old order and build a new one." In the words of the People's Daily, Red Flag and Liberation Army Daily they were an "iron broom" with the task "to annihilate mercilessly all hotheads of revisionism." Commanders and politcoms of military units were assigned to these guards as instructors. Formed into combat units and regiments, they received their own headquarters and command.

Their wave of terror first turned against the "overlooked" middle class and national bourgeoisie, social classes which were legally "guaranteed." In Red China's national flag of five stars, these classes are represented by two of these stars. The terrorists bursted into private apartments, smashed many valuable things, beat up and arrested the inhabitants, and hauled them out as well as sacked their houses. They put on their victims dunce caps and derisory placards with humiliating inscriptions. Then they were paint-bedaubed. This work done, they were reduced to a slave status, forced to work in the streets or sent to the countryside. Some of them were killed. The same fate befell communists and anti-communists alike.[60] Following the reports of Soviet newspapers, red guards launched a wave of kangaroo show trials. There was nothing spontaneous in all those outrages, since the roving bands were directed by Maoists.[61] The persecution and execution of the unhappy people had the appearance of a combination of the Russian *pogrom* and the Chinese torture.

The red guards were provided by the armed forces with old uniforms, food, accommodation, transportation and communication. Millions of them traveled to Peking and other cities to establish "revolutionary contacts and exchange experience." Premier Chou confirmed that 30 percent of the transport was currently used by them. The whole "revolution" was financed by the treasury. This was for them actually a synthetic experience, a large-scale military exercise in preparation for a "people's war." The zealots were longing for military glories. They wanted a big war, which if necessary would stain the whole Pacific with blood.[62]

The Russians disclaimed that the red guards had anything in common with the Red Guard soldiers fighting in their own civil war. Their view of the Chinese red guards, or rather of the *hung weiping*, for they always used the Chinese expression in designating them, was expressed as follows: "These Chinese teen-agers, who are politically ignorant, naive and inexperienced, and who have quickly adopted fanaticism, have become the driving force of the cultural revolution. These gangs of vagabonds have disorganized life in China and created a situation of physical and moral terror against the people."[63]

The red guards recklessly destroyed China's cultural heritage and historical relics like destructive locusts, said Lu Tsi, a nationalist commentator in his analysis of this movement. The citizens themselves and their communities were deprived of what remained of old Chinese ways and Western influence, and everything was terribly simplified. Books of non-communist Chinese and of all foreign authors were collected and burnt or used as mash. Only Mao's works and some other communist publications remained on display. Priceless ancient Chinese art treasures were smashed. In the Central Institute of Arts in Peking fire was made to destroy the sculptures of emperors, kings, generals, artists, scholars and works of art of old China as well as images of Buddha.[64] Churches and temples of all religions were blasted. In parts of China inhabited by Turkic and Moslem peoples the young terrorists covered the local Moslem clergy with paint and led them through the streets in shame. Moslem societies were dissolved, and their leaders persecuted. Burhan Shahidi, leader of the Islamic community in China, was imprisoned, and their national heritage ruined. In this way, the Russians reported the *hung weiping* burnt millions of books, destroyed countless outstanding paintings, tore down hundreds of pagodas and mosques, and demolished monuments of antiquity.[65]

Walls of houses, fences and store windows in the capital and in other cities were covered by big-character newspapers (*tatzu pao*) or wall-posters consisting of information, attacks, criticism, warnings, orders, ultimatums and denunciations.

Big-character posters as tools of struggle were initiated personally by Mao himself, when he instructed Mme Nieh Yüan-tzu, a teacher at Peking University to criticize university president Lu P'ing. Later this lady became chairman of the revolutionary committee at the University, and vice-chairman of the Peking revolutionary committee. As Mme Mao's cat's paw she was stabbed at a rally and became one of the victims of the factional struggle.[66] She was promoted to a candidate-member of the new CC.

The first poster of the Mao-Lin group appeared on the campus on May 25, 1966. Thereafter Mao wrote to the red guards of the *Tsinghua* University (a polytechnic school) describing the nation's first Marxist-Leninist big-character poster the "declaration of the Peking's People's Commune in the sixties of the twentieth century." He requested them to attack the Liu-Teng headquarters by means of posters which should be spread throughout the whole country. Two months later Mao put up his own poster. It bore the title "Bombard the Headquarters" (of the CPC). This happened on August 5, during the session of the rump CC. Praise was lavished on the first poster and on the comment of the People's Daily.[67]

Some posters were defaced by others. Readers complained in the Liberation Daily about the situation on Shanghai streets where "some people scribble and scrawl and paste other slogans on the criticism and repudiation columns unmolested, put on new slogans attacking certain organizations and in this way mutilate and damage many special columns and posters."

For people who have been denounced and attacked in the *tatzu pao* this form of public opprobrium had a Kafka-like character of a proscription known in ancient Rome, or of a proclamation in the French revolution before Robespierre's downfall, says Moravia.

The Frenzied Hunt of the "Smiling Tigers"

The witch-hunting frenzy was a striking evidence of resistance to Mao's personal dictatorship as well as of the insecurity of the ultra-orthodox clique which rules the country. It was Mao's last attempt to preserve his own image of China, made in the moment when China sank to the lowest point. The next generation could not be trusted. That was the real reason why Lin Piao created a private army of youngsters. What will become of these young people with their half-study, half-work education repeating, *ad nauseam,* political slogans? In fact the red guards introduced a mob rule of lawlessness, putting the constitution, the laws and the Party statutes in jeopardy. Basic human rights became non-existent, Maoism destroying all human concepts and the traditional morality of the Chinese society.

The red guards turned quickly to their main task—to fight the "establishment", the "battered Party bureaucracy" throughout the country called the "smiling tigers." This turned out to be much more difficult than mobbing the old "capitalists." Party functionaries and committees were routed, beaten up, and sometimes tortured, mutilated and killed. People who died under torture were officially certified to have died natural deaths. In this way, through wanton brutalities and atrocities, they shook up and purged many Party committees—availing themselves of the Red Chinese army's tactic "to beat the enemy piece by piece." Yury Kosyukov, an expelled *Izvestia* correspondent from China, told a press conference in Moscow that "numerous prominent Chinese Party leaders and statesmen had disappeared without a trace."[68]

In many places the Party functionaries were backed by rank-and-file communists and sometimes even by anti-communists, when they advocated better living conditions and tolerance. In some places, however, the anti-communists were only glad to see the downfall of the old powerholders, though they soon became aware that their lot has changed to even worse than before.

It is no wonder that it often happened that there were many wounded and dead people on both sides. Sparks of anti-Maoist actions produced their own victims. Such incidents were never reported in the central press, and could be mentioned only on posters in Peking's streets. The red guard press reported many serious encounters among the "little generals" or rather little commissars and Party functionaries, as well as large-scale scuffles with workers and between the rival groups of the red guards themselves. Japanese and Russian correspondents reported massacres in Changsha, Chengtu, Wuhan, Shanghai, Nanking, Tientsin, Sian, Lanchow, Harbin, Changchun, Shengyang, all of these being provincial capitals, in Kweilin (Kwangsi-Chuang province), and other cities. There was also a serious clash between red guards of the Peking University and cadets of the capital's Military Academy. Armed clashes in general were admitted by the CPC's theoretical organ. An appeal was made to the

masses not to fight the students.[69]   Troops were used to break up
large brawls. People's Daily issued a warning that opposition to the
red guards would be met with the "mighty state machine" and with
"heavy legal punishments."

The red guard activities were first limited in the people's communes, industrial enterprises, mining, construction organizations,
trade services, and scientific research institutes.   They were not
allowed to interfere in their affairs, nor take part in their discussions.
Here the resistance bore fruit as it was in the interest of the regime
for economic reasons.

In the presence of Mao and the reshuffled leadership, Lin Piao,
as the commander in chief's deputy of the red guards, at their second
and third mass rallies advised to "carry out the contest by reasoning
rather than by recourse to force," emulating the military discipline at
Tien-an-men (Square of the Gate-Tower of Heavenly Peace). This
call was echoed by the official press. Yet at the same time Lin ordered
them to "break all resistance." He described the upheaval as extending its scope to politics and economics.[70] In his mid-September speech
to the red guards he complained that their opponents were inciting
worker and peasant masses to fight the revolutionary students.

The Defense Minister spoke at several of these 1966 eight
manifestations, "meeting" the red guards, which took the form of
mass adoration of Mao and were meant to show his full endorsement
of the cultural revolution. During these meetings the Party leadership
which was present waved red cover booklets containing quotations
from the works of the "great teacher," and so did the red guards
themselves. The Russians called these booklets "the pocket Talmud
of Mao Tse-tungism."   In the official reports of these meetings, the
Standing Committee, Politburo, Secretariat and Central Committee
members were listed according to their new ranking.

The Chairman, wearing a PLA uniform, remained silent during
the meetings with the red guards, probably because of ill health or
some disorder. His look was glassy, his body bloated. Westerners
who had an opportunity to see Mao of late describe him as an
inanimated dummy, resembling a totem. The Japanese photographed
him with a telescope film camera. He looked on these pictures to be
a physically exhausted man with a face as tense as a mask. Other
people hold that Mao refrained from public speaking because his

voice is cracked and high-pitched, and consequently makes a poor impression.[71]

When the Chairman's spouse delivered her important address to Anhwei province delegations, which was broadcast by radio, Premier Chou made a remark that "Chiang Ch'ing's speech insured that the *voice of Mao* was transmitted throughout the country."

The vandalism of the red guards was limitless. The rule was that those who complained of lawlessness were immediately denounced as "capitalist henchmen."

The red guards in their posters sharply criticized the chief of state, the secretary general of the Party, several Politburo members, many vice-premiers, other cabinet members, many Party committees at ministries, the new propaganda chief, the leadership of the new Peking city committee and a host of other organizations. The zealots recited passages from Mao's works at the top of their voices, and staged regular and sit-down demonstrations and sometimes hunger strikes. They also occasionally wrote their petitions in blood. One of their papers, *Hung Weiping Pao,* wrote that the only correct attitude was to defend Mao and the Central Committee, which should not include its individual members but only those who were loyal to the "great helmsman." Everybody else may be subject to "bombing." Regret was expressed at the lack of unity of ideas and action in the top leadership as well as in the rank and file.[72]

The Chinese revolutionary writer Lu Hsun, who died in the mid-thirties, was celebrated both by the Chinese and the Russians at his birthday anniversary, but for opposing reasons. The Chinese hailed him as a fore-runner of the cultural revolution. The Russians, on the other hand, praised him as a bard of brotherhood: "He fought—they said—relentlessly against chauvinist scribblers who called upon the 'Asian knights' to sally forth against the Soviet state 'under the banner of Genghis Khan'." He acquainted the Chinese readers with the immortal works of foreign classics on which revolutionary culture had to be built. Such was his *Leitmotif.*

The Soviets complained that the red guards were imbued with vicious anti-Sovietism. In Russian they were called *okhranniki,* an expression used to describe the Tsarist secret police. In several places books in Russian, which were found in libraries and schools, were burnt. A mass anti-Soviet indoctrination of Chinese youth is indeed still going on. Anti-Soviet slogans in the streets of Peking and other Chinese cities are their distinguishing mark. The Russians are convinced that the *okhrana* was masterminded by experienced directors which abused the immature youth.[73] Also the nuclear blasts in China were used for further whipping up anti-Soviet hysteria.

Disruption of the whole transport system as well as cold weather temporarily brought to a halt the "exchange of experience" of the red guards. The Central Committee and the State Council decreed that everybody must return to his home. From November 21, 1966 their travels to Peking were banned. There is an estimate that from the second half of August to mid-November thirteen million red guards had converged on Peking, and on the day when the ban was issued two million of them were still in the capital.[74] Many of them disobeyed the order, which had to be repeated several times, even in the following year.

Following the above-mentioned rallies of the red guards, Maoist leaders received more than hundred thousand commanders, army men and functionaries of Party and government organizations (the new political police included), who took part in the "colossal work" and who took care of "Chairman Mao's guests from all parts of the country",[75] another evidence that the "revolution" was stagemanaged.

Moravia, who saw the Chairman as a romantic, or nostalgic and naive person described the cultural revolution in the summer of 1967 as follows:

> Fifty million Red Guards who in one year rush out from one end of China to another like in another children's crusade; millions of wall papers; hundreds of thousands of marching past, parades, demonstrations, rallies; more than ten million Red Guards received personally in Peking; and furthermore the whole of China turned upside down, agricultural and industrial production reduced, the officialdom confused, the Party bureaucracy destroyed, some provinces in the hands of Maoists, others in the hands of anti-Maoists. This is a rather incomplete list of the explosive results of Mao's turning to the masses.[76]

On his visit to Bucharest in the summer of 1966, Premier Chou in a luncheon speech said that the issue was "whether the dictatorship of the proletariat and the socialist economic basis of the country could be consolidated and carried forward."[77] The new revolution was to insure that China will never become revisionist and will never allow a peaceful evolution. This was the explanation given by Chou and Foreign Minister Ch'en. For the Maoist line to survive this was a question of "to be or not to be." It was a power and succession struggle in a sectarian feud which shook China during an all-embracing purge. The Maoists admitted that powerful elements within the Party were bracing for a contest of power against Mao and Lin. They foresaw that the enemy would be crashed.[78]

There are in the CPC two diametrically opposed lines, according to the Red Flag. In fact there was one more line. This included people who were waiting for the outcome of the struggle to side with the victor. The Maoist proletarian line serves the purpose of the ideological revolutionization. The "bourgeois counterrevolutionary line" on the other hand is followed by a "considerable number of foolish people within the Party."[79] For the developments in China the Maoists give the following explanation: "There can be no construction without a destruction." This is an old Bakuninist idea. Mao's opponents are divided between those who "being unwilling to change their minds, persist in error", and those "who are willing to correct themselves." The first category, whatever their merits, are an antagonistic contradiction which must be prosecuted. It was revealed that those who persist in error call the Maoists "counterrevolutionary, anti-Party elements, rightists and pseudo-leftists, but in reality, rightists."

Chinese nationalists described these intricate and complex feuds as organized grand purges and an organized mass resistance against the brutal features of Mao's ruthless policy and capricious rule.[80]

Had there been a majority in the Central Committee and in the CPC for Mao, no cultural revolution would have been necessary to overcome his enemies. Everything could have been solved by decree on the basis of the so-called democratic centralism. But such a dependable majority for his extreme policies had been missing for many years. To keep his power he had to abuse the Party statute. The red guards and red rebels were therefore set up as a counterforce to the established order of the CPC. This was conceded by the Red Flag, which argued that otherwise "an usurpation" could have taken place, in other words the revisionists might have taken over.[81]

Along with P'eng Chen other prominent leaders were subjected to humiliating "struggle meetings." The most important among them were Lo Jui-ch'ing, the former chief of the general staff, Lu Ting-yi, a former propaganda chief of the CC and minister of culture, and Yang Shang-k'un, then a CC member and alternate secretary, a vice-premier in charge of security affairs, and director of the CC's executive office (one of the 28 Chinese Bolsheviks.) The latter was accused of having provided the Russians with highly confident information. Later on photos appeared of the four once leading communists with placards of disgrace on their chest, kneeling with bent heads, pushed around by red guards. The photos were posted in the center of Peking. Lo and Yang were accused of impermissible contacts with foreign countries, meaning the Soviet embassy. Yang was particularly charged with having planted microphones in Mao's private quarters and providing in this way useful information for the Soviets.[82] Later it was reported that Lo, Lu and Yang committed suicide.

Ubiquitous big-character posters and mobile loudspeakers step by step identified Chief of State Liu Shao-ch'i and the Secretary General of the CPC, Teng Hsiao-p'ing, as leaders of the anti-Maoist line. These people also were pilloried and disqualified at mass rallies. Both appeared at Mao's meetings with the red guards between August and November without red armbands.

On the other hand, Lin Piao assumed the role of Mao's prophet and hatchet man, and with his approval was designated for succession, a position held for two decades by Liu. He became the Leader's trusted man to rally military support.

"Who will beat whom" in the ideological and power struggle between the orthodox and the revisionist wings of the Party became the overriding concern in the ordeal of Red China. Official press comments presented the turbulence as a struggle between socialism and capitalism, the latter identified with revisionism. They admitted that this struggle is far from ended and that it will last a long time.

In view of the many setbacks, Peking maintained the line that an offensive has been set on foot against Mao's policies by the "imperialists and modern revisionists" with whom the members of the overthrown social classes in China and the right-wing opportunists within the Party are acting hand in hand in a life-and-death struggle.

This explains best the stress laid on contradiction and the class struggle, calling for the domination of the Maoist faction, and for unrestrained adulation of Mao and his writings as a guideline in all manifestations of life. In sum, the new revolution was launched in order to break all resistance to extremism in Chinese internal and foreign policy. It was the most recent phase of Red China's blundering policy.

It has now become obvious that the majority of the CPC has viewed the action of the political desperados with strong resentment, and that it had at times offered them bloody resistance when it was able to obtain army support in resisting the purges. The Red Flag issued a warning to the left not to fear the temporary isolation and encirclement by the reactionary, and this appeal was reprinted by all dailies.

The historical background of the purged leaders was analyzed by a young Chinese doctoral candidate at Columbia University. He found out that they were linked to the disgraced chief of state in one way or another, and belonged to four separate cliques: 1) The P'eng Chen December 9th 1935 movement; 2) the "prison cadres" who are described in Volume II; 3) the "white area" cadres before 1945, who differed from the "liberated area" cadres; 4) those belonging to the Northwest Red Army before the Japanese aggression, or to the Northwest CC Bureau during that war under the leadership of Kao Kang, and the Marshals P'eng Teh-huai and Ho Lung, discussed in the previous chapter and in Volume II.[83] The first group embraced college and secondary school students who participated in the December student storm in Peking, and who successively went to Yenan after the start of the anti-Japanese war.

The Maoists are fighting against the thermidorian forces in their own ranks. The CPC will never recover the virility it had before the "mass line" was applied against it in such a drastic way, all on account of Mao's misgivings and then distrust of his own traditional cadres when they emerged from the Yenan crucible. The opposition turned out to be strong enough to check Mao's policies, and could not be brought to heel by the militant youth corps and the "rebels." In fact, only a handful of the top leaders participated in the cultural revolution, and they were far outnumbered by the opposition. There is little doubt that the resistance to the "revolution" was more serious than was expected.

Unity of their big country and strict order established under the rigorous control of the CPC were boasts of the Chinese communists. In order to regenerate the revolution, to make it permanent—a hopeless undertaking—disorder was created from above, a unique procedure indeed. As a result, the stability of the communist authority was undermined. The Maoists joined battle with the CPC which made room for the military. The young and older thugs would certainly fall short without the effective backing of the army. It is an old communist strategy to repeat a thousand times the same slogan in the hope that the populace will swallow it in the end. This strategy reached its peak with Mao's quotations emblazoned as a guidance for the whole country and repeated everywhere so loudly and blatantly in order to make it impossible for anyone to protest. The future of China depends on the outcome of this struggle.

Chinese Youth's Great Leap Backward

The cultural revolution was meant as a school for the young generation, which, as in all communist countries, has become alienated. There were not enough hardships in Red China to steel the youth. In the opinion of Maoists war would provide the "best" trial, but it could also spell the end of communism in China. The cultural revolution was conceived as a desperate effort to recapture the youth for the Spartan life known in the Yenan caves. To this end the re-opening of the schools was postponed until the next year by the decree of the Central Committee and the State Council of June 13, 1966. The ancient, democratic Chinese institution of selecting competent students through impartial examinations was abolished.[84] This was a great leap backward for China's expanding scientific, technological and educational élite, entailing grave consequences for professional standards. The progress of China suffered a severe blow by this measure. Japanese sources estimated that it meant a loss of at least 400,000 specialists in 1967/68.

Universities were to be filled by ideologically pure students of proletarian origin, regardless of their poor academic records. Hitherto a third of Chinese students came from what was called bourgeois families. In the future, selection and grading would follow recommendation based primarily on political grounds. The entire educational reform had to ensure the Maoist orthodox line.

The change would embrace all aspects of the educational process: the curricula, the textbooks and the teachers. It would be the supreme task of the latter to train revolutionary successors in Mao's doctrine. Graduates of senior high-schools would receive an "ideological graduation certificate" from workers, peasants and soldiers once they have gotten their training from them. The curricula would provide perfunctory education touching a variety of problems, but lacking depth in any discipline.

Some elementary schools and high schools resumed classes in mid-March 1967 with the slogan: "Re-open classes and make revolution." Teachers and students responded slowly. Some pupils held that school is not what it used to be, because there was nothing much to do after going back. The answer which was given to this objection was that the cultural revolution in schools had not yet been carried out thoroughly and in depth. The schools would become "red guard barracks."

According to Russian sources, only a few schools managed to resume their activity at that time. Many teachers "disappeared" and school desks and teaching aids had been destroyed. In fact, many teachers had been humiliated by their pupils, and some were beaten to death. The re-opened schools introduced political and military training by the army. A wall-poster proclaimed "we don't need brains —our heads are armed with Mao Tse-tung's ideals." These replaced science, culture and education.

The PLA was entrusted with re-opening of schools. It was admitted that there were no immediate, visible results due to the obstacles.[85] The Shanghai revolutionary municipal committee, the new powerholders, advised the elementary schools that the content of studies should consist primarily of mass criticism and repudiation, "liberating the great number of responsible students duped and poisoned by the bourgeois revolutionary line." They must resolutely oppose civil war. Seniors should participate in a specific amount of manual labor. Revolutionary teachers will be entrusted with the selection or editing of textbooks.

Mao's programmatic directive of May 7, 1966 in a letter to Lin Piao was held up as a guideline for education. It decreed that the main task for students is to study, but they should learn, in addition, industrial work, farming and military affairs (their role in the cultural revolution was then not yet mentioned). In the same way army men, workers and peasants should learn everything, too. An education reform group headed by Ch'en Po-ta was set up to create a revolutionary school system.[86] Meanwhile free course was given to revolutionary practice.

. How serious the situation was when the task was faced to bring the students back to study was illustrated by Premier Chou himself. Addressing the committee for the preparation of the 1967 take-over festival, he threatened students who would not return to school in a month that is, at the end of October, with the canceling of their school registration. He went on to rule that those who have already graduated but did not return home would face forfeiture of their degree, and no arrangements would be made to get them jobs. However, the following months revealed that the ultimatum of the State Council's Chairman was disregarded by the youngsters whom Mao's thought had turned berserk.

Again, by the end of October 1967, revolutionary pupils and teachers were appealed to by a CC directive to end the 16-month recess. They "must be aware that they are educators and, at the same time, persons undergoing a process of education. In many cases the students are more competent. They must go among the students, mingle with them, and establish new-style teacher-student relations."

The problems connected with the resumption of classes were staggering. Many teachers did not like the idea to meet their former pupils, the red guards, who at times had subjected them to torture. At the same time many pupils objected to the re-instatement of their former teachers. Their was a scarcity of revolutionary teachers, that is, Maoists. The curricula were vague and teaching material was missing. In the end, army members had to be called to force both pupils and teachers to go back to school. They were not much more successful.

The *T'ung-chi* University in Shanghai started an educational reform. It converted itself into the "7th May" Commune, composed of the University, a construction unit and a designing unit. In each class teachers, students, workers, engineers and technicians were organized into a military team. In this way the leadership of the University was captured by the Maoists who sought to co-ordinate education with production. This system was praised as good for the ideological reform of the intellectuals and for the elimination of the difference between mental and manual labor, between workers and peasants, and between urban and rural areas.

The mood of the teachers and pupils after the 18 month vacation and the vain appeals to resume classes was described as follows: "Some teachers feared of entering classrooms lest they be labeled as reactionaries. There were also some students who just could not settle down: They were busy on their far-flung trips to join battles or staying idly at home."[87]

Two years after the closing of schools some colleges still had not opened their gates and only a part of the secondary schools were able to do so. The "great teacher's" latest instructions decreed that colleges are "still necessary," but only science and engineering were mentioned in this connection. Mao stressed shortened schooling, revolutionizing education and giving proletarian politics a commanding post. Subsequently, Maoist anti-intellectualism was reflected in comments to the effect that "people are stupefied by books" and knowledge "is weakening the initiative." The eight-year long study at the Institute of Medicine was stigmatized as "counterrevolutionary and revisionist." There was a Maoist axiom which was given wide circulation. It stated that "the lowly are the most intelligent, the élite, however, most ignorant." The Chairman's anti-intellectualism was further expressed in such maxims as revealed in the Mao papers: "It is not absolutely necessary to go to school", "the more one reads, the more foolish one becomes", and "it is always those with less learning who overthrow those with more learning."[88]

At the same time a new youth-to-the-countryside campaign was launched. It was the third in the decade. Its purpose was to disperse idle youth and teachers to lifetime work assignments on farms and in factories, mines and reclamation projects. That was for many the end of the "resumption of classes to make a revolution." Almost the country's entire student population was affected. Working conditions for the urban youth in the countryside were compared to labor camps. A small paper, Revolutionary Youth, smuggled into Hong Kong, reported the suicide of eight young people on a state farm in Hunan.[89] The Soviet educational system in its turn was criticized by the Maoist press as "bringing up of intellectual aristocrats seeking fame and wealth."

Intellectuals were advised to re-educate and remold according to the proletarian world outlook in order to integrate with the worker and peasant masses and with the soldiers. This was the tenor of an editor's note in Red Flag,[90] presenting "the voice of the great leader." The editor added that even if they are "die-hard capitalist henchmen", a way should be found for them once they have properly purged themselves.

Actually, a new revolutionary road should be considered for training of technical personnel and other skilled people and for the selection of students from among workers and peasants with practical experience in production, and from soldiers. This seems to put higher education practically out of reach for many young people educated with a "bourgeois" world outlook.

For Maoists, all learning appears as darkness and a poisonous concoction. The only exception is study of the Chairman's thought. This may be seen from a compilation and satire made by a Russian commentator from several Chinese radio broadcasts:

Reactionaries of the type of Newton, Einstein, Rutherford and Popov have shown their true faces. They have exposed themselves as agents of international imperialism, as chained dogs of all kinds of reformism, opportunism, nihilism, constructivism and bourgeois humanism. Their malicious, slanderous formulas in Latin letters, Arabic numerals and mathematical symbols deliberately conceal the universal nature of Mao Tsetung's idea. Tolstoi, Goethe, Pushkin, Lu Hsun and Rolland have exposed themselves even more eloquently. Their thick, so-called 'literary' books, using the pretext of 'humanism,' glorify so-called freedom and other abnormalities. Freedom from what? From the ideas of Mao Tse-tung. How insidious and dangerous the actions of these standard-bearers of rightwing ideas and White Guard thoughts can be is indicated by the example of the so-called Newton, who, having discovered the so-called law of universal gravity, deliberately and provocatively kept quiet about the fact that the point of the matter is the gravitation of the whole world toward the ideas of Mao Tse-tung.

All this revisionist and imperialist scum, beginning with

Homer, who pretended to be blind in order to deceive the masses, and ending with Beethoven, who pretended to be deaf for the same purpose, has engendered blindness and deafness among certain unstable elements with respect to Mao Tse-tung's ideas.

Only by tearing up by the roots all this insolent mutiny against Mao Tse-tung's ideas, by destroying it in embryo, is it possible to embark on the high road of revolution, to destroy the old and build the new. It is especially disgusting that the Chinese reactionaries, who have wormed their way into all the cracks and are following the capitalist path, are supporting their actions with the formula, borrowed from the backyards of foreign history, 'ignorance is darkness, learning is light.' Our task is thoroughly to expose the malicious anti-Chinese nature of this formula. Guided by the life giving rays of Mao Tse-tung's ideas, we must realize that all learning, except the study of the ideas of Mao Tse-tung, is a poisonous mixture, a poison that gradually turns healthy and simple workers and peasants into rotten intellectuals. And therefore the complete victory of Mao Tse-tung's ideas is possible only after the complete liquidation of all kinds of learning.[91]

The same source reported that for the Maoists words are not at variance with deeds. This was proved by a secondary school in Heilungkiang province which was disbanded on the request of the pupils "in order to turn Mao Tse-tung's ideas into reality," and to allow them to go to factories and villages.

At the 12th plenary session of the so-called Central Committee, held in the second half of October 1968, the revolutionizing of schools and education was "solved" by the following decision: "As regards intellectuals, they must be re-educated by the workers, peasants and soldiers so that they can integrate with the workers and peasants. The workers' propaganda teams should stay *permanently* (emphasis provided) in the schools and colleges, take part in all the talks and struggle-criticism-transformation there, and always lead these institutions. In the countryside, schools and colleges should be managed by the poor and lower-middle peasants ... The workers, the poor and lower-middle peasants and the commanders and fighters of the PLA ... are undertaking this glorious task."[92]

The task of the worker-soldier or peasant-soldier Mao's thought propaganda teams—as they are called—was first of all to take control of educational and cultural institutions in order to struggle against factionalism and to form everywhere triple alliances of rebels, Maoist cadres and military. This was a steady goal of the cultural revolution, one which evidently was not reached everywhere.

To do so they had to gather weapons which remained after the civil war. In Canton's *Chungshan* University, for instance, they dismantled armed defense works, ferreted out students from other areas, and in the garrets, toilets, ponds and trees discovered large quantities of machine guns, primitive cannons, carbines, explosive charges, iron files, hand grenades, daggers, spears, choppers, sulphuric acid and other lethal weapons.[93]

The favorable targets of these teams were any institutions or enterprises where educated people were employed. This included the press, broadcasting and TV, literature and the arts, science, technology and political indoctrination. Later it expanded to the economic management and to all departments of the superstructure which were out of tune with the socialist economic basis. The 16-point decision had to be fully implemented. In schools the chief objective was to break "five obstacles," namely grading, fees, examinations, promotion and age-limit, and to create thus an egalitarian system of education.[94] This was in fact a challenge issued to anyone who dared to think for himself. Mao's thought became a mental straitjacket killing all creativity, a setback in education and culture.

In reality the educational "revolution" was only another anti-intellectual campaign striving to repress all channels of expression under the pretext of "re-educating" the youth. This time it was directed not only against the opposition, but also against the faithful student red guards. In some institutions the new mentors met with resistance. Members of some propaganda teams were beaten up, wounded and sometimes killed, and in turn there were casualties among the students. Thus resistance was cut down by force, Mao's injunction to the contrary notwithstanding. Many of the red guards were sent to the countryside or to remote border areas to share physical labor for "integration" with the masses.

The worker-peasants-soldiers teams wrested control of schools from the educated people who had been previously roughly handled

by red guards, which were now denounced as unreliable and vacil-
lating. At the October 1st festival of 1968 a small group of red
guards was officially cited on the 15th place among the 16 groups
mentioned. Their halcyon days were over.

For the teams "outstanding representatives" were selected and
a large number of commanders and soldiers were assigned to them.
A Shanghai high school even discarded school classes and instead
organized the school into squads, platoons and companies, based on
neighborhoods and streets. In urban areas provision was made to
have the schools run by factories. Resistance and sabotage from the
professional educators was expected. In the countryside, that is in
more than four fifths of the mainland, management committees of the
production brigades were put in control of the school system. The
traditional learning was reduced to a modicum. Political indoctrination, the study of Mao's thought, productive labor, peasant-led in-
struction in farming, vocational and military training dominate the
field.[95]

The Russians are highly critical of these teams, which are largely
composed of servicemen with a sprinkling of workers and peasants.
In their view these teams of "semi-literate workers and soldiers ...
perform the functions of a unique police guard" introducing in the
schools and elsewhere a garrison regime.

Four years after the educational process was interrupted, there
was no regular teaching at many colleges and universities with some
exception for science and engineering. Teaching slowly returned to
lower schools, some of which are now training centers for narrow
specialization. Red Flag had to repudiate the wide-spread theory of
"no future for teachers."

All that time not a single literary, musical or theatrical work was
published, not a single feature film was made, while museums and
libraries were closed. Chinese books dating before the cultural revolution were withdrawn branded as "bourgeois and feudal." A full
tabula rasa took place. *Trybuna Ludu* asserted that in the field of
education, the cultural revolution is still in the stage of destruction.

In the fifth year of the schooling system's disruption, only the
Maoist reform of primary education seemed to be completed. Even
in Shanghai most secondary schools continued partially unreformed.
At the model *Tsinghua* University difficulties were acknowledged in

a self-criticism by the much reduced workers-soldiers team who had to make concessions to the humilated and confused teachers. China will pay dearly for this experiment.[96]

NOTES

CHAPTER I:

CONFLICTING NATIONAL-REVOLUTIONARY INTERESTS

(pp. 1-21)

1. T. H. Rigby, "The Embourgeoisement of the Soviet Union and the Proletarization of Communist China," in Kurt London, editor, *Unity and Contradiction, Major Aspects of Sino-Soviet Relations*; Third International Conference on Sino-Soviet Bloc Affairs at Lake Kawaguchi, Japan, September 1960, 40 scholars from 11 countries, p. 35.

2. France Popit, "Ista Fronta" (Same Front), *Komunist*, Belgrade, September 5, 1968; Mao, *Selected Works*, Vol. I, pp. 318, 320.

3. Stephen Clissold, *Whirlwind*, pp.238-240.

4. Letter dated May 4, 1948, of the Central Committee of the Communist Party of the Soviet Union (CPSU hereafter) to its counterpart. Published in *The Soviet-Yugoslav Dispute*, p. 38.

5. Vladimir Dedijer, *Tito*, pp. 411, 417, 318. Djilas confirmed same in his *Conversations with Stalin*, p. 143.

5a. *The New York Times*, February 19, 1970; *Pravda*, December 23, 1969; Andrey A. Amalrik, *Will the Soviet Union Survive Until 1984?*, pp 45, 49.

6. A. Bovin, "Internatsionalnye printsipy sotsializma," *Izvestia*, September 21, 1966.

7. Hsinhua, international service in English, quoting *Red Flag*, February 10, 1966.

8. *Die Welt*, Hamburg, March 21, 1966. "Peking plant den Weltkrieg". Received "von berufener Seite".

9. *The New York Times* ,April 17, 1966.

10. *Sino-Soviet Conflict*, p. 3 (see Selected Bibliography.)

11. T.V. Program, "Howard K. Smith—News and Comment," December 2, 1962.

12. Edwin O Reischauer: *Beyond Vietnam*, p. 62.

13. UPI, November 13, 1967; *U.S. News and World Report,* June 22, 1970.

14. *New York Herald Tribune,* April 9, 1962.

15. Edgar Snow: *The Other Side of the River—Red China Today,* p. 101.

16. *The New York Mirror,* August 14, 1962, p. 18.

17. "Marksizm-Leninizm—nashe pobednoye znamya" (Marxism-Leninism—Our Victorious Banner), *Pravda,* January 10, 1963.

18. *The New York Times,* November 27, 1968.

19. *Asian Outlook,* February 1967.

20. Robert S. Elegant: "China's Next Phase," *Foreign* Affairs, October 1967, p. 150.

21. *U.S. News and World Report,* February 28, 1966.

22. Morton Halperin: "China's Strategic Outlook," in *China and the Peace of Asia,* pp. 99-100.

23. *Rad,* Belgrade, September 2; *Borba,* September 9, 1966.

24. *The New Republic,* Washington, December 18, 1961, p. 15. From an extension of portions of the second edition of Prof. Brzezinski's book: *The Soviet Bloc, Unity and Conflict.* A revised edition appeared in 1967. *East Europe* magazine published an article adapted from the later in March 1967, p. 511.

25. Donald S. Zagoria, "The Sino-Soviet Conflict and the West," *Foreign Affairs,* October, 1962, p. 190.

26. Hans J. Morgenthau: *Vietnam and the United States,* p. 55.

27. "Whence the Differences? A Reply to Thorez and Other Comrades", *Peking Review,* No. 9, March 1, 1963, based on *Jen-min Jih-pao* of February 27, 1963; *Time* magazine, December 12, 1969; *The New York Times,* March 1, 1970.

28. *Link,* New Delhi, October 16, 1960.

29. This writer opted for the abbreviation CPC emphasizing its multi-national character; Peter S. H. Tang: *Communist China Today,* p. 84.

30. Nikolay Kapchenko: "On Origins of the Political Course of the CPC Leaders," *International Affairs,* Moscow, March 1967.

31. Radio Moscow, Peace and Progress, in Mandarin, January 11, 1968, and May 6, 1969; Paul Wohl in *The Christian Science Monitor,* February 8, 1968; Radio Moscow in Mandarin, April 6, and May 9, 1967; NCNA, October 10, 1967.

32. Frane Barbieri, "Simultanka sovjetske diplomacije" (Simultaneous Game of Soviet Diplomacy), *Vjesnik,* Zagreb, December 31, 1961; Zvonimir Kristl, "Stanje odnosa u socijalistickom lageru. Razliciti stavovi SSSR i Kine: o ratu i miru, razoruzanju, koegzistenciji, putu u socijalizam" (The State of Relations in the Socialist Camp. Different Positions of the USSR and China: on War and Peace, Disarmament, Co-Existence, the Road to Socialism), *ibid.,* January 19, 20, 21, 1962; Frank O'Brien, *Crisis in World Communism; Marxism in Search of Efficiency,* pp. 119-120.

33. Nikolay Galay, "Geopolitical and Strategic Importance," *Studies on the Soviet Union*, 1962, No. 4, p. 17.
34. L. Shapiro, "The Chinese Ally from the Soviet Point of View," in K. London, *op. cit.*, pp. 364-5.
35. *The Times*, London, January 6, 1961, p. 11.
36. Donald S. Zagoria, *The Sino-Soviet Conflict*, pp. 14, 78; Stefan T. Possony, "The Chinese Communist Cauldron," *Orbis*, fall 1969, p. 791; *Kommunist*, Moscow, Nos. 6-7, 1968.
37. Stuart R. Schram, *The Political Thought* of Mao Tse-tung, pp. 81, 112-114.
38. Viktor Rudin, "Triumph of the Leninist Principles of Party Life," *World Marxist Review*, February 1962, p 8; "Velikoe internatsionalnoe uchenie" (A Great International Teaching), *Kommunist*, No. 6, 1969.
39. *The China Quarterly*, January-March, April-June 1960.
40. Franz Borkenau: "The Peking-Moscow Axis and the Western Alliance," *Commentary*, December, 1954, p. 513.
41. George Paloczi-Horvath: *Mao Tse-tung*.
42. *East Europe*, January, 1965, p. 5.
43. Franz Borkenau: "Mao Tse-tung," *The Twentieth Century*, August 1952.
44. Schram, op. cit., p. 63.
45. Franz Michael: "Common Purpose and Double Strategy," in Clement J. Zablocki's *Sino-Soviet Rivalry*, p. 18.
46. Tito's speech at the 5th plenary session of Yugoslavia's League of Communists' CC, *Borba*, May 19, 1963.
47. B. Schwartz, *Chinese Communism and the Rise of Mao*, pp. 196, 201-2.

CHAPTER II:

DIFFERENT AVENUES OF APPROACH (A PACIFIC PACT)

(pp. 23-35)

1. *Hinter Russland, China*, pp. 35, 65, 30, 47, 60, 63.
2. *United States Relations with China*. With special reference to the period 1944-1949, pp. 564-576.
3. *People's Daily*, October 16, 1967.
4. Edgar Snow, *Red Star Over China*, p. 110.
5. *Hinter Russland, China*, p 42; see also John E. Tashjean, *Where China Meets Russia*: An Analysis of Dr. Starlinger's Theory. Central Asian Collectanea, No. 2, Washington, D.C., 1958, Ph.D. thesis.
6. *Sino-Soviet Conflict*, p. 230.
7. Richard L. Walker, "Collectivization in China: A Story of Betrayal," *Problems of Communism*, 1955-1, pp. 1-12.

8. *Peking Review,* No. 36, September 6, 1963, after *Jen-min Jih-pao* August 30, 1963, "Further Exposure of Soviet Leaders' Acts of Betrayal," p. 27; The same daily, October 1, 1965.

9. *International Free Trade Union* Bulletin, December 1952; *New York Herald Tribune,* February 24, 1954; *The China News,* Taipei, August 4, 1957; Jacques Guillermaz: *La Chine Populaire,* p. 47; K.A. Wittfogel, "Agrarian Problems and the Moscow-Peking Axis," *Slavic Review,* 4/1962; *Free China Review,* June 1968, p. 72; Radio Moscow Peace and Progress in French to Asia, April 7, 1969; *Literaturnaya gazeta,* August 27, 1969; Branko Lazitch, "Combien de vies humaines le regime a-t-il couté à la Chine?", *Est & Ouest,* December 1-15, 1969; Stefan T. Possony *op. cit.* p. 792. See note I-36.

10. "The Chinese Equation," *The Sunday Times,* London, January 23, 1966; "A Study of the Chinese Mainland Population," *Issues and Studies,* Taipei, November 1968; *The New York Times,* January 25, 1970.

11. Leo Orleans, "Troubles with Statistics," *Problems of Communism,* January, 1965, after *China News Analysis,* No. 324, quoting from *Chi-hua Yu T'ung-chi* (Planning and Statistics), No. 8, 1959. The article was reprinted and commented upon in *Asian Outlook,* October, 1965; Dick Wilson, "China's Population," *The World Today,* May, 1966.

12. *The New York Times,* April 27, 1966; Radio Moscow in Mandarin, November 30, 1967; AP, September 18, 1968.

13. *Hinter Russland, China,* p. 106; *The New York Times,* December 28, 1965.

14. *The New York Times,* August 22, 1965 and August 16, 1966.

15. Victor S. Frank: *Problems of Communism,* March-April, 1964; C.P. Fitzgerald: "Tension on the Sino-Soviet Border," *Foreign Affairs,* July 1967, p. 689; *The New York Times,* November 27, 1968.

16. "Po povodu besedy Mao Tsze-duna gruppoi yaponskih sotsialistov" (On Occasion of the Conversation of Mao with a Group of Japanese Socialists). *Pravda,* September 2, 1964.

17. *International Boundary Study,* Department of State, The Geographer Report No. 64, p. 1, February 14, 1966; S.M. Dawson, "A Recent History of Sino-Mongolian Relation," *Asian Review,* April, 1964, p. 45.

18. C.P. Fitzgerald: "The Chinese View of Foreign Relations," *The World Today,* January 1968, p. 9; C.L. Sultzberger in *The New York Times,* October 31, 1965 and May 29, 1968.

19. *Sino-Soviet Conflict,* p. 112; Donald S. Zagoria: "A Strange Triangle: China, Soviet Union, United States," in Zablocki's book *Sino-Soviet Rivalry,* p. 44; *The New York Times* Magazine, November 21, 1965.

20. R.V. Burks "The Thaw and the Future of Eastern Europe," *Encounter,* August, 1964, p. 31.

21. *Department of State Bulletin,* July 3, 1967; Harrison E. Salisbury: "China Tops Soviet List of Potential Dangers," *The New York Times,* November 3, 1967; *Life* magazine, May 1, 1970.

22. Oliver M. Lee: "Communist China and West Europe," *Current History,* September, 1964.

23. *East Europe,* November, 1966, p. 15; *Sino-Soviet Conflict,* p. 120.

CHAPTER III:

THE CHINESE COMMUNIST IDEOLOGICAL CHALLENGE

(pp. 37-62)

1. *Pravda,* February 2, 1964, *ibid.*
2. *Hsinhua,* in English Morse to North America, November 23, 1949.
3. Stuart R. Schram, *op. cit.,* pp. 61, 256.
4. "Rech Lyu Shao-tsi" (his speech as Vice President of the WFTU and Honorary President of All-China's Federation of Trade Unions), January 4, 1950.
5. *For a Lasting Peace, For a People's Democracy,* No. 33, January 27, 1950.
6. Yü Chao-li, "Excellent Situation in the Struggle for Peace," *Peking Review,* No. 1, January 5, 1960.
7. G. Glezerman: "Velikoe znachenie Leninskih idei borby za demokratiyu i sotsializm", (The Great Meaning of Lenin's Ideas for the Struggle for Democracy and Socialism), *Pravda,* January, 21, 1965.
8. N. Kapchenko, *op. cit.;* "Korni nyneshnikh sobytii v Kitae" (The Roots of Current Events in China), *Kommunist,* No. 6, 1968.
9. L. Schapiro, "The Chinese Ally from the Soviet Point of View," in K. London, *op. cit.,* p. 364.
10. Address to the National Assembly in Belgrade, *Borba,* December 27, 1960.
11. *Peking Review,* No. 4, January 24, 1964, after *Jen-min Jih-pao* of January 21; *Pravda,* September 2, 1964.
12. "O borbe KPSS za splochennost mezhdunarodnovo kommunisticheskovo dvizheniya. Doklad tovarishcha M.A. Suslova na plenume CK KPSS." (On the Struggle of the CPSU for the Solidarity of the International Communist Movement. Report by Comrade Suslov on February 14, 1964, at Plenary Session of CPSU Central Committee), *Pravda,* April 3, 1964, pp. 1-8.
13. D.N. Aidit: *Set Afire the Banteng Spirit! Ever Forward, No Retreat,* Peking Foreign Languages Press, 1964 (pamphlet).
14. Lin Piao, "Long Live the Victory of People's War!," *Peking Review,* No. 36, September 3, 1965.
15. Branko Lazitch: "Une thèse prétendu chinoise," *Est & Ouest,* Paris, September 16-30, 1965; Claude Harmel: Du prétendu 'revisionisme' de Mao Tse-toung," *id.,* February 1-15, 1967; K. A. Wittfogel in *Free Trade Union News,* February 1967.
16. *Kommunist,* editorial, No. 15, October 1963.
17. T. Timofeyev, "Nauchny sotsialism i melkoburzhuaznaya ideologiya"

(Scientific Socialism and Petty-Bourgeois Ideology), *Pravda,* October 24, 1966; *Mao's Selected Works,* Vol. 1, p. 64.

18. Raymond L. Garthoff, editor: *Sino-Soviet Military Relations,* pp. 168-182, comment on a Soviet critique "The Peking Version of 'Total Strategy' " by I. Yermashev in the journal *Voennaya mysl* (Military Thought), October 1963.

19. Radio Moscow in Cantonese, November 19, 1967.

20. Commentary by General Petrochevsky over Radio Moscow in Mandarin, November 30, 1967.

21. B. Zanegin: "Proval vneshniepoliticheskovo kursa Pekina," (The Failure of Peking's Foreign Policy), *Izvestia,* May 23, 1968.

22. Mao, *Selected Works,* Vol. II, pp. 219, 224, 225.

23. Fernand Nicolon, "West European Integration: Trends and Contradictions," *World Marxist Review,* November 1965, p. 31.

24. See also Donald S. Zagoria, "China's Strategy, A Critique," *Commentary,* November 1965.

25. V. Kudryavtsev: "Opasnye podstrekateli" (Dangerous Instigators), *Izvestia,* April 13, 1968.

26. *The New York Times,* September 9, 1966.

27. *Diplomat,* September 1966.

28. *U.S. Policy With Respect to Mainland China,* Hearings before the Committee on Foreign Relations, U.S. Senate, 1966, p. 557.

29. *The New York Times,* February 24, 1967.

30. *Peking Review,* No. 36, September 1, 1963, Chinese Government Statement.

31. *Pravda,* September 21-22, 1963.

32. *Borba,* June 16, 1958.

33. *Id.* January 24, 1963.

34. Marvin L. Kalb: *Dragon in the Kremlin,* pp. 241-42.

35. Mao, *On the Correct Handling of Contradictions Among the People, Current Background,* No. 458, June 20, 1957. American Consulate General, Hong Kong.

36. "Long Live Leninism," *Hung Ch'i's* editorial, No. 8, 1960, *Peking Review,* No. 17, April 26, 1960.

37. *People's Daily,* March 19, 1966.

38. "Ukrepim edinstvo kommunisticheskovo dvizheniya vo imya torzhestva mira i sotsializma," (Strengthen the Unity of the Communist Movement in the Name of the Victory of Peace and Socialism), *Pravda,* January 7, 1963; *Sovietskaya Rossiya,* August 30, 1969.

39. Karl Marx, *Kapital,* Russian edition, Vol. I., p. 751.

40. V. I. Lenin, *Sochinenia,* Vol. XXVI, p. 350 and XXVII, p. 136.

41. *The New York Times,* October 27, 1961.

42. Hwang Tien-chien: *Communist China's Setbacks and International Tensions in 1965,* p. 92.

43. D. P. Mozingo and T. W. Robinson: "Lin Piao on 'People's War': China Takes a Second Look at Vietnam," RAND Memorandum 4814-PR, November 1965, Santa Monica, Calif.

44. Lo Jui-ch'ing: "Commemorate the Victory Over German Fascism: Carry the Struggle Against U.S. Imperialism Through to the End!" *Red Flag,* No. 5, 1965, *Peking Review,* No. 20, May 14, 1965, *passim.*

45. Mao's talk with African friends on August 8, 1963.

46. Ishwer C. Ojha, "China's Cautious American Policy," *Current History,* September 1967.

47. Lo Jui-ch'ing: "The People Defeated Japanese Fascism and They Can Certainly Defeat U.S. Imperialism, Too," *Peking Review,* No. 36, September 3, 1965, pp. 31-39.

48. *Rodo Mondai* (Labor Problems), Tokyo, October 1966.

49. *Vjesnik,* June 5, 1966. *Swiss Review of World Affairs,* December 1966, p. 11.

50. *China Report,* New Delhi, June-July 1966; Tanyug, December 23, TASS, December 18, 1966.

51. Radio Moscow in English to South Asia, July 24, 1967.

52. *Le Nouvel Observateur,* July 27, 1966.

53. Franz Michael: "Moscow and the Current Chinese Crisis," *Current History,* September 1967, p. 146.

54. *Paris-Match,* March 11, 1967.

55. *Peking Review,* No. 19, May 6, 1965.

56. *Izvestia,* February 2, and *Pravda,* February 16, 1967.

57. *Rude Pravo,* February 19, and Radio Moscow to Hungary, February 18, 1967.

58. *The New York Times,* April 12, 1967.

59. "Soviet Revisionist Ruling Clique Are Rank Traitors to Vietnamese Revolution," *People's Daily,* April 30, 1967.

60. *AFP,* July 21, 1967.

61. *Yomiuri Shimbun,* July 27, 1967.

62. Radio Moscow in Cantonese, April 3, and in French to Asia, April 9, 1968; Radio Budapest, MTI in Hungarian, July 13, 1968; Radio Moscow in Mandarin, March 19, 1969.

63. *Hung-Ch'i Tung-hsin* (Red Flag Bulletin), *The New York Times,* July 10 and 30, 1968; *Pravda,* July 14, 1968.

64. Radio Moscow in Mandarin, April 5; TASS, April 8; Radio Peking in Mandarin, April 9, 1968.

65. Radio Peking NCNA in English, April 5, 1968.

66. *People's Daily,* April 6, and July 5, 1968.

67. Radio Seoul in Korean; Radio Delhi in English, May 12, 1968.

68. *Literaturnaya gazeta,* June 26, 1968, G. Ushakov's commentary.

69. Radio Moscow in Mandarin, May 28, 1968.

70. *The New York Times,* July 26, and December 27, 1969; Allen Whiting, "How We Almost Went to War With China," *Look,* April 16, 1969.

71. *Kultura,* Warsaw, June 16, 1968; *Charts Concerning Chinese Communists on the Mainland,* April 1968, No. 17.

72. *The New York Times,* September 3, 1968.

73. *Hoc Tap,* May 1967, after André Tong: "Hanoi entre Pékin et Moscou," *Est & Ouest,* January 1-15, 1969; *Magyarorszag,* August 30, 1970.

74. A. Arzumanyan, V. Korionov: "Noveishie otkroveniya revisionista" (The Latest Revelations of a Revisionist), *Pravda,* September 2, 1960.

75. J. V. Stalin: *Problems of Leninism,* p. 32.

76. *KPSS—v rezolyutsiyah i resheniyah sezdov, konferentsii i plenumov CK,* chast I (The CPSU in the Resolutions and Decisions of Congresses, Conferences and Plenary Sessions of the CC), Part I, p. 414.

77. Cf. also Arthur A. Cohen, "How Original is Maoism," *Problems of Communism,* November-December 1961, p. 39.

78. Harry Schwartz in *The New York Times,* December 3, 1961.

79. *Borba,* January 1, 1955.

80. Zoran Zujovic, "Treci program KPSS," (The Third Program of the CPSU), *Politika,* Belgrade, August 2, 1961.

81. *Yugoslavia's Way,* The Program of the League of the Communists of Yugoslavia, p. 21.

82. R. Ulyanovsky, "Nekotorye voprosy nekapitalisticheskovo razvitiya osvobodivshikhsya stran" (Some Problems of the Non-Capitalist Development of the Liberated Countries), *Kommunist,* January 1966; "Avangard naroda Mali" (Vanguard of Mali's People), *Pravda,* April 10, 1965; K. Ivanov, "Natsionalno-osvoboditelnye dvizheniya i nekapitalistichesky put" (The National-Liberation Movements and the Non-Capitalistic Way), *Mezhdunarodnaya Zhizn,* 5/1965; Elizabeth Kridl Valkenier, "Changing Soviet Perspectives on the Liberation Revolution," *Orbis,* winter 1966; "Sino-Soviet Rivalry in the Third World," *Current History,* October 1969; Philip E. Mosely, "Communist Policy and the Third World," *The Review of Politics,* Notre Dame, Indiana, April 1966.

83. *Peking Review,* No. 11, March 12, 1965; *People's Daily* August 24, 1967.

84. *Program of the CPSU* (New Times), p. 7; R. Ulyanovsky: "Na novykh rubezhakh—O nekotorykh chertakh etapa natsionalno-osvoboditelnovo dvizheniya (At New Frontiers—On Some Characteristics of the Present Stage of the National-Liberation Movement), *Pravda,* January 3, 1968.

CHAPTER IV:

MAO'S DOCTRINE EXPOSED BY YUGOSLAV COMMUNISTS

(pp. 63-82)

1. *The New York Times,* July 1, 1957.

2. "Modern Revisionism Must Be Repudiated," *People's Daily*, May 5, 1958, *Peking Review*, No 11, May 13, 1958.

3. Published in English in Belgrade, by Methuen in London, and by Mc-Graw-Hill in New York.

4. Excerpts from lectures delivered in the seminar of Prof. Bogdan Raditsa of the Fairleigh-Dickinson University in New Jersey and at the former Tuesday Panel of the ACEN in New York City in 1961, published in *The China Quarterly*, London, April-June, 1962.

5. Kardelj, *op. cit.*, pp. 25 et seq. and pp. 71 et seq. Belgrade edition.

6. *Ibid.*, p. 189, 197, 198, 21.

7. *Ibid.*, pp. 78-79.

8. *Ibid.*, pp. 44, 90, 111.

9. *Fourth International*, No. 9, Spring 1960, p. 39.

10. Tito, *Report to the 5th Congress of the Socialist Alliance of the Working People of Yugoslavia*, p. 54; *Yugoslavia's Way*, p. 77.

11. Kardelj, *op. cit.*, pp. 74-75, 100 and 167-68.

12. Parts of this and the following sub-chapters were first printed in the *East-Central European Papers* of the ACEN, 1963, and are reprinted here in a revised form.

13. *World Marxist Review*, November 1960, p. 36.

14. *Pravda*, ibid., September 2, 1960.

15. "Losa usluga moskovske Pravde", ("A Bad Service of Moscow Pravda") *Borba*, September 12, 1960.

16. "Wild Anti-Marxists and Servants of Warmongers," Radio Tirana, September 25, 1960.

17. Trifun Mickovic: "Albanske impresije: Preorientacija na 'sopstvene snage'; Izneverene nade, koje su polagane u obim kineske pomoci" (Albanian Impressions: Reorientation Toward 'One's Own Forces'; Hope in the Volume of Chinese Aid Foiled), *Borba*, July 8, 1966.

18. Wu Chiang, "Our Age and Edvard Kardelj's 'Dialectic'." *Selections from China Mainland Magazines*, American Consulate General, Hong Kong, No. 306, March 26, 1962, pp. 14 et seq.

19. Mao's speech of November 21, 1957; *Survey of China Mainland Press*, No. 1656.

20. Predrag Vranicki, *Historija marksizma*, pp. 499-516; Mao: *Iz iskre moze da bukne pozar*, Izabrana djela I (A Single Spark May Start a Prairie Fire, Selected Works I), Serbo-Croatian edition, pp. 101-102.

21. Mao, *Nova faza*, govori i clanci (New Phase, Speeches and Articles), pp. 48-50, 70-71, and *Kineska nova demokracija* (New Chinese Democracy), p. 95; Serbo-Croatian edition; Mao, *Kineska revolucija i Kommunisticka partija Kine* (The Chinese Revolution and the CPC), a supplement to the work of V. Teslic's *Kineska revolucija i Moskva* (The Chinese Revolution and Moscow), p. 358.

22. Djilas, *Conversations with Stalin*, p. 181.

23. *Kommunist*, No. 6, April, and No. 9, June 1968.

24. W. A. Douglas Jackson, *Russo-Chinese Border Lands*, p. 59.

25. Sonja Dapcevic-Orescanin, *Sovjetsko-kineski spor i problemi razvoja socijalizma*, p. 210.

26. Yury Garushyants, "Tshechetnye potugi klevetnikov" (The Futile Efforts of the Slanderers), *Pravda*, September 12, 1967.

27. Peter S. H. Tang, *Communist China Today*, pp. 45-46.

28. Mao: *Selected Works*, Vol. IV, p. 100; *Pravda*, January 7, 1963, May 9, 1970.

29. Zlatko Cepo: "Spor a Kinom" (Conflict with China), *Vjesnik*, November 23, 1968.

CHAPTER V:

THE MOSCOW-PEKING-BELGRADE TRIANGLE

(pp. 83-126)

1. *The New York Times*, October 19, 1968.

2. *Trybuna Ludu*, November 12, 1968.

3. Yu. Georgiev: "Yugoslavia: 'Novi variant sotsializma?' " *Kommunist*, No. 15, October 1968, pp. 82-97.

4. D.I. Chesnikov, "Obostrenie ideino-politicheskoi borby i sovremenny filosofskii revisionizm" (Exacerbation of the Ideological-Political Struggle and the Contemporary Philosophical Revisionism), *Voprosy filosofii*, December 1968; *Mezhdunarodnaya zhizn*, 1/1969; S. Titarenko, "Borba V.I. Lenina protiv anarkho-sindikalizma" (Lenin's Struggle Against Anarcho-Syndicalism), *Pravda*, March 4, 1969; P. Kostin, "Gosudarstvennaya vlast i samoupravlenie pri sotsializme," (Government Rule and Self-Government Under Socialism), *Sovietskoe gosudarstvo i pravo*, February 1969; A.G. Titov, "Razgrom antipartiynoi gruppy demokraticheskovo tsentralizma" (Destruction of...), *Voprosy istorii KPSS*, 6/1970; O. Vasilev, "Nesostoyatelnost ekonomicheskikh kontseptsy anarkho-sindikalizma" (Insolvency of...), *Ekonomicheskie nauki*, 5/1970; *Politika*, March 5, 1969, and June 4, 1970.

5. *Borba*, September 20, 1968. From a speech delivered in Nova Gorica.

6. V. Feodosyev, "O chem shumit jugoslavskaya pressa" (What is the Yugoslav Press Talking About), *Sovetskaya Rossiya*, April 5, 1969.

7. *Borba*, November 15, *Politika*, December 1, 1968.

8. Radio Moscow, Soviet home service, June 11, 1956, Tito speaking in Russian; *Borba*, June 12, 1956.

9. *The New York Times*, June 12, 1956.

10. *Review of International Affairs*, Belgrade, December 16, 1959.

11. *Borba*, December 24, 1960.

12. Tanyug in English, October 25, 1961.

13. Radio Moscow in Serbo-Croatian, July 2, 1962,

14. *Politika,* October 30, 1966.

15. *Peking Review,* No. 38, September 21, 1962. "The Infamy of Modern Revisionism" in *People's Daily.* September 17, 1962.

16. "Postoje povoljni uslovi i prijateljski uzajamni interesi za dalje sirenje ekonomske, politicke, naucne, kulturne i drugih vidova saradnje medju dvema zemljama" (There are Favorable Conditions and Mutual Friendly Interests for a Further Development of the Economic, Political, Scientific, Cultural and Other Forms of Cooperation Between the Two Countries—title taken from the communiqué); *Borba,* October 5, 1962.

17. *Ibid.,* June 3, 1955.

18. *Politika,* June 21, 1956.

19. "Sovremenoe mezhdunarodnoe polozhenie i vneshnaya politika Sovietskovo Soyuza" (The Contemporary International Situation and the Foreign Policy of the Soviet Union), *Pravda,* December 13, 1962.

20. Some paragraphs of this sub-chapter are taken from a comparison between the Soviet and Yugoslav Party programs published in the *East-Central European Papers,* 1962.

21. *Christian Science Monitor,* December 20, 1962; *Politika,* December 17, 1969, and February 16, 1970; Radio Zagreb local, December 23, 1969; *Istoriya Kommunisticheskoi Partii Sovietskovo Soyuza,* third, revised edition, 1969, p. 555.

22. "Stvaraju se realisticki odnosi i poverenje" (Realistic Relations and Trust are Created), *Borba,* December 14, 1962.

23. Radio Moscow, TASS in Russian to Europe, December 10, 1962.

24. *Borba,* January 19, 1963.

25. *Washington Post,* January 19, 1963.

26. *Borba,* December 30, 1962.

27. *Politika,* March 24, and May 19, 1963.

28. *Medjunarodna Politika,* November 3, 1966.

29. *Borba,* July 2, 1967.

30. Philip E. Mosely, "The Kremlin and the Third World," *Foreign Affairs,* October 1967, p. 74.

31. Viktor Meier, "Yugoslav Communism" in *Communism in Europe,* Vol. I, pp. 79, 80.

32. C.L. Sulzberger's report, *The New York Times,* December 31, 1967.

33. *Borba,* February 19, 1968.

34. *Krasnaya Zvezda,* December 21, 1967.

35. *Borba,* July 2, 1965.

36. *Izvestia,* June 2, 1966.

37. *The Reporter,* September 28, 1961, p. 23.

38. *Yugoslavia's Way,* pp. 233, XIX.

39. D. Sevyan: "Prazdnik sotsialiticheskoy Yugoslavii" (Holiday of the Socialist Yugoslavia), *Pravda,* November 29, 1965.

40. *Politika,* June 29, 1968.

41. Sergey Kovalev: "Suverenitet i internatsionalnie obyazannosti sotsia-listicheskih stran" (Sovereignty and International Obligations of So-cialist Countries), *Pravda,* September 26, 1968; TASS, July 10, 1969; Radio Moscow in Serbo-Croatian, September 6; *Vjesnik,* October 11, 1969.

42. *Tanyug,* December 5, 1962.

43. *Politika,* October 30, 1966; TASS September 8, and NCNA, September 7, 1970.

44. I. Belyaev, E. Primakov: "Obshchie vzglyady, vzaimnoe doverie" (Com-mon Views, Mutual Trust), *Pravda,* May 20, 1966; Radio Belgrade, domestic service in Serbian, same date.

45. *Politika,* September 18; *Komunist,* September 19, 1968.

46. *Congressional Record,* June 6, 1962, p. 9134.

47. Milorad M. Drachkovitch and Adam Bromke: *United States Aid to Yugoslavia and Poland,* Analysis of a Controversy, pp. 97, 96.

48. Janez Stanovnik, *Socijalisticki elementi u ekonomskom razvoju nerazvi-jenih zemalja* (Socialist Elements in the Economic Development of Underdeveloped Countries), *passim; Zemlje u razvoju u svjetskoj privredi* (Developing Countries in the World Economy); Dj. Jerkovic, "Legiti-mate Defense of the Threatened," *Review of International Affairs,* Bel-grade, April 20, 1962; *The New York Times,* February 19, 1970.

49. Obren Milicevic, *ibid.,* p. 61.

50. *Komunist,* February 15, 1968, p. 20; Tito's Pristina speech, *Borba,* March 27, 1967.

51. *Yugoslavia's Way,* p. 54.

52. Milovan Djilas: "Subjektivne snage" (Subjective Forces), *Borba,* De-cember 27, 1953.

53. Viktor Meier, *op. cit.* pp. 51-52.

54. *Peking Review,* No. 39, September 27, 1963, pp. 14-27.

55. Dedijer, *op. cit.,* p. 432.

56. Jan Librach: *The Rise of the Soviet Empire,* pp. 303, 310.

57. *Yugoslavia's Way,* pp. 122, 118, 235-6.

58. *Borba,* April 27, 1967.

59. *Ibid.,* September 5, 1966, Murska Sobota speech; *ibid.* March 29, 1967, Pec speech; *ibid.* March 27, 1967. Pristina speech.

60. *Neue Zuercher Zeitung,* March 15, 1967; *Pravda,* February 20 and 27, 1967.

61. *Politika,* June 14; *Borba,* June 9; *Vjesnik,* June 6, 1968.

62. *The New Class,* p. 190.

63. *East Europe* magazine, June 1966, p. 48.

64. *Foreign Policy Bulletin,* Belgrade, January 31, 1963.

65. Djilas, *op. cit.,* p. 174.

66. *Praxis,* September 1967.

67. *Hsinhua,* in English, June 9, 1968; *Wall Street Journal,* June 4, 1971.
68. Tito's Labin speech in *Borba,* June 16, 1958.
69. *Yugoslav Communism,* p. 294.
70. *Congressional Record,* July 7, 1962, p. 9185.
71. Librach, *ibid.,* p. 305.
72. Jurij Gustincic in *Politika,* October 18, 1967.
73. *Yugoslavia's Way,* p. 154.
74. *Review of International Affairs,* Belgrade, August 25, 1965, pp. 368-369.
75. Excerpts from a lecture at the ACEN Latin American seminar, held in Medellin, Colombia, in December 1964..
76. George F. Hoffman and Fred Warner Neal, *Yugoslavia and the New Communism,* p. 171.
77. "O radnickom samoupravljanju" (On Workers' Self-Management), *Arhiv za pravne i drustvene nauke,* Belgrade, No. 2/3, 1957, pp. 377-386; *Historija marksizma,* pp. 48, 304, 317, 420; Joze Goricar: "Radnicko samoupravljanje u svetlu znanstvenog socializma" (Workers' Self-Management in the Light of Scientific Socialism), *Arhiv,* as above, p. 177.
78. A.P. Butenko, "Natsionalny kommunizm-ideologicheskoe oruzhie burzhuazii" (National Communism, the Ideological Weapon of the Bourgeoisie), *Voprosy filosofii,* Moscow, No. 6, 1958. p. 10.
79. *Program of the CPSU,* adopted by the 22nd congress on October 31, 1961. Supplement to the *New Times,* Moscow, No. 48, November 29, 1961, pp. 32, 36, 37. Cited hereafter as Soviet Party program.
80. *Borba,* August 22, 1963.
81. PAP, Warsaw, in Russian, May 16, 1957.
82. Vlajko Begovic, "Ostvarivanje prava radnicke klase u privrednim oganizacijama" (The Realization of the Rights of the Workers' Class in Economic Enterprises), *Komunist,* Belgrade, April 2, 1964.
83. Dusan Calic, "Socijalna funkcija, glavni problemi, i dalnji razvitak radnickih savjeta" (The Social Functions, Topical Problems, and the Further Development of Workers' Councils), *Ekonomski Pregled,* Zagreb, No 2/1958, p. 78.
84. Joze Goricar *op. cit.,* pp. 175-77; Dusan Calic, *op. cit.,* p. 83.
85. *Vjesnik,* September 21, 1964.
86. "Stvaranje i razdioba viska vrijednosti rada su bitni elementi za razvitak samoupravljanja" (Formation and Distribution of Surplus Value of Labor Are Essential Elements for Development of Self-Management), *Vjesnik u srijedu,* November 22, 1967.
87. Dr. V. Bakaric speech, *Vjesnik* April 27, 1968.
88. *Tanyug* in Serbo-Croatian, March 15, 1969.
89. *Praxis,* Zagreb, January-February 1967, pp. 34, 35, 37.
90. Desimir Tochitch: "Workers' Control in Yugoslavia—Fact or Fiction?", *Free Labour World,* September 1966, p. 20.
91. *Borba,* January 8, 1967.

92. *Ibid.*, October 26, November 6, 1967, and November 26, 1969; *Vjesnik*, December 5, 1969; Drago Tovic in *Vjesnik u srijedu*, December 13, 1967; Radio Belgrade domestic, September 21, 1970.

93. *Politika*, March 15, 1969.

94. "Sto ima novogo u novim statutima" (What is New in the New Statutes), *Vjesnik u srijedu*, September 16, 1964; *Borba*, April 30, May 1-2, 1970. Top Trade Union functionary Boro Romic in a round-table discussion.

95. *The Hinge of Fate*, Churchill's Memoirs, pp. 498-99.

96. *Yugoslavia's Way*, pp. 130, 141, 212.

97. Radio Belgrade, domestic service, November 13, 1961; *Ibid.*, August 30, 1963.

98. Radio Belgrade in Serbo-Croation, April 1, 1967.

99. *Foreign Agriculture*, published by the Department of Agriculture, Washington, D.C., October 1966.

100. *Yugoslavia's Way*, p. 143; *Politika*, June 18; *Vjesnik u srijedu*, July 12, 1967.

101. Radio Zagreb, domestic service, March 24, 1966.

102. "Rukovodstvima i clanovima SKJ" (To the Leadership and Members of the League of Communists of Yugoslavia), indicated as "a document of permanent value." *Komunist*, June 14, 1962.

103. Statement by Maks Bace in *Vjesnik u srijedu*, September 23, 1966.

104. *Tanyug*, April 7, 1967; *Borba*, July 2, 1968.

105. Grey Hodnett, "The Debate over Soviet Federalism," *Soviet Studies*, 4/1967, *passim*.

106. *Politika*, January 10, 1968.

107. Aleksandar Nenadovic, "Svi zajedno ili sve za Kinu" (All for One or All for China), *Politika*, October 3, 1965.

108. *Oslobodjenje*, Sarajevo, March 24; *Borba*, October 17; *Peking Review*, No. 45, November 7, 1969.

CHAPTER VI:

THE UNEQUAL TREATIES AND HISTORICAL BORDERS

(pp. 127-149)

1. For full text of General Griffith's statement see: *China, Vietnam and the United States*, pp. 61-74.

2. "Seven Letters Exchanged Between Central Committees of CPC and CPSU", *Peking Review*, No. 19, May 8, 1964.

3. "A Comment on the Statement of the CPUSA", *Jen-min Jih-pao*, March 8, 1963, *Survey of China Mainland* Press, No. 2936, March 12, 1963.

4. Statement made at a joint session of the Standing Committee of the National People's Congress and the plenary meeting of the State Council

on occasion of Chou En-Iai's report on the results of the visit to 13 Afro-Asian countries and Albania, *Peking Review*, No. 18, May 1, 1964, p. 12.

5. All figures of Russian territorial conquests are taken from the People's Republic of China Government Statement of May 24, 1969 and changed into square miles; F. Engels, "The Progress of Russia in the Far-East", *Collected Works of Karl Marx and Friedrich Engels,* Chinese ed., Vol. 12, p. 662.

6. Ch'eng T'ien-fong: *A History of Sino-Russian Relations,* pp. 32, 35, 36, 37, 49, 50; Owen Lattimore, "Russo-Chinese Imperialism", *New Statement,* March 21, 1969.

7. *Bolshaya Sovietskaya Entsiklopediya,* Moskva 1949, 2nd edition, Vol. I, pp. 552-53.

8. Peter S. Tang: *Russian and Soviet Policy in Manchuria 1911-1931,* p. 5.

9. *SSSR-Administrativno-Territorialnoe Delenie Soyuznih Respublik* (... Division of the Union's Republics); *Bolshaya Sovietskaya Entsiklopediya,* Vol. 32, pp. 290-91.

10. W.A. Douglas Jackson, *op. cit.,* pp. 113-117.

11. *Bolshaya Sovietskaya Entsiklopediya,* Vol. 32, p. 574.

12. *Pravda,* September 2, 1964.

13. *Bulletin,* Institute for the Study of the USSR, Muenchen, January 1964, p. 5.

14. *Asahi Shimbun,* January 18, 1965.

15. Danish News Agency, May 24, 1966.   The quotations come from the official version issued by the Chinese Embassy in Stockholm; J. Palavrsic: "Zasto Kina trazi sovjetska podrucja" (Why does China Claim Soviet Territory?), *Vjesnik,* December 11, 1966; *Le Monde* from Peking, November 8, 1966.

16. Risto Bajalski: "Ugrozena granica" (Endangered Frontier), *Borba,* January 29; *Pravda,* January 22; *Komsomolskaya Pravda,* February 15; Radio Vladivostok in Russian, February 11, 1967; *Krasnaya zvezda,* August 6, December 7; Reuters, November 18, 1969.

17. *Hsinhua* in Russian, March 10; TASS, March 11; *Izvestia,* March 30, 1969; *Sbornik dogovorov Rossii s Kitayem 1689-1881,* (Collection of Agreements Between Russia and China), Sanktpeterburg 1889.

18. *Hsinhua,* May 24, 1969.

19. Lenin: "Socialism and War", *Collected Works,* Chinese ed., Vol. 21, pp. 280-81.

20. *Izvestia,* June 15; *The New York Times,* August 31, October 1; *New Statesman,* London, September 19; Victor Louis (Vitaly Yevgenevich Lui), "Will Russian Rockets Czech-Mate China?" *Evening News,* London, September 16, 1969.

20a. *Peking Review,* No. 41, October 10; TASS October 18; Radio Kiangsu, October 17; *Hsinhua,* November 4; UPI, December 30, 1969; Radio Budapest, January 3, 1970.

21. I. Andronov: "Mao and the Celestial Empire", *New Times,* Moscow, July

10, 1968, pp. 13-17; Radio Moscow, Peace and Progress, in English, May 23, 1969.

22. Chow Shu-kai: "Significance of the Rift Between the Chinese Communist Regime and the Soviet Union", *The Annals of the American Academy of Political and Social Science,* July 1967, p. 70.

23. Ellis M. Zacharias (Rear Admiral USN, retd.): *Secret Missions,* pp. 148-149.

24. *The China Quarterly,* April-June 1964, p. 241; *AP* from London, April 5, 1969.

25. *Magyar Ifjusag,* March 14, 1969.

26. The conversation took place on July 10, 1964, and was first published in Hong Kong two days later, but was immediately denied by Peking. It appeared in the magazine *Sekai Siuho* (World Weekly) on August 11th.

27. "Beseda Mao Tsze-duna s yaponskimi sotsialistami" (Conversation of Mao Tse-tung with Japanese Socialists), *Pravda* September 2, 1964.

28. *Wall Street Journal,* September 2, 1964; Victor Zorza in *The Guardian,* October 9, 1964.

29. *Peking Informers,* January 16, 1968; Andro Gabelie, "Sta Kina zeli da kaze" (What China Wants to Say), *Borba,* March 8, 1969; *The Military Balance,* 1969-70; Jean Pergent, "Aspects militaires du conflit sino-soviétique en 1969," *Est & Ouest,* February 1-15, 1970; "Probable Developments of the Chinese Communist—Soviet Border Conflict," *Asian Outlook,* September, 1969; *The New York Times,* April 12, 1970; *Strategic Survey 1969;* Radio Moscow in Mandarin, June 9, 1970.

30. Hwang Tien-chien: *The Overall Disintegration of Chinese Communists in 1966,* p. 70.

31. Radio Bratislava domestic service, August 24, 1967.

32. "Kitaiskie vlasti prepyatstvuyut normalnomu sudohostvu na pogranich-nykh rekakh" (Chinese Authorities Obstruct Normal Navigation on Border Rivers), *Pravda,* September 1, 1967; NCNA, August 11, 1969, and December 23, 1970.

33. Ts'ai Ping-yüan: *An Analytical Survey of Border Disputes Between Soviet Russia and Communist China,* p. 25.

34. Soviet-annexed territories once belonging to Czechoslovakia, Poland and Romania total some 146,000 square miles.

35. *Washington Post,* May 1; *The New York Times,* May 12, and October 16, 1966.

36. *Scinteia,* October 15, 1966.

37. *The China Quarterly,* October-December 1964; report of Okada, Japanese socialist MP, August 1, 1964.

38. Frank N. Trager, "Communist China—The New Imperialism", *Current History,* September 1961, p. 136.

39. Schram, *op. cit.,* p. 61.

40. Mao, "The Chinese Revolution and the Chinese Communist Party", *Selected Works,* II, p. 311.

41. Chiang Kai-shek, *China's Destiny,* p. 34.

42. Ernst Henri (Semyon Nikolayevich Rostovsky), "Glyadya s Pamira... razoblachaet pretensii Maoistov rukovodit mirom" (The View from the Pamirs...Discloses the Pretensions of the Maoists to Rule the World), *Literaturnaya Gazeta,* No. 39-40, September 27, and October 4, 1967.

CHAPTER VII:

THE GREAT WHITE COLONIAL POWER IN ASIA

(pp. 151-168)

1. *Pravda,* September 2, 1964.

2. Robert Payne: *The Life and Death of Lenin,* p. 555.

3. Herbert Ritvo, *The New Soviet Society,* pp. 191, 192; "Soviet Revision-ist Renegade Clique is Biggest Exploiter and Oppressor of Central Asian and Kazak Peoples." *Peking Review,* No. 34, August 22, 1969, pp. 31-34; See also *Voprosy istorii KPSS,* 2/1970, p. 31.

4. *Pravda, ibid;* NCNA, June 24, and July 18, 1969.

5. Hugh Seton-Watson: *From Lenin to Khrushchev,* pp. 88, 164; "The Communist Powers and Afro-Asian Nationalism," in K. London, *op. cit.,* p. 200.

6. K. Pavlov: "At the Meeting-Point Between Two Communist Empires", *Bulletin,* Institute for the Study of the USSR, January 1964, p. 17; *The New York Times,* July 24, 1970.

7. C. P. Fitzgerald: "Tension on the Sino-Soviet Border," *Foreign Affairs,* July 1967, p. 693; *Izvestia,* April 17, 1971 (1970 census).

8. Robert Conquest: *Soviet Nationalities Policy in Practice,* p. 104.

9. V. Perevedentsev: "Voprosy territorialnovo pereraspredeleniya trudovykh resursov" (Problems in Territorial Turnover of Labor Resources), *Voprosy ekonomiki,* May 1962, pp. 48 *et seq.;* S. Yarmolyuk: "Kak stat sibiryakom" (How to Become a Siberian), *Izvestia,* September 5, 1967; Victor Zorza in *Manchester Guardian Weekly,* March 6, 1969.

10. TASS in English, November 24, 1966; *Izvestia,* March 11, 1970.

11. *Ekonomicheskaya gazeta,* December 1967; F. Bezruchko, " 'Dalyoky vostochnik'—gordy titul" ('Far Easterner'—Proud Title), *Sovietskaya Rossiya,* May 13, 1970.

12. Nikolay Galay, "Siberia in the Light of New Geopolitical and Strategical Realities," *Studies on the Soviet Union,* 1965, No. 1, p. 16.

13. A.P. Okladnikov, "Sovietsky Dalny Vostok v svete noveyshikh dosti-zheny arkheologii" (The Soviet Far East in the Light of Recent Archeolo-gical Achievements), *Voprosy istorii,* January 1964, p. 57.

14. "Tayny sela Sakachi-Alyan. Sibirskie uchenye oprovergayut legendy o proiskhozhdenii dalnevostochnykh narodov," (Secrets of the Village of Sakachi-Alyan. Siberian Scholars Refute Legends About the Origins of Far Eastern Peoples), *Pravda,* September 4, 1964; A.P. Okladnikov,

"Stranitsy istorii beregov Amura" (Pages of the History of Amur's Shores), *Izvestia*, September 5, 1964.

15. "Kitaisky 'skot po reyestru' i pravda istorii" (The Chinese "Evidence" and the Historical Truth), *Mezhdunarodnaya zhizn*, October 1964, pp. 21-27.

16. R. V. Vyatkin, S. L. Tiklivinsky: "O nekotorykh voprosakh istoricheskoi nauki v KNR" (On Some Problems of Historical Science in the Chinese People's Republic), *Voprosy istorii*, October 1963, pp. 14-15.

17. Konstantin Simonov: "Priznanie v lyubvi" (Declaration of Love), *Pravda*, July 19, 1967 (filed from Khabarovsk).

18. Hugo Portisch: "Rot Russland-Rot China—die borstige Grenze" (Red Russia-Red China—The Bristling Border), *Kurier* (Vienna), June 14-15, 1967.

19. *Literaturnaya gazeta*, May 29, 1968.

20. "Falshivye karty" (False Maps), *Pravda*, July 30, 1964; "Geografiya na pekinsky lad" (Geography, Peking Style), *Izvestia*, same date; *Tanyug* from Ulan Bator, May 21, 1969.

21. Bazaryn Shirendyb: "Mongolskie kommunisty razoblachayut shovinis-ticheskii kurs Pekina" (Mongolian Communists Unmask Peking's Chauvinist Course), *Izvestia*, January 7, 1968.

22. Radio Zagreb domestic, September 9, 1964.

23. Ibid., January 27, 1965; *The China Quarterly*, July-September 1964, p. 199.

24. "Temnye zamysly kitaiskikh rukovoditeley" (Shady Schemes of the Chinese Leaders), *Pravda*, September 10, 1964.

25. TASS, August 11, 1967.

26. *Chinese Communist Affairs*, August 1968.

27. Colonel X: "Symptoms of a Sino-Soviet Rift," *NATO's Fifteen Nations*, August-September, 1962.

28. Text of the Treaty, *Pravda*, January 16; *Izvestia*, January 19, 1966.

29. *Novosti Mongolii* (Ulan Bator), April 10, 1965.

30. Radio Peking in Mongolian, June 20, 1966; H. E. Salisbury from Ulan Bator, *The New York Times*, May 20, 1969.

31. Tamurbek Davletshin: "The Autonomous Republic of Tuva", in *Studies on the Soviet Union*, 1965, No. 1, p. 97.

32. Interview granted to John Dixon, Australian Television producer, December 8, 1963.

33. TASS, January 24, 1962.

34. Yury Zhukov: "Kitaiskaya stena" (The Great Wall of China), *Pravda*, June 21, 1964.

35. "O kharaktere otnosheny mezhdu sotsialisticheskimi stranami: Sochetat natsionalnye i internatsionalnye interesy" (On the Nature of Relations Between Socialist Countries: Combining National and International Interests), *Izvestia*, June 4, 1964.

36. Radio Singapore in English, May 24, 1966; *Sankei Shimbun*, June 28, 1967.

37. *The New York Times*, August 17, 1966.

38. *(Joint) Hearings on Military Procurement Authorization Fiscal Year 1968*, p. 13; UPI, January 26, 1967.

39. M. Domogatskikh and V. Karymov: "Pouchitelny urok" (An Instructive Lesson), *Pravda*, July 7, 1962; Kikuzo Ito and Minoru Shibata: "The Dilemma of Mao Tse-tung," *The China Quarterly*, July-September 1968, p. 62; Walter C. Clemens Jr.: *The Arms Race and Sino-Soviet Relations*, p. 20.

40. *Mainichi Shimbun*, March 9, 1967. By courtesy of the East Asian Institute, Columbia University; *Vjesnik*, May 25, 1969.

41. Manuel E. Mora-Valverde, member of the Costa Rican Communist Party's leadership: "Slova i dela rukovoditeley KPK" (Words and Deeds of the CPC's Leaders), *Izvestia*, June 19, 1964.

42. *Pravda*, October 6, 1958.

43. Harold C. Hinton: "The Chinese Attitude," in Morton H. Halperin's *Sino-Soviet Relations and Arms Control*, p. 174.

44. *Peking Review*, No. 13, March 29, 1968.

45. K. S. Karol, *Le Nouvel Observateur*, November 9, 1966, p. 17.

46. *Rodo Mondai*, October 1966; "Politika gruppy Mao Tsze-duna na mezhdunarodnoi arene" (The Policy of Mao Tse-tung's Group in the International Arena), *Kommunist*, No. 5/1969.

47. Morton H. Halperin, *op. cit.*, p. 9.

48. "Kampf den Mongolen", *Der Spiegel*, Hamburg, August 3, 1964.

49. Andrey Voznesensky: "Iz tsikla 'Uoki-Toki', prolog k poeme," *Literaturnaya Rossiya*, March 24, 1967, p. 15; Yevgeny Yevtushenko, "Na krasnom snegu ussuryskom" (On the Red Snow of the Ussuri), *Literaturnaya gazeta*, March 19, 1969.

50. Leopold Labedz and G. R. Urban: *The Sino-Soviet Conflict*, p. 179.

51. Radio Moscow, domestic service, September 6, 1964.

52. *Peking Review*, No. 38, September 17, 1965.

53. Tanyug, international service in English, November 2 and 3, 1965.

54. Editorial: "Peking Defeats Moscow," *The New York Times*, August 18, 1964.

55. "Protiv fraktsionnosti, za splochenie antiimperialisticheskikh sil—Zayavlenie sovietskovo pravitelstva" (Against Factionalism, For the Unity of All Antiimperialist Forces—Soviet Government Statement to Afro-Asian Countries), *Pravda*, August 14, 1964.

CHAPTER VIII:

THE SINIFICATION OF MINORITIES

(pp. 169-180)

1. *Peking Review*, No. 38, September 17, 1965, p. 26; *Kommunist*, July, 1968; State Statistical Bureau of the People's Republic of China, com-

muniqué on the census, November 1, 1954, NCNA; Helmut G. Callis, *China Confucian and Communist*, pp. 334-37; Theodore Shabad, *China's Changing Map*, pp. 33-35; *Peking Review*, No. 44, October 30, 1964, p. 20; G. Rakhimov in *Komsomolskaya pravda*, May 20, 1969.

2. George Moseley, "China's Fresh Approach to the National Minority Question", *The China Quarterly*, October-December 1965, pp. 15-27.

3. A. Dymkov, "Pekinskie shovinisty", *Izvestia*, April 2, 1967; Radio Moscow, domestic service, April 8, 1969.

4. *China Report*, New Delhi, October 1965, p. 12; Tang, *op. cit.*, p. 242.

5. *Hung Ch'i*, No. 12, June 30, 1964, Liu Ch'un: "The Current Nationality Question and Class Struggle in Our Country", *Selection from China Mainland Magazines*, No. 428, August 4, 1964.

6. Dennis Bloodworth, "Sino-Soviet Frontier Confrontation", *Chicago Sun-Times*, March 5, 1967.

7. *Sotsialistikh Kazakhstan*, quoted in *The New York Times*, September 14, 1964; *Pravda*, September 20, 1964.

8. Peter S. H. Tang, "Sino-Soviet Border Regions: Their Changing Character", in K. London (ed.), *op. cit.*, pp. 278, 285; J. P. Lo, "Five Years of the Sinkiang-Uighur Autonomous Region", *The China Quarterly*, October-December 1961, pp. 103-104; Address by Dr. Ku Ch'eng-kang at the 11th annual conference of the Asian People's Anti-Communist League held in Manila, on September 7-12, 1965; *Congressional Record-House*, September 23, 1965; *The New York Times*, June 12, 1969, and August 16, 1970.

9. *Peking Review*, No. 37, September 13, 1963, p. 18, "The Origin and Development of the Rift Between the Leaders of the CPSU and Ourselves". Start of a succession of nine *Jen-min Jih-pao* and *Hung Ch'i* (September 6) joint editorials, commenting on the "open letter" of the CPSU's Central Committee of July 14, 1963; Süleyman Tekiner: "Sinkiang and the Sino-Soviet Conflict," *Bulletin*, Muenchen, August 1967, *passim;* Radio Moscow Peace and Progress in Mongolian May 30, 1969.

10. Kuldja is the capital of the Ili-Kazakh autonomous *chu* (the size of Italy).

11. *Izvestia*, September 21 and 22, 1963, "Zayavlenie sovietskovo pravitelstva" (Statement by the Soviet Government); *Japan Times*, March 8, 1964; NCNA, May 24, 1969.

12. *Peking Review*, No. 19, May 8 1964; NCNA, international service in English, December 30, 1964.

13. *L'Unità*, May 20; Slobodan Vujica, "Sta se desava na reci Ili?" (What is Happening on the River Ili?), *Borba*, May 17; *UPI*, May 13; *AFP*, May 10, and 14; Niu Sien-ch'eng, "Sinkiang", *NATO's Fifteen Nations*, April-May 1969.

14. *Far Eastern Economic Review*, July 30, 1964; June 17, 1965; *China News Analysis*, Hong Kong, No. 591, December 3, 1965; H. E. Salisbury in *The New York Times Magazine*, November 23, 1969.

15. *The New York Times*, October 12, 1964; *The China Quarterly*, October-December 1963, p. 59; *Kazakhstankaya Pravda* September 22, 1963,

"Pismo v redaktsiyu: 'Ne mogu molchat'" (A Letter to the Editor: "I Cannot Be Silent"); *Ibid*, September 24, a reportage "Ryadom s granitsei" (Along the Border); A Mirov, "Sintszyanskaya tragediya", *Literaturnaya gazeta*, May 7; *Los Angeles Times*, May 5, 1969.

16. *Neue Zuercher Zeitung*, February 3, 1967; Stanley Karow, "Sinkiang: Soviet Rustlers in China's Wild West", *The Reporter*, June 18, 1964; Zumun Taipov, "Po tu storonu barrikady, glazami ochevidtsa" (On the Other Side of the Barricade, an Eye-Witness), *Kazakhstanskaya Pravda*, September 29, 1963; *Hsinhua* in English, August 15, 1969.

17. *Yeni Istanbul*, January 9; *Yeni Gazete*, February 20, 1966.

18. TASS, February 10, 1967.

19. "Eto-neprikrity shovinizm rasskazivaet pokinuvshy Kitai pisatel Bukhara Tishkanbayev" (It is Overt Chauvinism, Says the Writer B. T. on Leaving China), *Literaturnaya gazeta*, September 26, 1963, from Alma Ata; *Ibid.*, January 25, 1967, Anouar Alimzhanov: "Tragicheskaya istoriya odnovo lozunga" (The Tragic History of a Slogan), meaning the "hundred flowers" and the minorities in China; *Peking Review*, No. 37, September 11; Radio Urumchi, regional service, November 1; *The New York Times*, November 19, 1964.

20. *Hsinhua*, December 5, and December 28; Radio Moscow international service in Russian, September 23, 1964.

21. Radio Peking, *Hsinhua*, international service in English, September 29; *Ibid.*, domestic service, September 30, 1965.

22. Radio Peking, NCNA, domestic service, October 7, 1965.

23. Reuters from Moscow, December 8, 1965; *Red Flag*, July 1; *People's Daily*, October 1, 1969.

24. Richard A. Pierce, *Russian Central Asia*, pp. 297-8. Taken from Kuropatkin: "Vosstanie 1916 g.v Srednei Azii" (The situation in Central Asia in 1916), *Krasny Arkhiv* (Red Archive), XXXIV (1929), p. 74.

CHAPTER IX:

AGAINST KHRUSHCHEVISM AND ITS SUCCESSORS

(pp. 181-218)

1. "Otkrytoe pismo Tsentralnovo Komiteta KPSS partiinym organizatsiam, vsem kommunistam Sovietskovo Soyuza (Open Letter of the CC of the CPSU to Party Organizations, to All Communists of the Soviet Union), *Pravda*, July 14, 1963.

2. "A Comment on the March Moscow Meeting", a joint article of *People's Daily* and *Red Flag*, in *Peking Review*, No. 13, March 26, 1965.

3. *People's Daily*, November 21, 1960.

4. Jean Terfve, "A propos des divergences de vues entre Partis Communists", *Le Drapeau Rouge*, Bruxelles, January 5-17, 1962.

5. *New York Herald Tribune*, October 6, 1962.

6. *The China Quarterly,* January-March, 1967, p. 186.
7. Speech delivered at the Moscow meeting devoted to Soviet-Czechoslovak friendship, on July 12, 1958.
8. *Deadline Data on World Affairs,* India Foreign Relations, April 29, 1954.
9. *The New York Times,* November 27, 1968.
10. Radio Moscow, domestic service, October 14, 1959.
11. Letter of the CPSU'CC to its Chinese counterpart of March 30, 1963.
12. *Pravda,* December 22, 1963.
13. "Mirnoe sosushchestvovanie ne oznachaet oslableniya ideologicheskoi borby" (Peaceful Coexistence Does Not Mean Weakening of the Ideological Struggle), *Kommunist,* Moscow, No. 8, May 1962, pp. 60 et seq.
14. N.S. Khrushchev, "New Victories for the World Communist Movement", *World Marxist Review,* January 1961, p. 15.
15. N. Inozemtsev, "Mirnoe sosushchestvovanie—vazhneyshy vopros sovremennosti", (Peaceful Coexistence—the Most Important Contemporary Problem), *Pravda,* January 17, 1962.
16. Professors Ye. A. Korovin, F.I. Kozhevnikov, G.P. Zadorozhny, "Mirnoe sosushchestvovanie i mezhdunarodnoe pravo" (Peaceful Coexistence and International Law), *Izvestia,* April 18, 1962.
17. *Pravda,* January 7, 1963.
18. "Nezyblemaya osnova vneshney politiki SSSR" (The Unshaken Basis of the USSR's Foreign Policy), *Izvestia,* January 18, 1966.
19. *Politika,* October 30, 1966.
20. *Izvestia,* July 9, 1966.
21. S. Kovalev, *Pravda,* April 25; A. Butenko: "Pod falshibym flagom 'navedeniya mostov' " ('Bridge Building' Under a False Flag), *Izvestia,* May 16; V. Kozyakov: "Kuda tselit amerikanskaya politika 'navedeniya mostov' " (What is Behind the American 'Bridge Building' Policy?), *Krasnaya zvezda,* May 24, 1968; TASS, June 17, 1969; Z. Brzezinski, "East-West Relations After Czechoslovakia", *East Europe,* November-December 1969.
22. *New York Herald Tribune,* September 22, 1962.
23. *The New York Times,* November 16, 1962.
24. National Educational TV Network, "The President's Men", December 7, 1965.
25. W. W. Kulski, *Peaceful Coexistence; An Analysis of Soviet Foreign Policy,* p. XX.
26. Henry M. Pachter, *Collision Course,* p. 116.
26a. Wolfgang Leonhard: "Politics and Ideology in the Post-Khrushchev Era", in Dallin-Larson *Soviet Politics Since Khrushchev,* p. 52.
27. Ernst Kux in a lecture, *Swiss Review of World Affairs,* February, 1961.
28. F. Engels: *Druga Internacionala* (in Serbo-Croatian), p. 102.
29. Professor M. Rozental: "Evolyutsionnaya i revolyutsionnaya formy razvitiya obchestva" (...Forms of Society's Development), *Pravda,* September 30, 1966.

30. "La thèse du 'passage pacifique' en 1920" *Est & Ouest,* February 1-15, 1966.

31. *Ibid.,* October 16-31, 1966, quoting an article by the then Hungarian Prime Minister Gyula Kallai in the October 1965 issue of *La Nouvelle Revue Internationale.* Rakosi's lecture was delivered on February 29, 1952.

32. *Neues Deutschland,* January 17, 1963.

33. *Unità,* September 28, 1962.

34. *Humanité,* January 9, 1967.

35. *Peking Review,* No. 1, January 4, 1963.

36. *People's Daily,* May 11, 1968.

37. *Red Flag,* editorial, February 11, 1966.

38. George D. Damien: "On the Philosophy of Contradictions", *Orbis,* winter 1968, p. 1211.

39. "The Leaders of the CPSU are Betrayers of the Declaration and the Statement", *People's Daily,* December 30, 1965 in *Peking Review,* January 1, 1966.

40. Soviet Party Program, (New Times) p. 54; N. Lomakin: "O rukovodia-shchei roli Kommunisticheskoi Partii v stroitelstve sotsializma," (On the Leading Role of the CP in Building Socialism), *Pravda,* September 19, 1968.

41. *Problems of Communism,* September-October 1961.

42. P. Kopnin: "K voprosu o protivorechiyakh obshchestvennovo razvitiya", (To the Problem of Contradictions of the Social Development), *Pravda,* February 10, 1966.

43. *Ibid.,* November 4, 1967.

44. *Ibid.,* March 30, 1968, and December 23, 1969.

45. Ting Hsüeh-lei: "No Distortion of the Road of the October Revolution by the Soviet Revisionist Renegades", *People's Daily,* November 11, 1967.

46. Radio Peking, NCNA international service in English, November 11, 1967; "Revolutionary Soviet People Will Rise Up to Overthrow Reactionary Rule of Kremlin's New Tsars", *Peking Review,* No. 6, February 9, 1968.

47. L. Shapiro, "The Party and the *State*", Survey, October, 1961, p. 116; *Soviet Party Program,* p. 44.

47a. Ivo Lapenna, *State and Law: Soviet and Yugoslav Theory, passim; Khronika tekushchikh sobitii* (Chronicle of Current Events), No. 13, April 28, 1970.

48. "Komu eto vygodno—Po povodu vystupleniya tov. Edvarda Kardelja na sessii Soyuznoi narodnoi skupshchiny Yugoslavii" (To Whom is This Convenient—On Occasion of Comrade E. K.'s Engagement at the Session of the Federal Assembly of Yugoslavia), *Pravda,* December 18, 1956.

49. Mao, "On the People's Dictatorship", *Selected Works,* vol. IV, p. 418.

50. Edvard Kardelj, "Deset godina narodne revolucije" (Ten Years of Peo-

ple's Revolution), *Komunist*, No. 2-3 1951, p. 97; Diskusija na VI. Kongresu KPJ, Zbornik VI. Kongres (Anthology), pp. 183-192.

51. Kardelj: "Postoji li u nasim uslovima klasna borba?" (Is There a Class Struggle in Our Conditions?), *Borba*, February 25, 1968.

52. M. Djilas, *ibid.*, pp. 38, 39.

53. Professor D. Chesnokov: "O byurokratii deistvitelnoi i mnimoi" (On the Real and Apparent Bureaucracy), *Mezhdunarodnaya zhizn*, April 4, 1967.

54. Professor Doak Barnett: Seminar on international communism at Columbia, November 2, 1966.

55. *Yugoslavia's Way*, p. 146.

56. Dragoljub Milivojevic, *Politika*, August 10, 1966; D. Bilandic, *Komunist*, November 2, 1968, p. 11; S. Stojanovic, *Socijalizam*, Nos. 1-2, 1968, p. 192; Krste Crvenkovski, *Nova Makedonija*, April 2, 1969.

57. *The New York Times*, October 10, 1967.

58. E. Zhukov, V. Trukhanovsky, V. Shunkov: "Vysokaya otvetstvennost istorikov" (High Responsibility of the Historians), *Pravda*, January 30, 1966; V. Golikov, S. Murashov, I. Chkhikvishvili, N. Shatagin, S. Shaumyan, "Za leninskuyu partiinost v osveshchenii istorii KPSS" (For a Leninist Party-Mindedness in the Illumination of the CPSU's History), *Kommunist* No. 3, 1969, pp. 67-82.

59. R. Bajalski: "Uskladjena kritika Staljina" (Coordinated Criticism of Stalin), *Borba*, May 6, 1966; *Pravda*, December 21, 1969.

60. *People's Daily* and *Red Flag* editorial, August 14, 1967.

61. *Pravda*, September 28, 1965.

62. Yevsei Liberman: "Plan, pribyl, premiya", Sovershenstovovat hozyaistvennoe rukovodstvo i planirovanie (Planning, Profit and Bonus, To Improve Economic Management and Planning), *Pravda*, September 9, 1962.

63. G. Lisichkin: "Pribyl ih i pribyl nasha" (Their Profit and Ours), *Pravda*, January 22, 1968.

64. C. Olgin: "The 'Economic Reform': The Political Aspect", *Bulletin*, Institute for the Study of the USSR, November 1967, *passim*.

65. Anatoly Efimov and Valery Rutgaizer: "The Soviet Economic Reform—Initial Results and Perspectives", *World Marxist Review*, August 1968, pp. 32-38; Aleksandr M. Birman in *Novy Mir*, March 5, 1969.

66. Yevsei Liberman: "The Soviet Economic Reform," *Foreign Affairs*, October, 1967.

67. Same author: "Ochered: anamnez, diagnoz, terapiya. O somnitelnoi teorii 'polnoi zagruzki' " (Queux: Their Case History, Diagnosis, and Therapy, On the Dubious Theory of 'Full Capacity'), *Literaturnaya gazeta*, March 20; *Planovoye khozyaistvo*, January 1968.

68. S. Strumilin: "Pribyl" (Profit), *Komsomolskaya pravda*, February 16; and "Ot Oktyabrya k kommunizmu", *Voprosy ekonomiki*, November, 1968.

69. Gyoergy Lukacs: "The Great October Revolution 1917 and Contemporary Literature", *Man and Society*, Paris, July-September, 1967; Radio Zagreb domestic, February 2, 1971.

70. *Sputnjik,* February, 1967.
71. C. Olgin, *op. cit.,* p. 19.
72. I. Berkhin: "Novaya ekonomicheskaya politika i yeyo rol v perekhodny period ot kapitalizma k sotsializmu. Iz opyta sotsialisticheskovo stroitelstva v SSSR" (The New Economic Policy and its Role in the Transition Period from Capitalism to Socialism. From the Experience of the Construction of Socialism in the USSR), *Kommunist,* No. 4, 1967; *Pravda,* April 23, 1966.
73. *Izvestia.* December 29, 1968; *Borba,* February 15, 1969; *Pravda,* July 3, 1970.
74. "Refutation of the New Leaders of the CPSU on United Action", a joint article by *People's Daily* and *Red Flag,* November 11, in *Peking Review,* No. 46, November 12, 1965.
75. "Ekonomicheskaya politika i borba za komunizm" (Economic Policy and the Struggle for Communism), *Pravda,* January 14, 1966.
76. A. Rumyantsev, T. Khachaturov and A. Pashkov: "Plan i tovarnoe proizvodstvo pri sotsializme" (The Plan and Commodity Production under Socialism), *Pravda,* March 4, 1968.
77. *The New York Times,* May 19; *Politika,* May 14; *Borba,* May 22; *Ekonomicheskaya gazeta,* Nos. 21 to 31, 1968.
78. *The New York Times,* June 9, 1968.
79. Radio Zagreb in Croatian, September 7, 1968.
80. A. Avtorkhanov: "From Khrushchev to Brezhnev: The Problems of Collective Leadership", *Bulletin,* Muenchen, September 1968, pp. 14, 15; Radio Moscow domestic, April 13, 1970.
81. Yin Ch'ing-yao: "Is the Soviet Union on the Way Toward Capitalism?", *Issues and Studies,* November 1967, pp. 33, 34.
82. Lucien Laurat: "Bref historique des transformations économiques en U R SS." *Est & Ouest,* November 1-15, 1967.
83. Georg von Wrangel: *Wird der Ostblock kapitalistisch?,* p. 247.
84. *People's Daily* article of November 10th of 2½ pages under the bold headline "Anti-Chinese Comments by the New Leadership of the CPSU and Its Followers Since the Schismatic March Meeting", *Peking Review,* No. 46, November 12, 1965.
85. "Odnosi SSSR-Kina—Protest protiv kineskog ispada—Prvi puta posle sedam meseci u javnom dekumentu KPSS govori se o razbijackoj politici Pekinga" (USSR-China Relations—Protest Against the Chinese Outburst —A Public CPSU Document Speaks for the First Time After Seven Months About Peking's Splitting Policy), *Borba,* June 8, 1965.
86. "Boevaya solidarnost," (Fighting Solidarity), editorial, *Pravda,* December 26, 1967; Radio Moscow in Mandarin, September 10, 1968, Peace and Progess.
87. Seymour Freidin: "Inter-Red Cloak-and-Dagger Fights", *New York Herald Tribune,* October 2, 1965.
88. *Peking Review,* January 1, 1966,
89. *Ibid.,* No. 25, June 18, 1965.

90. *Ibid.,* No. 11, March 12, 1965.

91. Radio Peking, NCNA, international service in English, February 25, 1965.

92. A revised syndicated article to the North American Newspaper Alliance, March 5, 1965.

93. Branko Bogunovic's sixth installment on the cultural revolution in China, *Politika,* December 23, 1967.

94. *Hsinhua,* international service in English, March 1, 1965.

95. "Refutation of the New Leaders of the CPSU on 'United Action'", *Peking Review,* No. 46, November 12, 1965.

96. "Antisovietskaya publikatsiya v kitaiskoy pechati", (Anti-Soviet Publications in the Chinese Press), *Pravda,* November 16; "Internatsionalny dolg kommunistov vseh stran", (International Duty of the Communists of All Countries), *ibid.,* November 28, 1965.

97. *People's Daily,* November 18, 1965. "There is No Silver Buried Here".

CHAPTER X:

PRESAGES OF THE TEMPEST

(pp. 219-240)

1. Mao, *On the Correct Handling of Contradictions Among the People,* pp. 44, 45, 71.

2. George W. Ball, *The Discipline of Power,* pp. 172, 174, 175.

3. *People's Daily,* August 7, 1957, in Roderick MacFarquhar, *The Hundred Flowers,* p. 75.

4. *Chinese Communist Affairs,* August, 1968, pp. 10-11.

5. *Vjesnik,* May 17, 1962; Vasil Magdeski, *Politika,* April 24, July 15; *Borba,* April 28, 1962; N. Marjanovic, "The Adjustment Phase in China," *Review of International* Affairs, Belgrade, May 20, 1962.

6. Valentin Chu, "The Famine-Makers," *New Leader,* June 11, 1962.

7. NCNA, December 9, 1967, after n.d. *People's Daily* article.

8. Li Tien-min, *Whither Goes the People's Communes, passim.*

9. Sonja Dapcevic-Orescanin, *op. cit.,* p. 118.

10. *Asahi Shimbun,* January 7, 1967.

11. Franz Michael, "Common Purpose and Double Strategy," in C. J. Zablocki's *Sino-Soviet Rivalry,* p. 20.

12. David A. Charles, "The Dismissal of Marshal P'eng Teh-huai," *The China Quarterly,* October-December 1961, p. 75; J. D. Simmonds, "P'eng Teh-huai: A Chronological Re-Examination," *ibid,* January-March, 1969.

13. Peter Tang, *Communist China Today,* Vol. I, pp. 81-83.

14. *Peking Review,* No. 34, August 18, 1967; P'eng Teh-huai's "Letter of Opinion," *Current Backgroud,* Hong Kong, April 28, 1968.

15. *Peking Review*, No. 36, September 1; *People's Daily*, August 16; NCNA, August 27, 1967.

16. "From the Defeat of P'eng Teh-huai to the Bankruptcy of China's Krushchev," *Hung Ch'i* editorial, No. 13, 1967; CTK, January 3, 1967.

17. Title of an important article in the *People's Daily*, March 29, 1962, dealing in an allegorical fashion with the Urumchi River regulation. Reprinted, significantly, by *Pravda*, April 3, 1962.

18. *The New York Times*, September 29, 1962; *Time*, May 20, 1966.

19. Benjamin I. Schwartz, "Upheaval in China," *Commentary*, February, 1967, p. 58; Harry Gelman, "Mao and the Permanent Purge," *Problems of Communism*, November-December, 1966, p. 5.

20. Quoted in "On Krushchev's Phoney Communism and Its Historical Lessons for the World," pp. 71-72. (9th anti-Soviet comment); *Politika*, January 7, 1966.

21. *Bolshaya Sovietskaya Entsiklopediya, Godishnik* 1965, Yearbook.

22. Wei Li, "Peiping's Third Five-Year Plan," *Chin-jih Shih-chien* (World Today), Hong Kong, April 1, 1966.

23. Mao, *Selected Works*, Vol. I, p. 344.

24. *The China Quarterly*, April-June, 1964, *passim*; *Chieh-fang-chün Pao*, July 24, 1965.

25. Mao's remarks of May 1963 when the 10-point CC decision for the socialist education movement was worked out, repeated by Lin Piao in his report to the 9th Party Congress; *Peking Review*, No. 4, January 21, 1966.

26. *Peking Review*, No. 32, August 6, 1965.

27. *Chinese Communist Affairs*, Special Issue: Peiping's "Cultural Revolution" August, 1966, p. 1-2.

28. *Issues and Studies*, compiled by Liu Hsiang, February, 1966, pp. 3-36.

29. *Charts Concerning Chinese Communists on the Mainland*, April, 1968, Chart 17.

30. *Chinese News Agency*, Taipei, April 7, 1969; *The Nation*, March 2, 1970; *The New York Times*, July 21, 1970.

31. *Peking Review*, No. 28, July 10, 1964.

32. *Survey of the China Mainland Press*, No. 3255, July 10, 1964; *Interpreter* August, 1964; An Tzu-wen, "The Education of Successors for the Revolution is the Strategic Goal of the Party," *Red Flag*, Nos. 17, 18, 1964; "To a Big Struggle With the Bourgeoisie for the Next Generation," *People's Daily*, March 31, 1966.

33. *Chung-kuo Ch'ing-nien Pao*, December 9, 1964.

34. Dai Shen-yu, "Peking's Cultural Revolution," *Current History* September 1966, p. 137; *People's Daily*, December 9, 1965; *Tanyug*, May 28, 1968; *Komsomolskaya Pravda*, October 15, 1966; Radio Moscow in Russian, February 1, 1967.

35. Wm. Malden, "A New Class Structure Emerging in China?", *The China Quarterly*, April-June, 1965.

36. Mao, *Contradictions* etc. pp. 51-52; *Quotations of Mao*, p. 15.

37. *Peking Review,* No. 29, 1964, pp. 24-26.
38. Edgar Snow, "No War with U.S. Over Vietnam," *The Sunday Times,* London, February 14, 1965, p. 12.
39. *Neues Deutschland,* May 3, 1966.
40. Justus M. van der Kroef, "The Sino-Indonesian Rupture," *The China Quarterly,* January-March, 1968, *passim.*
41. Voice of the Proletariat, 10th issue, January 1, 1968, rebel organ of Wuchow (Kwangsi-Chuang province).
42. Statement by CPR Government, NCNA, October 27, 1967.
43. Radio Djakarta, domestic service in Indonesian, September 16; V. Shurygin, "Zhestoky urok" (Cruel Lesson), *Pravda,* September 14, 1968.
44. *Pravda,* September 14; TASS, international service in English, October 10, 1968.
45. Radio Peking, NCNA, in English, December 1, 1967.
46. *People's Daily,* November 6, 1967.
47. *Le Monde,* March 7, 1968.
48. CTK in English, July 28; Kzhevnikov and Blishchenko, "Peking is Trampling on International Law," Radio Moscow domestic, September 13, 1967; M. Saranovic, "Izmedju diplomacije i parola" (Between Diplomacy and Slogans), *Borba,* July 31, 1968; L. La Dany, "China: Period of Suspense," *Foreign Affairs,* July 1970; M. Ukraintsev, "Asia and the Peking Empire-Builders," *New Times,* June 9, 1970.
49. *The New York Times,* August 12, 1967.
50. I. Andronov, *New Times, op. cit.* pp. 14, 16. See Chapter VI, note 21.
51. *People's Daily,* February 22, 1966, editor's note to "Cuban Premier Fidel Castro's February 6 Anti-Chinese Statement"; *Survey of China Mainland Press,* February 25, 1966, pp. 28-29.
52. N. Simonia, "Maoisty shantazhiruyut" (Maoists Use Blackmail), *Izvestia,* September 7, 1967.
53. Radio Moscow in English to Africa, December 6, 1967; "O politicheskom kurse Mao Tsze-duna na mezhdunarodnoi arene" ("On the Political Course of Mao at the International Arena"), *Kommunist,* No. 8, May 1968.
54. M. S. Kapitsa, *Leveye zdravovo smysla,* O vneshnei politike gruppy Mao, (To the Left of Common Sense, on the Foreign Policy of Mao's Group).

CHAPTER XI:

THE GREAT PURGE: MAOISTS FIGHT THE "RUSSIAN DISEASE"

(pp. 241-285)

1. *People's Daily,* April 8, 1964; *Red Flag,* 3/1971.
2. George D. Damien: "The Dialectical Structure of the Chinese Great Proletarian Cultural Revolution", *Orbis,* spring 1970.

3. NCNA, November 8, 1967, quoting *People's Daily; Peking Review*, No. 5, February 2, 1968, pp. 20-21.

4. P. Feduseyev in *Pravda*, April 22, 1968.

5. *Peking Review*, No. 25, June 17, after *Red Flag*, No. 8, June 10, 1966.

6. *Red Flag*, No. 10; *Peking Review*, No. 45, November 4, 1966, p. 15.

7. *Liberation Army Daily*, April 18, May 14, June 6, 1966.

8. *People's Daily*, July 1, 1966.

9. *Red Flag*, No. 15, *Peking Review*, No. 52, December 23, 1966, p. 21.

10. *People's Daily*, February 16; "Borba obostryaetsya" (The Struggle is Aggravating), *Izvestia*, December 11, 1966.

11. "Literary and Art Workers Must Go to the Countryside to Readjust Themselves," *People's Daily*, February 12; *Kwang-ming Jih-pao*, February 22, 1966.

12. L. Sergeyev: "Chto oznachayut 'novye ustanovki' v Kitae (What do the "New Installations" in China Mean), *Agitator*, January 1967: "Mezhdu dvuh ognei" (Between Two Fires), *Izvestia*, May 6, 1968.

13. *China Report*, New Delhi, April-May 1966.

14. *Japan Times*, May 17; Branko Bogunovic, "Dve pekinske senzacije" (Two Peking Sensations), *Borba*, May 1, 1966.

15. *Tanyug*, May 28; *Vjesnik*, June 5; *Swiss Review of World Affairs*, December: *People's Daily*, June 4: *Izvestia*, December 11; Reuters, December 15, 1966.

16. *Peking Review*, No. 21, May 19, 1967, pp. 6-12.

17. *Hsinhua*, October 12; M. Saranovic, "Zlocini Peng Cena" (P'eng Chen's Crimes), *Vjesnik*, July 10, 1967.

18. *People's Daily*, October 17, 1967.

19. *Ibid.*, April 17; *Kwang-ming Jih-pao*, June 9, 1966.

20. *Wen-hui Pao*, November 10; *Liberation Army Daily*, November 29, 1965, and April 18, 1966.

21. *Hung Ch'i*, November 13, 1967.

22. Klaus Mehnert: "Mao's zweite Revolution," *Osteuropa*, November-December 1966, p. 751. Later printed in book form.

23. *People's Daily*, May 6, 1966.

24. *The New York Times*, May 6 and 9, 1966; Tass, September 25, 1967.

25. *Hsinhua*, June 3: *People's Daily*, March 25, and June 19, 1966.

26. "Vehemently Repudiate the Revisionist Educational Line of China's Khrushchev and Lu Ting-yi," NCNA, December 13, 1967, after *People's Daily*.

27. *Red Flag*, No. 9, July 1, 1966.

28. *People's Daily* and *Liberation Army Daily*, July 17, 1966.

29. *Hupeh Daily*, June 30, 1966.

30. *Liberation Army Daily*, September 6, 1966; *Free China Review*, May 1968.

31. *People's Daily,* August 8 and 27; *Hsinhua,* November 14; J. Palavrsic: "Nove ideje u kineskoj ekonomici" (New Ideas in the Chinese Economy), *Vjesnik.* December 13, 1966.

32. Hwang Tien-chien: *Chinese Communist Power Struggle in 1967,* Part I p. 7. Part II, *passim.*

33. Hwang, ibid., Part I, pp. 37, 38.

34. *Liberation Army Daily,* June 6, 1966.

35. Li Tien-min: "People's Communes: A Basic Cause of the Mao-Liu Conflict," *Issues and Studies,* February 1968, pp. 6-12; *Collection of Documents Seized in Guerrilla Attack on Lien-Chiang* (hsien), Fukien province. Taipei: Ministry of Defense, 1964.

36. Liu Ta-yüan: *The "Four Cleanness Movement" and Ideological Purge on Chinese Mainland, passim.*

37. NCNA, December 13, 1967.

38. *Peking Review,* No. 33 and 34, August 12 and 19, 1966.

39. Hwang Tien-chien: "A Great Purge on the Chinese Mainland in the Name of the 'Great Cultural Revolution,'" *Asian Outlook,* June 1966, p. 13.

40. Radio Moscow in Mandarin to China, October 16, 1966.

41. Hwang Tien-chien: *Transformation of Mao-Lin Faction's Tactical Line for Power Seizure,* p. 72; *The New York Times,* December 9, 1968.

42. Same author: *1967—A Year of Precariousness for Chinese Communists,* p. 50.

43. Fang Chun-kuei: "Anatomy of the Eight CPC CC," *Chinese Communist Affairs,* August 1967, pp. 32-63; Paris H. Chang: "China's New Phase," *The New Leader,* November 18, 1968.

44. *Charts Concerning Chinese Communists on the Mainland,* April 1968, Chart 6; *Chinese Communist Affairs,* August 1968, pp. 41-50; Radio Moscow in Mandarin, September, 1967; Donald W. Klein: "The State Council and the Cultural Revolution," *The China Quarterly,* July-September 1968, *passim.*

45. Minoru Shibata: "I was Deported," *Sankei Shimbun,* October 4, 1967.

46. Hwang, *1967, etc., op. cit.,* pp. 43, 51, 52, 57; "Bombard Ch'en Yi, Liberate Foreign Affairs Circles." *Hung Ch'i,* April 4, 1967.

47. Hwang, *Chinese Communist Power Struggle,* Part II, p. 39.

48. *Sankei Shimbun,* April 28; *AFP,* May 15, 1967; Hwang, *op. cit.,* p. 61.

49. *The New York Times,* May 4, 1968; Melvin Gurtov, "The Foreign Ministry and Foreign Affairs During the Cultural Revolution," *The China Quarterly,* October-December 1969. *passim.*

50. Ku Ch'eng-kang, "The Advent of a New Situation in the Anti-Communist Struggle on the Chinese Mainland," *Asian Outlook,* June 1966, p. 2.

51. Wang Chang-ling, "Peiping's 'Great Cultural Revolution' and Red Guards," *Issues & Studies,* November 1966, pp. 14-23; *People's Daily,* August 22, 1966.

52. *Chinese Communist Affairs,* June 1967, p. 56.

53. *Hsinhua,* August 31; *Tanyug,* August 24, 1966.

54. Robert S. Elegant, "China Leaps Where?", *The Reporter,* September 22, 1966, p. 37.

55. *Tanyug,* November 21; "Hunveibiny zametayut sledy" (Hung Weiping Cover Their Traces), *Pravda,* December 18; "Chernye spiski 'kulturnoi revolyutsii,'" (Black Lists of the 'Cultural Revolution'), *Komsomolskaya Pravda,* September 29, 1966.

56. TASS, December 18, 1966.

57. *People's Daily,* September 12, 1967.

58. Yao Wen-yüan, "Comments on Tao Ch'u's Two Books," *Peking Review,* No. 38, September 5, 1967.

59. Tass, August 30, 1966.

60. *Ibid.,* August 26 and 27, 1966.

61. "Hunveibiny deistvuyut" (The Red Guards in Action), *Pravda,* September 23, 1966.

62. *Tanyug,* October 30, 1966.

63. Radio Moscow in Albanian, June 23, 1967.

64. *Hsinhua,* August 25, 1966.

65. *Literaturnaya gazeta,* July 17, 1968.

66. *Chinese Communist Affairs,* October 1968, p. 49.

67. *Red Flag,* Nos. 2 and 9, 1967; *Kyodo,* August 30; *Peking Review,* No. 33, August 11, 1967.

68. Radio Shanghai City in Mandarin, October 28; Tass in English, January 4, 1967; "The Making of a Red Guard," *The New York Times Magazine,* January 4, 1970.

69. Leonid Sergeyev, Radio Moscow's political observer, in English to South Asia, November 26; *Red Flag,* December 12; *Tanyug,* November 21; *People's Daily,* September 11, 1966.

70. *Hsinhua,* August 3; "Na podmostkakh Tyan'an'men" (On T'ien-an-men's Scaffolding), *Komsomolskaya Pravda,* October 4; "A chto yest buden? 'Hunveibiny' vtorgayutsya ekonomiku KNR" (What is a Workday? The 'Red Guards' Interfere With PRC's Economy). *Ibid.,* September 28, 1966.

71. Tillman Durdin from Hong Kong, *The New York Times,* December 27, 1967.

72. *Tanyug,* October 20, 1966.

73. V. Sorokin: "Pevets borby i bratstva. K 85 letiu Lu Sinya" (Bard of Struggle and Brotherhood. On occasion of Lu Hsun's 85th Anniversary), *Izvestia,* September 25; "Novye ataki Hunveibinov" (New Attacks of the Red Guards), *Izvestia,* October 17; "S kulakami i tsitatami" (With Fists and Quotations), *Komsomolskaya Pravda,* October 29; "Hunveibiny na ulitsah Pekina" (Red Guards on Peking's Streets), *Pravda,* October 30, 1966.

74. *Japan Times, Asahi Shimbun, Tass,* November 18, 1966.

75. *Hsinhua,* December 20, 1966.
76. Alberto Moravia: *La Rivoluzione Culturale in Cina,* p. 59.
77. *The New York Times,* June 19, 1966.
78. *Red Flag,* September 17, 1966; *People's Daily* editorial January 22, 1967.
79. Radio Peking in Mandarin, November 1, 1966, quoting *Red Flag,* No. 14.
80. *The Peking Informers,* October 16, 1966.
81. *Red Flag,* December 12, 1966.
82. Tanyug, January 16; Reuters January 19; *Borba,* February 1, 1967; *Chinese Communist Affairs,* October 1968, p. 38.
83. "Never Forget the Class Struggle," editorial of the *Liberation Army Daily,* May 4, 1966, cited by all Peking dailies, *Peking Review,* No. 20; *Borba,* August 11; *Tanyug,* October 31, 1966; Parris H. Chang, "Mao's Great Purge: A Political Balance Sheet", *Problems of Communism,* March-April 1969.
84. *Hsinhua,* June 18, 1966.
85. *Wen-hui Pao,* March 15, "Fight Well This Hard Battle of Reopening Classes and Making Revolution"; Tass, March 11; *People's Daily,* May 16, 1967; *Peking Review,* No. 11, March 15, 1968.
86. Radio Shanghai in Mandarin, June 10; *Tokyo Shimbun,* August 8, 1967.
87. "Universities, Middle and Primary Schools Should All Resume Classes to Make Revolution," *People's Daily,* October 25, editorial; Radio Peking in Mandarin, November 2; *Wen-hui Pao,* editorial: "Comments on Resumption of Classes and Restoration," December 18, 1967.
88. *Peking Review,* No. 31, August 2, and No. 47, November 22; *The New York Times,* October 31, 1968.
89. *People's Daily,* July 22; Tass, July 28, 1968.
90. "On the Question of Re-educating Intellectuals," joint commentators' article of *Red Flag* and *People's Daily,* September 11, 1968.
91. A. Ter-Grigoryan: "Yadovitaya smes" (Poisonous Mixture), *Izvestia,* September 12, *Current Digest of the Soviet Press,* October 2, 1968.
92. NCNA, November 1, 1968.
93. Peggy Durdin, "The Bitter Tea of Mao's Red Guards," *The New York Times Magazine,* January 19, 1969.
94. *Red Flag,* August 31; *People's Daily,* August 18 and October 24; *Wen-hui Pao,* September 21 after Radio Shanghai local, September 20; *Peking Review,* No. 35, August 30, 1968.
95. *Ibid.,* No. 36, September 6; Radio Shanghai City service, October 29; Radio Peking domestic, October 26; *People's Daily—Liberation Army Daily,* August 15; *Red Flag,* August 25, 1968; *Chinese Communist Affairs,* April 1969, pp. 25-27.
96. "Na kazarmennom rezhime" (Garrison Regime), *Izvestia,* October 8; Radio Moscow in English, October 10, 1968; *China News Analysis,* January 2, 1970; *Trybuna Ludu,* April 24; Radio Moscow domestic, May 27; *Red Flag,* 4 and 8/1970, 10/1971.

GLOSSARY

ACEN	Assembly of Captive European Nations
AFP	Agence France Press
Akahata	Red Flag, Tokyo
AP	Associated Press
APACL	Asian People's Anti-Communist League
apparatchik	functionary of a Communist Party or socialist country
Arhiv za pravne i drustvene nauke	Archive for Juridical and Social Sciences, Belgrade
Asahi Shimbun	Morning Sun Newspaper, Tokyo
BTA	Bulgarian News Agency
Borba	Struggle, Belgrade
CC	Central Committee of a Communist Party
Chieh-fang Chün-pao	Liberation Army Newspaper, Peking
Chieh-fang Jih-pao	Liberation Daily, Shanghai
Chinese personal names	First family name, then usually two-character, sometimes one-character given name
Chung-kuo Ch'ing-nien Pao	Youth Newspaper of China, Peking
Cominform	Communist Information Bureau (1947-1956), composed of the Communist Parties of the Soviet bloc as well as of France and Italy
Comintern	Communist International (1919-1943) of all Communist Parties
CP	Communist Party
CPC	Communist Party of China as of a multi-national country

319

CPSU	Communist Party of the Soviet Union
CPY	Communist Party of Yugoslavia, forerunner of the League of Communists
CTK	Czechoslovak News Agency
GDR	German Democratic Republic, East Germany
GFR	German Federal Republic
gosplan	Soviet Union's central economic plan
hsia fang	sending down, actually deportation, mass rustification
Hsinhua She	New China News Agency, NCNA
Hukbalahap	communist guerrilla in the Phillipines, from national army fighting the Japanese
hung weiping	red guards, Maoist student rebels, sometimes anti-Maoists
Hung Ch'i	Red Flag, Peking
Izvestia	News, Moscow
Jen-min Jih-pao	People's Daily, Peking
kolkhoz	Soviet collective farm
Komsomol	Soviet communist youth league
kray	Soviet administrative territory
kulak	Peasant opposing collectivization
Kung-shang Pao	Industrial, Commercial Newspaper, Hong Kong
Kuomintang, KMT	(Chinese) Nationalist Party
Krasnaya Zvezda	Red Star, Moscow
Kwang-ming Jih-pao	Bright Daily, Peking
Kyodo	Japanese News Agency
Magyar Hirlap	Hungarian Newspaper, Budapest
Mainichi Shimbun	Daily Newspaper, Tokyo
Mezhdunarodnaya Zhizn	Foreign Affairs, Moscow
MP	Member of Parliament
MTI	Hungarian News Agency
MVD	Ministry of Internal Affairs, also political police, Moscow
Nan-fang Jih-pao	Southern Daily, Canton
Nedelya	Week, Moscow
NEP	New Economic Policy

Nepszabadsag	People's Freedom, Budapest
Nhan Dan	People, Hanoi
Nihon Keizai Shimbun	Japanese Economy Newspaper, Tokyo
Nowe Drogi	New Ways, Warsaw
oblast	Soviet administrative region
PAP	Polish News Agency
Party	Communist Party
Paritinaya Zhizn	Party Life, Moscow
Pathet Lao	Laos communists
Peiching Jih-pao	Peking Daily
Peiping	northern peace, renamed by the KMT. Peking means northern capital
PLA	People's Liberation Army (all three armed forces of Communist China)
Planovoye Hozyaistvo	Planned Economy, Moscow
Politburo	supreme leadership of a CP
politcom	political commissar of a communist military unit
Politizdat	Izdatelstvo politicheskoi literatury, a Moscow publisher
Pravda	Truth, Moscow
PRC	People's Republic of China
Rabotnichesko Delo	Worker's Action, Sofia
regional bureau of the CPC's CC	the old CPC was geographically divided in six entities
Rinascità	Regeneration, Rome
ROC	Republic of China on Taiwan
RSFSR	Russian Soviet Federated Socialist Republic
Rude Pravo	Red Right, Prague
Russian way of address among friends	given and middle name (a diminutive form of father's given name)
SALT	strategic arms limitation talks
samizdat	self publishing, Russian underground literature
SFRY	Socialist Federal Republic of Yugoslavia
Sankei Shimbun	Industry, Economy Newspaper, Tokyo
Scinteia	Sparkle, Bucharest
Soviet	people's committee, administration

Sovietskoe Gosudarstvo i Pravo	Soviet Government and Law, Moscow
sovkhoz	Soviet state farm
sovnarkhoz	Soviet regional economic administration
Sputnjik	Fellow-Traveler, Moscow
Svobodne Slovo	Free Word, Prague
Ta-kung Pao	Impartial Newspaper, Hong Kong
Tanyug	Yugoslav News Agency
TASS	Soviet News Agency
tatzu pao	big-character wall newspaper
Trybuna Ludu	People's Tribune, Warsaw
tsaofan p'ai	Maoist rebel mass organization
Trud	Labor, Moscow, Sofia
UPI	United Press International
uravnilovka	egalitarianism, wage leveling
USSR	Union of the Soviet Socialist Republics
Vecherni Novini	Evening Newspaper, Sofia
Vietcong	Vietnamese communists
Vjesnik u srijedu	Messenger on Wednesday, Zagreb
voprosy	problems
Wen-hui Pao	Gathering of Information Newspaper, Shanghai
Wen-wei Pao	same meaning in Cantonese, Hong Kong
WFTU	World Federation of Trade Unions (pro-communist)
Yomiuri Shimbun	Reading and Selling Newspaper, Tokyo
Za Rubezhom	Abroad, Moscow
Zeri i Poputlit	The Voice of the People, Tirana
Zycie Warszawi	Warsaw's Life

INDEX

323